The Matriarchs of Genesis

The Matriarchs of Genesis

Seven Women, Five Views

BY

David J. Zucker

AND

Moshe Reiss

WIPF & STOCK · Eugene, Oregon

THE MATRIARCHS OF GENESIS
Seven Women, Five Views

Wipf & Stock
An Imprint of Wipf and Stock Publishers
199 W. 8th Ave., Suite 3
Eugene, OR 97401

www.wipfandstock.com

ISBN 13: 978-1-62564-396-4

Manufactured in the U.S.A.   08/06/2015

Dedicated to the memory of
Miriam Reiss, Miriam (Mary) bat Sarah Leah,
and Lilian R. Zucker, Rachel bat Alisa,

and in honor of Donna D. Zucker, Alma bat Rachel Leah,
Pallas Athene Reiss, Hannah bat Devorah bat Ruth

as well as in honor of all those who learn
and teach ללמוד וללמד.

Contents

Acknowledgments | ix

Authors' Note | xi

Chapter 1   Introduction | 1

                     General Introduction | 1

                     Sources | 11

                     Themes | 22

                     A Final Note | 28

Chapter 2   Sarah | 29

                     Biblical Sarah | 29

                     Early Extra-Biblical Literature's Sarah | 36

                     The Rabbis' Sarah | 44

                     Contemporary Scholarship | 69

                     Feminist Thought | 78

                     Addition/Excursus | 84

                     Summary and Conclusion | 86

Chapter 3   Hagar | 88

                     Biblical Hagar | 88

                     Early Extra-Biblical Literature's Hagar | 97

                     The Rabbis' Hagar | 104

                     Contemporary Scholarship | 115

                     Feminist Thought | 122

                     Summary and Conclusion | 127

Chapter 4   Rebekah | 129
              Biblical Rebekah | 129
              Early Extra-Biblical Literature's Rebekah | 136
              The Rabbis' Rebekah | 144
              Contemporary Scholarship | 151
              Feminist Thought | 159
              Addition/Excursus | 164
              Summary and Conclusion | 166

Chapter 5   Leah | 169
              Biblical Leah | 169
              Early Extra-Biblical Literature's Leah | 174
              The Rabbis' Leah | 177
              Contemporary Scholarship | 184
              Feminist Thought | 189
              Summary and Conclusion | 192

Chapter 6   Rachel | 195
              Biblical Rachel | 192
              Early Extra-Biblical Literature's Rachel | 202
              The Rabbis' Rachel | 206
              Contemporary Scholarship | 214
              Feminist Thought | 219
              Summary and Conclusion | 224

Chapter 7   Bilhah and Zilpah | 227
              Biblical Bilhah and Zilpah | 227
              Early Extra-Biblical Literature's Bilhah and Zilpah | 229
              The Rabbis' Bilhah and Zilpah | 236
              Contemporary Scholarship | 239
              Feminist Thought | 241
              Summary and Conclusion | 244

Chapter 8   Conclusion | 247

Bibliography | 255

Acknowledgments

Throughout the writing of this book, we have tried to be aware of patriarchal biases and androcentrism in the biblical texts and their traditional interpreters. As two males (and on top of that, two male rabbis) writing about the Matriarchs, we are aware of our masculine subjectivity. Consequently, as we progressed with the book, we sought the advice and comments of a number of women scholars, women pastors, and women rabbis; we also consulted with male scholars. We have benefited from their criticism and appreciate their insights and suggestions. Special thanks to Gwen Cain, Sandra Cohen, Julie W. Dahl, Hélène Dallaire, Tamara Cohn Eskenazi, Chananya (Andrew) Goodman, Laurie Jeddeloh, Daniella Krause, Amy-Jill Levine, Jan McCormack, Susan Miller Rheins, Patrice Von Stroh, Donna D. Zucker, and Ian Michael Zucker for reading various chapters in an earlier form and offering valuable observations and recommendations. We also are particularly appreciative of the excellent suggestions offered by Amy-Jill Levine. Of course, as the usual declaimer has it, all errors are ours alone.

Authors' Note

WE CAN IMAGINE YOU, the reader, picking up this volume and saying, "*The Matriarchs of Genesis* . . . but why *seven* Matriarchs? Surely there are only four!" We can also imagine you asking, "Why five views, and how can there be five views? Doesn't Genesis just present one view of these women?"

The answer to the first question as to why *seven* Matriarchs is that these women are all married to those men traditionally termed the Patriarchs of Genesis: Abraham, Isaac, and Jacob. These seven women, then, are their respective wives: Abraham's Sarah, but also Hagar; Isaac's Rebekah; and Jacob's Leah and Rachel, but also Bilhah and Zilpah. Yes, Jacob had four concurrent wives, and together they produced thirteen children—twelve sons and one daughter. Six of these women (Sarah, Rebekah, Leah, Rachel, Bilhah, and Zilpah) are Matriarchs of Judaism, and therefore Christianity. Hagar is the Matriarch of Islam.

The book of Genesis, like the Bible as a whole, focuses on the lives of males, not females. The lives of men—who they were, what they did, what they said, and what was said to them—dominates the narratives we read in the Bible. At the same time, undoubtedly, about half of the people who lived in biblical times were women. Yet, less than 10 percent of the names mentioned in the Bible belong to women, and not all of them voice their views. Indeed, when looking at the seven Matriarchs of this volume, not all of them had a speaking part in Genesis. That said, when certain women like Sarah and Hagar, Rebekah, Leah, and Rachel do speak, their voices are clear and strong.

As to the second initial question concerning why we include five views if Genesis presents these seven Matriarchs as they were, the view from Genesis is the first level of our inquiry. We locate each woman where she appears in Genesis and, episode by episode, chapter by chapter, offer context for her appearance (who she was, what she did, what she said, or what was said to—or about—her). It is possible that even at this point, there may be details that are new to you, or that you may not have considered before.

The second level or view takes the same Matriarchs (accordingly, readers will find chapters devoted to Sarah, Hagar, Rebekah, Leah, Rachel, and Bilhah and Zilpah) as she appears in the literature of the early extrabiblical period. These are works written in the late Second Temple period and a bit thereafter, ca. 200 BCE–200 CE. For example, we cite material written about these women by the historian Josephus and from those books known as the Pseudepigrapha. The Pseudepigrapha is comprised of Jewish writings that never attained canonical status and were not included in the official books of the Bible. Specifically, we offer examples of the Matriarchs' treatment in such works as the book of *Jubilees* and the *Testaments of the Twelve Patriarchs*; then we provide readers with context and scholarly commentary on these examples. Both *Jubilees*, and then the *Testaments of the Twelve Patriarchs* are examples of what is termed Rewritten Scriptures. The book of Genesis is the source for those works, but their portrayals of the Matriarchs are very different from the women we know from the Bible. These Re-written Scriptures both excise and add to the words of the biblical account found in Genesis. The Matriarchs in these works often have very different, much more active roles and voices than in the first book of the Bible. They are strong and powerful figures. For example, in *Jubilees* there is no mention of Rebekah's courtship or her childlessness, but she is featured taking a prominent role in advising with Jacob about his future marriage partner. Likewise, *Jubilees'* Rebekah has many powerful speeches and seems to have an unusually prominent standing in the community; she is a woman standing alongside the men.

Next, we turn to a third source that presents yet a different view of these Matriarchs: the writings of the classical rabbis. The rabbis share their ideas through the medium of midrash (pl. midrashim), short explanations rooted in the biblical text. The rabbis wanted to teach certain values, such as what was or was not proper behavior, or address how to be in right relationship with God. To do this, the rabbis reached into the Bible, and for our purposes, into the lives of the Matriarchs, lifting the biblical story out of its original context and applying it to another context. The rabbis both quoted the biblical text and invented new dialogue for the Matriarchs. In presenting their view of the Matriarchs, the rabbis both taught their values and kept the Bible alive. We offer dozens of examples from the writings of the rabbis, providing a wide variety of views and clearly citing the sources for each of these quotations.

The fourth view of each Matriarch is taken from contemporary (late twentieth- and early twenty-first century) biblical scholarship. These scholars—Jewish, Christian, other religions, and secular alike—present and analyze the materials found in Genesis. They offer commentary from various perspectives, such as a cultural, political, linguistic, or sociological vantage point. The fifth view is that of feminist thought. Feminist authors clearly are not categorized by gender identity, because there are both male and female feminists. Feminist writers seek to understand the Matriarchs and their significance as they experienced life *as women* in the biblical world. We admit that whether an author is quoted in the "contemporary scholarship" section or the "feminist thought" section is sometimes a subjective, arbitrary decision on our part.

We have written a book that avoids technical language. We understand that many readers may lack intimate familiarity with the biblical narratives, much less be fluent in Hebrew. We have kept that in mind in providing our explanations. This book is largely a collection of materials taken from both ancient and modern sources, readily accessible materials that focus on the Matriarchs of Genesis. Our approach is unique in that we know of no other work that brings together in one volume such diverse views that are nevertheless linked in a common purpose. The bibliography and notes refer to works for the reader who wants to explore further into the fascinating lives of the Matriarchs of Genesis.

David J. Zucker, Moshe Reiss

1

Introduction

General Introduction

A PEOPLE'S SELF-UNDERSTANDING IS fashioned on its heroes and heroines.

Sarah. Rebekah. Leah. Rachel. As well as Bilhah and Zilpah. Together these four (or more accurately, six) women are the Bible's Matriarchs, the earliest mothers of the people of Israel. Sarah is married to Abraham and is Isaac's mother. Rebekah is married to Isaac and is the mother of Esau and Jacob. Leah and Rachel, along with Bilhah and Zilpah, are concurrently married to Jacob. These four women produce many children—twelve sons and at least one daughter. These twelve sons nominally form the traditional twelve tribes of Israel.

The Matriarchs are the wives of those men we call the Patriarchs. We also include a chapter that focuses on Hagar, because as we explain below, Hagar is Abraham's second wife. Abraham and Hagar are the parents of Ishmael. Genesis records Hagar's voice and some of her actions. Through Ishmael, Hagar becomes the Matriarch of Islam, just as Sarah, Rebekah, Leah, Rachel, Bilhah, and Zilpah are the Matriarchs of Judaism.[1] Hagar interacts with both Sarah and Abraham; she is a crucial part of the story of these two important figures.

The narratives featuring the Matriarchs Sarah, Rebekah, Leah, Rachel, Bilhah, and Zilpah (and those featuring Hagar) are all found in the book of Genesis.[2] Time and again, the first four of these women are featured as

---

1. Some of the Matriarchs of Genesis are featured in the Christian Scriptures. Although not mentioned by name, the figure of Sarah appears in an allegory in Gal 4. Hagar is directly mentioned twice in Gal 4. Sarah and Rebekah are mentioned in Rom 9, and there are other references to Sarah in Rom 4, Heb 11, and 1 Pet 3. Jeremiah's reference to Rachel appears in Matt 2.

2. Biblical writers make mention of the Matriarchs in later texts. Sarah will also appear as an example in Isa 51:2. Leah is mentioned in Ruth 4:11. Rachel will be mentioned in 1 Sam 10:2, Jer 31:15, and Ruth 4:11. A number of the Matriarchs' names appear in the Christian Scriptures, as noted above. None are mentioned directly by

powerful characters whose strong personalities influence the lives of their husbands, who confer with them. At one point the Bible[3] records that God instructs Abraham to listen specifically to the words of Sarah (Gen 21:12). These women are exceptional. They are special because we know their names, and often we hear their voices and learn what they do, even if not as frequently as we in a modern and more equal age might wish. Too often the Bible simply refers to someone's wife, mother, sister, or daughter but erases her individuality by neglecting to present her name, much less to record her voice or describe what she does. "Rarely if ever do women in the Bible get to speak for themselves. Rather, they are portrayed from the perspective of male authors and in the context . . . where men's experience was the norm."[4] Seeking to know more about these women is difficult because, to use the felicitous phrase of Judith Plaskow, one is "exploring the terrain of silence." These "women are not absent, but they are cast in stories told by men."[5]

Women's voices in the Bible come in three forms. The most common is through the omniscient voice of the narrator, or someone describing women or women's actions: "Then Rebekah and her maids rose up, mounted the camels, and followed the man" (Gen 24:61). "Sarah shall bear you a son" (Gen 17:19). Secondly, women sometimes speak to share information: "Rebekah said to her son Jacob, 'I heard your father say . . .'" (Gen 27:6). Thirdly, and most infrequently, women describe their own feelings: "God has brought laughter for me; everyone who hears will laugh with me" (Gen 21:6). Yet even within these examples, there remains the ultimately unanswerable question: Are these women's voices speaking, or are these examples of men representing women's voices?

The Matriarchs and the Patriarchs (Abraham, Isaac, and Jacob) lived between three-and-a-half to four thousand years ago, at least a millennium-and-a-half before the Common Era[6] began. They functioned within a patriarchal society, which is hierarchical rather than equal.[7] Under such a

---

name in the Qur'an, although there is a reference to Abraham's (Ibrahim's) wife. See James, "Sarah, Hagar, and Their Interpreters," 52.

3. In this book, the word "Bible" only refers to the Jewish/Hebrew Bible, unless there is specific reference to the Christian Scriptures. The words "Jewish Bible," "Jewish Scriptures," "Hebrew Scriptures," and "Hebrew Bible" are used interchangeably.

4. Ringe, "When Women Interpret the Bible," 3.

5. Plaskow, *Standing Again at Sinai*, 2–3.

6. The Common Era (CE) and Before the Common Era (BCE) correspond to the same time as the religiously exclusive terms Anno Domini (AD) and Before Christ (BC).

7. "Patriarchy" derives from the rule of the father. It is a system through which men are already privileged and which relies on the subordination of women. This system has a long historical and political background. A manifest political consequence is the

patriarchal society, men are generally considered superior to women and children. Males are regarded as stronger, and they are more likely to be involved in public religious matters.[8] Priests are male, and their duties are only permitted to those who are consecrated. Male animals are regarded as superior to female animals for ritual sacrifices. Unblemished people and animals are superior to blemished ones. Certainly men take the forefront when it comes to matters of negotiation, whether it is land or grazing issues or matters concerning the selection a wife or husband (see Gen 12:15, 18–19; 20:2, 8ff.; 21:25ff.; 24; 26:17–31; 34:13ff.) and so on.

Praise of women is not unknown in the biblical text, but it is rare. In some of the later prophetic and wisdom literature of the Bible, sexist language and, at times, misogynist viewpoints are expressed,[9] which may well reflect attitudes from the earlier biblical period. Isaiah says, "Women rule over . . . my people, your leaders mislead you" (Isa 3:12).[10] Later in that book, the prophet describes sinners as "children of a sorceress . . . offspring of an adulterer and a whore" (Isa 57:3). Jeremiah depicts an unfaithful Zion as a woman dressed in crimson decking herself out in golden ornaments, enlarging her eyes with paint, and beautifying herself for lovers (Jer 4:30). Ezekiel uses two prostitutes as symbols for Jerusalem and Samaria (Ezek 16 and 23). Following the destruction of the temple in 586 BCE, Zion is

---

emphasis on male linage (patrilineality). Through this system, males control women's sexuality to protect linage and property rights. Many feminist and gender theorists seek to critique and analyze how patriarchy functions within social, political, economic, and historical contexts. Importantly, however, just as women do not benefit in this system, some men do not benefit from patriarchy; this can be seen with respect to patriarchal understandings of gender(ed) roles, as not all men can or do fit within the social and political expectations of what it means to be a "man" in this system.

There are challenges to the extent of patriarchy's influence in biblical life. See Groothuius and Merrill, *Equality*; Otwell, *And Sarah Laughed*; Davidson, *Flame of Yahweh*, 34–35, 223ff.

8. Although it deals with the biblical period as a whole, for a discussion about "Women's Religious Life in Ancient Israel," see the chapter by that title in Newsom, Ringe, and Lapsley, *Women's Bible Commentary*, 354–61.

9. We define "sexist" as behaviors or attitudes that favor stereotyping of social roles based on gender, which oftentimes are discriminatory towards women. "Misogyny" is dislike, hatred, or contempt for women.

10. Unless otherwise noted, translations used for this book are taken from *The New Oxford Annotated Bible with the Apocrypha: Revised Standard Version* (NRSV). This Bible was chosen because it presents both a modern translation and inclusive, gender-neutral language. Hereafter referred to as *NOAB*.

Reference will be made to differences in verse numbering as reflected in the Masoretic (traditional Jewish) Text of the Hebrew Bible. The NRSV translation will be followed by the Hebrew tradition in brackets and marked with an "H" for Hebrew (for example, Ps 83:6 [7H]).

represented as a withered widow, a woman who is being punished for her past sinfulness and rebelliousness (Lam 1:1–2, 8, 18; 5:1, 3; Jer 18:21). In Proverbs, while there is the paean to the capable wife (Prov 31:10–31), there are sections that speak of Woman Folly (Prov 7, 9).

One way that the concept of greater male power and responsibility is expressed is through the depiction of biblical characters. Limiting her example to the unannounced visitors to Abraham and Sarah's encampment depicted in Gen 18, Esther Fuchs observes how differently people are described:

> Abraham's activity outside of the tent is contrasted by Sarah's passivity. Seventeen verbs predicate Abraham's dedication to his guests. The verbs 'run' and 'hasten' are repeated twice. Sarah, on the other hand, is the subject of four verbs, none of which demonstrates a high level of exertion: to hear, laugh, deny, and fear. Although there is reason to believe that Sarah obeyed her husband's instructions and, like a good housewife, baked cakes for the guests, the text does not mention this fact explicitly. Sarah emerges from the scene as confined, passive, cowardly, deceptive, and unfaithful.[11]

Biblical life's male-dominated patriarchal society is noted for gender asymmetry: "The patrilineal nature of Israelite society, with land and property transferred across generations via the male line, is likely the reason for the stringency of biblical precepts dealing with female sexuality. A woman's fiancé and then her husband had exclusive rights to her sexuality; and her parents guarded it before betrothal."[12] Women generally were in a subservient position to men within the same class structure. Yet the master's wife clearly had rights over male servants. This arrangement was not unique to the Bible; it was also true of ancient societies in general, including Egypt, Canaan, Assyria, Babylonia, Persia, and Greece. Women are largely adjuncts

---

11. Fuchs, "Literary Characterization," 129. When Abraham asks Sarah to prepare the food, he turns over that responsibiliy to her. She sees to it that the bread is baked; she does not necessarily bake the bread herself, for it is a task performed by her servants.

12. Meyers, "Women in Ancient Israel," xlii. Yet even that statement needs explanation and explication, for as Meyers goes on to elucidate, men and women were interdependent. In biblical times, women had a variety of economic, educational, managerial, and religious roles. In terms of household life, "the relationship between a woman and her husband was one of interdependence and complementarity in most household functions" (ibid., xliii). The narratives of the Matriarchs and Patriarchs, however, do not deal with these more prosaic domestic matters.

of their men.[13] The Bible was (primarily) written and edited by men within a patriarchal society—certainly a society dominated by males.[14]

Males may dominate, yet biblical women can also be powerful figures. In the Bible, beginning with the book of Exodus, there are occasional examples of women who serve as military and religious leaders, prophets, and wise women from whom men seek counsel. There also are depictions of women saving the lives of men. The focus of this book, however, is on Genesis. There too, as we shall see, certain women stand strong, taking on important and life-changing roles that will affect their lives and the lives of their husbands and their families. The "matriarchs of Genesis are all strong women. As independent personalities, fiercely concerned for their children, they often are informed of God's plans for their sons [Gen 18:9–15; 25:22–23]. Indeed, it appears from the stories of Sarah and Rebekah that they understand God better than their husbands."[15] The women and men featured in Genesis are both heroic and flawed. "They are husbands and wives, parents and children, constantly torn between their highest aspirations and their basest instincts. They are at once bold visionaries engaged in direct dialogue with God and frail human beings trapped in their own self-destructive behavior."[16] They, like us, struggle between who they really are and who they would wish to be.

Finally, a word about God. The dominant image of God in the Bible is that of a male figure. Due to the structure of the Hebrew language, there is no neutral case; nouns, pronouns, and verbs are either masculine or feminine. References to God use the masculine forms for nouns, pronouns, and verbal expressions. Yet there also are occasional images in which God takes on more female characteristics:

> Even if ancient Israelites imagined Israel's God primarily as male, the Torah and the rest of the Hebrew Bible do enable readers to understand God in gender-inclusive terms. Support for thinking about God not only in masculine terms comes in part from the metaphors that depict Israel's God. The biblical writers

13. "The laws contained in the Pentateuch appear to be addressed to a society in which only the male was regarded as a legally responsible person [see Num 30:3–15; 27:1–11; 36:1–12; Lev 12:2–5; 27:2–8; Deut 22:13–21; Num 5:11–31]" (Davies, *Dissenting Reader*, 1).

14. That women may have written parts of the Bible, such as the Song of Songs and/or Ruth, is discussed in a variety of sources. See Bloom, *The Book of J*; Eskenazi and Frymer-Kensky, *Ruth*, xvi, xvii.

15. Plaskow, *Standing Again at Sinai*, 3–4.

16. Rosenblatt and Horowitz, *Wrestling with Angels*, xxvi, quoted in Shapiro, "Approaching the Avot," 1.

sometimes refer to God using male imagery: for example as a warrior (see at Exodus 15:3), father (see at Deuteronomy 32:6), or king (see at Deuteronomy 33:5). But biblical texts also portray God with female imagery, as one who gives birth (see at Numbers 11:12, Deuteronomy 32:13, 18).[17]

With the *exception of direct quotations* from the NRSV text, we try to avoid using the word LORD (i.e., "Master," or in Hebrew, *Adonai*), a term that has masculine overtones. Instead, we use the non-gender-specific word "God." To replace the pronouns "he," "him," and "his" when referring to the Deity, at times we use the locution [God].

The Structure of This Book: A Fivefold Presentation

In addition to the introduction and conclusion, this work features chapters devoted to Sarah, Hagar, Rebekah, Leah, Rachel, and Bilhah and Zilpah. Each chapter is divided into five sections: how the Matriarch is presented in the Bible, early extra-biblical literature, rabbinic literature, contemporary scholarship, and feminist thought.

The Bible

The first section discusses how the Bible presents each specific Matriarch in the book of Genesis.

Early Extra-Biblical Literature

The second section presents a description of the specific Matriarch as found in the early extra-biblical literature, primarily that of the Pseudepigrapha. "From a Jewish standpoint, these texts [the Apocrypha and the Pseudepigrapha], along with the Dead Sea Scrolls and the writing of Philo, Josephus, and other Hellenistic Jewish authors, all belong to a single corpus of Jewish writings of the Second Temple period. Some of these writings clearly were considered to be sacred texts, but for one reason or another they were not incorporated into the canonical collection that makes up our current Jewish Bible."[18] In this category, one finds additional sections or traditions not

---

17. Eskenazi and Weiss, introduction to *Torah: A Women's Commentary*, xxxiv.

18. Kugel, "Apocrypha and the Pseudepigrapha," 7.

included in the eventual biblical canon. For example, *Jubilees* and the *Testaments of the Twelve Patriarchs* comment upon

> well-known biblical narratives from Genesis, seeking to resolve
> inconsistencies . . . as well as to flesh out details in the story,
> and, often, to bring out some new teaching or lesson from the
> biblical narrative. *Jubilees* and the *Testaments of the Twelve Patri-
> archs* [explain and expand] the stories of Genesis [they do not]
> cite a verse and then offer an explanation, but rather [choose]
> to explain via *retelling*. Commentators would rewrite a text in
> their own words, inserting into it their own understanding . . .
> Sometimes these insertions went on for pages . . . In many cases,
> it seems that the writer is simply reflecting what he or she has
> heard or learned from others—teachers or preachers or other
> public figures.[19]

We also occasionally refer to the writings of Philo and Josephus.

The Rabbis

The third section features each specific Matriarch as portrayed and interpreted by the rabbis and sages in classical Jewish texts such as the Talmud
and various collections of midrash (pl. midrashim). The classic rabbinic
period is ca. 200 to 500 CE in the lands of Israel and (Parthian and Neo-Persian) Babylon,[20] although several midrashic collections were collected and
edited for centuries after that time. The rabbis were teachers and expositors
of Jewish tradition. We also take note of some material in the collections
known as the Targum to the Bible (pl. Targumim; Aramaic translations or
re-interpretations of the Bible). In addition to citing midrashim, we shall
occasionally offer the insights of some of the traditional rabbinic commentators on the biblical text such Rashi, Ramban (otherwise known as Nachmanides or Nahmanides), and Sforno. Most of these commentators lived
during the Middle Ages through the Renaissance period. See the "Sources"
section later in this chapter.

---

19. Ibid., 8, emphasis in original. Although Kugel mentions the Apocrypha, we do
not quote from that source.

20. The area of land between the Tigris and Euphrates Rivers became an area of
great cultural significance for the dispersed Jewish community in the third century CE.
This was more than seven hundred years after the biblical Exile to ancient Babylonia.

Contemporary Scholarship

Fourth, we draw on the perception of contemporary scholarship, including Jewish and non-Jewish scholars, both men and women, writing on the book of Genesis in the twentieth and twenty-first centuries. Among them are E. A. Speiser, Gerhard von Rad, Nehama Leibowitz, Nahum M. Sarna, Claus Westermann, Susan Niditch, Phyllis Trible, Athalya Brenner, Bruce Vawter, Gordon J. Wenham, Tamara Cohn Eskenazi, Avivah Gottlieb Zornberg, David W. Cotter, Tammi J. Schneider, Yairah Amit, Robert Alter, Amy-Jill Levine, and many others.

Feminist Thought

The fifth and final section we present is the perspective of feminist scholars who bring additional insights to the material at hand. Some women would claim the term "feminist"[21] for themselves while others would not. We understand feminist thought to be part of contemporary scholarship, but a specialized section within that grouping. Feminism is not a matter of gender identity, for there are both male and female feminists. Feminism is both a body of theory and a mode of viewing the world that places significance on the experiences of women, as well as a political movement that seeks to end sexism. *Some writers are both contemporary and write from a feminist viewpoint.* There are works that specifically claim a feminist orientation in their very title, such as *A Feminist Companion to . . .* Other books or articles simply reflect a feminist viewpoint. Whether a given source appears in the "Contemporary Scholarship" section or the "Feminist Thought" section is sometimes an arbitrary, subjective choice. What distinguishes feminist from non-feminist scholarship is the primary concern for women as the major subject of analysis, as well as women's experiences and how they are represented. This means, for example, as Esther Fuchs has suggested, that going beyond issues of survival and security, a feminist view centers on "interpersonal politics, and [moves] from the public to the private" sphere.[22] Amy-Jill

---

21. Feminists, both female and male, reflect the theological spectrum. These include "evangelical women" who make "an important contribution to feminist hermeneutics, albeit from a more conservative position" (Kroeger and Evans, *IVP Women's Bible Commentary*, xv).

22. Fuchs, "Feminist Hebrew Literary Criticism," 195. See Brenner and Van Dijk-Hemmes, *On Gendering Texts*, 1–13. See also relevant chapters in Brenner and Fontaine's *A Feminist Companion to Reading the Bible*: Reinhartz, "Feminist Criticism and Biblical Studies," 30–38; Milne, "Toward Feminist Companionship," 39–60; and McKay, "Future of Feminist Biblical Criticism," 61–83.

Levine explains that feminist analysis "extends to questions of religion, class, race, ethnicity, and sexual preference, among others, and it often remarks on the interrelated or systematic nature of oppressive behaviors."[23] These oppressive behaviors, as we note, can be directed by either men or women.

Feminist thought (Jewish, Christian, other religious, or non-religious) has helped all of us recognize the degree to which patriarchy operates in the ancient (and contemporary) world. The work of the authors of the early extra-biblical texts, as well as the rabbis' conservative and often androcentric political and religious scholarship, is congruent with their era. We, therefore, have gained a new vision of the Bible through the scholarship and insights of feminist writers.

In the introduction to the excellent resource, *Women's Bible Commentary* (third edition, 2012),[24] the editors point out that with "increasing self-confidence and sophistication, feminist study of the Bible has blossomed to become one of the most important new areas in contemporary biblical research." Women have raised new questions and "have posed . . . new ways of reading" that "have challenged the very way biblical studies are done," and as these authors point out, feminist biblical studies take many different directions:

> Some commentators have attempted to reach 'behind the text' to recover knowledge about the actual conditions of women's lives in the biblical period . . . Still others have tried to discover the extent to which even the biblical writings that pertain to women are shaped by the concerns and perspectives of men and yet how it can still be possible at times to discover the presence of women and their own points of view between the lines.[25]

These perspectives have enriched our understanding by giving us another picture of biblical life. Yet, as readers we have to read carefully, for at times feminist analyses—as with analyses from any specialized viewpoint—can have their own particular perspectives. Levine observes, "Negative resonances that accompany the character in question are not infrequently ignored or excused. In some cases, the previously marginalized, the 'other,' becomes regarded as invariably right and good."[26] For example, in some

23. Levine, "Beer-lahai-roi," 14.

24. Newsom, Ringe, Lapsley, introduction to *Women's Bible Commentary*, xxi–xxxi. The original volume is listed in the bibliography under Newsom and Ringe, *Women's Bible Commentary*.

25. Newsom, Ringe, and Lapsley, introduction to *Women's Bible Commentary*, xxviii.

26. Levine, "Beer-lahai-roi," 18.

analyses that focus on Hagar, she is the "innocent victim" who is exploited by Sarah and Abraham. Again, in Levine's words, one has to be aware of the "power and perniciousness of interpretation."[27]

Certainly, as mentioned earlier, in the biblical era men were hierarchically privileged over women and were regarded as superior, stronger, and—at the very least for the people of Israel in the public arena (i.e., the priesthood and their assistants)—more spiritual. Yet, certain women benefited from their social position under the law: women who were free were held in higher regard than women who were slaves. For example, in Genesis and in the allegory found in the New Testament in Paul's Epistle to the Galatians, which is based on the figures of Sarah-Hagar (Gal 4:22–5:1), Sarah is "emblematic of what is desirable, promised, and legitimate and . . . [those texts] view Hagar as alien, atavistic, and rejected." Yet on the other hand, there are contemporary feminist "readings that celebrate Hagar as representative of the oppressed: [as a woman who] struggles against elite privilege and social abuse"[28] and epitomize Sarah as dominating and violent.

Levine points to Phyllis Trible's groundbreaking work, *Texts of Terror: Literary-Feminist Readings of Biblical Narratives* (1984), where in the introduction to her chapter on Hagar, Trible features this epitaph for Hagar: "She was wounded for our transgressions; she was bruised for our iniquities." These words are a paraphrase from Isaiah's description of the Suffering Servant and evoke images, certainly for Christians, of Jesus of Nazareth (see Isa 53:5; Matt 8:17; 1 Pet 2:22–24). Therefore, they associate with Hagar's image someone who is completely innocent and fully exploited. Trible writes that when read

> in light of contemporary issues and images, her [Hagar's] story depicts oppression in three familiar forms: nationality, class, and sex . . . As a symbol of the oppressed, Hagar becomes . . . the faithful maid exploited, the black woman used by the male and abused by the female of the ruling class, the surrogate mother, the resident alien without recourse, the other woman, the runaway youth.[29]

Yet, at the same time, Levine points out that often such "positive reevaluation of one figure signals the denigration of another." She then goes on to ask who is to be understood as among Hagar's oppressors: "Hebrews? Israelites? Jews? The authors of the text? Men? Are they real people? . . . For some readers, the 'obvious' answer—anachronistically and overgeneralized—is

27. Ibid., 15.

28. Ibid.

29. Trible, *Texts of Terror*, 27–28.

'the Jews.' For others, the answer is 'the text.'"[30] The net effect is less to understand the biblical words in their context than to exchange one example of exploitation/victimhood for another. "Thus, while Hagar's various activities can be celebrated and her various persecutors condemned, it is unhelpful to view her solely as victim or unequivocally as 'good.'"[31] In short, Genesis' presentation of Hagar is that of someone who is very human. Like all of us, she has her good qualities and her failings.

In the example of the Sarah-Hagar relationship, in the New Testament, the Apostle Paul privileges Sarah, who for him represents the example to argue for the new faith. Many, but not all, classical midrashim favor Sarah because she is the senior Matriarch of Judaism. Conversely, Trible and others favor Hagar because she is a figure that they suggest illustrates certain concepts they wish to highlight. The Genesis text is more complex. Each woman shows both her better and her less desirable character traits. They can each behave with generosity of spirit or pettiness. As we explain in the chapter on Hagar, Hagar is treated sympathetically in both Gen 16 and 21. Nahum M. Sarna has noted that in the Genesis text itself, the narrator's voice sympathizes with the plight of Hagar: "God, the guardian of the weak and the suffering, reveals Himself to the lowly Egyptian maidservant, bringing her a message of hope and comfort."[32] Although in the latter chapter, God tells Abraham to "do what [Sarah] tells you," the heavenly response to Hagar's plight again shows God as the guardian of the weak and of those who suffer deprivation.

Sources

Bible

Christians often think of the Bible as the dual volumes, to use Christian terminology, of both the Old Testament and the New Testament. When referring to the Bible, Jews mean something different. For Jews, the Bible is only those books that most Protestant Christians refer to as the Old Testament. These are what Roman Catholics, Anglicans, and Eastern Orthodox Christians refer to as the Old Testament, but without the Apocrypha/deuterocanonical books. Jews may also call it the Jewish Bible, the Jewish Scriptures, the Hebrew Scriptures, the Hebrew Bible, or the Tanakh, which is an acronym for the Torah (Teaching, Instruction), the Neviim (Prophets),

30. Levine, "Beer-lahai-roi," 19.
31. Ibid., 18.
32. Sarna, *Genesis*, 120.

and Ketuvim (the Writings). The adjective "Old," as in the phrase "*Old* Testament," suggests that there is a new, updated, and improved version. For Jews, the *original* covenant-contract-testament with God remains in force. God's covenant with the Jewish people is eternal. For Jews, Judaism is neither the prototype nor the roots of another religion that is "improved." For Jews, the Jewish Bible and Judaism are complete. Judaism has a full life of its own. For Jews, the Bible—one of the most hallowed and revered objects in Judaism—is not the "Old Testament," which has been replaced by a newer version. It is *the* irreplaceable Testament.

The Jewish Bible (*TaNaKh*) divides into three parts: the Teaching (the *Torah*, sometimes translated as "the Law"), the Prophets (*Neviim*), and the Writings (*Ketuvim*). While Jewish and Christian Bibles contain the same books, there are important differences in their order. Christian Bibles follow an historical sequence, but Jewish Bibles are set in the order in which the books were canonized (recognized as official). (As noted earlier, Roman Catholic, Anglican, and Eastern Orthodox Bibles also contain the Apocrypha/deuterocanonical books.)

The Teaching (*Torah*):

Genesis, Exodus, Leviticus, Numbers, Deuteronomy

The Prophets (*Neviim*):

Joshua, Judges, 1, 2 Samuel, 1, 2 Kings, Isaiah, Jeremiah, Ezekiel, Hosea, Joel, Amos, Obadiah, Jonah, Micah, Nahum, Habakkuk, Zephaniah, Haggai, Zechariah, Malachi

The Writings (*Ketuvim*):

Psalms, Proverbs, Job, Song of Songs, Ruth, Lamentations, Ecclesiastes, Esther, Daniel, Ezra, Nehemiah, 1, 2 Chronicles.

Early Extra-Biblical Literature

Pseudepigrapha

The Pseudepigrapha, like the Apocrypha, comes from the time of the later Second Temple period and a bit thereafter, ca. 200 BCE to 200 CE. While the Apocrypha was incorporated into the Roman Catholic, Anglican, and Eastern Orthodox churches, the Pseudepigrapha was not. There are occasional references to the Matriarchs in the books of the Pseudepigrapha. The major source comes from *Jubilees*, but there is also some material in other books, primarily the *Testaments of the Twelve Patriarchs*.

Testaments of the Twelve Patriarchs

The *Testaments of the Twelve Patriarchs*, written in the second century BCE, "bears witness to the diversity of outlook that developed in Judaism in the period prior to the Maccabean Revolt and flourished throughout the Maccabean period."[33] The words of these testaments are credited to each of the twelve sons of Jacob and are modeled on his last words as reflected in Gen 49. As shall be noted when quoting from these works, they often reflect a very misogynist viewpoint.

Jubilees

The book of *Jubilees*

> was composed some time in the second century BCE or possibly even earlier. The *Book of Jubilees* recasts *Genesis* and the first [twelve] chapters of *Exodus* in the form of an angelic revelation to Moses [while he is on Mount Sinai] and emends the biblical stories. Many biblical passages are entirely omitted, while others are expanded either by the addition of narratives concerning the biblical characters or by the incorporation of numerous halakhic injunctions.[34]

This means that *Jubilees* is probably one of the earliest extant commentaries on the Bible.[35] The "title well reflects one of the book's outstanding features: its frequent assigning of a date to the events of Genesis by referring to the jubilee and year in which they took place . . . The length of a jubilee is [forty-nine or fifty years] . . . each jubilee easily divides into seven subgroups of seven years . . . conventionally called 'weeks.'"[36] Their authorship is unknown. Most scholars believe the author(s) referred to copies of the

33. Kee, "Testaments of the Twelve Patriarchs," 778.

34. Bohak, "Book of Jubilees," 381. The explanation about Moses receiving this revelation, which is dictated by an angel on Mount Sinai, is found in the prologue to *Jubilees* and at the beginning of its second chapter.

35. While known about for more than a century, *Jubilees* was only available in the Ethiopian Christian Church texts in their ancient language. When fifteen Hebrew copies were found among the Dead Sea Scrolls, the book of *Jubilees'* importance to Jewish scholarship became apparent.

36. Kugel, "Jubilees," 273; Kugel, *Walk through Jubilees.*

Samaritan Pentateuch (or an earlier version of it), the Masoretic Hebrew
Pentateuch (the authoritative Hebrew text of the Pentateuch/Torah), the
Septuagint, Aramaic Targumim (translations), and the Dead Sea Scrolls,
written in Hebrew and Aramaic, the Peshittas (translations into Syriac) and
other books of the Pseudepigrapha and Second Temple literature, such as
the *Testaments of the Twelve Patriarchs* or an earlier version of it.[37] *Jubilees*
is "arguably the most important and influential of all the books written by
Jews in the Second Temple period."[38]

Jubilees is characterized as an example of reworked or "Rewritten
Scripture."[39] It is unique in that it records "the biblical story as a record of
couples . . . [thus it] significantly expands and enriches the depiction of the
female characters."[40] Indeed,

> One of the more eye-catching aspects of *Jubilees* is the important
> place it assigns to women. Whereas in Genesis the patriarchal
> wives [do act and speak,] in *Jubilees* they are more prominent
> and in some cases play key roles in the sacred drama . . . [This
> is especially true in terms of Rebekah.] The place of women in
> *Jubilees* is a sub-category of a larger theme regarding the pu-
> rity of the chosen line—that holy and priestly nation . . . which
> required proper marriages and separation from the inherently
> impure nations . . . In order to guarantee the integrity of the
> genealogy that leads to Israel and its priests, the ancestors had
> to marry women from the right stock. The point was so impor-
> tant that the family connections of the women are detailed in
> the genealogies, and when they came from non-approved clans
> trouble resulted."[41]

The author's themes include the ideal of endogamous marriages and
the prohibition of exogamy (*Jub.* 30:7–14.) There is a clear polemic against
foreign wives, which is likely related to the developing issue of matrilineal descent. (For example, biblically, both of Joseph's sons, Manasseh and

37. VanderKam, *Textual and Historical Studies*, 103–205; VanderKam, *Book of
Jubilees*, 17–21; Segal, *Book of Jubilees*, 1–41, 317–24.

38. Kugel, *Walk through Jubilees*, 1.

39. Rewritten Scriptures (Rewritten Bibles) can also be seen as midrashim on the
Bible. An example of a late Rewritten Scripture is the *Pirke de Rabbi Eliezer*, composed
about the seventh or eighth century CE. The *Pirke de Rabbi Eliezer* is more usually
referred to as midrash.

40. Halpern-Amaru, "First Woman, Wives," 609.

41. VanderKam, "Recent Scholarship," 420. In his article, VanderKam actually
wrote that in "Genesis the patriarchal wives bear children and do little else (apart from
some domestic scheming)" (ibid.). Regretfully, this is an example of a sexist dismissal
of the important roles played by the Matriarchs in the Genesis text.

Ephraim, as well as Moses' sons are regarded as Hebrews; this is based on patrilineal descent, for their mothers were not Hebrews.) Matrilineal descent versus patrilineal descent appears to have been finally codified by the time of the completion of the Mishnah, ca. 200 CE.[42] This concern over exogamy is first mentioned in Ezra-Nehemiah as the Exilic community returned to Judah from Babylon (ca. 538–400 BCE). During the Babylonian exile, and certainly among those who returned, some men married local "non-Jewish" women, in several cases no doubt divorcing their Jewish wives. Ezra and Nehemiah show concern about foreign wives in general, and more specifically with priests who took non-Jewish wives (Ezra 10:1–17; 9:12; Neh 13:1–3, 23–27). Whether the *Jubilees* statements are directed against the Samaritan community or the more assimilated Hellenized Jewish community of the third century BCE is unclear. The author of *Jubilees* "believed that Judah in his own day was plunged in fornication and impurity [this] . . . impurity arising largely from sexual immorality and contact with 'foreigners,' that is, non-Jews."[43] Marriage to foreign men does not appear to be a problem in either Ezra-Nehemiah or *Jubilees*. Perhaps the tribal inheritance through the male line made Judean women who were lacking in inheritance less of an issue. "There is no explicit reference to the ethnically assimilated *ger* and no mention of a process of religious conversion in *Jubilees*." The word used in *Jubilees* for *ger*, or "foreigner," is *nakir*, or "otherness," a term more exclusive than foreigner and certainly not a resident alien.[44]

Additionally, *Jubilees* values both spouses as supporting partners in covenant history. The female spouses' "knowledge of the promised future . . . empowers these women [the Matriarchs of Genesis] so that they function in a way that is independent of the men in their lives . . . Their actions serve as correctives for a male whose vision or understanding is somehow misguided or distorted . . . Rather, it is an assertiveness, an independence of mind and spirit that enlightens, redirects, and/or rectifies."[45] The author of *Jubilees* generally describes almost perfectly functioning families. The author limits the roles of Judah and even Joseph (despite his rejection of Potiphar's wife) possibly because of their marriages to outsiders. The author likewise assigns a smaller part to Jethro and Zipporah in Moses' life, even as there is more attention paid to Levi and the Levites because of the importance of the priesthood and their marrying endogamously.

---

42. Cohen, *Beginnings of Jewishness*, 273.

43. Kugel, "Jubilees," 276–77.

44. Halpern-Amaru, *Empowerment*, 157.

45. Ibid., 75.

As Betsy Halpern-Amaru notes, "the task of reconstruction is a formidable one."[46] In Genesis, there are serious tensions between Sarah and Hagar when Sarah feels that she has been mocked or scoffed at by Hagar. This episode is excised in *Jubilees*, which wants to offer a picture of happy families. Years later, at Isaac's weaning ceremony, Ishmael is present, and Abraham rejoices because he has sons. At the weaning ceremony—or perhaps later, for the *Jubilees* text is ambiguous on this point—Ishmael is portrayed as "playing and dancing." There is no sense that he is mocking, scoffing, or in any way diminishing the role of Isaac. Yet, Sarah demands that he and his mother be driven away, for she is "jealous of Ishmael." The potential rivalries among the children, Ishmael and Isaac, itself encourages conflict between the spouses, Abraham and Sarah, and between Sarah and Hagar. In Genesis, Sarah's call for the expulsion of mother and son carries with it her hostility toward Hagar. She appears to be thinking, "Just as his mother mocked me, so he is mocking my son." By way of contrast, in *Jubilees* it is only Ishmael's positive role that is at issue. The *Jubilees* author often rewrites the biblical text when doing so is perceived to be necessary. For example, when the issue is about Jacob seeking a wife from his uncle Laban's family, not only does he get this particular instruction directly from his mother Rebekah, but he also had this selfsame advice to marry his maternal cousins from his grandfather Abraham. The unseemly "deception" and the implied division or disagreement between Isaac and Rebekah as to the proper son to bless, which is so prominent in Gen 27 (see the description devoted to this matter in the chapter on Rebekah below) is simply eliminated. In its place is relative family harmony. Further, given the patriarchal nature of the ancient Near-Eastern society, *Jubilees*' respect for women and the importance and vitality given to its descriptions of women is remarkable.

Flavius Josephus

Flavius Josephus (ca. 37–100 CE) was a Judean general who defected to the Roman legions after realizing the likelihood of losing the Jewish War against Rome. Josephus suggests that Greco-Roman culture and Hellenistic Judaism might coexist. His most famous works are *The Jewish War*, the *Antiquities of the Jews*, and *Against Apion*. Josephus writes for a Roman audience, but he clearly respects his own people and traditions. His intent is to mediate between his contemporary Jewish and Greco-Roman, Greek-speaking audiences. Josephus relates some incidents and ideas not seen elsewhere. His writings about the characters in Genesis are influenced by Hellenism

46. Ibid., 47.

and may also have been swayed by midrashic traditions that have since been lost. He idealizes women as viewed by Greco-Roman culture. They show affection to their husbands and actively seek to protect their children. Yet, on the whole, Josephus tends to downplay the role of biblical women as did his near-contemporary, Philo of Alexandria.[47]

Rabbinic

Targums (Targumim)

The Targum is an Aramaic version of the Hebrew Bible compiled from the Second Temple period until the early centuries of the Common Era. Aramaic was the dominant Jewish language or lingua franca for hundreds of years in many of the major Jewish communities in the Near East. To facilitate the study of the Bible and make its public reading understood by the common people, authoritative translations were required. As translations, the Targumim are sometimes paraphrases and sometimes fairly literal, yet they also contain many midrashic expansions. We refer primarily to the *Targum Onqelos.*

Midrash Collections

There are many midrash collections. The best-known may be *Midrash Rabbah*,[48] which is a commentary on the Torah and the five scrolls, or Megillot (Song of Songs, Ruth, Lamentations, Ecclesiastes, and Esther). There are, however, many other collections, such as *Pesikta Rabbati, Pesikta de Rab Kahana, Pirke de Rabbi Eliezer,* and so forth. Midrash is a product of the rabbis who flourished from ca. 200 to 500 CE, but collections may have been added to and compiled centuries after that time. Midrash, which is always grounded in the biblical text, is a uniquely Jewish way of interpreting the Bible.[49] "Midrash" means to study, to search, to investigate, to go in quest of, and to give account for what is written.[50] While midrash is rooted in the

---

47. Philo, however, does value Sarah on an allegorical level (Niehoff, "Mother and Maiden," 413–44).

48. All references to *Midrash Rabbah* are taken from the Soncino edition.

49. "Midrash is a type of literature, oral or written, which has its starting point in a fixed canonical text, considered the revealed word of God by the midrashist and his audience, and in which this original verse is explicitly cited or clearly alluded to" (Porton, "Midrash," 4:819).

50. Bruns, "Hermeneutics of Midrash," 190. The Hebrew for sermon, *derasha*, is

text, it often moves far from the plain meaning of that text. Since the "Bible is a laconic, elliptical, and at times ambiguous text; thus it is open to a variety of interpretations of any one [word, phrase, or] verse."[51] For example, in Gen 12:17 the Hebrew words are *'al d'var Sarai*. This could correctly be translated "because of Sarai," or, as the rabbis suggest, "according to the *word* of Sarai."[52] The rabbis suggest that she actually spoke at this juncture.

Adele Berlin captures the intent of this special form of teaching when she explains that "midrashic comments help us see the meaning more clearly, if more imaginatively." She goes on to say, "The rabbis were not interested in what we call 'the original meaning of the text.' They were more intent on the meaning for their own time, and they engage in obviously anachronistic readings. They thereby lift the biblical story out of its original context and apply it to another context. In so doing, they keep the Bible alive."[53] One example to illustrate this point is when the rabbis praise Rebekah. They credit her with being pious. She performs several traditional ritual acts associated with women, such as separating dough from the *hallah* and lighting candles, virtues that are extolled in rabbinic Judaism, many hundreds of years after her lifetime (*Genesis Rabbah* 60.16).[54]

In the mind of the rabbis, each biblical statement carried many meanings.[55] As this was so in terms of legal legislation, so it was applicable to narrative sections, which include the stories of the Matriarchs and the Patriarchs. Genesis' actual words concerning the Matriarchs were limited; what might be said about them was virtually limitless. Midrash is the "'unconsciousness' of the text."[56] It is "a creative process through which the rabbis arrived at a new perception about the world. By saying that scripture is like the manna, the rabbis were suggesting that it nourishes, sustains and enlivens the people of God."[57] Midrash involves many genres: tales and allegories, ethical reflections, epigrams and legends. Through midrash, the "sacred words became an inexhaustible mine . . . of religious and ethical teaching."[58] In the words of the

based on the word "midrash" (Hyman, *Biblical Women in the Midrash*, xxvii–xxxiii).

51. Bronner, *From Eve to Esther*, xv.

52. See "The Rabbis' Sarah" below.

53. Berlin, "Writing a Commentary," 15.

54. The volumes of *Midrash Rabbah* are referred to by the name of the book, the word *Rabbah*, and then the specific midrash itself (i.e., *Genesis Rabbah* 94.9, *Exodus Rabbah* 1.1, or *Lamentations Rabbah* 2.2.4).

55. Babylonian Talmud *Sanhedrin* 34a.

56. Paul, *Moses and Civilization*, 93.

57. Callaway, *Sing, O Barren One*, 7. The reference is to the *Targum Onqelos* for Eccl 12:11.

58. Cohen, *Everyman's Talmud*, xviii.

rabbis, each word in the Torah has seventy possible interpretations—*Shiv'im panim ba-Torah* (*Numbers Rabbah* 13.15, 16).

Through their midrashim, the rabbis teach about the values of their time, such as the nature of God, opposition to idolatry, proper modesty, the importance of studying sacred texts and of generosity, hard work, chastity, and loyalty, as well as discussing differences between the Jewish and non-Jewish communities. Furthermore, according to the midrashic tradition, linear time does not exist when it comes to the Torah. Past, present, and future time periods are seamless; they are all part of one ongoing continuum.[59] Midrashic literature first appears in spoken form in the land of Israel and in the great communities of Parthian and Neo-Persian Babylonia between the third to sixth centuries CE. The rabbis that are quoted in the midrash often disagree among themselves. To say that something is *a* rabbinic view, or even *the* rabbinic view, does not mean that all rabbis support that position or that interpretation.[60] Though redacted at later points, these rabbinic teachings draw on sources that both precede the time of the New Testament and continue for several centuries thereafter. Midrash composing continued as late as the twelfth and thirteenth centuries CE.[61]

A COMMENT ABOUT THE RABBINIC LITERATURE:
TIME AND CONTEXT

It is important to understand the rabbis in their own time and context: "The shapers and expositors of rabbinic Judaism were men, and the ideal human society that they imagined was decidedly oriented toward men. [The rabbis

---

59. "'*Ayn muqdam um'uḥar baTorah*—There is neither later nor previous time in the Torah" (Babylonian Talmud *Pesahim* 6b).

60. There often are differences of opinion among the rabbis. Furthermore, there may be variations in some of the details of a given midrash from one midrash collection to another. Some midrash collections repeat a midrash that appeared earlier in that same volume. Though we quote a specific midrash, there may be variations to be found.

61. In this book we cite many midrashim. These come from midrash collections, as well as from midrashic (*aggadic*, i.e., homiletic) materials from the Talmud. These documents were redacted at differing periods. A specific midrash may attribute a certain view to a given scholar. As with the Talmud, the certainty that such an attribution is absolutely accurate is doubtful: "Just because a particular document claims that a certain authority said a certain thing . . . should we believe that it is so? Many documents in antiquity attribute opinions or words falsely; ancient historical sensibilities saw nothing wrong with such artificial attributions" (Kraemer, *Responses to Suffering*, 11). We also quote occasionally from the *Zohar*. The *Zohar* is a mystical commentary on the Torah. It dates from about the thirteenth century CE. Technically not part of midrashic literature, nonetheless it contains midrash-like statements.

assumed that women had] lesser intellectual, spiritual, and moral capacities
. . . Rabbinic texts do not grant women a significant role in any aspect of
rabbinic Judaism's communal life of leadership, study, and worship."[62] When
Rabbi Ulla said, "Women are a nation/people unto themselves" (Babylonian
Talmud *Shabbat* 62a), his observation was not meant as a compliment. In
the sexist, sometimes misogynist, worldview of the rabbis, women were less
valued. In the Mishnah, the first part of the Talmud, it states, "Whoever
teaches his daughter Torah, it is as if he taught her frivolity [or lascivious-
ness]" (Mishnah *Sotah* 3.4). One also finds the view that women were regarded as of insufficient spiritual strength to pursue religious texts: "Rabbi
Eliezer believed that women were unfit for Torah study . . . [Babylonian
Talmud *Sotah* 21b]. His opinion expressed the dominant rabbinic attitude
which limited women's access to traditional Jewish learning for centuries.
The sage Ben Azzai expressed the opposite point of view, 'A man is obligated
to teach his daughter Torah' . . . [Babylonian Talmud *Sotah* 20a]; however,
this remained a minority view."[63]

The rabbis both praise and criticize the behavior of the Matriarchs.
There is a midrash that suggests the Matriarchs partnered with the
Patriarchs,[64] while in another midrash, Sarah is criticized for dominating
Abraham.[65] The rabbis were not monolithic in their views; there are often
a variety of opinions expressed, although on the whole, when it comes to
matters of gender and sexuality, there is a clear sexist bias. Nonetheless,
there are comments about Rabbi Akiva and his wife Rachel, as well as his

62. Baskin, "Women and Post-biblical Commentary," l–li. See "Aggadic Attitudes
toward Women" in Bronner, *From Eve to Esther*, 1–21. There she notes, "In talmudic life
and literature, the proper role of women was restricted to that of wife and mother—en-
abling roles. Talmudic sources praise women for being supportive of their menfolk and
for obeying their husbands and fathers" (Bronner, *From Eve to Esther*, 3).

63. Sohn, "Post-biblical Interpretations, *Vayak'heil*," 539.

64. An example of the Matriarchs and Patriarchs partnering together is the midrash,
"Abraham's coinage was widely distributed . . . What was on his coinage? An old man
and an old woman (Abraham and Sarah) on one side, and on the other, a young man
and a young woman (Isaac and Rebekah)." As the word "greatness" and "blessings" are
repeated frequently in the text in Gen 12, the midrash explains that "greatness" refers to
the Patriarchs and "blessing" to the Matriarchs (*Genesis Rabbah* 39.11). Furthermore,
there is a tradition that just as Abraham brought male converts into Judaism, so did
Sarah work alongside him to convert women (*Genesis Rabbah* 39.14; *Song of Songs
Rabbah* 1.3.3).

65. *Genesis Rabbah* 47.1. "Abraham was crowned through Sarah, but not Sarah
through Abraham. She was her husband's ruler. Abraham derived honor from Sarah,
but not she from him." Sarah entered into litigation with Abraham; therefore, her life-
span was less than that of Abraham (*Genesis Rabbah* 45.5; Babylonian Talmud *Rosh
Hashanah* 16b).

disciple, Rabbi Meir, and the learned Bruria, his wife, which suggest that these women were loved and respected by many. Likewise, rabbinic literature recognized the indispensability of women to provide essential support for family wellbeing and even family peace. Women were essential to social cohesion and sustenance.

Talmud

The Talmud is the vast compendium of Jewish thought developed in the post-biblical world between ca. 200 BCE and 500 CE. The word "Talmud" means "study" or "learning." It is a central source of Jewish teaching; it is a record of rabbinic discussions taking place over those centuries. It covers Jewish law, philosophy, ethics, customs, history, and narratives about the Bible. It has two components: first, the *Mishnah*, codified in 200 CE, which is written in rabbinic Hebrew and is a code of Jewish law; and second, the *Gemara*, which is written in Aramaic. For many centuries Before the Common Era and well into the Common Era, Aramaic was the common language of many people in that era living in the land of Israel (including Jesus), in Judea, and other communities in the Near East where Jews lived. The *Gemara* was developed in the next three centuries. It was written simultaneously in two locations (Parthian and Neo-Persian) Babylon, which is the more authoritative text (termed the "Babylonian Talmud," or the *Bavli*) and in the land of Israel (often called the "Jerusalem Talmud," or the *Yerushalmi*). Although it is now in written form, it continues to be called the "Oral Law," and it remains an important source of Jewish study today.

Medieval/Renaissance Commentators

The preeminent medieval commentator on the Bible is Rabbi Shlomo ben Isaac, known by the acronym Rashi (1040–1105 CE, France). He offers a simple explanation of the biblical text and often refers to midrashim. Over the next several hundred years, as the Dark Ages declined in the second millennium of the Common Era, a renaissance took place. It featured the studies of Greek and Latin at centers of Christian and Islamic learning. This renaissance had an impact on Jewish life. Beyond the focus on midrashim in the early medieval times, a new form of Jewish commentary developed based on studies of Greek and Latin in the Christian and Islamic centers— an inter-confessional influence—that was resurrected through Arabic translations. This new Jewish scholarship was more related to literary and grammatical structure than to midrashic narrative. Other important Jewish commentators we cite include Nachmanides, otherwise known as Nah-manides or by the acronym Ramban (1194–1270 CE, Spain), and Obadiah ben Jacob Sforno (ca. 1475–1550 CE, Italy). We also refer to the *Zohar*, the thirteenth-century Kabbalistic text that is a mystical commentary on the Torah (Pentateuch).

Themes

Infertility[66]

Sons are indeed a heritage from the LORD, the fruit of the womb a reward.

—Ps 127:3[67]

In the biblical mind, children, and more generally, fertility, were rewards from God. The first commandment to humans was "Be fruitful and multiply." The psalm verse that praises the man who fears God and walks in God's ways says that he will be happy, matters will go well, and he shall have a "wife like a fruitful vine . . . children like olive shoots" around his table (Ps 128:3). Issues of infertility also apply to the land. In Leviticus, the people are told that if they follow God's commands, there will be rain in the proper seasons, "the land shall yield its produce, and the trees of the field shall yield their fruit . . . threshing shall overtake the vintage, and the vintage shall overtake the sowing" (Lev 26:4–5; cf. Deut 28:11). As fertility is linked to God's blessing and approval, so infertility is understood as a sign of divine disfavor. Not following God's ways brings "consumption and fever . . .[which will] cause life to pine away" (Lev 26:16). For those who turn from God, "Cursed shall be the fruit of your womb, the fruit of your ground, the increase of your cattle and the issue of your flock" (Deut 28:18). Infertility on a general level

66. The twin themes of infertility and its opposite, motherhood, are major subplots in the narratives of the Matriarchs of Genesis. Although beyond the scope of this book, these themes in one form or another continue as issues in biblical life. Subsequently, in Genesis these themes weave into the accounts that deal with Tamar, Judah's daughter-in-law, and very possibly into that of Potiphar's wife and her interest in Joseph. Later in the Bible, there are the examples of Manoah's wife (Judg 13); Hannah, Elkanah's wife (1 Sam 1); Michal, David's wife (2 Sam 6:23); and Ruth. There are references to infertile women in the prophets and the Psalms. In rabbinic literature, Zion is labeled as childless; however, like Sarah, Rebekah, and their sisters, she will bear fruit in old age.

67. NRSV translates the noun as "sons" instead of the more generic word, "children." While this may offend a gender-inclusive sensitivity, it probably reflects accurately how the biblical audience heard the words of the Psalm.

meant that the family, tribe, clan, or nation could not reproduce itself. It would mean the end of that group. The drastic punishment that temporarily befalls the people of Gerar is infertility. God "had closed fast all the wombs of the house of Abimelech because of Sarah, Abraham's wife" (Gen 20:18). The Bible assumed that a couple's inability to conceive was not the result of the husband's sterility, but rather God's decision in this matter concerning the wife's womb. Yet, the focus is on the woman's body: God *closed her womb* is the way that the Bible (and later rabbinic statements) explained the phenomenon of infertility. As understood by the ancient rabbis, the creative role in birth is the "seed," which is the term used as a metaphor for an offspring (Gen 21:13; or the "drop," see Mishnah *Avot* 3.1). The womb is the vessel—the earth in which the seed is planted. "It seems reasonable to conclude, therefore, that in the Hebrew Bible a child belongs to the father in a way it does not to the mother."[68] That men were not generally considered to be infertile (which might have meant simply a low sperm count), and that women were often labeled infertile (Gen 11:30; 25:21; 29:31) is part of the sexist view of the biblical text.

The rabbis praise Sarah because she realizes that her inability to conceive is divinely decreed. She does not revert to magic or amulets, as pagan women would. Sarah said, "I know the source of my affliction; it is not as people say [of an infertile woman] 'she needs a talisman, she needs a charm,' but rather behold now, [God] has restrained me from bearing" (Gen 16.2; *Genesis Rabbah* 45.2). Consequently, an infertile woman's eventual ability to conceive was understood as a sign of God's special blessing (viz. Sarah, Rebekah, Rachel, Leah, and later, Manoah's wife and Hannah). As the psalmist says, God "gives the barren woman a home, making her the joyous mother of children" (Ps 113:9; cf. Isa 54:1). "God's primary role in fertility is . . . emphasized. Men may be like God in their ability to generate new life, but the similarity has its limits. Men may plant their seed but only God can open the womb, and God does so according to a divine calculus beyond human understanding. The only way in which humans can play a role in the process is through prayer. The childless matriarchs provided an important model of the efficacy of prayer and they also became important metaphors for consolation and comfort. Over time, rabbinic enumerations of infertile biblical women whose prayers were answered evolved."[69]

Although he may be reflecting biblical thinking on the matter, it is with enormous insensitivity that Jacob replies to Rachel's plea to impregnate

---

68. Gellman, *Abraham! Abraham!*, 93. Gellman refers to Delaney, *Abraham on Trial*.

69. Baskin, "Infertile Wife." See also the "Sarah's Infertility" section in "The Rabbis' Sarah."

her, "Am I in the place of God who has withheld from you the fruit of the womb?" (Gen 30:2). A much more caring approach is taken a generation earlier by his father, Isaac: "Isaac prayed to the LORD for his wife, because she was [infertile]; and the LORD granted his prayer, and his wife Rebekah conceived" (Gen 25:21). Rachel is Jacob's favored wife, but for many years she lacks direct heirs, while Leah, the less favored wife, is fruitful but emotionally frustrated. Likewise, Sarah, Abraham's longtime first wife, is infertile, while the woman of lesser status, Hagar, conceives easily. The theme of a loved wife who eventually gives birth is a continuing thread in the biblical narrative.

Motherhood

The converse of infertility is motherhood, and bearing sons is even more praiseworthy. Being a mother is probably the most important role women play in the biblical world. Karla G. Shargent suggests that daughters and wives who do not give birth simply disappear, as in the case of women such as Dinah; Jephtha's daughter; Michal, David's wife; and Tamar, David's daughter.[70] Given ancient life spans, it was likely that for many women, motherhood (including domestic functioning) and adulthood were practically coterminous.

Abraham has two or three wives, eight sons, and no daughters. Isaac has one wife and two sons. Ishmael has one wife, twelve sons, and one daughter. Jacob's twelve sons and at least one daughter are conceived by four wives. His brother Esau fathers seven sons with three wives. The number of male versus female children seems remarkable and unlikely unless one accepts a divine plan, or explains this phenomenon through a patriarchal bias; that is, the conscious decision not to list all of the female children born. How else can it be that 91 percent of all names mentioned in the Bible refer to men?[71]

---

70. Shargent, "Living on the Edge," 34–36. Three exceptions are Deborah; Miriam, who has no children in the text (although she does in the midrashim); and Serah, the daughter of Asher (Serah /Serach bat Asher), who also has no children, but who in a midrash sang to Jacob that Joseph had not died (Ginzberg, *Legends of the Jews*, 2:115–16, 5:356–57; Reiss, "Serach bat Asher," 45–51). Serah, Jacob's granddaughter, according to midrashic tradition, entered Egypt with Jacob and miraculously left to go to the promised land centuries later (Gen 46:17; Num 26:46). She is also associated with the wise woman of Abel at the time of King David (2 Sam 20:16; *Genesis Rabbah* 94.9). See Jacobi, "Serach bat Asher."

71. Meyers, "Every Day Life," 245. In Gen 22:20–24, Abraham is informed that his brother Nahor fathered twelve children: eight by his wife Milcah and four more by his concubine (*pilegesh*) Reumah. The last child mentioned is Maacah, which sometimes refers to a female (for example, one of David's wives, as in 2 Sam 3:3) but in this context could be male or female, although probably male, since it likely refers to a tribal head,

Conception and birth—actually bringing forth children, especially sons—is a prime virtue for motherhood. Caring for, and more specifically, caring for the interest of those children is also important. There are examples among the Matriarchs that address just this issue. The first instance that highlights mother-as-child-protector is Sarah. At a certain point (Gen 21), Sarah acts to protect the interests of her son, Isaac. Fearing the religious or psychological influence on Isaac posed by his stepmother, Hagar, and his older half-brother, Ishmael, or possibly fearing that Ishmael might physically harm Isaac in order to become the sole heir, Sarah forces their mutual husband to expel Hagar, and Ishmael as well, from the Abrahamic encampment. Later in that selfsame chapter, Hagar fears for the life of her son when she and Ishmael appear to run out of water in the inhospitable wilderness. She places him under some foliage and calls out in sadness (Gen 21:16). Surely it is not coincidental that in *both* cases, God recognizes the "protective child-centered" actions of Sarah and Hagar and personally intervenes. In the case of Sarah, God instructs Abraham to listen to her voice; in the case of Hagar, God sends an angel to reassure her, and then the text explains specifically that "God was with the boy, and he grew up" (Gen 21:20).

Later we learn that Isaac loved Esau and Rebekah loved Jacob (Gen 25:28). Then, at a crucial moment, Rebekah takes on the mother-as-protector role when shielding her son, Jacob, from the wrath of his brother, Esau. She understands that Esau is furious over the "theft" of the blessing. Rebekah tells Jacob to leave. She then complains to Isaac about the situation. As a result of her urging, Isaac sends Jacob to Rebekah's brother Laban in faraway Paddan-aram (Gen 27:42–28:2). The biblical text does not explain in so many words that Rebekah urged Isaac to send Jacob to her brother's home, but that is exactly what he does. It is likely that Isaac understood the import of what Rebekah meant when she expressed her anger and disappointment about Esau marrying local Hittite women. Several chapters later in Genesis, Jacob's wife Leah appears to be protective of the gift of her son, Reuben. Reuben is bringing her a present, some mandrakes. Rachel—probably following a folk belief that mandrakes can be used as an aphrodisiac—wants to take some of the mandrakes. Leah only agrees to the bargain with her sister once Rachel temporarily concedes to Leah their mutual husband Jacob's presence in the marriage bed. Jacob does sleep with Leah; she is rewarded with conceiving a fifth son for him, and soon, a sixth (Gen 30:14–19).

---

similar to the twelve sons or tribes that stem from Jacob.

Power/Lack of Power

Men and women were interdependent upon each other. Women had roles in economic life as well as in educational, managerial, and religious life. In ancient Israel, daily "life centered on what can be called the 'family household,' which was the basic unit of society."[72] Women may have had less power than men, but nonetheless, they

> figured prominently as authority figures in intrafamily matters
> . . . The Bible calls the household 'mother's household' rather
> than the usual 'father's household' in several passages concerned
> with marriageable daughters (Gen 24:28; Ruth 1:8; Song 3:4; 8:2)
> . . . Such a role took women out of their own domestic contexts
> and gave them input into matters affecting land and property. It
> gave them direct influence over aspects of life that transcended
> their own immediate milieu.[73]

As Carol Meyers points out, "there are no absolute statements in the Hebrew Bible of categorical male supremacy over women." The statement in Gen 3:16, "your desire shall be for your husband, and he shall rule over you," needs to be understood in terms of "sexuality in the context of a sanction for increasing the birthrate, not with general social dominance."[74]

In the Hebrew Bible, there are many examples of powerful women. Deborah is both a judge and a prophet. Miriam, Huldah, Isaiah's unnamed wife, and Noadiah are all termed prophets (Exod 15:20; 2 Kgs 22:14; 2 Chr 34:22; Isa 8:3; Neh 6:14). Esther is a queen, and other queens are also mentioned, including Jezebel and Athalya. The Bible mentions two "wise women" (2 Sam 14; 20) who advised David and his chief general, Joab, respectively. Both of these women use tact and negotiation to help solve family and political problems. Abigail saves her husband's life through her wise appeal to David, and David will later marry her (1 Sam 25). Yet, generally compared to their male companions, women's authority and power is inferior within the overall pattern of patriarchy of the biblical world. Consequently, they often have to resort to deception to achieve their goals. Deception is a highly apparent theme in Genesis and is practiced by such women as Sarah, Rebekah, Rachel, and Leah, among others (Lot's daughters and Potiphar's wife). Some scholars believe that powerless characters use deception and that deception is not limited to women. Jacob (whose name can be interpreted as "trickster," see Gen 27:36) resorts to trickery, and David also

72. Ibid., 246.
73. Ibid., 249.
74. Ibid., 250. See also Adler, *Engendering Judaism*, 121–25.

resorts to trickery (1 Sam 21:13).[75] For example, in Gen 27, at least in the plain reading of the text, Rebekah may have used deception instead of some other means because she felt powerless in a patriarchal society.[76] In the end, her deception only furthers the divine plan.

Endogamy: Marriage within the Tribe or Family

Commenting on the statement Laban makes to Jacob, "It is better that I give her [Rachel] to you than I should give her to any other man" (Gen 29:19), Sarna explains, "Marriage between relatives was regarded as highly desirable in that it safeguarded 'purity of blood,' tribal property, and the welfare of the daughter."[77] The question of endogamy versus exogamy is theologically complicated, depending on the biblical source: Exod 34:15–16; Num 31:17–19; Deut 7:3–4; 21:10–14. There is no general biblical prohibition concerning marriage between Jews and non-Jews.[78] Specific prohibitions are stated, for example, concerning Canaanites and Moabites (Deut 7:1–3; 23:3–4 [4–5 H]). Nonetheless, there are exceptions to these rules, notably Judah's Canaanite wife, Bat Shua, and his daughter-in-law, Tamar (Gen 38), as well as Ruth the Moabite. Some particular marriages concerning Abraham's descendants are frowned upon, although not necessarily excluded from the biblical text: Ishmael and Esau's descendants are an example, and Esau is a direct descendant of Abraham and Sarah. For Ezra and Nehemiah, who come from an exilic community, the problem of intermarriage is greater than for previous generations. The matrilineal-line principle, which would only become the norm in the third century CE at the time of the rabbis, may have been debated during the biblical postexilic period. The ancient book of *Jubilees*, written during the Hellenistic period, views Moses' marriage to Zipporah with disfavor.

* * * *

75. Jeansonne, *Women of Genesis*, 67. See Niditch's remarks regarding tricksters in Niditch, "Genesis," 36.

76. "Rebekah's deception of the old and blind Isaac does not so much as hint at the wife's powerlessness versus her husband. It does not take into account that deception is Rebekah's only means of granting her preferred son a blessing. The fact is that Isaac, despite his dramatized impotence, is superior to Rebekah in power, yet it is Rebekah who is presented as a powerful woman who outsmarts an ailing old man" (Fuchs, "Who Is Hiding the Truth?" 137).

77. Sarna, *Genesis*, 204.

78. See Cohen, *Beginnings of Jewishness*, 260. At a later point in the Talmud, the biblical prohibition of marriage to certain non-Jews was expanded beyond some of the specific nations mentioned; see Babylonian Talmud *Avodah Zarah* 36b.

A Final Note

We have provided a wide variety of sources in our research so that the interested reader can delve further into the subject of the Matriarchs of Genesis.[79] While we have not attempted an exhaustive study of feminist thought, we hope that we have been representative of this important perspective, and sympathetic to it. At times we draw attention to the context of the sources that we quote and remark on their possible "perspectives" as we understand them. *Occasionally we consciously restate unfamiliar ideas of material presented earlier, such as the rabbinic concept—for the didactic purpose of their midrashim—of the absence of traditional linear time during the biblical period. This allows a character in Genesis to know of or refer to legislation found later, such as in Exodus. Likewise, in some cases the same or similar material can be found in the Sarah and Hagar chapters, or the Leah and Rachel chapters, but the focal point will differ. Furthermore, some observations or concepts apply to more than one Matriarch.*

79. See bibliography.

2

Sarah

Biblical Sarah

Introducing Sarah

SARAH IS THE BIBLE's first Matriarch. More broadly, Sarah is the mother of the Jewish people.[1] Commentaries on Genesis deal with Sarah's place within the biblical narrative, her life within the context of ancient Near Eastern customs, laws, and mores, and other matters as well. As the first Matriarch in Jewish (and Christian) tradition, Sarah and the world in which she lived hold special interest to women. She is the focus of female commentators and feminist commentators in particular.[2] Sarah plays a pivotal role in the unfolding drama of Genesis. She is Abraham's wife and Isaac's mother. Hagar the Egyptian is Sarah's slave. Sarah's actual words in Genesis are few in number. She is portrayed as a supportive, largely silent wife, although she states quite clearly her views on matters of importance to her.

---

1. As Abraham, Isaac, and Jacob are regarded as the Patriarchs within Jewish tradition, so Sarah, Rebekah, Leah, and Rachel (and possibly Bilhah and Zilpah) are deemed the Matriarchs of Judaism. This tradition has its roots in Isaiah's words, "Look to Abraham your father and to Sarah who bore you" (Isa 51:2). "Sarah our mother" (*Sarah imeinu*) is used both in rabbinic writings and in common speech (*Pesikta de Rab Kahana*, Piska 20.1).

2. To cite but a few examples: Athalya Brenner, Leila Leah Bronner, Amy-Jill Levine, Tamara Cohn Eskenazi and Andrea L. Weiss, Elaine James, Susan Niditch, Mayer I. Gruber, Ilona N. Rashkow, Savina J. Teubal, Phyllis Trible, Avivah Gottlieb Zornberg, Danna Nolan Fewell, and David Gunn.

Teubal takes an idiosyncratic view that is not widely shared. She suggests that Sarah is a priestess. Although Teubal does not claim that Sarah was a devotee of the goddess Astarte, she nevertheless points out that plaques of the goddess Astarte were found at Kiriyat-Sepher, which is in close proximity to Kiriyat Arba, Hebron, and Mamre (cf. Gen 13:18). "For Sarah . . . there are major elements in the episodes which are characteristics of a priestess" (Teubal, *Sarah*, 99).

Genesis 11: Sarah Begins as Sarai, an Infertile Wife

Although there are some other references to Sarah in the Bible, she appears in chapters 11 through 23 of Genesis.[3] When first introduced, she is named Sarai, meaning "my princess." She holds this name for more than half of her life. She is listed as the daughter-in-law of Terah as the wife of Abram (who will become Abraham, just as Sarai becomes Sarah in chapter 17). The Bible explains that Terah was planning to take his family from Ur of the Chaldeans to Canaan, but that when they came to Haran they settled there, and after some time Terah died (Gen 11:31–32). The text also notes, "Now Sarai was barren; she had no child" (Gen 11:30). The "Hebrew 'akarah simply means 'childless,' but not necessarily infertile."[4]

Genesis 12: The Call, Travels, and a Sojourn in Egypt

This is the tenth generation since the time of Noah. God's voice has been silent. Suddenly, without warning or preamble, God calls to Abram and commands him to leave Haran, where he and his immediate family have settled. At this point, Abram is seventy-five years old, Sarai sixty-five.[5] They are to go to a new and unspecified land: "Go from your country and your kindred . . . to the land that I will show you" (Gen 12:1). God promises that Abram will be the progenitor of a great nation and that his name will become great. Furthermore, "in you all the families of the earth shall be blessed." Technically, the biblical text reads that "The LORD said *to Abram*, 'Go from your country . . .'" Yet this is a command to both Abram and Sarai.

---

3. Sarah's life is depicted in Gen 11–23. The other references to her in the Hebrew Bible are Gen 24:36, 67; 25:10, 12; 49:31; and Isa 51:2. Sarah is mentioned by name in the New Testament in the Epistles in several places: Rom 4:19, 9:9; Heb 11:11; 1 Pet 3:6; and she is referred to, but not named, in Gal 4:21–31. These references do not fall within the purview of this book.

4. Sarna, *Genesis*, 87 n. 30. NRSV uses the term "barren." Unless we are quoting a text which uses that word, we substitite the less offensive word, "infertile." Friedman uses "infertile" in place of "barren." See Friedman, *Commentary on the Torah*.

5. Abraham is listed as seventy-five, and therefore Sarah is sixty-five (cf. Gen 17, where Abraham is nearly 100 and Sarah nearly ninety). Old age was seen as a sign of divine favor, but these figures seem unrealistic. Although not a hard-and-fast rule, in many cases when the ages of people found in the post-diluvian era in Genesis are halved, the narrative makes greater sense. This would translate into Sarah being merely forty-five when she became pregnant (not ninety) and Abraham being only fifty (not 100) years old. This explanation does not resolve the issue of Sarah's claim to be post-menopausal and then becoming pregnant. See Zucker, "Ages of the Matriarchs and the Patriarchs."

This will be clarified later in Genesis when God makes it manifest that it is not through Abraham alone but rather through his and Sarah's child that the covenant will continue (Gen 17:19).

The family travels leisurely. Lot, their nephew, as well as their large household of many servants and retainers, accompanies them. In the absence of any direct heirs, Abram probably thinks that the covenant would continue through Lot. (Later, in Gen 15:2–3, Abram, still childless, will complain to God that it will be his servant Eliezer who will be the chief inheritor.) In time, they settle in the land of Canaan. Not long thereafter, due to a major famine, the family and its entourage relocate to Egypt for a time.

When they are approaching Egypt, Sarai's husband explains that he fears for his life. "When [Abram] was about to enter Egypt, he said to his wife [Sarai], 'I know well that you are a woman beautiful in appearance; and when the Egyptians see you, they will say, "This is his wife;" then they will kill me and let you live. Say you are my sister, so that it may go well with me because of you, and that my life will be spared on your account'" (Gen 12:11–13).[6] This is the first of three similar situations related in Gen 12 and 20 concerning Abraham and Sarah and in Gen 26 regarding Isaac and Rebekah.[7] There is some difference of opinion among scholars as how to understand this episode, as well as its later parallels. This shall be discussed in the "Contemporary Scholarship" and the "Feminist Thought" sections below.

At its most direct level, this means that Sarai is marginalized as a person. Abraham and the Egyptians regard her merely as her "brother's" property. He seems to get her to agree and to submit to Pharaoh. She apparently acquiesces to this changed status. Sarai does not claim that she is Abraham's lawful wife. Shortly after their arrival, Sarai is taken into Pharaoh's palace. There is no indication in the biblical text that she objects to or challenges

6. Technically, Sarai is Abram's sister. According to Gen 20:12, they share a common father, but not the same mother. As a note in *NOAB* explains, "Marriage with a half-sister was permitted in ancient times (2 Sam 13:13) but later was forbidden (Lev 18:9, 11; 20:17)" (comment on Gen 20:12). This note notwithstanding, it is unclear in the Samuel passage whether Tamar voices these words in an attempt to avoid rape.

According to Josephus and rabbinic tradition, Sarah is also the same person known as Iscah—or Yiscah, perhaps meaning "regal," or something to do with "sight" (see the discussion below in the section on "Josephus" in "The Rabbis' Sarah"). Iscah is the daughter of Haran, Abraham's dead brother, whose other daughter is Milcah. Abraham's other brother Nahor married Milcah. If they were the same persons, then Rebekah, Leah, and Rachel would be related by blood to both Abraham and Sarah. Lot then would be a brother to Milcah and Sarah/Iscah.

7. This episode (and parallel episodes in Gen 20 and 26) have been termed the "wife-sister" motif. While Speiser suggests connections with Nuzi documents (Speiser, *Genesis*, 91–94), that view has been challenged. See Greengus, "Sisterhood Adoption," 5–31.

this wife-sister deception. As shall be discussed in a section below, "The Rabbis' Sarah," there is rabbinic material that features her prayers to God seeking release and rescue from the Pharaoh's advances towards her. In Egypt, Sarai's husband prospers, and he acquires "male and female slaves" for their household (Gen 12:16). Yet God takes notice of what is happening and brings plagues unto Pharaoh and his house, "because of Sarai, Abram's wife" (v. 17). Finally, Pharaoh releases her, expelling them both from Egypt along with Abram's newly acquired wealth.

Genesis 16: Sarah, Hagar, and Abraham

Sarai is not mentioned in chapters 13, 14, or 15. Ten years have passed since Sarai and Abram first settled in Canaan. They still lack direct heirs. In desperation, following ancient Near Eastern custom,[8] Sarai takes one of her household servants, Hagar the Egyptian, and convinces Abram to take Hagar as a wife/concubine. Hagar's role is to function as a surrogate mother in place of Sarai.

Hagar conceives almost immediately, and she then apparently acts contemptuously towards Sarai. Tensions mount. Sarai confronts her husband who, in effect, relinquishes any authority he has in this matter. He says to Sarai, "Your slave-girl is in your power; do with her as you please" (Gen 16:6). Sarai mistreats Hagar, who then leaves the encampment and flees to the desert. There, Hagar has an angelic encounter. She is told to return to Sarai. She is also informed that she will bear a son whom she is to name Ishmael. This name is then directly connected to the angel's explanation that God has heard her affliction (Ishmael translates as "God hears," *yishm'a 'el*). Hagar does return and apparently tells Abram about her experience in the desert wilderness, for he names his son Ishmael.

Genesis 17: Sarai Becomes Sarah; The Promise of a Son

Sarah does not appear as an active character in this chapter. She is spoken about, but she is not physically present. In this chapter, Abram receives a new name from God, Abraham. God renames Sarai, giving her the name Sarah. Furthermore, God says that she will be doubly blessed: Sarah will give birth to a son, and she shall give rise to nations. Noting that he is one hundred years old, while Sarah is ninety, Abraham is incredulous and laughs when he

---

8. See the section below on "Contemporary Scholarship" for an explanation of this custom of surrogate motherhood.

hears this news. Patiently, God repeats the information to him. God further explains that the covenant will be through their mutual son Isaac, but that Ishmael will also become the father of many princes. God then reiterates that in about a year's time Abraham's wife will give birth: "Sarah shall bear to you" (Gen 17:21).

Genesis 18: Visitors Appear, Sarah Is Told She Will Give Birth; Sarah's Reaction

Chapter 18 begins with some unexpected visitors presenting themselves when the family is encamped by the oaks at Mamre. Abraham rushes to meet them, then goes to Sarah's tent and asks her to help him prepare food. The meal is served to the three visitors outside of the tent near a tree. Sarah is standing inside the entrance near the tent opening. She overhears their conversation (Gen 18:9–10). The visitors explain that in a year's time Sarah will give birth. Now it is Sarah who is skeptical, perhaps bitter. She is bemused thinking that this is too little, too late, for as the text explains, she is post-menopausal (v. 11). "So Sarah laughed to herself, saying, 'After I have grown old, and my husband is old, shall I have pleasure?'" (Gen 18:12).[9] Despite this remark, or perhaps due to the bitterness of her response, or because she has doubts about Abraham's abilities or God's, God chides Sarah: "The LORD said to Abraham, 'Why did Sarah laugh? . . . Is anything too wondrous for the LORD?'" Sarah overhears this question. She is embarrassed and afraid. She denies the fact that she laughed, saying, "'I did not laugh'. . . He said, 'Oh yes, you did laugh'" (Gen 18:13–15). God's response to Sarah's remark may be a gentle rebuke. On the other hand, is God exasperated with her lack of faith, tingeing the word "laughter" with divine bitterness? It is notable that when Abraham is equally incredulous (Gen 17:17), God is considerably more patient with the Patriarch. This is a remarkable passage. The plain reading of the text suggests that God is one of the visitors to the encampment, and quite clearly that God is in dialogue with Sarah.[10] As shall

---

9. Please note these alternate readings: "Now that I am withered" (NJPS) and "Now that I've lost the ability" (CJPS). As shall be explained in the section on rabbinic literature below, the rabbis have an answer for this remarkable phenomenon.

10. Teubal suggests that God may have been more than in dialogue with Sarah: "Isaac was conceived through divine agency. '[God] took note [pqd] of Sarah as [God] had promised, and [God] did for Sarah as he had spoken. Sarah conceived and bore a son to Abraham in his old age, at the set time which God had spoken' [Gen 21:1–2] . . . the verb paqad is used for a husband visiting his wife for coitus in Judges 15:1. Use of this word in conjunction with the visit of [God] to Mamre seems to bring vestiges of a tale of supernatural conception in which a male deity impregnates a human woman . . .

be noted below, the rabbis suggest (Hagar in Gen 16:13 and Rebekah in Gen 25:23, notwithstanding) that this is the only instance in the Hebrew Scriptures where God speaks to a woman.

Genesis 20: Sarah, Abraham, King Abimelech of Gerar; Sarah as Sister

Sarah does not appear in chapter 19 of Genesis. As chapter 20 begins, Sarah and her husband continue to wander in the land of Canaan. They leave Mamre and move for a while to the Negev area—to the Philistine stronghold of Gerar, located between Kadesh and Shur. In a situation reminiscent of the deception in Egypt, Abraham once again presents Sarah as his sister, not his wife (Gen 20:2). She is then taken into the ruler's harem. God suddenly intervenes and warns Abimelech that he is in mortal danger: "God came to Abimelech in a dream by night, and said to him, 'You are about to die because of the woman whom you have taken; for she is a married woman'" (Gen 20:3). The next verse states clearly that Abimelech had not yet approached Sarah. The king is anguished. He explains to God that both the woman and the man had claimed that they were siblings. God confirms that Abimelech is innocent of intentional wrongdoing but warns him to return Sarah upon pain of death.

The next morning, Abimelech warns his community about these events. He confronts Abraham, who claims that it was his fear of being killed that caused him to misrepresent his true relationship with Sarah. Abraham then continues to explain that on some level they are siblings, for "she is indeed my sister, the daughter of my father but not the daughter of my mother, and she became my wife" (Gen 20:12). Abraham claims responsibility for his deceitful words. As in Egypt, Abraham prospers because of the deception, for Abimelech gives him sheep and oxen as well as male and female slaves, then returns Sarah to him. Abimelech next turns to Sarah and says, "Look, I have given your brother a thousand pieces of silver; it is your exoneration [alternatively, "your unblemished virtue," or "vindication"] before all who are with you; you are completely vindicated" (Gen 20:16).[11]

---

hieros gamos" (Teubal, *Sarah*, 126).

11. See "Sarah's Exoneration, Vindication" in the "Contemporary Scholarship" section.

Genesis 21: Sarah Gives Birth; Expulsion
of Hagar and Ishmael

As Gen 21 begins, Sarah conceives and gives birth. Abraham names their son Isaac, a name that literally means, "one will laugh." Reaching back to the announcements of Isaac's future birth in chapters 17 and 18, in this chapter, as later in chapter 26, laughter and Isaac are connected, but often it is bitter laughter.[12]

There are two major episodes in Gen 21 that concern Sarah. The first seven verses describe Sarah's joy at becoming a mother. This is followed by five verses that reflect Sarah's protective stance regarding Isaac's personal welfare. Genesis 21:8–12, which probably takes place around the time of Isaac's weaning, suggests that Sarah desires to banish Hagar and Ishmael, for they threaten Isaac's present and future well-being. At this point Isaac is approximately three years old,[13] and Ishmael is about sixteen or seventeen. Sarah approaches Abraham and demands that he expel Hagar and her son from the family encampment. Sarah explains that the "son of this slave woman shall not inherit along with my son Isaac" (Gen 21:10). In the previous verse, the biblical text says, "Sarah saw the son of Hagar the Egyptian whom she had borne to Abraham, playing" (v. 9). The Septuagint, and therefore most Christian Bible translations, add a few words so that the sentence reads, "playing *with her son Isaac*."[14] It is not at all clear what the word "playing" means in this context.[15] Were Ishmael's actions, with or without Isaac, connected to Sarah's decision to expel Hagar and Ishmael? Did Sarah see Ishmael acting this way at Isaac's weaning ceremony, or before, or after? Could it have been months or years later? Considering that Ishmael was his father's firstborn son, surely he was entitled to some inheritance. Two generations later, Jacob's sons by the secondary wives, Bilhah and Zilpah, become full tribal leaders (Dan and Naphtali, Gad and Asher, respectively). The Bible is silent on most of these matters. Although upset by this turn of events, Abraham capitulates when God tells him to defer to Sarah's wishes. God is explicit: "Whatever Sarah says to you, do as she tells you, for it is through Isaac that offspring shall be named for you" (v. 12). God also

---

12. See Speiser, *Genesis*, 125 n. 17; Alter, *Genesis*, 97; Zucker, "Isaac," 105–10.

13. "Extant documents suggest that . . . in the ancient Near East, mothers usually weaned their children at around the age of three" (Berlin, "Central Commentary, *Sh'mot*," 312). See Gruber, "Breast-Feeding Practices," 69–107.

14. Emphasis added.

15. This particular issue shall be discussed at some length in the next sections, "The Rabbis' Sarah," "Contemporary Scholarship," and "Feminist Thought."

explains that because Ishmael is Abraham's offspring, he will know God's support; Ishmael will be the progenitor of a nation (Gen 21:13, 18, 20).

Genesis 23: Sarah Dies and Is Buried

Sarah does not appear in Gen 22, the Binding of Isaac. Given Sarah's protective stance toward Isaac, her absence from the biblical narrative is nearly incomprehensible. A midrash offers an explanation as to why she is absent.[16] The last time Sarah appeared was in Gen 21, at about the age of ninety-three. Thirty-four years pass without comment.[17] Then, at the end of a long life, at the age of 127, Sarah dies at Kiriyat Arba/Hebron; she is buried there (Gen 23:1–2).

Early Extra-Biblical Literature's Sarah

Jubilees

Sarah appears as Abraham's wife in the book of *Jubilees*. While *Jubilees* broadly reflects the information found in Genesis, it includes additional materials, and much is deleted or retold. The family conflict that is so visible in Genesis is largely downplayed by the author(s) of *Jubilees*. A more important theme for *Jubilees* is family or tribal endogamous marriages, which seem required for the often partner-like relationships described.

While Sarah's childlessness is mentioned early in the Genesis tradition (Gen 11), *Jubilees* mentions her infertility at a later point. Sarah is taken into Pharaoh's house, but details about this differ from the Genesis account. At a later point in *Jubilees*, Abraham informs Sarah of the covenantal promise of heirs and land. Furthermore, Sarah is present when the visitors mention her future pregnancy, unlike in the Genesis version, in which she is eavesdropping in a tent. In *Jubilees*, Sarah and Abraham together, following the *Aqedah*, or Binding of Isaac (Gen 22), move to Kiriyat Arba/Hebron, which appears to contradict the account in Genesis where Abraham lives in Beersheba. Finally, Sarah's death is listed as Abraham's tenth trial; these trials, almost mythic in themselves, are a post-biblical tradition.[18] Sarah is

16. See "'Protecting' Sarah from the Truth" in "The Rabbis' Sarah" section later in this chapter. See also the examples that address Gen 22 in the "Feminist Thought" section.

17. A discussion of the missing years is found in the "Addition/Excursus" section at the end of this chapter.

18. Abraham's ten trials or ten tests are part of rabbinic lore (see *Mishnah Avot* 5.3;

featured in *Jub.* 12–17 and 19. The *Jubilees* chapters center on Abraham; however, the material listed below focuses on Sarah.

Jubilees 12

This chapter paraphrases parts of Gen 11 and 12. As in Genesis, the names of the main characters are Abram and Sarai.[19] At the end of Gen 11, Sarah (Sarai) is first mentioned as Abram's wife, along with the information that she is childless. Chapter 12 includes the call to the new locale, meandering through the land, and the temporary sojourn in Egypt. It also includes Abraham's request that Sarah pretend to be his sister and the consequences of her being taken into Pharaoh's house.

In terms of Sarah-related material, *Jub.* 12:9 explains that "Abram took a wife, and her name was Sarai, daughter of his father, and she became a wife for him." This sibling connection will only come to light in Gen 20:12, when Abraham explains this matter to King Abimelech of Gerar. As in Gen 12, the *Jubilees* text includes a similar call to move to a new land, with the promise that the families of the earth would be blessed through Abraham. What is pointedly different is that Abraham is told that God will be God not only to Abraham, but also to his son, grandson, and all his descendants: "And I shall be God for you and your son and for the son of your son and for all of your seed. Do not fear henceforth and for all the generations of the earth. I am your God" (*Jub.* 12:24). Since Abraham is married to Sarah, the inference at this point is that they shall have children together.

Jubilees 13

As a result of a famine, Abraham and Sarah move to Egypt. The *Jubilees* text adds that they are there for half a decade (v. 11), while no such number is found in Gen 12. The "wife-sister" motif that appears in Gen 12, 20, and 26, when the spouse is presented as a sibling, does not appear in *Jubilees*. In Genesis, Abraham claims that he fears for his life because of his wife's beauty and effectively "sells" her to the Pharaoh of Egypt. The *Jubilees* author

---

Avot de Rabbi Natan, 33; *Numbers Rabbah* 15.12). These trials include the command to leave his homeland, and the command to sacrifice Isaac. There are variant traditions as to the specific nature of these trials, but all agree that Abraham triumphed in all of them. *Pirke de Rabbi Eliezer* chs. 26–31 enumerate one version of the trials, and *Midrash Psalms*, Ps 18.25 offers a different version.

19. Please note that in the following sections, a brief overview of the biblical account precedes a description of the material in *Jubilees*.

eliminates the beauty issue. *Jubilees* has the Pharaoh take Sarah by force after the couple has resided in Egypt for five years. The text explains, "his wife was taken from him . . . when Pharaoh took Sarai" (*Jub.* 13:11, 13). As in Genesis, God retaliates by bringing plagues to harass Pharaoh and Egypt. Pharaoh then returns Sarah to Abraham and sends them away.[20]

Jubilees 14

Chapter 14 of *Jubilees* contains information that is conveyed first in Gen 15 and 16. In Gen 15, God speaks to Abraham, and Abraham brings an elaborate sacrifice. God explains that in the fullness of time, Abraham's descendants will inherit the land. In broad outline, similar information is conveyed in *Jub.* 14. The *Jubilees* account, however, unlike Genesis, adds that Abraham conveys this message of heirs and land to Sarah. (In the Bible, Sarah will not learn of her future pregnancy until she overhears the "visitors"—not Abraham—announce this fact in Gen 18:9–10.) In *Jubilees*, Sarah and Abraham enjoy a much more mutually supportive relationship than is found in the Genesis account. That she cannot bear children is a problem that they share; it is not simply Sarah's problem. It is at this point that the *Jubilees* text finally informs the reader that Sarah is childless: "And on that day we made a covenant with Abram . . . And Abram renewed the feast and ordinance for himself forever. And Abram rejoiced and he told all of these things to Sarai, his wife. And he believed that he would have seed, but she did not give birth" (*Jub.* 14:20–21).

Genesis 16 features the early Sarah-Abraham-Hagar narratives. This chapter includes Sarah's suggestion to enlist Hagar to produce a child, Hagar's pregnancy, her difficulties with Sarah, and eventually the birth and naming of Ishmael. Similar material is found in *Jub.* 14, including Sarah's suggestion that she might procure an heir through Hagar, Abraham taking Hagar for a wife, Hagar's pregnancy, as well as the eventual birth and naming of Ishmael:

> And Sarai advised Abram, her husband, and she said to him: "Go into Hagar, my Egyptian maid. It may be that I will build seed for you from her." And Abram heard his wife Sarai's word, and he said, "Do (it)!" And Sarai took Hagar, her Egyptian maid,

20. By contrast, Abraham asking Sarah to pretend to be his sister rather than his wife, Sarah's great beauty, and Abraham's prayers after Sarah is forced into the Pharaoh's house are all part of the *Genesis Apocryphon* (columns 19 and 20), a "fragmentary work from the Second Temple period, discovered at Qumran" (Morgenstern and Segal, "Genesis Apocryphon," 237).

and she gave her to Abram, her husband, so that she might be a
wife. And he went into her. And she conceived and bore a son
and he called him Ishmael. (*Jub.* 14:22–24)

Hagar becomes pregnant and gives birth, all in one verse (*Jub.* 14:24).
None of the Sarah-Hagar conflict is mentioned, nor is Sarah's criticism of
Abraham, which we find in Genesis: "May the wrong done to me be on
you!" (Gen 16:5). In the *Jubilees* account, Sarah is portrayed as much more
invested in the surrogate pregnancy *for their mutual benefit*, telling Abraham: "Go into Hagar, my Egyptian maid. It may be that I [Sarah] *will build
seed for you* [Abraham] from her" versus the Genesis account: "I shall obtain
children by her" (Gen 16:2).

Jubilees 15

This chapter in *Jubilees* features information taken from Gen 17, including
name changes and the promise of an heir through Sarah herself. In Gen 17,
God speaks again to Abraham about the covenantal relationship. Abram's
name becomes Abraham, and Sarai becomes Sarah. In addition to mentioning the requirement of circumcision, God promises that Sarah will bear a
child to Abraham. In *Jubilees*, God likewise changes their names, speaks
of circumcision, and promises a child through Sarah. God "said, 'Yes, but
Sarah will bear a son for you and you will call him Isaac. And I shall raise
up my covenant (as) an eternal covenant with him and with his seed after
him'" (*Jub.* 15:19).

Jubilees 16

This chapter initially addresses the angels' visit to the Abrahamic encampment and the announcement that in a year's time, Sarah would give birth.
In Gen 18, visitors suddenly appear, and Abraham goes out to greet them.
He then asks Sarah to prepare a meal. After they have eaten, they announce
that Sarah will give birth in a year's time. She laughs with incredulity. When
called out for her reaction, Sarah denies her laughter, but she is reminded
that she did indeed laugh. *Jubilees* 16 repeats the visitors' announcement.
Whereas in Genesis Sarah is positioned inside her tent as she listens by the

opening, in the *Jubilees* text she seems to be present when the statement is made: We[21] "appeared to Abraham at the oak of Mamre and we talked with him and we also caused him to know that a son would be given to him by Sarah his wife. And Sarah laughed because she heard that we discussed this matter with Abraham" (*Jub.* 16:1–2).

In Genesis, God asks Abraham why Sarah laughed. In *Jubilees*, God seems to address Sarah, and then "admonishes" her for her response. Unlike the Genesis account, here the angels inform Sarah that her son's name will be Isaac: "And we reproached her. And she was afraid and denied that she laughed about the matter. And we told her the name of her son Isaac—just as his name was ordained and written in the heavenly tablets" (*Jub.* 16:2–3).[22] The next section in *Jubilees* that mentions Sarah is based on the early verses of Gen 21 detailing that God fulfilled the earlier promise and that Sarah therefore conceived and bore a child. God

> visited Sarah and did for her as [God] had said. And she con-
> ceived and she bore a son . . . in the time when [God] told Abra-
> ham. Isaac was born on the feast of the firstfruits of the harvest
> [*Shavuot*]. And Abraham circumcised his son on the eighth
> day. He was the first one circumcised according to the covenant
> which was ordained forever. (*Jub.* 16:12–14)

As Kugel points out, "what more appropriate time for Isaac, the 'first fruit' of Sarah's womb, to be born!"[23] The author(s) of *Jubilees* may have had a slightly different version than the current Masoretic Text. *Jubilees* suggests that an additional angelic visit to both Abraham and to Sarah takes place following Isaac's birth. During this second encounter, first Abraham and then she is informed of what the angels had told Abraham, namely that the descendants of Isaac would be God's special "possession from all people,

21. As explained in the introductory chapter, the book of *Jubilees* takes the form of an angelic revelation to Moses while he is on Mount Sinai (see chapter one, footnote 34). Consequently, in this section the "we" of "we appeared to Abraham at the oak of Mamre . . ." means an angel is relating this information to Moses.

22. This reference to "heavenly tablets" is not part of the Genesis tradition. In the *Jubilees* text, reference to these "heavenly tablets" suggests that the Torah is already written and resides in heaven. It allows for the Matriarchs and Patriarchs to know about later legislation, such as is found in Exodus, even though it has not yet been revealed. As noted earlier in the introductory chapter of this volume, hundreds of years after the time of *Jubilees*, the rabbis will offer the explanation that in the biblical era there is no such thing as linear/chronological time. *'Ayn muqdam um'uḥar baTorah*, "There is neither later nor previous time in the Torah" (Babylonian Talmud *Pesahim* 6b). Kugel explains that these references to the heavenly tablets are the later work of an anonymous writer, whom he terms the "Interpolator" (Kugel, "Jubilees," 278).

23. Ibid., 345.

and so that he might become a kingdom of priests and a holy people" (*Jub.* 16:18; cf. Exod 19:6).

Jubilees 17

This chapter reflects information that appears in Gen 21, including the birth of Isaac and his subsequent weaning, as well as the expulsion of Hagar and Ishmael at Sarah's demand:

> Abraham celebrated a great feast . . . on the day that his son, Isaac, was weaned. And Ishmael, the son of Hagar, the Egyptian woman, was in the presence of Abraham, his father, in his place. And Abraham rejoiced and he blessed [God] because he had seen his sons and had not died without sons . . . And he rejoiced because [God] had given him seed . . . so that they might inherit the land . . . And Sarah saw Ishmael playing and dancing and Abraham rejoicing very greatly. And she was jealous of Ishmael and she said to Abraham, "Drive out this girl and her son because the son of this girl will not inherit with my son, Isaac." (*Jub.* 17:1–4)

The *Jubilees* version adds certain information not found in Genesis. In the view of one contemporary scholar, Ishmael is definitively present at the weaning ceremony, which is only inferred in Genesis.[24] In *Jubilees*, Abraham rejoices because he sees his *sons*. It might be that Abraham assumes that both of his sons will inherit the land and produce progeny for him. At this point, Sarah sees Ishmael playing *and dancing*; she also sees Abraham rejoicing. *Jubilees* mentions that Sarah becomes "jealous of Ishmael" and demands that Abraham send away the girl and her son.[25] The reason for Sarah's jealousy is not stated. Was it because Ishmael was playing, because he was dancing, or both? Or are his playing and dancing coincidental? Was she jealous of Ishmael because Abraham rejoiced and blessed God at the sight of both his sons? The *Jubilees* text also fails to explain why Sarah's emotions turn to jealousy. Why not some other emotion? Further, *Jubilees*—like Genesis—does not address why, as part of the "non-inheritance," Hagar and

24. "In the text in Genesis there is no explicit connection made between the feast of Isaac's weaning and Ishmael and Isaac playing together, although it is implied. In *Jubilees*, however, this connection is explicit" (Van Ruiten, "Hagar," 127).

25. "The emotions of Abraham and Sarah seem to be placed in greater contrast than in Genesis. On the one hand, the author of *Jubilees* stresses Abrahams' extreme happiness (*Jub.* 17:2b, 3b, 4b), and on the other, Sarah's jealousy is also made explicit (*Jub.* 17:4c)" (ibid., 134).

Ishmael had to be expelled from the Abrahamic encampment. Were there no other alternatives?

Jubilees 19

Sarah does not appear in *Jub.* 18. Chapter 19 of *Jubilees*, like Gen 23, reports that Sarah died at Kiriyat Arba and that Abraham buried her there:

> Abraham returned [from the *Aqedah*, or Binding of Isaac, in Gen 22] and dwelt two weeks of years opposite Hebron, i.e., Kiryath Arba. And . . . the days of Sarah's life were completed and she died in Hebron. And Abraham went to weep for her and bury her . . . he spoke with the sons of Heth so that they might give him a place in which to bury his dead. (*Jub.* 19:1–4)

In Gen 22, Abraham returns to Beersheba, not Kiriyat Arba/Hebron. Indeed, according to Gen 23, Abraham is at Beersheba and needs to go to Hebron to mourn Sarah and purchase a burial site for her. Finally, in *Jubilees*, Sarah's death is listed as the tenth trial of Abraham as opposed to the rabbinic version, in which the *Aqedah*, or Binding of Isaac, is Abraham's tenth trial: "And all the days of the life of Sarah were one hundred and twenty-seven . . . These (are) the days of the life of Sarah. This (is) the tenth trial with which Abraham was tried. And he was found faithful, controlled of spirit" (*Jub.* 19:7–8).

Josephus

Sarah Is Iscah

Josephus claims that Sarah is the same person as Iscah, the sister of Milcah and Lot, Abraham's niece (*Ant.* 1.6.5).[26] Whereas Gen 11:29 states that Haran had two daughters, Milcah and Iscah, Josephus states that the daughters were Milcah and Sarah.[27] Furthermore, Josephus writes that Abraham marries his niece Sarah, whereas in Gen 20:12 Abraham claims that they are siblings who share a father but not a mother in common.

---

26. Josephus' *Antiquities of the Jews* will be cited parenthetically hereafter as *Ant.*

27. See also *Targum Pseudo-Jonathan* on Gen 11:29; Babylonian Talmud *Megillah* 14a, *Sanhedrin* 69b; *Genesis Rabbah* 38.14.

Sarah Is in Danger

Genesis 12, unlike *Jubilees*, mentions Sarah's great beauty. Josephus describes Sarah's good looks as legendary and comparable to Eve. He assumes that Sarah is in real danger because of "the Egyptians' frenzy for women" (*Ant.* 1.8.1).

Disease and Politial Disturbance

While the rabbis claim that an angel of God intervened in preventing Pharaoh from abusing Sarah, Josephus suggests that it was "disease and political disturbance" brought by God that convinced the Egyptian monarch of the error of his ways (*Ant.* 1.8.1).

Sarah Loved Ishmael

Josephus explains that while "Sarah at the first . . . cherished [Ishmael] . . . with an affection not less than if he had been her own son . . . when she herself gave birth to Isaac, she held it wrong that her boy should be brought up with Ishmael, who was the elder child and might do him an injury after their father was dead" (*Ant.* 1.12.3). This insight about Sarah's fondness for Ishmael is unique to Josephus.

Joseph and Aseneth

In the opening chapter of the pseudepigraphical work *Joseph and Aseneth*,[28] Aseneth is compared to the Matriarchs of old. In contrast to other Egyptian women, Aseneth "was in no way like the Egyptian *parthenoi* [young, unmarried women][29] but was in every way like the daughters of the Hebrews; she was tall like Sara, attractive like Rebekka, and beautiful like Rachel" (*Jos. Asen.*, 1:5).

---

28. Ahearne-Kroll, "Joseph and Aseneth." Dating of this work is unclear; most scholarly estimates range from ca. 100 BCE to 115 CE in Egypt.

29. For a fuller explanation of the term *parthenoi*, see ibid., 2530 comment on 1:4.

Testament of Abraham

The *Testament of Abraham*[30] is thought to come from the first or second century CE and was most likely written in Egypt. It has survived as two recensions, an A and B version. At one point in the A version, Sarah recognizes that a visitor to their home is an angel; Abraham did not realize this (*T. Ab. A* 6.1–6). Just prior to this, God had sent a message to Isaac in a dream saying that before long, his father would die. Isaac then goes into Abraham's room and tells him so. Both men start to cry. Sarah, who is in her own tent, overhears this. She joins them and also bewails Abraham's impending death. In the A version, unlike in Genesis, Abraham's death precedes that of Sarah (*T. Ab. A* 5.6–14; 20.6–7).

In the second version, Abraham goes off on a long journey with the angel Michael. They are gone a long time. Sarah, in the meantime, "since she had not seen what had become of Abraham, was consumed with grief and gave up her soul. And after Abraham returned to his house, he found her dead, and he buried her" (*T. Ab. B* 12.15–16).

The Rabbis' Sarah

The rabbis of the Talmudic period sought to teach values that would enhance Jewish life and bring people closer to their religious traditions as well as to the presence of God. One way to do this was through legislation by means of carefully worded interpretations of biblical laws. To supplement this legal material, the rabbis created a more flexible set of writings known as midrash. Through midrash, the rabbis teach their values. The tradition of midrash often takes biblical narratives and uses them as a springboard to develop additional materials about the lives of familiar ancient figures. Some of the early extra-biblical Second Temple literature noted above became sources for rabbinic commentary. It is through midrash that the rabbis created a whole other side of Sarah's persona. This is the Sarah portrayed in classical Jewish texts, the Talmud, and many collections of midrashim.

As explained in the introductory chapter, the rabbis reflect a worldview under which males are privileged over females. In their minds, the ideal human society is decidedly oriented toward men, whom the rabbis believe to possess superior intellectual, spiritual, and moral capacities. The rabbinic attitude toward women is often sexist and sometimes misogynistic. Women are often compared to children and slaves. Every morning, men would thank

---

30. The *Testament of Abraham* Recensions A and B will hereafter be cited as *T. Ab. A* and *B*, respectively.

God for not making them a woman, a slave, or a heathen. On the other hand, we find extraordinary statements about the importance of women: "As the reward for the righteous women who lived in [the generation of the Exodus] the Israelites were delivered from Egypt" (Babylonian Talmud *Sotah* 11b). This range of attitudes is present in the rabbis' writings about Sarah. Sometimes they are quite obvious, such as when the rabbis articulate their surprise that God spoke directly to a woman. They explain that this incident with Sarah is the one exception in which such express communication with a woman is recorded.[31] At another point, they suggest women are incapable of deep thought. Abraham, in his explanation to Sarah for taking Isaac away (to sacrifice him on the mountain), falsifies his true intent, for he considers women to be light-headed.[32] At other occasions, the rabbis' ambivalence about women lies beneath the plain meaning of their comments.

Genesis 11

Sarah is introduced to the reader of the Bible in Gen 11. At this point, she is called Sarai. Her seeming inability to bear progeny is stated clearly: she is childless.

Sarah's Relationship to Abraham

Genesis 11:29 describes Sarah as Abraham's wife. In Gen 20:12, Abraham claims that she is his half-sister, the daughter of his father but not of his mother. A variant tradition describes Sarah as the same person as Iscah, Abraham's niece and the sister of Milcah (Babylonian Talmud *Megillah* 14a; *Sanhedrin* 69b; *Genesis Rabbah* 38.14).

Sarah's Childlessness

Sarah is the first in a series of childless women. Not only the Matriarchs of Genesis, but also others follow in this line. In addition to Sarah, Rebekah, Rachel, and Leah, there is Manoah's wife, who is Samson's mother, as well as Hannah, who is Elkanah's wife and Samuel's mother. Hence, the words from Ps 113:9, God "gives the *infertile* woman a home," apply to Sarah, just as they will also apply to these other female figures: "Now Sarai was infertile;

31. Referencing Gen 18:15, see "A Singular Experience: God Spoke Directly to Sarah" below.

32. See the section below on "'Protecting' Sarah from the Truth."

she had no child" (Gen 11:30). The words "making her the joyous mother of children" also apply to Sarah: "Sarah would nurse children . . . I have borne him a child" (Gen 21:7; *Pesikta de Rab Kahana, Piska* 20.1).

Sarah's Period of Childlessness: A Paradigm for Zion[33]

The sages build on the verse, "Now Sarai was infertile; she had no child" (Gen 11:30; cf. 16:1). The rabbis equate Sarah's delayed childbearing to Zion. Zion, which is understood as a metaphor for the people Israel, is described as a woman. Zion (or the people of Israel), while momentarily childless, will know fruitfulness. Zion shall give birth; the people of Israel will be reborn in their own land: "Zion is the seventh in the number of notable mothers in Israel who were barren a long time before God blessed them with children. Like the others, Zion's time will come: no longer barren, no longer uprooted from the Land, she will find peace."[34]

Genesis 12

The call from God to go to a new land begins this chapter. After some time in Canaan, due to a serious regional famine, Abraham and Sarah travel to Egypt.

Sarah and Abraham Were Proselytes and Actively Proselytized Others

Sarah and Abraham were the first proselytes to the new faith (*Numbers Rabbah* 8.9). They brought others to know the one God. Sarah converted the women, while Abraham converted the men: "Abram took his wife Sarai . . . and the persons whom they had acquired in Haran" (Gen 12:5; *Genesis Rabbah* 39.14; 84.4; *Song of Songs Rabbah* 1.3.3; Babylonian Talmud *Avodah Zarah* 9a). This understanding is based on reading the word "acquired"—the literal Hebrew is "they made"—as a synonym for "converted," not merely adding members to the household. In a different midrash collection, the rabbis point out that the actual words "they made" cannot be taken literally.

33. The connection to Mother Zion is based on two verses in Isaiah: "Sing, O barren one" (Isa 54:1) and "Then you will say . . . 'Who has borne me these?'" (Isa 49:21). Some of the material in this section appears in a different form in Zucker, "Sarah: The View," 221–52.

34. See Braude and Kapstein, *Pesikta de Rab Kahana*, 330.

Humans are incapable of creating even an insect. Rather, what is meant here is that God credited Abraham and Sarah as if they had "made" new *souls* when they brought these converts into the faith of the one God.[35]

Sarah's Great Beauty

Eve was a beautiful woman. She transmitted her beauty to the reigning beauties of each generation. Yet Sarah was even more beautiful than Eve, explains one midrash (*Genesis Rabbah* 40.5). According to the rabbis, even in her mid-sixties Sarah was extraordinarily good-looking. Her husband affirms this when he says to her, "I know well that you are a woman beautiful in appearance" (Gen 12:11). Elsewhere, despite her advanced age, we are told that Sarah was as beautiful as a bride on her wedding day (*Genesis Rabbah* 45.4). Another midrash features four stunningly attractive women, naming Sarah as the first example. The other three women were Rahab, a prostitute (Josh 2:1); Abigail, one of David's wives (1 Sam 25:3); and Queen Esther (Esth 2:15) (Babylonian Talmud *Megillah* 15a).

Traveling is arduous work that affects travelers physically. Nonetheless, despite their many journeys, Sarah remained beautiful (*Genesis Rabbah* 40.4; *Zohar, Lech Lecha,* 1.81b).[36] The Egyptians praise Sarah's beauty. When "the Egyptians saw that the woman was very beautiful . . . they praised her to Pharaoh" (Gen 12:14–15). The rabbis explain that the light of Sarah's beauty filled all of Egypt (*Genesis Rabbah* 40.5).

Sarah Seeks Divine Support

When Sarah and Abraham were approaching Egypt, Sarah's husband focuses on his—not her—wellbeing. He says, "Say you are my sister, so that it may go well with me because of you." How did Sarah respond to this strange request? Did she argue with her husband? Was she distraught? Neither Genesis nor the rabbis offer clues to Sarah's feelings, nor is there any suggestion of what her reply may have been. When, however, Sarah "was taken into Pharaoh's house" (Gen 12:15), the rabbis explain that she turned to God for help. She says words to the effect that this is not something she is doing of her own volition. Sarah claims she is innocent of wrongdoing. She is there because Abraham trusted in God. Implicit in her comments is the request

---

35. *Avot de Rabbi Natan*, ch. 12.

36. As noted earlier, the *Zohar* is a mystical commentary on parts of the Bible. It dates from about the thirteenth century CE. (Please note that in the edition of the *Zohar* from which we quote, direct biblical quotations appear in capital letters.)

that God save her. The Genesis text reads: 'al d'var Sarai, which NRSV translates as "because of Sarai." The word d'var can mean "matter," "thing," or "word." The rabbis take d'var to mean "word"; they suggest Sarah spoke up at this point, either praying to God or instructing an angel in what to do to prevent Pharaoh from molesting her. Sarah said:

> Sovereign of the World, Abraham came with you under a promise, since you had said to him (in Gen 12:3): I will bless those who bless you. Now I did not know anything except that, when he told me that you had said to him (in Gen 12:1): go, I believed your words. But now, <when> I have been isolated from my father, my mother, and my husband, this wicked man [Pharaoh] has come to mistreat me. He (Abraham) had acted because of your great name and because of our trust in your words. The Holy One said to her: By your life, nothing evil shall harm you, as stated (in Prov 12:21): No harm shall befall the righteous, but the wicked are full of evil. So in regard to Pharaoh and his house, I will make an example of them. Thus it is written (in Gen 12:17): then [God] afflicted Pharaoh and his house with great plagues at the word of Sarai. (Midrash Tanhuma, Genesis. Lekh-Lekha, 3.8 Gen 14:1ff., Part 3)[37]

Sarah in Pharaoh's Palace

When Sarah "was taken into Pharaoh's house . . . the LORD afflicted Pharaoh and his house with great plagues because of Sarai, Abram's wife" (Gen 12:15, 17). The Bible does not provide details as to what transpired. Was she forced into an adulterous relationship? Was she raped? The rabbis are quick to defend Sarah's virtue. Although he desired to do so, the Pharaoh was unable to touch her:

> Because [Pharaoh] dared to approach the shoe of that lady . . . the whole of that night Sarah lay prostrate on her face, crying, "Sovereign of the Universe! Abraham went forth [from his land] on your assurance, and I went forth with faith; Abraham is without this prison, and I am within!" The Holy One said to her, "Whatever I do, I will do for your sake, and all will say, 'It is because of Sarai, Abram's wife.'" (Genesis Rabbah 41.2)[38]

---

37. Midrash Tanhuma, Genesis. Please note that in the Ktav edition translated by John T. Townsend, direct biblical quotations appear in capital letters.

38. Note that in the Soncino edition of Midrash Rabbah edited by Freedman, Simon, and Slotki, direct biblical quotations appear in capital letters.

Another midrash collection describes what happened at that fateful encounter between Sarah and Pharaoh:

> In that very hour an angel came down from the heavens with a rod in his hand. <When> Pharaoh came to take off her shoe, he smote him with his hand. <When> he came to touch her clothes, he would smite him. And the angel would consult with Sarah on each and every blow. If she said that he should be afflicted, he was afflicted. When she would say: Wait for him until he recovers himself, the angel would wait for him, as it is stated (in Gen 12:17): at the word of Sarai. What is the meaning of at the word of Sarai? That <here> is not stated "On the matter of," nor "over the cause of," nor "for the sake of," nor "in consequence of," but at the word of Sarai. Thus, if she said he should be afflicted, he was afflicted; and if not, he was not afflicted. R. [Rabbi] Yehudah b. [bar] R. [Rabbi] Shallum the Levite said, The Holy One did not allow a wicked man to occupy himself with a righteous woman. Our masters have said: <When> he came to take off her shoe, leprosy immediately overcame him, and his governors were also afflicted with him—also the princes, also the servants, and also his family. And the walls also were afflicted along with him, as stated (in Gen 12:17): then [God] afflicted Pharaoh and his house. Why? (ibid., cont.): at the word of Sarai, Abram's wife." (*Midrash Tanhuma, Genesis. Lekh-Lekha,* 3.8 Gen 14:1ff., Part 3)

Was Pharaoh aware of Sarah's marital status? Had he not been told that the two were siblings, not spouses? A midrash suggests that the severity of Pharaoh's punishment was deserved, because Sarah had told him the truth: "She told him [Pharaoh], 'I am a married woman,' yet he would not leave her" (*Genesis Rabbah* 41.2). In this midrash, Sarah is portrayed as having revealed her true relationship to Abraham.

Given the devastating famine that affected Canaan, were there alternatives open to Abraham and Sarah? Why did they not turn back from Egypt and go somewhere else? It may have been possible for them to go back towards Mesopotamia. A medieval manuscript, the *Zohar*, directly addresses this matter. Rabbi Yesa said:

> Abram knew that all the Egyptians were full of lewdness. It may therefore seem surprising that he was not apprehensive for his wife and that he did not turn back without entering the country. But the truth is that he saw her [Sarah] with the Shekinah [*Shekhinah*, God's feminine presence, sometimes associated with

Wisdom],[39] and therefore was confident. *That it may be well with me for your sake*: these words were addressed to the Shekinah, as if to say: "that God may entreat me well for your sake." *And that my soul may live because of you*: because through this (the Shekinah) man ascends and becomes privileged to enter on the path of life. (*Zohar, Lech Lecha*, 1.81b–82a)

This explanation that Abraham saw Sarah with God's feminine presence, the *Shekhinah*, is high praise for Sarah. Nonetheless, when Abraham claimed that they were merely siblings, he knowingly placed Sarah at great risk. Abraham's request, which was really a demand, is severely criticized by the medieval commentator Ramban (Nahmanides), who points out that Abraham committed a serious sin when he endangered Sarah's honor. Scripture does not record that Sarah agreed to this deception. When they arrived in Egypt, she was taken to Pharaoh's palace without being asked about her relationship with Abraham. Abraham only gave this information after she was taken to the palace, and then only after Pharaoh blamed him when her identity became known.[40]

Sarah's Chastity: An Example for Later Generations

Sarah's chaste behavior in Egypt benefited later generations. She inspired women during the time of the Egyptian oppression. When Sarah

> went down to Egypt, she took pains to [avoid] unchaste conduct of any kind; thereafter, all Israelite women, inspired by her example, also took pains to [avoid] unchaste conduct of any kind. According to Rabbi Hunya, citing Hiyya bar Abba, such [avoidance of] unchastity was in itself of sufficient merit to bring about the redemption of Israel. (*Pesikta de Rab Kahana*, Piska 11.6)

39. Abraham "saw with her [Sarah] the Shekinah. It was on this account that Abram made bold to say subsequently, 'she is my sister,' with a double meaning: one the literal, the other figurative, as in the words 'say to Wisdom, you are my sister' (Prov 7:4). Say now you are my sister" (*Zohar, Lech Lecha*, 1.81b).

40. See Nahmanides, *Genesis*, comment on Gen 12:10, 13. See also Borgman, *Genesis*, 43; Niditch, "Genesis," 36.

Sarah Was Not Affected by the Plague

Sforno explains that although Pharaoh's household was afflicted with plagues, Sarah was saved from the pestilence so that all would recognize that she was not guilty of wrongdoing.[41]

Pharaoh Intended to Marry Sarah

Pharaoh showered Sarah with gifts, including the land of Goshen, where a later generation of Israelites would settle: "Rabbi Joshua ben Korhah said: Because of his love for her, (Pharaoh) wrote in his marriage document (giving her) all his wealth, whether in silver or gold, or in manservants, or land, and he wrote (giving) her the land of Goshen for a possession" (*Pirke de Rabbi Eliezer* ch. 26).

Pharaoh Gave His Daughter Hagar to Sarah

In his marriage contract with Sarah, Pharaoh gave her his daughter Hagar: "He (also) wrote (giving) her Hagar, his daughter from a concubine, as her handmaid" (*Pirke de Rabbi Eliezer* ch. 26). That Hagar is Pharaoh's daughter by a concubine parallels the notion that Hagar is a concubine to Abraham. Other rabbis term her a wife.[42] Another midrash gives a different explanation for Hagar's presence: "When Pharaoh saw what was done on Sarah's behalf in his own house [the intervention of the angel and the consequent plagues] he took his daughter and gave her to Sarah. He said, 'Better let my daughter be a handmaid in [Sarah's] house than a mistress in another house'" (*Genesis Rabbah* 45.1). In both instances, this means that Hagar is not just *an* Egyptian woman, but rather that she is of royal blood, which indirectly points to Abraham and Sarah's importance.

Genesis 16

Sarah does not appear by name in Gen 13–15. Chapter 16 relates the early Sarah-Hagar narratives.

41. See Sforno, *Commentary on the Torah*, 65 comment on Gen 12:17.

42. See our discussion below and relevant material in the chapter on Hagar.

"Perhaps I Will Be Built up through Her"

Sforno interprets Sarah's words in a very different way. He says that her statement "that I [Sarah] shall obtain children by her" does *not* mean that she intends to adopt Hagar's son. Rather, it means that Sarah believes that through
her own jealousy of Hagar, this will enable Sarah herself to conceive.[43]

Sarah Claims Her Childlessness Is Divinely Ordained

The Sarah-Hagar relationship is initially driven by Sarah's need and desire
to produce an heir for herself and her husband. The chapter begins by repeating the fact that Sarah has been unable to bear children, mentioning
seemingly in passing that she has an Egyptian slave, Hagar. In the second
verse, Sarah turns to Abraham and explains that God has prevented her
from having children. The rabbis praise Sarah for taking this position. Sarah
said, "I know the source of my affliction; it is not as people say [of a childless
woman] 'she needs a talisman, she needs a charm,' but rather behold [God]
has restrained me from bearing" (Gen 16:2; *Genesis Rabbah* 45.2).

Sarah and Hagar: Early Encounters

Sarah gives Hagar to Abraham to serve as his second wife[44] and surrogate
mother of a forthcoming heir. On the whole, the rabbinic/midrashic tradition presents Hagar in a negative light. Likewise, the rabbis have little good
to say about Ishmael.[45] Negative portrayals dominate, but there are positive
comments as well. Sarah approaches Hagar and urges her to cohabit with
Abraham, telling her slave that Hagar herself will benefit spiritually. According to one midrash, Sarah "persuaded her with words, 'Happy are you to be
united with such a holy man'" (*Genesis Rabbah* 45.3).

　　While Hagar gains by marrying Abraham, Sarah does not lose any
rights. Hagar conceives immediately, and her value, certainly psychologically, is enhanced. Once she is pregnant, Hagar belittles Sarah: "Hagar . . .

---

43. See Sforno, *Commentary on the Torah*, 76 comment on Gen 16:2.

44. His second wife or his concubine? Speiser and Sarna make the case that Hagar
is a concubine, not a wife (Speiser, *Genesis*, 117; Sarna, *Genesis*, 119). For an alternative
view of "wife" versus "concubine," see Alter, *Genesis*, 68. One midrash proclaims, "to be
a wife, but not a concubine" (*Genesis Rabbah* 45.3). For a perspective on these issues
from the viewpoint of Hagar, see the chapter on Hagar later in this volume.

45. As explained below in this chapter, Ishmael represented the "Other," the outsider, and therefore a probable threat to the family or community. See Zucker, "Conflicting Conclusions"; Reiss, "Ishmael, Son of Abraham").

conceived; and when she saw that she had conceived, she looked with contempt on her mistress" (Gen 16:4). According to a midrash, Hagar points out the length of time Sarah had been married and her inability to become pregnant. As mentioned above, Sarah herself claims that she is at fault. Hagar then infers Sarah deserves to be childless because she is unworthy. The unspoken message is clear: *I, Hagar, am a "moral" person; I conceived immediately.* According to this midrash, female visitors would come to spend time with Sarah. Sarah would then refer them to Hagar: "Hagar would tell them: 'My mistress Sarai is not inwardly what she is outwardly: she appears to be a righteous woman, see how many years have passed without her conceiving, whereas I conceived in one night!'" (*Genesis Rabbah* 45.4; *Midrash ha Gadol*, Genesis 1.244).

In her anger, disappointment, and frustration—no doubt directed towards Hagar and inwardly to herself—Sarah complains to Abraham, who abdicates any responsibility in the matter. He effectively turns over the matter to Sarah, who then deals "harshly" with Hagar (Gen 16:6). Consequently, despite her pregnancy, Hagar flees into the desert. Since Genesis does not offer an example of how Sarah's anger manifests itself, the rabbis come forward to offer suggestions. Sarah prevented Hagar and Abraham from sleeping together. She slapped Hagar's face with a slipper. Then, disregarding Hagar's newfound status as a second wife to Abraham, Sarah treated her as a slave. She forced Hagar to carry water buckets and towels to the bathing area (*Genesis Rabbah* 45.6). There may be psychological or social dimensions to the tensions between the women, likely exacerbated by each woman's feelings of inferiority or superiority, her sense of self as a real woman who can bring forth children, or jealousies in terms of competition for Abraham's affections and over the ability to give him an heir.

Sarah's Harsh Treatment of Hagar Has Repercussions

The medieval commentator Naḥmanides (Ramban), in his comment to Gen 16:6, writes that Sarah's harsh treatment of Hagar (and later Ishmael) becomes the reason why the Egyptians enslaved the Israelites in Egypt.

Genesis 17

Sarah is not physically present in Gen 17. She is the subject of a conversation that God has with Abraham. God tells him to change her name from Sarai to Sarah, even as the Patriarch is to change his own name from Abram to Abraham. In this chapter, God also explains that in due time Sarah will become pregnant and produce an heir for Abraham. The Bible does not explain the meaning of the name change from Sarai to Sarah, but the rabbis offer their thoughts.

Sarah and Abraham: Interdependent, Not Independent

According to the Rav, Rabbi Joseph B. Soloveitchik, the name change for Sarah took place at the same time as the name change for Abraham. This

> involved the addition of a letter from God's name, the Tetra-grammaton [*yud hey vav hey*], signifying that they will share a spiritual role which will reach out unto the nations of the world. He was to become . . . "the father of a multitude of nations" (Gen 17:4) and she "a princess to the entire world" (Rashi [Gen 17:15], ibid., [Babylonian Talmud *Berakhot*] 13a). Abraham could not be a "father of multitudes" if Sarah were not crowned as a "mother" of this multitude.[46]

Sarah Is a Princess

The Hebrew word *sar* means "prince" (see Isa 9:6 [9:5 H], *Sar shalom*, or "Prince of Peace"). Sarah, the feminine version of *sar*, therefore translates as "princess": "Formerly she was a princess [Sarai] to her own people only, whereas now she is a princess [Sarah] to all humans" (Babylonian Talmud *Berakhot* 13a; *Genesis Rabbah* 47.1).

Why Sarai Became Sarah

Originally, her name was Sarai. When she performed good deeds, [people] added to her name by putting in a large letter so that she was called Sarah [the Hebrew letter "*hey*" is larger than the Hebrew letter *yud*] (*Mekilta de Rabbi Ishmael*, Tractate Amalek, 3.43–45).

A Change of Name Can Bring a Change of Fortune

"Rabbi Ḥunya said in the name of Rabbi Joseph: A change of name can . . . avert a harsh decree. A change of name is shown by the instance . . . 'As for Sarai your wife, you shall not call her Sarai, but Sarah shall be her name'

46. Soloveitchik, *Man of Faith*, 86.

(Gen 17:15). Sarah as Sarai could not bear children, but renamed Sarah she could bear them" (*Pesikta Rabbati, Piska* 52.3).

Sarah's Time of Childlessness Was Equal to Her Strength to Bear It

Proverbs states, "The crucible is for silver, and the furnace is for gold, so a person is tested by being praised" (Prov 27:21). Like a refiner of metals such as gold and silver, God refines the righteous according to their strength. Sarah was married for many years before she gave birth. "The Holy One . . . tried her according to her strength" (*Pesikta Rabbati, Piska* 43.5).

A Double Miracle

A midrash explains that God says to Abraham, "I will bless her, and moreover I will give you a son by her; I will bless her, and she shall give rise to nations" (Gen 17:16). Sarah is first blessed so that a miracle can occur and so she can then become pregnant, despite being postmenopausal.[47]

Genesis 18

Genesis 18 features the three visitors that come to the family encampment. After they have eaten, they inquire about Sarah. They then explain that "in due season . . . Sarah shall have a son" (Gen 18:10).

Sarah and the Visitors

As noted in the first part of this chapter, Sarah is skeptical, perhaps even irked, about the anonymous visitors' statement that in a year's time she will give birth. She feels that now it is too late for a family. She is nearly ninety and postmenopausal. She laughs bitterly to herself, saying, "Now that I have lost the ability, am I to have enjoyment—*with my husband so old*?" (Gen 18:12).[48] Jewish tradition notes that when sharing Sarah's comment with Abraham, God slightly changes her words so not to give offense to

---

47. See Rashi's comment on Gen 17:16 in *Sifsei Chachamim Chumash*.

48. Stein, *Contemporary Torah* (CJPS translation). NJPS reads, "Now that I am withered, am I to have enjoyment—with my husband so old?" The NRSV translation reads, "After I have grown old and my husband is old, shall I have pleasure?"

him. Unvarnished truth can be needlessly hurtful.[49] When God reports
Sarah's words to Abraham, God explains that she claimed *she* was too old
to bear children: "Bar Kappara said: Great is peace, for even Scripture made
a misstatement in order to preserve peace between Abraham and Sarah"
(*Genesis Rabbah* 48.18; Babylonian Talmud *Baba Metzia* 87a).

A Singular Experience: God Spoke Directly to Sarah

God conversed with Sarah, teasing or perhaps rebuking her for her lack
of faith (Gen 18:13–15). This is the one and only time, contend the rabbis,
when God spoke so clearly and directly to a woman. This greatly enhances
Sarah's reputation: "Rabbi Yehudah bar Rabbi Simon, and Rabbi Yohanan in
the name of Rabbi Eleazar ben Rabbi Simon said: The Holy One . . . never
condescended to hold converse with a woman save with that righteous one
[viz. Sarah]" (*Genesis Rabbah* 45.10; 48.20; 53.5; *Midrash Psalms*, Ps 9.7).[50]
It is noteworthy that Abraham's laughter in Gen 17:17 goes unremarked
upon. Sarah's laughter, however, receives God's notice. According to the
Talmud, in the Greek translation of the Hebrew Bible, the Septuagint, the
translators changed the words from "Sarah laughed to herself" to Sarah
laughing publicly (Babylonian Talmud *Megillah* 9a). Some commentators
suggest that Abraham rebuked Sarah, not God.[51]

Both Abraham and Sarah Were Childless

While most midrashic sources regard Sarah as the spouse that was infertile,
according to a Talmudic passage, both Sarah and Rebekah were unable to
bear children because they were androgynous [*tumtummin*]. In this same
section, a rabbi suggests it was Abraham who was infertile (Babylonian Talmud *Yevamot* 64a–b). These statements are notable because they are exceptions to the general view of the rabbis.

---

49. See the explanations in Lieber et al., *Etz Hayim*, 101–102.

50. *Genesis Rabbah* 45.10 goes on to say that God spoke directly to Sarah. The
rabbis say that in Gen 16, God spoke to Hagar through the medium of an angel. Hagar
claims she saw God, hence the name of the place. Although it would seem that God
spoke directly to Rebekah in Gen 25:23, the rabbis in this particular midrash suggest
otherwise. Different rabbis understand the matter in diverse ways. In *Midrash Psalms*,
Ps 9.7, several rabbis suggest God addresses Rebekah, but this is the exception to the
general view.

51. See Sforno, *Commentary on the Torah*, 88 comment on Gen 18:15; Schneider,
"Central Commentary *Vayeira*," 89.

Genesis 20

Sarah does not appear in Gen 19, for that chapter deals with Lot and his family, as well as with the fate of Sodom and Gomorrah. Genesis 20 is the second time that Sarah is portrayed as Abraham's sister, not his wife. This time, the monarch is King Abimelech of Gerar. Although similar to the situation with Pharaoh in Egypt, the Abimelech encounter differs in critical ways.

Sarah and Abimelech

The rabbis are somewhat sympathetic to Abimelech, who, in principle and perhaps in practice, is innocent of conscious wrongdoing: "God came to Abimelech . . . and said to him, 'You are about to die because of the woman whom you have taken; for she is a married woman'" (Gen 20:3). When Abimelech protests, God acknowledges that the ruler is blameless: "Then God said to him . . . 'Yes I know that you did this in the integrity of your heart'" (Gen 20:6). In one midrash, Abimelech explains to God that he looked into the matter at some length. Nonetheless, he was given false information. The midrash explains, "Abimelech said: I asked Abraham, 'What is she—your wife?' He replied, 'She is my sister.' Then I asked Sarah, 'Are you his wife?' She replied, 'No, I am his sister.' Nevertheless, I went on to ask the people of his household, and they likewise said that she was his sister" (*Pesikta Rabbati, Piska* 42.3).

According to Genesis, God "had closed fast the wombs of the house of Abimelech because of Sarah, Abraham's wife" (Gen 20:18). There was more to this matter. A midrash explains that in addition to the reproductive organs, God also stopped up all the other orifices of their bodies. Their tear ducts were blocked, so they could not weep. God closed their ears, and they could not hear. The plague affected Abimelech's flocks, herds, and cattle (*Pesikta Rabbati, Piska* 42.3, 6).

Another source suggests that the impact was more widespread. Abimelech became impotent. Even insect life was affected (*Pirke de Rabbi Eliezer* ch. 26).

Abraham Accused of Pimping Sarah

Following the disclosure of Abraham and Sarah's marital relationship, Abimelech not only returns Sarah to Abraham, he makes a kind of indemnity payment. According to an extraordinary rabbinic insight, Abimelech accuses Abraham of pimping Sarah: "Rabbi Yehudah bar Rabbi Ilai said, [Abimelech reproached Abraham:] 'You went to Egypt and made merchandise of [Sarah], and you came here and traded in her'" (*Genesis Rabbah* 52.12). This midrash is unique in its criticism of Abraham on this matter.

Genesis 21

Chapter 21 covers the birth of Isaac and relates the later Sarah-Hagar narrative. At long last, Sarah conceives and gives birth to Isaac. According to Genesis, given that Sarah is ninety years old at this point, this conception is miraculous.[52]

Mother Sarah

In her delight, Sarah laughs, saying, "'God has brought laughter for me; everyone who hears will laugh with me.' And she said, 'Who would have said to Abraham that Sarah would nurse children? Yet I have borne him a son in his old age'" (Gen 21:6–7). For too many years, Sarah had been the object of other people's derision. Many governors and governors' wives had jeered at her, calling her a "barren woman" (*Pesikta Rabbati, Piska* 42.5). A year earlier, unexpected visitors promised that Sarah would give birth. Months had passed. They spent time in Gerar, and still she did not conceive. The rabbis explain that the angels were frustrated on her behalf. They spoke to God, advocating for her. "The angels rose up, complaining: '[Ruler] of the universe, all these years Sarah was barren [and for a brief period] Abimelech's wife was barren . . . Now that Abraham has prayed [on behalf of Abimelech],'" the angels went on, "'Abimelech's wife was remembered; even his maidservants were. These were remembered, but Sarah remains barren. Justice demands that she also be remembered' . . . Thereupon, says Scripture, And [God] remembered Sarah" ["[God] dealt with Sarah as [God] had said" (Gen 21:1) and she gave birth to Isaac] (*Pesikta Rabbati, Piska* 42.3).

52. When Sarah and Abraham produced a child, this was considered extraordinary for their advanced ages (see Gen 17:16–19; 18:11–15; 21:1–2). Indeed, Sarah had spoken of herself as post-menopausal (Gen 18:11–12). It is miraculous and in contrast to the "normal" sexual relationship that produces Ishmael. It is also different from the situation when, in a later generation, God "remembered" from the root *z kh r* (*zayin khaf resh*) Hannah after Eli said God would grant her her wish of a child (1 Sam 1:19). When God remembered Sarah, the term used is very strange—not *zakhor*, the usual word for "remember," but from the root *p q d* (*peh quf dalet*). This root has a range of possible meanings, including "command," "remember," "enumerate," "visit," and "order." One interpretation is that God commanded or created this child as a miracle.

Unlike ordinary women, Sarah experienced no pain at Isaac's birth (*Midrash Tanhuma, Genesis. Wayyera*, Gen 4.37 Gen 21:1ff., Part 8).[53] This "gift" of no pain (cf. Gen 3:16) makes Sarah's labor different from the normal experiences of women. The rabbis see this as part of the miracle of Isaac's birth and God's beneficence. The rabbis go on to explain that Isaac's birth caused universal rejoicing and miraculous acts:

> All barren women everywhere in the world were remembered together with Sarah and were with child at the same time she was; and when she gave birth to a child, all of them gave birth to children at the same time she did. It was for this reason that Sarah said: God has given me occasion for laughter; every one that hears will laugh in joy with me (Gen 21:6) . . . And not only this remembrance, but much more besides. When Sarah bore her child, every blind [person] in the world was given sight; every cripple was made straight; every mute was given speech; and all mad [people] were healed of [their] madness.

On the day that Isaac was born, God also intensified the light of the sun (*Pesikta Rabbati, Piska* 42.4).[54]

Yet even so, there were those who raised questions about Isaac's parentage. People knew that Sarah and her husband had dwelt for a time in Gerar. Some suggested that Isaac was Abimelech's son, not Abraham's child. This was easy to disprove. Not only was Isaac the result of a full nine-month pregnancy, he also looked just like Abraham (*Genesis Rabbah* 53.6).[55] At the birth of Isaac, the text tells us that he was born *l'zikunav* (Gen 21:2), usually translated as "in [Abraham's] old age." The phrase can be construed as a contraction of *Ziv iKuNin*, "in the precise image of [Abraham]."[56] This reading continues to emphasize Isaac as the son of Abraham and Sarah.

53. The same was true of Jocheved, Moses' mother (*Exodus Rabbah* 1.20; Babylonian Talmud *Sotah* 12a).

54. This midrash is a good example of fantasy and hyperbole. The rabbinic "sages utilized every sort of literary and rhetorical technique to make this material attractive and compelling to their audience," explains Heinemann. As he notes earlier in that chapter, they also used "wit and humor" (Heinemann, "Nature of the Aggadah," 47, 42).

55. Another midrash explains that some of Abraham's contemporaries questioned Abraham's ability to father a child at his age. This midrash explains that when this allegation was made, Isaac immediately took on Abraham's features. Father and son looked so much alike that people confused them one for the other. The prooftext for this talmudic midrash is "*These are the descendants of Isaac, Abraham's son: Abraham*" (Gen 25:19), as if the text were saying "Abraham's son, Abraham" (Babylonian Talmud *Baba Metzia* 87a).

56. Tuchman and Rapoport, *Passions of the Matriarchs*, 53. The original source is *Genesis Rabbah* 53.6.

There are further statements: "Abraham gave the name Isaac to his son, whom Sarah bore him" and again, "Abraham circumcised his son Isaac" (Gen 21:3–4). All this language is to prevent anyone from thinking that Isaac's father might be Abimelech. There were those who even questioned the reality of Sarah's pregnancy. They said that the aged couple had found the child somewhere along the road (Babylonian Talmud *Baba Metzia* 87a). Others claimed that Isaac was Hagar's child, not Sarah's, and that Sarah was incapable of suckling Isaac (*Pesikta de Rab Kahana, Piska* 22.1).

To counter these allegations, Abraham asked Sarah to forgo her natural modesty and to nurse Isaac publicly. He "said to Sarah: 'Sarah, don't just stand there! This is not a time for modesty. For the hallowing of the Name [i.e., God] arise and uncover yourself!' Sarah arose and uncovered herself, and her two nipples were pouring out milk like two jets of water" (*Pesikta Rabbati, Piska* 43.4; Babylonian Talmud *Baba Metzia* 87a). Noblewomen the world over brought their children to partake of Sarah's nourishment (*Genesis Rabbah* 53.9). Her husband invited all the great men of the age to see this wonder, and Sarah invited the women. Sarah's super-abundance of milk was clearly well publicized: "Each [woman] brought her child with her, but not the wet nurse" (Babylonian Talmud *Baba Metzia* 87a). The children of those who came with sincere feelings became proselytes to Judaism (*Pesikta Rabbati, Piska* 43.4). Alternatively, the "children who nursed from our mother Sarah, all of them became proselytes" (*Midrash Tanhuma, Genesis. Wayyera,* Gen 4.38; Gen 21:1ff., Part 9).

How was it that Sarah had taken so long to become pregnant? What did the Bible mean when Sarah was described earlier as being childless (Gen 11:30)? The rabbis explained that she had been childless because she lacked ovaries, but then God fashioned them for her and returned her youthfulness to her (*Genesis Rabbah* 47.2; 53.5; 48.19; *Tanna debe Eliyyahu,* ch. [5] 6, ER p. 28 [p. 104]).[57]

When Did Sarah Wean Isaac?

Rashi suggests that Sarah weaned Isaac when he was two years old, based on a statement in the Talmud that this is the normal time for weaning (Babylonian Talmud *Gitin* 75b, comment on Gen 21:8).

---

57. God also fashioned an ovary for Rebekah (*Genesis Rabbah* 63.5). Jocheved, Moses' mother, is also miraculously given ovaries (*Exodus Rabbah* 1.19). It shows God's benign acts that finally make the "barren woman" sing. The word for "ovary," *'ikar,* is connected to one of the words for "womb," *'ikurah mibayit.*

Sarah and Hagar: Forced Departure

Genesis 21:9 reads: "Sarah saw the son of Hagar the Egyptian, whom she had borne to Abraham, playing [*metzaheq*]." The rabbis ask, what is the meaning of the word "playing" or *metzaheq* here? To answer that question, we first need to consider how the rabbis understood Ishmael. Ishmael was more than just Abraham's firstborn son; Ishmael was the progenitor of the Ishmaelites,

As is explained in greater detail in the chapter on Hagar, at a certain point in the biblical world, Ishmael becomes a general symbol for any of Israel's neighbors, whether they are Ammonites, Edomites, Hivites, Midianites, or Moabites. For example, Ishmaelites and Midianites seem to be used interchangeably (Gen 37:25, 27–28). Any or all of these tribes or peoples were suspect simply because they were "Others," non-Israelites, or in the rabbinic world, non-Jews. This kind of distrust of the "Other" was commonplace: "All foreign peoples were portrayed in a negative light, for example, in the Greco-Roman world the Roman satirists depicted Egyptians, Syrians, Jews and other non-Romans" in an unflattering light. This demonizing of "Others" was standard fare; it was not a uniquely Jewish trait. It was, in fact, "totally consistent with pre-modern thinking in the West and Middle East."[58] In the post-biblical world, the rabbis inherited this mindset. They continued this general negative attitude towards their Semitic neighbors, collectively known as "Ishmaelites," as an expression of the tensions between Israel and competing peoples. Ishmael—and by extension Hagar—personified evil behavior. Therefore, most rabbinic interpretations understood Ishmael's "playing" or *metzaheq* (Gen 21:9) in a negative light. Following the birth of Islam (ca. 650 CE) and the Muslim tradition that Ishmael is their historical progenitor, calumnies increase. "Ishmael" becomes a code word for Muslims in both midrashic collections such as the *Pirke de Rabbi Eliezer* and other Jewish writings.[59]

The following well-known midrash offers several different examples of how the term "playing" or *metzaheq* is interpreted in a negative light:

> Rabbi Akiba explained, It has been taught [regarding this verse] that "playing/*metzaheq*" means nothing else but immorality, as in the verse "The Hebrew servant whom you have brought among us, came in to me to insult[60] me" (Gen 39:17). Thus this teaches

58. Reuven Firestone, personal communication to David Zucker, September 1, 2000.

59. See further explanation about the *Pirke de Rabbi Eliezer* in our chapter on Hagar.

60. The original Hebrew, *letzaheq*, has alternatively been translated by the *Tanakh*:

[continues the midrash] that Sarah saw Ishmael ravish [young women as well as] seduce married women and dishonor them.

Rabbi Ishmael taught: This term "playing/*metzaheq*" refers to idolatry, as in the verse, [In front of the golden calf] "the people sat down to eat and drink, and rose up to revel" [*letzaheq*] (Exod 32:6). This teaches you that Sarah saw Ishmael build altars, catch locusts and sacrifice them.

Rabbi Eleazar said: The term "playing/*metzaheq*" refers to bloodshed, as in the verse "Let the young men come forward and have a contest before us" [*visahaqu*—(from the root *sin het quf*) actually a close homonym of the root word *letzaheq*—and then the biblical text explains that the opponents killed each other with swords] (2 Sam 2:14 [cf. 2:16]).

Rabbi Azariah said in Rabbi Levi's name: Ishmael said to Isaac, "Let us go and see our portions in the field" and then Ishmael would take a bow and arrows and shoot them in Isaac's direction, while pretending to be playing. Thus it is written, "Like a maniac who shoots deadly firebrands and arrows, so is one who deceives his neighbor and says 'I am only joking'" (Prov 26:18–19) [*mesaheq*—from the root *sin het quf*, again a close homonym of the root word *letzaheq*—to play."] But I [Rabbi Akiba—or possibly Rabbi Azariah] say: This term "playing/*metzaheq*" refers to inheritance. For when our Father Isaac was born all rejoiced, whereupon Ishmael said to them, "You are fools, for I am the firstborn and I shall receive a double portion." (*Genesis Rabbah* 53.11)[61]

Blaming Hagar

Sforno comments that in Gen 21:9, the text that leads up to the crucial word for "playing," "scoffing," or "mocking" defines Ishmael as the son of Hagar the Egyptian. Sarah assumed that Ishmael's scoffing or mocking was something he had learned from his mother. Sforno then refers to the rabbinic saying; "The talk of a child in the marketplace is either that of his father or that of his mother" (Babylonian Talmud *Sukkah* 56b, qtd. in comment on Gen 21:9).

The Holy Scriptures [NJPS]: *The New JPS* [Jewish Publication Society] *Translation* as "to dally with me," or more clearly, given the context of this narrative, "to seduce me."

61. This translation slightly modifies the English from the Soncino translation, which uses the term "sport" for playing. Cf. *Exodus Rabbah* 1.1; *Midrash Tanhuma-Yelammedenu*, Exod 1.1, 313–14; Exod 4:27, 347.

Sarah Was Not Jealous of Hagar or Ishmael

Jubilees had suggested that Sarah was jealous of Ishmael, an idea also mentioned in *NOAB*, in the comment on Gen 21:9–10. The *Zohar* takes the opposite view: "It cannot be supposed that Sarah was moved by jealousy of her [Hagar] or her [Hagar's] son. For if so, God would not have supported her by saying, 'listen to her [Sarah's] voice'" (*Zohar, Vayera*, 1.118b).

Sarah's Compartmentalized Thinking

In the *Zohar*, we read that a sage suggests Sarah saw Ishmael "as being the son not of Abraham but of Hagar the Egyptian" (*Zohar, Vayera*, 1.118b). This comment reflects a profound psychological insight. In her desire to protect the interests of her son, Isaac, Sarah disassociated Ishmael from his Abrahamic parentage, seeing him only as Hagar's progeny. This allowed her to go to Abraham and demand that he "Cast out the slave woman with her son." In that moment, Sarah felt he would acquiesce because, in effect, Ishmael was Hagar the Egyptian's son, not his own child.

Sarah Curses Ishmael

In Gen 21, when Hagar takes Ishmael into the desert wilderness, she loses her way and is fearful that Ishmael will die. According to a midrash, Sarah had put a curse on Ishmael, "whereupon he was seized with feverish pains" (*Genesis Rabbah* 53.13), leading medieval and renaissance commentators to criticize Sarah.[62]

Genesis 22

Genesis 22 begins with the narrative of the Binding of Isaac: "God tested Abraham. [God] said to him, 'Abraham ... Take your son ... and offer him ... as a burnt offering on one of the mountains that I shall show you'" (Gen 22:1–2). Sarah does not appear in Gen 22. Nonetheless, the rabbis are aware that it was unlikely that Abraham would take Isaac from their home and not say something to her.

---

62. See "Some Concluding Thoughts About the Rabbinic Views of Hagar" in the chapter devoted to Hagar.

"Protecting" Sarah from the Truth

At that very moment, Abraham thought,

> If I inform Sarah, women are light-headed about little things;
> all the more so about such a big thing. But if I don't tell her and
> steal him away, when she doesn't see him, she'll kill herself. He
> said to her, "Prepare us some food and drink, and we'll celebrate
> today." She said to him, "What's the reason for this celebration?"
> He said to her, "Old people like us give birth to a son—it is in-
> cumbent upon us to celebrate!" Amidst the celebration he said,
> "You know, I was three years old when I encountered [recog-
> nized] my Creator. This lad is getting older and hasn't been edu-
> cated. There is a place far away where they educate boys. I'll take
> him and educate him there." She said, "Go in peace." Without
> further ado, "He arose early in the morning." Why [so early] in
> the morning? He thought, Sarah may change her mind and not
> let me go. I'll get up early, before she does.[63]

Genesis 23

Chapter 23 relates the funeral arrangements following Sarah's death.

Sarah's Death

The final image we have of Sarah is in Gen 21, when she demands the expulsion of Hagar and Ishmael. She is then about ninety-three years old. Sarah is
absent in Gen 22, the narrative of the *Aqedah*, or Binding of Isaac. The next
time she is mentioned in Genesis is the announcement of her death at age
127 in Kiriyat Arba/Hebron (Gen 23:1–2). What happened in those thirty-
four intervening years? The Bible is silent about that matter. The classic rabbinic texts likewise do not mention it, although there are some comments
as to whether or not Sarah and Abraham were living together when she died
at Kiriyat Arba/Hebron.[64] Midrashic tradition offers ideas about the reason
for her death. These sources would require Isaac to be thirty-seven years old
at the time of the *Aqedah*, or Binding, contrary to the sense of the biblical

---

63. *Midrash Tanhuma*, Vayera 22 (also in *Yalkut Shimoni*, Vayera 98), quoted in
Zierler, "In Search of a Feminist," 13.

64. See the comments of Rashi and Ramban on Gen 23:2. For a fuller discussion
of what happened to Sarah and where she might have been during those years, see the
"Addition/Excursus" section at the end of this chapter.

text, which depicts him as a child innocently complying with this father's actions on the mountain.[65]

According to some sources, following the fateful Binding on Mount Moriah, Isaac himself returned home alone and reported what took place:

> When Isaac returned to his mother, she asked him, "Where have you been, my son?" He answered her, "Father took me, led me up mountains and down valleys, took me up a certain mountain, built an altar, arranged the wood, bound me upon it, and took hold of a knife to slay me. If an angel had not come from heaven and said to him, 'Abraham, Abraham, lay not your hand upon the lad,' I would have been slain." On his mother, Sarah, hearing this, she cried out, and before she had time to finish her cry her soul departed. (*Ecclesiastes Rabbah* 9.7.1; *Pesikta de Rab Kahana, Piska* 26.3)

In another source, Isaac brings Sarah the news, and she utters six cries and then dies (*Leviticus Rabbah* 20.2). A variant of this explanation features the evil angel Sammael (alternatively Satan), who goes to Sarah and tells her what took place on Mount Moriah:

> "Your husband Abraham has taken your son Isaac and slain him and offered him as a burnt offering upon the altar." She began to weep and cry aloud three times, corresponding to the three sustained notes [of the Shofar, the ram's horn sounded on the Jewish New Year], and (she gave forth) three howlings corresponding to the three disconnected short notes [of the Shofar] and her soul fled, and she died. (*Pirke de Rabbi Eliezer* ch. 32)[66]

The shofar is sounded on Rosh Hashanah, the day when the *Aqedah*, or Binding of Isaac (Gen 22), is recited as the Torah reading. This rabbinic explanation seeks to offer connections between the wailing sound of the shofar, which may sound like someone crying, and the fact that the next chapter in Genesis begins with notice of Sarah's death (Gen 23). There is also a tradition that when Satan comes to tell Sarah about the incident on the mountain, she answers him that Abraham is correct to follow God's will.[67]

65. If Gen 23 follows directly on Gen 22, then Isaac would be thirty-seven years old, for he was born when Sarah was ninety. If Gen 22, however, follows reasonably soon after Gen 21, then Isaac would still be a child. The figure of Isaac in Gen 22, moreover, appears to be that of a young person. The Bible does not address this vital issue of Isaac's age at the Binding.

66. In *Midrash ha Gadol* the messenger is Satan, not Sammael (Gen 1.327).

67. When Sarah hears that Abraham has taken Isaac to sacrifice him, she faints.

Sarah's Age at Her Death: 127

The literal Hebrew text in Genesis says that Sarah's years were a hundred years, twenty years, and seven years. According to the *Zohar*, each of these segments had supernal mystical meaning (*Zohar*, *Haye Sarah*, 2.122b–123a).

Sarah's Eulogy

Sarah, in the minds of many rabbis, is an ideal wife. Therefore the praise found in Prov 31, which describes the "capable wife," is attributed to Sarah. In the rabbis' view, this is Abraham's eulogy for her. The rabbis take the verses in Prov 31 and associate Sarah with the biblical text:

> Who can find a gallant wife? [Prov 31:10]. About whom were the words spoken? <They were spoken about Sarah> since it is written (in Gen 23:2): and Abraham proceeded to mourn for Sarah and weep for her, <i.e.,> he began to weep and eulogize. So he said: When shall I be able to get <another wife> like you? (Prov 31:10) A gallant wife: This was Sarah, as stated (in Gen 12:11): See here now, I know that you are a beautiful-looking woman. (Prov 31:10, cont.): Her value was far beyond that of rubies, in that you came from afar. Thus it is stated (in Isa 46:11): Summoning a bird of prey from the east, my confidant from a far country. (Prov 31:11): Her husband's heart had confidence in her: This was Sarah, as stated (in Gen 12:13): [Please say you are my sister] so that it may be well with me because of you. (Prov 31:11, cont.): And he has no lack of profit. This refers to our father Abraham, of whom it is stated (in Gen 13:2): now Abraham was very rich (Prov 31:12) She did good for him and not evil. This refers to Sarah, since it is stated (in Gen 12:16): And because of her, it went well with Abraham. (*Midrash Tanhuma, Genesis. Hayye Sarah*, 5.3 Gen 24:1ff., Part 3. *Midrash Tanhuma Yelammedenu, Genesis*, And the Life of Sarah, Gen 5.4, p. 157)

Sarah's Burial Place at Kiriyat Arba

Sarah died and was buried at Kiriyat Arba/Hebron (Gen 23:1–2). Abraham, apparently unaccompanied by Isaac, purchases land for a permanent

---

Then she rouses herself and says, "All that God told Abraham, may he do it unto life and peace" (Ginzberg, *Legends of the Jews*, 1:278). The source Ginzberg cites is *Midrash Vayosha* 36.

sepulcher. Kiriyat Arba translates as "City of Four," leading the rabbis to ask, Who were these four? Among the answers were four very special women— Eve, Sarah, Rebekah, and Leah—and four couples: Adam and Eve, Abraham and Sarah, Isaac and Rebekah, Jacob and Leah (*Genesis Rabbah* 58.4; Babylonian Talmud *Eruvin* 53a; *Sotah* 13a).

Sarah's Image Lives On

There is a tradition that, following her death, the image of Sarah appeared in her tent. Isaac drew comfort from this, as he looked upon it daily (*Zohar*, Haye Sarah, 2.133b).

Sarah's Special Place

As the Bible's first Matriarch, Sarah elicits special attention from the rabbis. Sarah is a considerable character in her own right. As the first Matriarch, she is the mother of the Jewish people, affectionately termed *Sarah imeinu*, or "Sarah Our Mother," just as Abraham is called *Avraham avinu*, "Abraham Our Father." Yet compared to the material written about Abraham in both Genesis and in midrash, she has a lesser role in the unfolding of the biblical drama. As a whole, the rabbinic material surrounding Sarah is positive. The rabbis favor and praise Sarah, but they point out her failings as they understand them in their time and place. The rabbis portray Sarah as a loyal wife who supports her husband in his journeys. Likewise, she is a proud mother. She is powerful—a princess, a prophet, and a provider. The rabbinic view of Sarah adds greatly to the biblical view of Sarah. Their expanded portraits offer a broader and deeper picture of a person who is more complex, strong, and positive. If the rabbinic view of Sarah does not always offer specific details, nevertheless it portrays someone with whom many contemporary women can engage.

Sarah Is a Prophet

The rabbis claim that Sarah and Iscah, Haran's daughter (Gen 11:29), are the same person: "Rabbi Isaac observed, Iscah was Sarai, and why was she called Iscah? Because she foresaw [the future] by holy inspiration" (Babylonian Talmud *Sanhedrin* 69b).[68] Sarah is regarded as one of seven women proph-

68. The Hebrew word "Iscah," which has a dubious etymology, may be connected to the Aramaic root *sacah* [*sin kaf alef*], which means "to gaze" or "to look."

ets (along with Miriam, Deborah, Hannah, Abigail, Huldah, and Esther) (Babylonian Talmud *Megillah* 14a). Sarah's gift of prophecy was superior to Abraham's; she was able to discern that Ishmael was wicked (*Exodus Rabbah* 1.1; *Midrash Tanhuma Yelammedenu, Exodus,* Now These Are the Names, Exodus 1.1, pp. 313–14).

Sarah's Influence on Abraham

Sarah's powerful influence over Abraham disturbed the rabbis. It went against their values and mores: "The Rabbis said: She is her husband's ruler. Usually, the husband gives orders, whereas here we read, 'In all that Sarah says to you, hearken unto her voice' (Gen 21:12)" (*Genesis Rabbah* 52.5; 47.1). Yet at the same time, there is a midrash that suggests Abraham profits from listening to his wife (*Deuteronomy Rabbah* 4.5).

The Perfect Couple

Sarah was blameless in her generation; she was a fitting mate for Abraham (*Midrash Proverbs*, Prov 19; *Numbers Rabbah* 14.11).[69] They made a perfect couple (*Numbers Rabbah* 2.12).

Sarah as Student

Among the biblical women, Sarah alone studied Jewish texts, including the Torah, Mishnah, and Talmud (*Ecclesiastes Rabbah* 7.28.1). In one sense, this makes her unique, and yet it perpetuates the notion that it is not necessary to teach women Torah. As to the question of how Sarah can engage in writings written years after her death, this is not a problem for the midrashic tradition. According to the rabbis, there is no such thing as linear or chronological time, since past, present, and future time all merge seamlessly.

Targum Onqelos

When Sarah is in Pharaoh's palace, as noted above, the rabbis read '*al d'var Sarai* as "according to the *word* of Sarai." *Targum Onqelos* follows the

---

69. Midrashim reflect the value system of the time in which they were composed. This midrash, as with the previous one addressing Sarah's influence over Abraham and likewise the next midrash, which suggests that Abraham and Sarah made a "perfect" couple, may be discordant in terms of twenty-first-century thinking.

Masoretic text and translates this with the word *'eysak*, which would mean "on account of" or "because of her."

Contemporary Scholarship

Living in the contemporary world, we see Sarah through the lenses of twenty-first-century life. This is again a different Sarah. The actual words the Bible devotes to Sarah are limited; what might be said about her seems limitless. There are many fine contemporary scholarly commentaries on the book of Genesis. Nonetheless, we shall limit our examples to specific insights scholars have made about material dealt with earlier in this chapter.

Sarah Is Part of God's Covenant with Abraham

In Gen 12:1, God technically addresses Abram, not Abram and Sarai. Is she not part of the covenant? Certainly, some time later God tells Abraham that the covenantal line will be through the joint lineage of Abraham and Sarah. To indicate this, God bestows new names upon them (Gen 17:5, 15–16). While in a narrow literal sense the command to Abram in Gen 12:1 is directed toward him, not them, it is likely that people in biblical times understood God's call was for both Abram and Sarai. Second Isaiah says quite clearly, "Look to Abraham your father and to Sarah who bore you, for he was but one when I called him but I blessed him and made him many" (Isa 51:2). The words in Isaiah are "called him" and "made him," but this is a generic "him" and effectively means "them." This is clear because the first part of the sentence expressly mentions Sarah.

Abraham's Statement to Sarah: "Say You Are My Sister"

When Abraham and Sarah are about to enter Egypt, he says to her, "I know well that you are a woman beautiful in appearance; and when the Egyptians see you, they will say, 'This is his wife'; then they will kill me and let you live. Say you are my sister, so that it may go well with me because of you, and that my life will be spared on your account" (Gen 12:11–13). In this passage, Abraham twice uses the term "please," or *n'a*. A more literal translation of the above words would be "*Please*, I know well that you are a woman beautiful in appearance . . . Say *please* you are my sister." Davidson suggests that Abraham begs Sarah to take on this role.[70]

Sarah and Abraham Entering Egypt: Tricksters

According to one body of thought, the wife-sister ruse is a plan devised by Abraham and Sarah together. This is a way that the relatively powerless can outwit the powerful, so "This passage is not a tale about unethical behavior, but a story of marginalized persons who succeed in roundabout, unorthodox ways."[71]

Sarah in Pharaoh's Palace

The Genesis text is ambiguous as to exactly what took place at Pharaoh's palace. A case can be made that Pharaoh intended to marry Sarah, to grant her wifely status. He tells Abraham that, on the assumption that she was the Patriarch's sister, the monarch wanted her as a wife (*l'isha*,[72] the same term is used later in Gen 16, when Sarah offers Hagar to Abraham as a wife).[73] Another modern commentator explains, "Abram's wife becomes another man's wife. Becoming a wife, in these narratives, always implies sexual relations."[74]

Nahum Sarna suggests that at the very least, Pharaoh wanted to approach Sarah sexually. Sarna explains, "there seems to be a word play behind the Hebrew expression . . . 'to afflict, plague,' as well as 'to come into physical contact with, to harass sexually.'" Both of these expressions feature the same verb root, *nun gimmel 'ayin*. Sarna also explains that there may be "a connection with Pharaoh's passion for Sarai . . . [and temporary] sexual impotence induced by some severe inflammation or acute infection of the genital area."[75]

---

70. Davidson, *Flame of Yahweh*, 227.

71. Niditch, "Central Commentary, *Lech L'cha*," 63. See also Niditch's remarks regarding tricksters in ibid., "Genesis," 36.

72. See Gen 12:19; 16:3.

73. Schneider, *Mothers of Promise*, 29. See also Alter's discussion of the word "wife" versus "concubine" (Alter, *Genesis*, 68).

74. Borgman, *Genesis*, 42; Shinan and Zakovitch, *From Gods to God*, 224.

75. Sarna, *Genesis*, 96–97.

The Norms in a Patriarchal Society

Sarah belongs to Abraham and therefore he could make her available to Pharaoh. The king [however] then understands that he violated a social rule, i.e., he took ownership of a married woman. It is nevertheless interesting to note that the story conveys the idea that a man has the right to impose his power over an unmarried woman or a widow, but is forbidden to take control or ownership of a married woman. According to the post-biblical commentaries, this story reestablishes the norms of the traditional patriarchal society, and both Abraham and Pharaoh, as two men in the ancient world, adhere to the same social order.[76]

Obtaining Children

The first time we hear Sarah's words are in Gen 16. Up to this point, Sarah has been spoken about; now we hear her voice. The phrase she uses creates a pun, for the literal Hebrew translation of her words, "*I shall obtain children by her*," is *ib-ba-neh*—a wordplay that could also mean "sonned" through her (the Hebrew *ben* is "son").[77]

Surrogate Motherhood

In the Ancient Near East during the period of the Matriarchs and Patriarchs, there were legal precedents that addressed issues surrounding childlessness.[78] As Niditch explains, "Surrogate motherhood allowed a barren woman to regularize her status in a world in which children were a woman's

76. Tohar, "Abraham and Sarah," 10.

77. Alter, *Five Books of Moses*, 77.

78. Surrogate motherhood is mentioned early in the Bible and may have been common practice. Examples include Sarah, Rachel, and Leah. It is also noted in the Code of Hammurabi para. 146, which addresses a situation where a noblewoman gives her slave to her husband as a surrogate womb (Westermann, *Genesis*, 239). It is also found in the Nuzi and Mari texts (ca. eighteenth century BCE) in Mesopotamia, but "The foremost example is a Nuzi text, translated by E. A. Speiser . . . Speiser concludes from this: 'What Sarah did . . . was in conformance with the family law of the Hurrians'" (Westermann, *Genesis*, 239).

Mesopotamian sources relevant to Gen 16:1–6 are found in Tsevat, "Hagar and the Birth," 70–72. See also Sarna, *Genesis*, 119. For further information, see Knobloch, "Adoption," *AYBD*, 1:76ff.

status and in which childlessness was regarded as a virtual sign of divine disfavor (see [Gen] 16:2; 30:1–2 . . . 38). Childless wives were humiliated and taunted by co-wives (Gen 16:4)" (See Peninah's treatment of Hannah in 1 Sam).[79]

Sarah in the Light of Hagar Belittling Her

Sarah is upset with Hagar. She blames her husband for this state of affairs. This is not how she imagined it would be. Sarah "who wanted to be built up by way of having offspring, feels torn down."[80]

A Legal Aspect?

There also may be a legal side to this matter of Sarah's accusation against Abraham. Tsevat suggests that when Sarah says to Abraham, "May the wrong done to me be on you" in v. 5, "the legal form has a litigious ring. A lawsuit is indicated with [Sarah's crying to Abraham that she has been wronged]. He, the master of the house, is permitting her handmaid to infringe on her position as mistress . . . Whatever protection under custom of agreement Hagar might have had before, she has forfeited by her conduct."[81] Sarah hands Hagar over to Abraham to be punished as the law required. As Speiser explains, Sarah was not acting on impulse; rather she is acting "in conformance with the family law of the Hurrians, a society whose customs the patriarchs knew intimately and followed often."[82]

Harsh Treatment, Which Leads to Harsh Treatment

"Then [Sarah] treated [Hagar] harshly" (Gen 16:6). Sarah mistreats her pregnant maidservant, who was intended to be a surrogate mother to produce an heir. The Hebrew for "treating harshly" is va-t'aneha. This word suggests physical as well as mental or emotional abuse. It "generally carries

79. Niditch, "Genesis," 34–35. For the cultural context of this legalized surrogate motherhood, see Sarna, Genesis, 119 comment on v. 2; Speiser, Genesis, 120. Material from Nuzi and Hammurabi is featured in Matthews and Benjamin, Old Testament Parallels, 47–53; 110.

80. Borgman, Genesis, 44.

81. Tsevat, "Hagar and the Birth," 55.

82. Speiser, Genesis, 121. See von Rad, Genesis, 192, in which von Rad mentions the Hammurabi Code para. 146.

the connotation of physical harm: it can mean . . . to oppress . . . as well as simply to humble or humiliate."[83] Abraham does not intervene. In a later generation, when Sarah and Abraham's descendants are enslaved in Egypt, they in turn will be oppressed (*'anoto* in Exod 1:11; *oni* in 3:7) as foretold earlier to Abraham (*'anu* in Gen 15:13)—all these verbs come from the same Hebrew word root, *'ayin nun hey*, meaning "oppression."

Ishmael's Legal Rights

Sarna addresses Ishmael's legal rights and suggests that even after the birth of Isaac, Ishmael's rights remained in place. Sarna explains:

> The legal position of Ishmael is quite clear. Sarah had under-taken to recognize as her own the male offspring of the union of Abraham with Hagar, a match that she herself had initiated and imposed on her husband (16:2). Abraham, for his part, undoubtedly recognized Ishmael as his legitimate son, a fact repeatedly attested by a variety of earlier texts (16:15; 17:23, 25f.) and affirmed here [Gen 21:11] as well as later on (25:9, 12). Did this status assure Ishmael automatic inheritance rights even after the birth of Isaac? Sarah's formulation of her demand and the extreme length to which she was prepared to go point to an affirmative answer.[84]

Yet there is a clause in the "laws of Lipit-Ishtar where it is stipulated that the father may grant freedom to the slave woman and the children she has borne him, in which case they forfeit their share of the paternal property . . . Sarah is asking Abraham to exercise that legal right."[85] Towards the end of his life, Abraham gave gifts to his sons by his concubines [*p'lagshim*] and sends them away. He designates Isaac as his sole successor (Gen 25:5-6).

The Tensions of Blended Families

There are tensions among Sarah, Hagar, and Abraham, and presumably these are heightened by the birth of Ishmael, and then Isaac's birth. They are

---

83. Hackett, "Rehabilitating Hagar," 14. Friedman translates the word in this verse (Gen 16:6) as degrade writing that "Sarai degraded [Hagar]" (Friedman, *Commentary on the Torah*). See also *Genesis Rabbah* 45:6; Trible, *Texts of Terror*, 13; Graetz, *Silence Is Deadly*, 23.

84. Sarna, *Genesis*, 146–47 n. 10.

85. Ibid.

examples of an all-too-human dynamic reflecting many of the additional strains that often exist in a household of stepparents and stepchildren—blended families.[86]

"With Her Son, Isaac" (Gen 21:9)

In many standard Christian translations of the Bible, at the end of the sentence in Gen 21:9 we find the additional words "with her son, Isaac."[87] That phrase appears in the Septuagint (LXX), the Greek version of the Hebrew Scriptures, but it does not appear in the traditional Hebrew (Masoretic) text [MT], which ends with the word "playing."[88] Sarah then goes to Abraham and demands that he "Cast out this slave woman with her son; for the son of this slave woman shall not inherit along with my son, Isaac" (Gen 21:10).

The Verb "Playing," or Metzaḥeq, Has Multiple Meanings

Was Ishmael "playing with her son, Isaac," or just "playing" (Gen 21:9)? Furthermore, what are the implications of the word "playing"? This has been the subject of much commentary and controversy. The word in Hebrew is metzaḥeq, which has multiple meanings. Depending on its context, metzaḥeq (mem tzadeh ḥet quf) can hold such diverse meanings as "laugh," "play," "fondle," "insult," "seduce," "dally," "mock," "be idolatrous," "revel," or "kill."[89] Gerhard von Rad explains that whatever Ishmael did, it "need not be anything evil at all. The picture of the two boys playing with each other on an equal footing is quite sufficient to bring the jealous mother to a firm conclusion: Ishmael must go!"[90] E. A. Speiser writes that Ishmael's "'playing'

86. Zucker and Reiss, "Abraham, Sarah, and Hagar."

87. NRSV, New American Bible (Roman Catholic), and The Jerusalem Bible (Roman Catholic) include the words "with her son Isaac." The New English Bible with the Apocrypha features the words "laughing at him" which is ambiguous. Does this refer to Isaac, or to Abraham? The New International Version follows the traditional Hebrew (Masoretic) text.

88. The New Jewish Publication Society (NJPS) version, Tanakah: The Holy Scriptures, reads, "Sarah saw the son whom Hagar the Egyptian had borne to Abraham playing" (Gen 21:9).

89. See Zucker, "What Sarah Saw." For a different view, that the "metzaḥeq" issue centers on a religious/idolatry controversy related to circumcision-as-an-Egyptian rite, see Teubal, Sarah, 37–41.

90. von Rad, Genesis, 232. A note in NOAB offers the suggestion that "The jealous mother [Sarah] could not stand seeing the two boys on the same level, even at play" (comment on Gen 21:9–10).

with Isaac need mean no more than the older boy was trying to amuse his little brother. There is nothing in the text to suggest that he was abusing him."[91] W. Gunther Plaut notes that some "commentators have suggested that it was sexual play that brought forth Sarah's strong reaction. There is nothing, however, to substantiate this."[92]

What Ishmael Represents to Sarah

What does Ishmael represent for Sarah? Why is she so intent on removing Hagar and Ishmael from the family compound? Sarah says explicitly that Ishmael "shall not inherit" along with Isaac (Gen 21:10). This could mean that Sarah did not wish for Ishmael to inherit Abraham's wealth, for it was she herself that was so instrumental in his achieving prosperity.[93] Yet it is likely that she means something else, that she does not want the physical, familial, and psychological presence of Ishmael around her son. The use of the word *metzaheq* or "playing," with its linguistic affinities to the name Isaac, or *Yitzhaq*, is intentional in the text: "The wordplay may suggest that Ishmael 'played at' being Isaac. Sarah, seeing him in this assumed role, fears that today's play may become tomorrow's serious rivalry, and therefore resolves to end the relationship by . . . sending . . . [Ishmael] away."[94]

Ishmael as Both an "Other" and an Egyptian

Sarah thinks of Ishmael as an "Other."[95] Ishmael, the son of Egyptian Hagar, reminds Sarah of that painful time in Egypt when, to save her husband's life, she became part of Pharaoh's harem and was likely subject to rape.

91. Speiser, *Genesis*, 155.

92. Plaut, *Torah: A Modern Commentary*, 139. See Rashi on Gen 21:9, citing Exod 32:6 and Gen 39:17. On the other hand, Schneider, in the note to Gen 21:9, states that while *metzaheq* [*m'tzachek*] can be translated as "playing," it "can also mean 'mocking,' 'fooling around,' and toying with him sexually" (Schneider, "Central Contemporary Vayeira," 98).

93. See Gen 12:16, "for her sake [Pharaoh] dealt well with Abram" and with King Abimelech of Gerar: "Look, I have given your brother a thousand pieces of silver; it is your exoneration before all who are with you; you are completely vindicated" (Gen 20:16).

94. Plaut, *Torah: A Modern Commentary, Revised Edition*, 132.

95. See the "Sarah and Hagar: Forced Departure" section above in "The Rabbis' Sarah."

Isaac's Physical Safety

Sarah has concerns about Isaac's physical safety. If Ishmael believes that Isaac threatens his position of inheritance, he may harm his younger brother.

Role Model

Ishmael is about fourteen years older than Isaac, and therefore is naturally an influential role model for Isaac. Sarah's concern is not for Isaac's physical safely, but for the undue influence Ishmael might have upon her son, both psychologically and emotionally. Sarah is worried that Isaac might fall under the excessive influence from his older, teenage brother.[96]

Religious and Cultural Concerns: Egyptianization

Sarah and her husband are years older than Hagar. In all likelihood, they will predecease her. As Isaac's stepmother, Hagar would have an enormous influence upon him both religiously and culturally. He would be "Egyptianized," and thereby lose the religious and cultural norms of his Mesopotamian-oriented parents. More specifically, as one scholar suggests, Sarah desires to prevent Isaac from adopting polytheistic religious ideas. Teubal writes what "the text implies is that Hagar was bringing up her son Ishmael in a traditional Egyptian way, and this was not the influence Sarah wanted around Isaac."[97] Sarah's intervention has a double effect. On one hand, it gives Isaac the opportunity to forge a relationship with God without any foreign influences in the family encampment. On the other hand, it also allows Ishmael a chance to develop his own future destiny.

Sarah's fear of pagan religio-cultural influences is realistic. This family was a small island surrounded by a sea of polytheistic religions with different value systems. For example, in the next generation, Esau upsets his parents when he marries foreign wives (Gen 26:34–35). Israel's biblical history is replete with examples where the community was negatively influenced by

---

96. "Sarah fears that the danger of Ishmael corrupting his younger brother is greater than the prospect of Isaac being a good influence on Ishmael" (Lieber et al., *Etz Hayim*, 114). Based on the teaching of the Ḥafetz Ḥayyim (Yisrael Meir Kagan, Lithuanian rabbi, nineteenth to twentieth century) (ibid.). This idea and other factors in this section are considered in Zucker, "What Sarah Saw."

97. Teubal, *Sarah*, 40. Although this is speculation on Teubal's part, her point is reflected in rabbinic thought; however, the rabbis say that only after she was in the desert did she revert to her pagan practices (see *Genesis Rabbah* 53.14; *Pirke de Rabbi Eliezer* ch. 30).

competing cultural and religious practices. For example, at Shittim, Phineas acts quickly to curb foreign practices (Num 25:1–9). Deuteronomy clearly states that upon entry to the promised land, Israel is to eradicate idolatry (Deut 12:2–4.) Syncretistic religious practices are an ongoing concern (See Jer 7:30–31; Ezek 14:6–9; Hos 7:11–13, etc. See also Ezra 10:2–5).

Sarah's Vision of Reality Is More Lucid than Her Husband's

Avivah Gottlieb Zornberg explains that "Sarah who could tell Abraham . . . 'Cast out that slave woman and her son' . . . demonstrates not only inflexible will but an apparent lucid vision of reality that is hidden from the more entangled emotions of Abraham: 'The matter disturbed Abraham greatly, for it concerned a son of his ([Gen] 21:10–11).'"[98]

Displacement and Affliction

The "Egyptian Hagar—whose name echoes the word *ger* ('stranger')—is taken from her home to Canaan. This cycle of displacement and enslavement will continue: Hagar's descendants (the Ishmaelites) will sell Joseph into Egyptian slavery (37:27–28), and Hagar's people (the Egyptians) will 'afflict' Sarah's descendants (Exodus 1:11–12) as Sarah 'afflicted' Hagar (Gen 16:6)."[99]

Cast out . . . Cast out

Sarah demands that Hagar and Ishmael be "cast out." Sarah's use of this particular verb will become ironic years later. In Egypt, Pharaoh first casts out Moses and Aaron, then all of the Israelites (Exod 10:11; 11:1; 12:39).

Sarah's Exoneration and Vindication

Since the episodes concerning Sarah, Hagar, Abraham, and Ishmael in chapters 16 and 21 are interconnected, we have placed them together. In chapter 20 of the Genesis narrative, Abraham and Sarah spend some time in Gerar. There, for a time, Sarah is taken into the palace of the ruler, Abimelech, who then restores her to Abraham. Abimelech sends along gifts to Abraham and says to Sarah, "It is your *exoneration* before all who are with you;

98. Zornberg, *Genesis*, 134–35. See *Genesis Rabbah* 53.11.
99. Levine, "Another View, *Lech L'cha*," 78.

you are completely vindicated" (Gen 20:16). The word "exoneration" is the NRSV translation for the phrase *kesut 'enayim*, literally "a covering of the eyes." As a note to this verse in *NOAB* explains, "*Exoneration*, i.e., a gift to induce everyone to overlook the injury done to Sarah." The revised edition of *The Torah: A Modern Commentary* and *The Torah: A Women's Commentary* translates this phrase as "unblemished virtue." Sarna comments that, taken literally, the term could mean that Sarah should not appear in public unveiled because of her great beauty. Interpreted figuratively and seen as vindication or exoneration, "the payment is a recognition that Sarah's honor was not violated" and that people's eyes should be closed to thinking that she was deserving of scorn.[100]

Sarah Dies at an Advanced Age

"Sarah is the only matriarch whose age is reported. Her age surpasses the ideal 120 with the sacred number of 7."[101]

Feminist Thought

As twenty-first-century readers, we are informed and enriched by the perspective of feminist writers—both female and male—who have brought additional insights to these ancient works. Jewish, Christian, other-religious, and non-religious feminist thought has helped us to understand more clearly the degree to which patriarchy operated in the ancient world. The conservative and androcentric political and religious sensitivity of the writers of the early extra-biblical period and of the classical rabbis reflected the norms of their time. We live in a different era. In this section, we offer feminist insights into the Matriarchs.

The God of Sarah

Was the covenant in Gen 12 made only with Abraham and not Sarah as well? "For centuries, Jews have looked to Sarah as the first of our foremothers. Women's *tekhines* (petitionary prayers) have called upon the God of Sarah, and pleaded in Sarah's name on women's behalf."[102]

100. Sarna, *Genesis*, 144 n. 16.

101. Amit, "Central Commentary, *Chayei Sarah*," 113.

102. Sohn, "Contemporary Reflection, *Lech L'cha*," 81.

Sarah Portrayed as Sister: Coerced by Her Husband, Part 1

How are we to understand the narratives of Abraham passing off his wife as his sister in Egypt and Gerar? One answer is that she is merely her husband's property, to do with as he wishes. Abraham's request of her is a formality on his part; he really is coercing her in this matter. He assumes that she will give her consent. This is a "crass, male-centered . . . [account] where it is clear that Abram has more to gain as the brother of an unattached, protected woman than the husband of a 'used' one . . . This is no woman-affirming tale. Sarai is an exchange item to be traded for wealth."[103]

Sarah Portrayed as Sister: Coerced by Her Husband, Part 2

Describing Sarah as a commodity to be effectively sold at Abraham's will, suggests that Abraham is *pimping* Sarah. This interpretation has support in rabbinic literature. As quoted earlier in reference to the parallel tale at Gerar in Gen 20, "Rabbi Yehudah bar Rabbi Ilai said, [Abimelech reproached Abraham:] 'You went to Egypt and made merchandise [*samech ḥet resh tav*] of [Sarah], and you came here and traded [*samech ḥet resh tav*] in her'" (*Genesis Rabbah* 52.12).

The Personal Is Political

Naḥmanides observes that Abraham's "inappropriate treatment of his female spouse . . . brings on the national servitude of the Israelites to Pharaoh" at the time of Moses.[104] Bonna Devorah Haberman suggests that this interpretation strengthens the phrase that "'the personal is political' . . . every individual experience of gender-based oppression [is] significant to the public and political discourse . . . [it] is the building block for the larger, societal, international, and global relationships of oppression."[105]

Sarah and Hagar Take on Symbolic Meaning

"'Sarai and Hagar's discord have [*sic*] reverberated until the present day' through the conflict between the peoples—Palestinians and Israelis—who

103. Niditch, "Genesis," 36.
104. See the discussion under "The Rabbis' Sarah" section above.
105. Haberman, "Divorcing Ba'al," 50.

trace their spiritual and even biological lineage back to the sons of Hagar and Sarah."[106] On the other hand, Lynn Gottlieb writes, "It is a tragedy that religion and ideology have transformed this story into a conflict of faiths and peoples. The ultimate irony is the consequent suffering of the hundreds of thousands of women and children who have died as a result of religious and national wars fought in the name of this text."[107] This statement about religious and national wars could refer to the wars from the Crusades in the Middle Ages to the present day, in which Christians and Muslims have fought bitter sectarian battles, often sexually abusing women in the process.

Sarah Acts Unilaterally

It is notable in chapter 12 that while in Egypt, Abraham acted unilaterally concerning Sarah's immediate future; he did not seek Sarah's views. Similarly, in chapter 16 Sarah acts unilaterally; she does not seek either Hagar's or Abraham's views. In both instances, neither "Abraham nor Sarah is concerned with what this intimate encounter might mean for the other parties involved [Sarah with Pharaoh, Hagar with Abraham], but only with what he or she stands to gain."[108] There is some irony in Sarah "giving" Hagar to Abraham "for a wife" (l'isha), for this is the same phrase Pharaoh uses when describing his intentions toward Sarah (Gen 12:19; 16:3).

Sarah's Anger Emerges

Sarah does not address her "victimization in Egypt" at that time. Yet, when

> Hagar conceives, and becomes haughty towards Sarah [Gen 16:4], Sarah decides to send her away . . . when asking Abraham to send Hagar away, she exclaims, "Chamasi Alecha" [Gen 16:5], "The wrong done to me is your fault!" Sarah's strong words here represent the first and only time that she expresses her innermost feelings about what Abraham did to her. Here, she finally allows her deep anger at Abraham's prior behavior to emerge.[109]

---

106. Graetz, *Unlocking the Garden*, 91, quoted in Reinhartz and Walfish, "Conflict and Coexistence," 115.

107. Gottlieb, *She Who Dwells Within*, 88–90, quoted in ibid., 120.

108. Exum, "Endangered Ancestress?'" 142.

109. Chesler and Haut, "Sacrifice of Sarah."

Sarah Did Not Know

At Gen 17:16, God tells Abraham that Sarah will have a child. Apparently Abraham did not share this information with Sarah. In chapter 18, she is taken by surprise when the visitors suggest that she will have a child in a year's time. Gunn and Fewell suggest that Abraham, in his concern for Ishmael, never told Sarah about God's statement, and that in effect he did not give assent to what God had said.[110]

Sarah Laughed to Herself

When Sarah overhears that she will conceive and give birth, she laughs (Gen 18:12). A few verses later, she is chided for her disbelief. We do not know for certain who calls Sarah out in this matter, whether it is God or her husband. Is this a rebuke or simply a gentle comment on her laughter? Tammi J. Schneider suggests it is Abraham and that he is chastising Sarah.[111] Ilona N. Rashkow suggests that it is God who addresses her and that "Sarah is condemned for laughing."[112] There surely is some irony here, for in a few years' time, Sarah will condemn Ishmael for laughing or playing (Gen 21:9ff.).

Sarah's Abusive Behavior

For feminists both male and female, this perpetuation of abusive behavior is painful to encounter. It is especially difficult because here, an abused female abuses another female. As a contemporary critic has written, the

> violence that is practiced by Abraham against Sarah, she now recapitulates in relation to the most vulnerable person in her own household. Thus, the cycle of abuse goes on . . . [The] Torah . . . makes clear that our ancestors are by no means always models of ethical behavior that edify and inspire us. On the contrary, often the Torah holds up a mirror to the ugliest aspects of human nature and human society.[113]

If Sarah is actually casting Hagar out into the inhospitable wilderness, then this raises difficult ethical issues: "From a feminist perspective, the call

---

110. Fewell and Gunn, *Gender, Power, and Promise*, 48.

111. Schneider, *Mothers of Promise*, 32.

112. Rashkow, *Phallacy of Genesis*, 97.

113. Plaskow, "Contemporary Reflection, *Vayeira*," 107. See also Shapiro, "Approaching the Avot."

for the expulsion of Hagar raises troubling questions. The story portrays the oppression of one woman by another."[114]

Sarah's Fierce Anger

David W. Cotter writes of "the fierce nature of Sarah's . . . anger." He explains,

> When Sarah looks at Ishmael, she does not see the teenaged son of her husband, half-brother to her own son . . . All she sees is Hagar. She remembers the humiliation she suffered at Hagar's hands (Gen 16:4) and finds that the time is ripe to wreak her revenge. So, robbing them of any shred of identity, refusing to name them or admit any relationship between these two boys, she demands that the slave and her son be driven out.[115]

Sarah Riled

A different commentator suggests that Sarah is upset because she mistrusts Ishmael's intentions: "Sarah was riled by Ishmael enjoying himself and playing happily on an occasion when the spotlight should be exclusively on her son . . . Perhaps she sees Ishmael . . . setting his sights on a familial position equal to that of Isaac."[116]

Sarah's Stature

A contemporary scholar points out that Sarah is a powerful figure in her own right:

> [Sarah] was of sufficient stature to be respected by kings in communities outside her own [Pharaoh and Abimelech]. (The kings reprimand Abram, not Sarah) . . . The matriarch was also held in high esteem by her husband. Abram is solicitous of her favors before their meeting with kings; he dutifully heeds her request to provide her with a child and accepts Sarah's decision to treat Hagar harshly when the handmaid is insolent to her. Also, Abram's attitude is differential and subservient to the three

---

114. Eskenazi and Weiss, *Torah: A Women's Commentary*, 98.
115. Cotter, *Genesis*, 140–41.
116. Hamilton, *Genesis*, 79.

mysterious visitors at Mamre, in contrast to Sarah, who argues
with one of them.[117]

This interpretation presents Sarah as someone of strength and high standing, someone who commands respect. It is a different view of Sarah than as
merely her husband's property.

Sarah's Exclusion from Genesis 22: The Aqedah, or Binding

Phyllis Trible laments Sarah's exclusion from Gen 22. She points out that this
"leaves the reader to remember as her last words only the harsh imperative"
of sending Hagar and Ishmael away. The "attachment of Gen 22 to patriarchy," with Sarah's "absence from the narrative and her subsequent death,
[suggests that] Sarah has been sacrificed by patriarchy to patriarchy."[118]

Sarah Follows Abraham and Isaac to Mount Moriah

In a modern midrash, Sarah follows Abraham and Isaac up to Mount Moriah. When she sees Abraham bind Isaac with the intent of slaughtering
him, Sarah challenges God and says, "Spare Isaac. Take me instead. Stop
Abraham's hand; remember your covenant with us." God acquiesces and
sends the ram. "The angel says to Abraham, Do not raise your hand against
the boy . . . Sarah pushed the ram into the clearing, and Abraham offered
it up as a burnt offering in place of his son (XXII, 13)." Consequently we
learn, "and Sarah's lifetime . . . came to one hundred and twenty-seven years
(XXIII, 1)—God heard her prayer on Mount Moriah, and honored her
request."[119] In effect, Sarah voluntarily gives up her life for Isaac.

Sarah Was Sacrificed, Not Isaac

When she links the announcement of Sarah's death in Gen 23 directly to
the *Aqedah*, or Binding of Isaac, in Gen 22, one modern writer states that a

> great sacrifice indeed, say the Sages, was made at Mount Mo-
> riah: the demand for Isaac's sacrifice was met by his mother.
> Out of the shadows and into the limelight of the *akeidah* they
> take Sarah. Isaac could not be the one to die on the mount; it

117. Teubal, *Sarah*, 136.
118. Trible, "Genesis 22," 287.
119. Witte, "Sacrifice of Sarah."

was through him that God had promised progeny to Abraham and Sarah. Our first foremother, Sarah, was the sacrifice taken in Isaac's stead.[120]

Parallels between Sarah and Hagar

There are remarkable parallels between the lives of Sarah and Hagar. Alone among the Matriarchs of Genesis, each bears only one child, and "each must surrender that child's fate to divine will, for both Ishmael and Isaac face death in the wilderness. Neither has control over her own body, and neither has support from her natal family. Both are resourceful; both are blessed. Neither is a purely positive role model; neither is a purely negative exemplar."[121]

Addition/Excursus

Searching Beneath the Surface: An Alliance between Sarah and Hagar

The Sarah-Hagar relationship is complicated. They are married to the same man. Sarah gave Hagar to Abraham to produce an heir and then was upset when she perceived Hagar belittling her. Nonetheless, for over a dozen years, Ishmael had been the heir apparent, with a legal standing recognized by Sarah. Then Sarah gave birth in her own right. It is reasonable to assume that the relationship among those five central characters—Sarah, Hagar, Abraham, Ishmael, and Isaac—all changed as a result of Isaac's birth. This does not mean that the Sarah-Hagar connection became a negative one. *A different answer, one that is more benign, may explain Sarah's demand that Hagar and Ishmael leave the family compound.* The plain meaning of the text may contain hidden messages. Many possibilities exist, possibilities that are in themselves both intriguing and full of intrigue. Biblical characters have multiple reasons behind their actions, just as is true of people today.

For many years, Sarah and Hagar honored Ishmael's place as the heir apparent. As former rivals for power and affection within the household, it is likely that Sarah and Hagar learned to live with each other. Each woman had a special place in Ishmael's life. One was his "heir mother" and one was his "birth mother." It was in the women's mutual interest to forge a

---

120. Halevy, "Sarah, the Enabler."
121. Levine, "Beer-lahai-roi," 20.

working relationship,[122] and so they become co-mothers for him.[123] Once Isaac is born, both women realize that the boy's presence changes the family dynamics. There is a concern that Abraham might take drastic action, for with this new heir, Hagar and Ishmael are no longer "needed" in the same way. Over the past years, Abraham has exhibited increasingly strange behaviors (e.g., a covenant ritual involving walking between carcasses and then swooning in Gen 15; adult circumcision in Gen 17; entertaining angels or men or strangers and debating or bargaining with God in Gen 18; and the interactions with Abimelech of Gerar in Gen 20). Their mutual husband seems so God-intoxicated, who knows what he will do next? These acts cause both Sarah and Hagar to question the future safety of their respective son and stepson. It is likely that Sarah consults and conspires with Hagar in an attempt to proactively protect their children.

The women believe that it is time to place a bit of physical distance between Abraham and the rest of the immediate family. Sarah and Hagar decide to seek out a safe place for themselves and for their sons. God promised that both their sons would become great nations (Ishmael in Gen 17:20ff.; Isaac in Gen 17:15ff.). This way, each son will realize his destiny.[124] They have some time to work out this plan. According to a midrashic source, Ishmael is twenty-seven at the time of the "expulsion," and Isaac is thirteen.[125] After a time, they decide on the destination of the natural oasis of Beer-lahai-roi.[126] They arrange that Hagar and Ishmael will go to this oasis first, and then in due time, Sarah and Isaac will join them. Their plan nearly goes amiss when Hagar loses her way in the desert, a very human error in the wilderness. Then an angel of God intervenes and sets them on the correct course. Genesis 16:14 refers to a well at Beer-lahai-roi. There, Hagar

---

122. Teubal, *Hagar*, 77.

123. The idea of co-mothers with shared responsibilities repeats as a theme in Gen 37:10. Joseph suggests that the sun and moon are to bow down to him. Jacob asks Joseph, "Are your mother and I to do this?" Yet Jacob's mother, Rachel, has been dead a long time. "Your mother" refers to Leah (or perhaps to Leah, Bilhah, and Zilpah, all of whom are Joseph's stepmothers), the other mother figure(s) in Joseph's life. Thanks to Rabbi Daniel M. Zucker for pointing out this parallel.

124. For a fuller treatment of this idea, see Zucker, "Mysterious Disappearance."

125. See n. 2 to *Genesis Rabbah* 53.13 (p. 472) and also n. 5 to *Genesis Rabbah* 53.10 (p. 468) in the Soncino English edition: "[Isaac] was thirteen years old."

126. Beer-lahai-roi is only mentioned in Genesis, and the name means "the Well of the Living One who sees me." It was located in the Negev, about twenty-five miles or so southwest of Beersheba, between Qadesh and Bered (Gen 16:14). In *Targum Jonathan* (Gen 16:14) Bered is associated with the Nabatean ruins at Halutza (Elusa), some twelve miles southwest of Beersheba (Avi-Yona, "Elusa," 6:690). Qadesh is probably some fifty miles southwest of Beersheba (Noth, *Numbers: A Commentary*, 106).

finds sustenance when she is in the desert. We can extrapolate that this well is an oasis, for as is mentioned later in Genesis, Isaac also will live there (Gen 24:62; 25:11).

* * * *

Summary and Conclusion

Biblical Sarah is first mentioned at the end of Gen 11. She is childless, or perhaps infertile. Her name is Sarai, the wife of Abram. In Gen 12, they travel to the land of Canaan. Due to a regional drought, the family moves to Egypt, where Sarai is taken into the Pharaoh's palace. Abram had asked her to say that she is his sister, not his wife. God intervenes, and the couple's true relationship is discovered. In chapter 16, Sarai urges Abram to take Hagar, her Egyptian slave woman, as a second wife and to impregnate her, which he does. This plan nearly comes apart when tensions develop between the two women. In chapter 17, God changes Abram's name to Abraham and Sarai's name to Sarah. In chapter 18, visitors announce that in a year's time, Sarah will give birth. In chapter 20, Abraham once again indicates that Sarah is his sibling, not his wife. As chapter 21 begins, God remembers Sarah, and she gives birth to Isaac. Later, Sarah demands that Abraham send Hagar and Ishmael away. She dies in Gen 23.

The primary early extra-biblical writings about Sarah appear in the book of *Jubilees*. *Jubilees* is a retelling of material found in Genesis and the first dozen chapters of Exodus. The tensions between Sarah and Hagar and between Sarah and Abraham are not mentioned in *Jubilees*. The expulsion of Hagar and Ishmael occurs at, or some time after, Isaac's weaning. *Jubilees* adds additional details to those events, including Sarah's jealousy of Ishmael. Josephus, in his *Antiquities of the Jews*, mentions Sarah, and references to Sarah also appear in the pseudepigraphical works the *Testament of Abraham* (versions A and B) and *Joseph and Aseneth*. In *Joseph and Aseneth*, Aseneth is compared favorably to Hebrew women, for she is tall, as was Sarah.

The rabbis in the classical midrashic material feature a range of views about Sarah. She is *Sarah imeinu*, "Sarah Our Mother," the first Matriarch of the Jewish people. The rabbis credit Sarah for bringing women proselytes into Judaism, just as Abraham brought men to the faith of the one God. The rabbis praise Sarah for her chastity in Egypt. Nahmanides criticizes Sarah for her ill treatment of Hagar. Later, when the visitors come to announce that in a year's time she will give birth, Sarah laughs and is incredulous, which earns her rabbinic rebuke. According to some midrashim, Sarah died when she learned what had happened at the *Aqedah*, or Binding of Isaac, on Mount Moriah.

Contemporary and feminist scholars offer differing views of what took place in Egypt and later in Gerar. They range from Abraham imploring Sarah to pretend to be his sister, to his coercing her, to the idea that the deception is a well-thought-out plan by Abraham and Sarah—a deception that those who are marginalized use to gain power in a hostile world. Scholars have written about the cultural context for Sarah's offering Hagar as a surrogate womb, as well as on the verb used to describe Sarah's harsh treatment of Hagar the Egyptian, and what sparked Sarah to demand that "the slave woman and her son" be sent away. Some feminist writers have offered parallels between Abraham acting unilaterally in Egypt by making demands on Sarah and Sarah's acting unilaterally to make demands on Abraham in terms of Hagar. In both cases, the woman who is offered is neither consulted nor given a choice in the matter. Sarah's whole relationship with Hagar is described as morally problematic because it perpetuates the cycle of violence aimed at women.

In conclusion, in the Genesis account of Sarah, certain patterns emerge—patterns that also will be seen in many, if not all, of the other of the Matriarchs. All are born in one land and will either live a substantial number of years in a different country or will at least die in a different land. The Matriarch's inability to become pregnant and its resolution (as in the case of Sarah, Rebekah, Rachel, and Leah), or her easy conceptions (as with Hagar, Leah, and Bilhah and Zilpah) are a major part of her story. Like the other primary Matriarchs (Rebekah, Leah, Rachel, and even Hagar), we hear Sarah's voice. She has strong opinions, especially about matters concerning her child(ren), and what she does directly influences the lives of her husband and her son(s). We see a different Sarah in the pseudepigraphical literature—one that, certainly in *Jubilees*, is less confrontational about family matters. This is also true of her sister Matriarchs. The rabbis' Sarah is active and purposeful in what she does, sometimes to the rabbis' admiration, sometimes not. Again, this generally will be true of the other primary Matriarchs. The rabbis credit Sarah, like the other primary Matriarchs, with being a prophet. Contemporary scholars and contemporary feminist scholars discuss Sarah both within the cultural context of the ancient Near East and from the perspective of the twentieth through twenty-first centuries. She is celebrated for her strengths and is criticized for her treatment of Hagar. She is viewed as either a trickster or as a casualty of patriarchy, having to pretend what she is not.

We turn now to Hagar to explore her life in Genesis, in early extra-biblical writings, rabbinic literature, contemporary scholarship, and feminist thought.

3

Hagar

Biblical Hagar

Introducing Hagar

HAGAR'S APPEARANCES ARE LIMITED in the Hebrew Bible; she is featured in Gen 16 and 21, and there is a short genealogical reference to her in Gen 25:12.[1] Hagar, an Egyptian, is one of Sarah's servants. In time, at Sarah's direction, Hagar becomes Abraham's second wife and the mother of his first child, Ishmael. Hagar does not volunteer for this role. Rather, Sarah suggests to Abraham that this way Sarah will "obtain children" by Hagar. Through this arrangement, Hagar's role is elevated in the Abrahamic household. Sarah instigates this arrangement, yet she soon has misgivings. The two women appear to have an ongoing difficult relationship (Gen 16:1–6). Eventually, Sarah compels Abraham to send Hagar and Ishmael away (Gen 21:9–21). In fact, "The narrator does not make unnuanced judgments about the behavior of the women in this narrative. The choice of words and the actions of the characters themselves indicate that their motives are complex . . . The narrator is sensitive to Sarai's frustration, yet the poignancy of Hagar's plight is recognized as well."[2] Hagar has a dual status in these chapters. She is both "Sarah's antagonist . . . and . . . the central character of

1. Later works provide a wide array of additional perspectives on Hagar's role and significance within the biblical narrative. In the Epistle to the Galatians in the New Testament, Paul utilizes Hagar as an allegorical symbol: "Hagar, a slave who bears children into slavery, represents the Sinaitic covenant" (Cohen, "Letter of Paul to the Galatians," 341). The church fathers (the Patristics) discuss Hagar in a distinctly different manner: "Patristic readings were heavily influenced by Paul" (James, "Sarah, Hagar, and Their Interpreters," 51). For example, John Chrysostom refers to Hagar as an example of arrogance and ingratitude. See Zucker and Brinton, "'Other Woman." Some of the material in this chapter appears there in a different form. See also Thompson, *Writing the Wrongs*. Each of these sources refers to Hagar. Each provides differing and sometimes (although not necessarily) competing views of her.

2. Jeansonne, *Women of Genesis*, 20–21.

a narrative in which she, not Sarah, is the heroine and matriarchal figure."[3] As we note in the introductory chapter, technically Hagar is the Matriarch of Islam. Islam draws its connection to the first Patriarch through Hagar and Abraham's son, Ishmael.[4]

Genesis 16: Hagar, Sarah, Abraham; Meeting the Angel

Hagar first appears in the opening verse of Gen 16. The biblical account is very terse: "Now Sarai . . . had an Egyptian slave-girl whose name was Hagar" (Gen 16:1). The text is silent about Hagar's age and her lineage. No mention is made about how this Egyptian woman became part of Sarah's household, although earlier, the Bible explained that Abraham and Sarah had sojourned for a time in Egypt. When in Egypt, Abraham acquired "male and female slaves" (Gen 12:16). It is likely that Hagar was one of these women.

As will be true of the later primary Matriarchs, Sarah has trouble conceiving a child: "Sarai, Abram's wife, bore him no children" (Gen 16:1, cf. 11:30). In an attempt to produce progeny, Sarah turns to Abraham and says, "You see that the LORD has prevented me from bearing children; go into my slave-girl; it may be that I shall obtain children by her" (Gen 16:2). This is a purposeful request. Both infertility or childlessness and fertility or children were ascribed to God in the ancient world. Childlessness "was regarded as a virtual sign of divine disfavor (see 16:2; 30:1–2 [33:5; 1 Sam 1:6])."[5] Sarah asks Abraham to take Hagar as a wife, "that I [Sarah] shall obtain children by her." The literal translation of the Hebrew says, *"that I will be built up by her."* Put in modern terms, Hagar is to be Sarah's surrogate womb.

Surrogate motherhood was enshrined in ancient Near-Eastern law and tradition, especially for the upper classes.[6] It was in the household's interest not only to produce an heir, but an heir who had an appropriately high lineage. It is likely that surrogate mothers often came from impover-

3. Nikaido, "Hagar and Ishmael," 221.

4. Although Islam reveres Hagar (Hajar) as the mother of Ishmael (Isma'il), Hagar is not mentioned by name in the Qur'an. Those connections are made through the *Qisas al-anbiya'*, a genre of literature that is similar to midrash. According to the Sahih Bukhari (nineth century CE), although it also occurs repeatedly in various Islamic collections of stories and ancient histories that include biblical characters, Abraham recognized the problem between his wives and chose to send Hagar and Ishmael away. Hagar asks if this is Allah's wish; Allah confirms it is.

5. Niditch, "Genesis," 35.

6. For the cultural context of such legalized surrogate motherhood, see Speiser, *Genesis*, 119–21; Sarna, *Understanding Genesis*, 127–29; Sarna, *Genesis*, 119; Niditch, "Central Commentary, *Lech L'cha*," 72; Niditch, "Genesis," 34.

ished but prominent families. This was purely a matter of business, property, and inheritance.

What did Hagar think about this? The Genesis text is silent, for Hagar is voiceless in this whole drama. She might have hoped that having sexual relations with her mistress' master and producing a child would elevate her status. In the meantime, Abraham appears aloof. He largely abdicates any responsibility in this very sensitive triad. Nonetheless, the dynamics and interpersonal relationships assume massive importance for the two women involved.

Abraham impregnates Hagar. Whether this relationship continued beyond the point of Hagar's conception is not stated. Was she expected—indeed, did Hagar expect—to have more children? Since Abraham had been promised descendants as many as the stars of the heaven (Gen 15:5), it is likely that despite his advanced age, that he would want more than one child. Consequently, it is possible that both expected to have a continuing sexual relationship. Earlier, God had promised Abraham that his descendants would inherit the land. No explicit mention was made of a wife; therefore Abraham (and Sarah and Hagar too) assumed that the child born to Hagar would be his promised son. Genesis simply states, "Sarai, Abram's wife, took Hagar . . . and gave her to her husband Abram as a wife ['ishah]" (Gen 16:3). Was Hagar in reality Abraham's spouse, or was she just a concubine? As one scholar explains, "The basic difference between a concubine and a wife is that no *mohar*, or bride-price, is paid for the former."[7] Several "English versions, following the logic of the context, render this as 'concubine,'" explains Robert Alter. "The word used, however, is not *pilegesh* [the normal Hebrew word for concubine] but *'ishah* [wife], the same term that identifies Sarai at the beginning of the verse."[8] In these verses, the Genesis narrative repeatedly emphasizes Sarah's role as the Patriarch's wife (Gen 16:1, 3). Yet Hagar is also Abraham's wife, or *'ishah*. Two generations on, Jacob has several wives at the same time—multiple concurrent spouses make for domestic discord. As will be the case with Bilhah and Zilpah, there are primary and secondary wives; Hagar was not a *pilegesh*, or concubine, but she was inferior to

7. Sarna, *Genesis*, 208.

8. Alter, *Genesis*, 68. Speiser and Sarna make the case that Hagar is a concubine, not a wife (Speiser, *Genesis*, 117; Sarna, *Genesis*, 119). Alter's comment about several "English versions" notwithstanding, many well-regarded English translations also use the term "wife." Cf. the NRSV, NEB, NIV, and JB (Jerusalem Bible), and NJB (New Jerusalem Bible). See also Fox, *Five Books of Moses*. In Gen 25:6, the text specifically terms Abraham's later-born sons as "the children of his concubines," using the word *p'lagshim*, the plural of *pilegesh*, or "concubine." Nahmanides also suggests the correct term is "wife" not "concubine." As shall be explained further on in this chapter in the section "The Rabbis' Hagar," many sages consider Hagar to be Abraham's wife.

Sarah even as a wife. This will become clear a bit later in the chapter, when Abraham cedes all authority over Hagar to Sarah. When children become involved, the difficulties grow exponentially, with all the challenges of what are today termed "blended families." The triad of Sarah-Hagar-Abraham will face many of these problems.[9]

Abraham has sexual relations with Hagar, who immediately conceives (Gen 16:4). Once she becomes pregnant, the relationships between Hagar and her mistress, as well with as her/their husband irreparably change. Again, the Bible is terse in its description. When Hagar "saw that she had conceived, she looked with contempt on her mistress" (Gen 16:4). Was this overweening pride on Hagar's part? I can do what you cannot do? Did Abraham then favor Hagar over Sarah? Did he encourage this behavior or suggest to Hagar that she would displace Sarah? How did Hagar express her feelings toward Sarah? Did she verbalize those thoughts, and if she did, to whom did she express them? Or did Sarah just intuit them? Again, the biblical text provides no answers, although as will be shown, the ancient sages provided their thoughts on these matters. In the meantime, there is the adage in the book of Proverbs: "Under three things the earth trembles . . . [one is] a maid when she succeeds her mistress" (Prov 30:21, 23).[10] In her anger and upset, and with righteous indignation, Sarah confronts not her rival, but her/their husband, for she feels that he has let her down.[11] Sarah challenges Abraham and suggests that it is he who is at fault: "May the wrong done to me be on you! I gave my slave-girl to your embrace, and when she saw that she had conceived, she looked on me with contempt. May the LORD judge between you and me!" (Gen 16:5). Sarah does not mention Hagar by name; she merely refers to her by her place in Sarah's household. Sarah uses a circumlocution ("I gave my slave-girl to your embrace"), thus avoiding the fact that Hagar is Abraham's second wife. Indeed, Sarah and Hagar never have direct communication.

Abraham succumbs to Sarah's scathing critique. He does nothing to explain, much less defend Hagar's possible unwise behavior or his own part in this situation. Likewise, Abraham abdicates any responsibility he has for Hagar's welfare as his second wife.[12] He distances himself from the whole situation and in effect throws up his hands and says, "Do what you think is best." In his reply to Sarah, Abraham also refuses to mention Hagar by

9. Zucker and Reiss, "Abraham, Sarah, and Hagar."

10. Alternatively, "The earth shudders at three things . . . [one is] a slave-girl who supplants her mistress" NJPS/*TANAKH*.

11. Teubal, *Hagar*, 77–81.

12. In Gen 21, Abraham will repeat this behavior, betraying his responsibilities toward Hagar and their mutual child (Zucker, "Betrayal (and Growth)").

name. Despite the fact that Hagar is carrying the heir-apparent, Abraham's future child, the Patriarch dismisses her. He marginalizes her, effectively referring to her as Sarah's property. He tells Sarah, "Your slave-girl is in your power; do to her as you please" (Gen 16:6). As Jo Ann Hackett explains,

> Abram responds with apparent calm, although with no sensitiv-
> ity whatsoever to Hagar's plight, and he tells Sarah that Hagar
> is in her power, "in her hand" literally . . . Sarai proceeded to
> oppress Hagar . . . and the Hebrew verb [va-t'aneha, from the
> root 'ayin nun hey] generally carries the connotation of physical
> harm: it can mean . . . to oppress . . . as well as simply to humble
> or humiliate.[13]

Sarah "dealt harshly with her, and she [Hagar] ran away from her" (Gen 16:6). Here again, the Bible is silent about the nature of this harsh treatment. As shall be shown below, however, the rabbis fill in some of these details. In response to Sarah's maltreatment, Hagar leaves and seeks refuge at some kind of oasis or spring in the nearby desert on the road to Shur. At this point, there is "total disaster for all concerned. Hagar has lost her home, Sarai her maid, and Abram his second wife and [his yet to be born] . . . child."[14] When she is by herself in the wilderness, quite amazingly, Hagar has a divine encounter. Genesis explains, an "angel of the LORD found her by a spring of water in the wilderness" (Gen 16:7). For ten generations, from the time of Noah to the time of Abraham, God had not communicated to humans. Up to this point, God had spoken to the Patriarch several times but had not engaged Sarah in conversation. Now, suddenly, an angel addresses runaway Hagar. Furthermore, this is the Bible's first mention of such a divine messenger. The biblical text is ambiguous. Robert Alter notes that this "'angel' (Hebrew, mal'akh; in Greek, angelos) . . . [is someone] who carries out a designated task . . . the divine speaker here begins as an angel but ends up (verse 13) being referred to as though he were God."[15]

The special messenger knows who Hagar is and her predicament as well. This is evidenced by the angel's opening words to her: "Hagar, slave-girl of Sarai."[16] Then the angel asks two vital questions. "Where have you

13. Hackett, "Rehabilitating Hagar," 14. See "Harsh Treatment, Which Leads to Harsh Treatment" in the "Contemporary Scholarship" section of the chapter on Sarah.

14. Wenham, *Genesis 16–50*, 9.

15. Alter, *Genesis*, 69. A similar movement in status of the speaker(s) takes place in Gen 18 and 19. In Gen 18, Abraham and Sarah's visitors appear first as humans, and then later, God is speaking. In Gen 19, the visitors to Lot's home are first called men, and later they are termed angels.

16. The angel addressing Hagar as "slave-girl of Sarai" underscores her precarious position. On one hand, she is Abraham's wife, or 'ishah, but at the same time, she is

come from, and where are you going?" (Gen 16:8). By labeling Hagar as a slave-girl, and even more specifically, Sarah's slave, these questions are rhetorical; they are not meant to elicit unknown information. In the words of Phyllis Trible, these "questions embody origin and destiny."[17] At the same moment, there is both a literal and existential dimension to those queries. On an existential level, the angel is asking Hagar to consider where she is on her spiritual life's journey. Hagar acknowledges her status, for whatever else she might be, she is Sarah's property. She answers the first part of the query put to her, but she does not address the rest—the question as to where she is going. She answers, "I am running away from my mistress, Sarai" (Gen 16:8). Perhaps Hagar has no idea to where she is going. Alternatively, she may consciously choose not to address the second part of the angel's words to her.

The description of the encounter and dialogue between the angel and Hagar covers seven long verses. The responses are thoughtful and measured. There is no sense of a hurried conversation. The Hebrew text intersperses spoken words with descriptions of who is speaking. The angel then acknowledges Hagar's pregnancy and goes on to tell her what she is to name the unborn child: "And the angel of the LORD said to her, 'Now you have conceived and shall bear a son; you shall call him Ishmael, for the LORD has given heed to your affliction'" (Gen 16:11).

The angel makes it clear that life will be difficult for Ishmael: "He shall be a wild ass of a man, with his hand against everyone, and everyone's hand against him; and he shall live at odds with all his kin" (Gen 16:12). The final words of this NRSV translation, "at odds with all his kin," place Ishmael in an adversarial relationship with others around him. That is not the only way the words can be translated. *The Contemporary Torah*, a recent gender-sensitive adaption of NJPS/*TANAKH*, translates the same phrase as "He shall dwell alongside of all his kin." Dwelling alongside one's kin often means forming alliances; it hardly suggests a relationship of continuous conflict.[18] Indeed, when Abraham dies, both Isaac and Ishmael are there to bury him (Gen 25:9). At the same time, Hagar's son will be free, not a slave. Furthermore, Hagar will have numerous descendants, a promise otherwise made only to the Patriarchs, who receive similar blessings.[19] The angel's statement

---

undoubtedly Sarah's slave, which allows Sarah to humiliate her.

17. Trible, *Texts of Terror*, 15.

18. See Zucker, "Conflicting Conclusions," 39.

19. For a discussion about Hagar's descendants as the Hagarites or Hagarenes, both terms are used in the relevant literature; see Hilhorst, "Ishmaelites, Hagarenes, Saracens." For biblical connections between Hagrites and Ishmaelites, see Ps 83:6 [7H] and 1 Chron 27:30f.

provides Hagar considerable comfort. She understands that she has had a divine encounter. Aware of a tradition that one cannot see God and remain alive, Hagar draws attention to this matter in her comments: "So she named the LORD, who spoke to her, 'You are El-*roi*;' for she said, 'Have I really seen God and remained alive after seeing him?' Therefore the well was called Beer-lahai-roi; it lies between Kadesh and Bered" (Gen 16:13–14).

This angelic-human encounter is extraordinary; it is the first biblical instance of an angelic "annunciation."[20] In addition, this annunciation is offered to someone who is the quintessential outsider as both a slave and a woman. Hagar in herself is not part of the Abrahamic line. Yet Hagar is the only person in the Bible, male or female, to "name" God.

Hagar returns to the familial encampment, and there she gives birth to Ishmael. Her name—Hagar—is mentioned three times without the qualifying words "Egyptian," "servant," or "slave" (Gen 16:15–16). At this point, Ishmael is the heir apparent. He is Abraham's son, and Sarah has said she will adopt him: "I shall obtain children by her" (v. 2). There is no desire at this juncture to speak disparagingly of Ishmael's birth mother. Abraham "named his son, whom Hagar bore, Ishmael," which translates to "God hears" (Gen 16:15). It is noteworthy that Abraham names the child and knows to name him Ishmael. Hagar likely told the Patriarch about the events in the wilderness. There are no divine instructions to Abraham concerning the name of the child, as there will be with Isaac (Gen 17:19). In times to come, Isaac will be the link to the Jewish people, and therefore to Judaism and Christianity. Ishmael, according to Muslim tradition, is the link to Islam. This important connection, while of great interest in its own right, is beyond the scope of this discussion.

Hagar does not appear in Gen 17–20. Ishmael appears, although in a non-speaking role, in Gen 17. In that chapter, God once again addresses the Patriarch, explaining that, in time, he would have a child by Sarah and that her name was to change from Sarai to Sarah. God also confirms what the angel told Hagar: Ishmael will be the progenitor of twelve princes; he will father a great nation (Gen 17:20). Circumcision will be the covenantal sign between Abraham and his descendants. Abraham then proceeds to circumcise Ishmael, aged thirteen; all of Abraham's household males, whatever age they were; and he himself, at the age of ninety-nine (Gen 17:23–27). It is thought that circumcision was practiced among upper-class Egyptians around this time.

---

20. At its simplest level, an "annunciation" is an announcement. In Christianity, "the Annunciation" refers to the angel Gabriel announcing to Mary that she would conceive a child that would be called the Son of God (Luke 1:26–38; see also v. 37).

Genesis 21: Continued Tensions and Aftermath

As with chapter 16, in chapter 21 the lead characters are Sarah, Hagar, and Abraham, with Ishmael serving as a secondary character. About fourteen years have passed since the earlier events surrounding Hagar's pregnancy and the birth of Ishmael. The Bible does not offer any insights into the continuing relationship between Sarah and Hagar. The text is also silent about the nature of the relationships between Sarah and Abraham and between Hagar and Abraham. Up to this point, the Genesis texts tell us nothing directly about Sarah's (or Abraham's) feelings about Ishmael, much less her (their) relationship with him. Until the birth of Isaac, Ishmael was the one who would "build up" Sarah (see Gen 16:2, but also Gen 21:10–11). Chapter 21 begins with God "remembering" the promise that Sarah would conceive, and soon Isaac is born. At Isaac's weaning ceremony, probably when he is about three years old[21] or sometime thereafter, Sarah sees Ishmael "playing," perhaps with Isaac.[22] Something appears to upset Sarah. She goes to Abraham and demands that he send away both Hagar and Ishmael: "Cast out this slave woman with her son; for the son of this slave woman shall not inherit along with my son, Isaac" (Gen 21:10). Here, as with earlier in chapter 16, Sarah effectively dismisses the relationship between Abraham and Hagar. Once again, she does not mention Hagar by name. Although this upsets the Patriarch, he bows to his wife's ultimatum. While the Patriarch's feelings are addressed with "the matter was very distressing to Abraham on account of his son" (Gen 21:11), no mention is made of Hagar's or of Ishmael's response to this sudden change of events. Susan Niditch comments, "This passage is a difficult one in biblical ethics. Abraham cares not at all about the maid he has bedded and Sarah is contemptuous of mother and child and would expose them to death. The author works hard to rationalize and justify the emotions and actions of Abraham and Sarah (21:12–13)."[23]

God suddenly addresses Abraham for the first time in this episode, saying, "Do not be distressed because of the boy and because of your slave woman; whatever Sarah says to you, do as she tells you, for it is through Isaac that offspring shall be named for you. As for the son of the slave woman, I will make a great nation of him also, because he is your offspring" (Gen 21:12–13). A different word is used here for Hagar, the term 'amah instead of shifhah. As shall be noted in the chapter on Bilhah and Zilpah, we "no longer know whether these terms are used interchangeably as a stylistic

21. Sarna, *Genesis*, 146.

22. As noted in the chapter on Sarah, a number of Christian translations add the words "with her son Isaac."

23. Niditch, "Genesis," 35.

concern or whether each term carries a different connotation."[24] Hagar, as an Egyptian and slave, is a double outsider, and Abraham does not even consider her ("the matter was very distressing to Abraham on account of his son," as opposed to his son and his son's mother, or his son and his wife). God tells Abraham to obey Sarah's request and then justifies it "for in Isaac will your descendants be remembered." A similar promise of multiple descendants previously made to Hagar (Gen 16:10) makes no reference to the father. Every part of this episode of Hagar's expulsion degrades her.

Desert travel is precarious. Hagar loses her way; soon she runs out of water. She finds shelter for Ishmael and places him under a bush.[25] In her anguish, she walks some distance away and bewails her situation. She has good reason to be upset. She is lost and fears for her life and for the life of her son. Second, she is bereft because the future she had imagined, in which she would continue in the Abrahamic household as an honored "second wife" and as the mother of the oldest son born to the master, it is not to be. Up to this point, it was clear that Ishmael was the legal son of Abraham; he could have expected to be the heir-apparent.[26] As Sarna writes, "The legal position of Ishmael is quite clear. Sarah had undertaken to recognize as her own the male offspring of the union of Abraham and Hagar . . . Abraham, for his part, undoubtedly recognized Ishmael as his legitimate son . . . ([Gen] 16:15; 17:23, 25f.)."[27]

Hagar, consequently,

> lifted up her voice and wept. And God heard the voice of the boy, and the angel of God called to Hagar from heaven, and said to her, "What troubles you, Hagar? Do not be afraid; for God has heard the voice of the boy where he is. Come, lift up the boy and hold him fast with your hand, for I will make a great nation of him." Then God opened her eyes and she saw a well of water. She went, and filled the skin with water, and gave the boy a drink. (Gen 21:16–19)

Toward the end of this narrative dealing with Hagar and Ishmael, the text refers to Hagar one more time, although not by name. The Bible explains

24. Schneider, *Mothers of Promise*, 134. Sarna refers to discoveries that suggest an *'amah* could be a slave girl to a married couple such that she is the wife of the husband and an *'amat* of the wife (Sarna, *Exodus*, 120).

25. See the comment below in the "Child or Lad? Or Both at the Same Time—2?" section under "Contemporary Scholarship."

26. See the comment below in the "Angry Hagar" section under "Contemporary Scholarship."

27. Sarna, *Genesis*, 146. See also the discussion about this in the chapter on Sarah, "Ishmael's Legal Rights."

that Ishmael dwelled in the wilderness of Paran and that "his mother got a wife for him from the land of Egypt" (Gen 21:21). Hagar's arrangements for an Egyptian spouse for Ishmael (an endogamous relationship) parallels Abraham's as well as Rebekah and Isaac's desire for their son to marry within the family.[28]

Genesis 25: A Final Note about Hagar

The Bible mentions Hagar once more. In chapter 25, she is identified as the mother of Ishmael: "These are the descendants of Ishmael, Abraham's son, whom Hagar the Egyptian, Sarah's slave-girl, bore to Abraham" (Gen 25:12).

Early Extra-Biblical Literature's Hagar

Jubilees

The book of *Jubilees* features a number of parallels with the primary Hagar narratives that appear in Gen 16 and 21. Those parallels are found in *Jub.* 14 and 17, respectively. What stands out most strikingly is that the author(s) of *Jubilees* consciously sought to downplay the family disharmony evident in these Genesis chapters. This is most evident in *Jub.* 14. The Genesis verses that detail the problems between Sarah and Hagar before Ishmael's birth and Hagar's subsequent visitation by the angel(s) or God are completely omitted. *Jubilees* shortens Gen 16, along with some interesting expansions, such as Abraham telling Sarah about God's promise to give the land to his descendants (*Jub.* 14:21). Just as there is one final reference to Hagar in Genesis in a later chapter, which mentions her in the Ishmael genealogical section (Gen 25:12), so too there is one additional mention of Hagar in *Jub.* 19, as shall be explained below.

---

28. Marrying within the family or clan—endogamy—is an important principle for the biblical world, although at times people ignored this guideline, often leading to disastrous results (e.g., Esau, King Solomon, King Ahab). "Given the frequency with which these [early] biblical personages marry within their family, it is fair to assume that the patriarchal family's tendency was endogamous—they married in [the same family] . . . This assumption receives further support from the urgency with which Abraham, in Isaac's case, and Isaac and Rebekah in Jacob's case insist that the sons marry in. The negative examples involve the pointed references to those of the family who 'marry out,' notably Ishmael, Esau, and Judah," explains Engelmayer. He goes on to write, "As the family of Abraham grew into a nation, the need for 'marrying in' [to the direct family] lessened and, eventually, disappeared . . . [when] there were more God-fearers immediately at hand" (Engelmayer, "Ivri: Naming Ourselves," 16, 23).

Jubilees 14

Chapter 14 of *Jubilees* is a condensed account of Gen 15 and 16. We find only twenty-four verses in *Jub.* 14, while there are thirty-seven verses in Gen 15–16. In Gen 15, God promises Abraham that he will father children: "'no one but your very own issue shall be your heir.' [God] brought him outside and said, 'Look toward heaven and count the stars, if you are able to count them.' Then [God] said to him, 'So shall your descendants be'" (Gen 15:4–5). The rest of Gen 15 describes the sacrifices that Abraham brings, his succumbing to a deep slumber, and his covenant with God.

The account in Genesis is similar to *Jub.* 14:13, which explains that God informs Abraham that he will have progeny and that they will be strangers in a land not their own: "Know this for certain, that your offspring shall be aliens in a land that is not theirs, and shall be slaves there, and they shall be oppressed for four hundred years" (Gen 15:13). Furthermore, Abraham is told that God is going to give the land to Abraham's descendants (*Jub.* 14:18; cf. Gen 15:18). A few verses later, the *Jubilees* text explains, "And Abram rejoiced and he told all of these things to Sarai, his wife. And he believed that he would have seed, but she did not give birth" (*Jub.* 14:21). That Abraham informs Sarah about the encounter and covenant with God is an addition not found in the Genesis text.

In Gen 16, Hagar is introduced, she marries Abraham, and she conceives. Then, due to an altercation with Sarah, Hagar flees to the desert, where she has an angelic encounter at an oasis. The angel counsels her to return, which she does. The chapter concludes with the birth and naming of Ishmael. In the *Jubilees* account, after Abraham tells Sarah about God's statement to him, the text continues with these words: "And Sarai advised Abram, her husband, and she said to him, 'Go into Hagar, my Egyptian maid. It may be that I will build seed for you from her'" (*Jub.* 14:22). There is similar wording in Gen 16:2: "And Sarai said to Abram, 'You see that the Lord has prevented me from bearing children; go in to my slave-girl; it may be that I shall obtain children by her.'" The accounts in *Jubilees*, as in Genesis, do not address how Hagar might feel about this, much less how Abraham may regard this request.

There are, however, important differences between the Genesis and *Jubilees* texts. In both cases, there are specific references to the surrogate mother's lower status. Yet, in Genesis her identity is erased, for the relevant line reads, "go into my slave-girl," while in *Jubilees* Hagar is mentioned by name, as is her country of origin; she is an Egyptian (Gen 16:2; Jub 14:23). In the Genesis account, while Sarah claims that her childlessness is a divine judgment, no such ascription is found in *Jubilees*. In Genesis, Sarah says that it may be that *she* would "obtain children" through this arrangement. In the *Jubilees* account, Sarah tells Abraham that through this process, Sarah will build up seed *for Abraham*. In this latter explanation, the focus is on the child that will be for their mutual benefit.

Genesis 16:3 not only records that Sarah gave the slave-girl to Abraham as a wife, but also that Abraham had been living in the land of Canaan for a decade. The *Jubilees* account omits this time sequence. In Gen 16:4–15, the Bible spells out in some detail the consequences of Hagar becoming Abraham's second wife. Hagar not only quickly conceives, she then looks with contempt upon Sarah. Sarah takes great umbrage. Initially, Sarah does not rebuke Hagar but instead goes to confront Abraham, blaming him for the turmoil in the family. She says to Abraham, "May the LORD judge between you and me!" (Gen 16:5). Abraham abdicates his responsibilities to his second wife and potential heir and tells Sarah that she can do as she pleases with Hagar. Sarah does retaliate at this point and "dealt harshly" with Hagar, who then runs off into the wilderness.

Genesis 16:7–14 describe the important encounter between Hagar and the agent from God. Then Ishmael is born and named by Abraham. Abraham's age is also listed as eighty-six (Gen 16:15–16). *Jubilees* 14:24 takes the opening phrase of Gen 16:4, that Abraham had intercourse with Hagar and that she conceived, but leaves out the conflict between Hagar and Sarah, Sarah's confrontation with Abraham, Sarah's abusive behavior toward Hagar, Hagar's flight from the encampment, Hagar's angelic encounters, and her naming God. The rest of *Jub.* 14:24 picks up the essential details of Gen 16:15–16, including the Patriarch's age at the time of Ishmael's birth: "And he went into her. And she conceived and bore a son and he called him Ishmael, in the fifth year of that week. And that year was the eighty-sixth year in the life of Abram." This retelling of the Genesis narrative is consistent with the tenor of *Jubilees*, which downplays family conflict. In its own way, *Jubilees* is similar to the rewriting that occurs in the book of Chronicles, where the Chronicler simply excised or ignored the unseemly narratives dealing with David's personal life with Abigail and later with Bathsheba. The details concerning how Solomon attained the throne as reported in Samuel and Kings are also expunged.

Jubilees 17

Jubilees 17, which has just eighteen verses, corresponds generally to Gen 21, although Isaac's birth, which is part of that Genesis account, was mentioned previously in *Jub.* 16. *Jubilees* begins with the weaning of Isaac and continues with Sarah's disquiet with Ishmael and her demand that Abraham expel Hagar and Ishmael from their encampment. *Jubilees* also describes Hagar and Ishmael and their plight in the desert, as well as the angel sent by God to rescue them. It concludes with praise of Abraham and notice that he has been tried and found faithful in a number of matters.

Genesis 21 begins with the announcement that God "dealt with Sarah as he had said." In short order, Sarah conceives and gives birth. Abraham names his child Isaac (as he had been instructed to do in Gen 17:19) and then circumcises Isaac on the eighth day. Sarah remarks that God has brought her laughter and that others will laugh with her, a sentence that puns on the word Isaac, or *Yitzhaq*, which translates, "one will laugh." During the weaning ceremony, or afterwards, Sarah sees Ishmael "playing." She then goes to Abraham and demands that he send away the "slave woman with her son" (Gen 21:10). Though distressed about this, Abraham complies, but only after God tells him to do as Sarah tells him, "for it is through Isaac that offspring shall be named for you" (Gen 21:12). God also reassures Abraham that the son of the slave woman will be the father of a great nation, for he is Abraham's child. The chapter continues with Hagar and Ishmael in the desert. When they run out of water, Hagar offers her plaint, and an angelic figure calls out encouragement to her. God then opens her eyes, and Hagar sees a well of water. Hagar eventually finds a wife for Ishmael from the land of Egypt (Gen 21:21). The chapter then features an unrelated pericope involving a dispute between Abraham and Abimelech, the king of Gerar (Gen 20). The two men establish a pact at the well at Beersheba (Beersheba means "Well of the oath"). The chapter concludes with a statement that Abraham calls on God's name and dwells there in the land of the Philistines for a long time.

The *Jubilees* account is notable both for what it contains and what it omits. Isaac's birth appears in an abbreviated form in *Jub.* 16. The seventeenth chapter of *Jubilees* commences with Isaac's weaning ceremony, linking it to the Jubilee year. It names both Ishmael and his mother, Hagar the Egyptian, and suggests that "Abraham rejoiced and he blessed [God] because he had seen his sons and had not died without sons" (*Jub.* 17:2). *Jubilees* then continues with the words "And Sarah saw Ishmael playing and dancing and Abraham rejoicing very greatly. And she was jealous of Ishmael and she said to Abraham, 'Drive out this girl and her son because the son of this girl will not inherit with my son, Isaac'" (*Jub.* 17:4). Although it is similar to the description in Genesis, *Jubilees* modifies Ishmael's actions, suggesting that he is "playing *and dancing*," possibly rejoicing at the festivities around his younger brother's weaning. It also explains that Sarah was "jealous" of Ishmael, something not found in Genesis. The text in *Jubilees* gives no clue as to the reason behind Sarah's emotion. It could be that she is jealous of the close relationship between Abraham and Ishmael.

The next part in *Jubilees* initially follows the Genesis text fairly closely, with one notable exception: the expulsion of the slave woman and her son. Unlike the Genesis account, which only mentions the words "his son," in *Jubilees* there is specific mention of the servant: "And the matter was grievous in the sight of Abraham because of his maidservant and because of his son" (*Jub.* 17:5). David Rothstein remarks that Hagar actually is noted, although not by name, and she precedes mention of the boy. This is exceptional, for by way of contrast, the Samaritan Pentateuch, which is "notorious for performing such harmonizations, makes no reference to Hagar at Gen 21:11, nor does the Septuagint (LXX)."[29] Rothstein continues by observing that Naḥmanides notices that Abraham had no difficulty separating from Hagar.

In Gen 21, although Abraham is upset, God comforts him and tells him to acquiesce to Sarah's demands. God explains that Abraham's name will continue through Isaac; in addition, Abraham's first son will be the father of a great nation. In both Genesis and *Jubilees*, Hagar and Ishmael wander in the desert but run out of water. She is distraught and calls out in distress. An angel speaks to Hagar, reassuring her of God's concern and protection. She then sees a well of water. Hagar fills her bottle and refreshes both herself and Ishmael. In both accounts, Hagar finds an Egyptian wife for Ishmael. In this section, however, there are several divergences from the biblical account. Genesis explains that even though it is Hagar who weeps, "God heard the voice of the boy,"—i.e., Ishmael's voice, not Hagar's (Gen 21:17). By contrast, *Jub.* 17:11 explains "And an angel of [God], one of the holy ones, said to her, "What are you weeping for, Hagar?" The biblical account explains that at this point, "*God* opened her eyes and she saw a well of water" (Gen 21:19). In *Jubilees*, it is Hagar who opens her eyes and sees the well of water. *Jubilees* mentions that after he is married, Ishmael fathers a son and then names him. Ishmael "called him Nebaioth because, she said, '[God] was near to me when I called to him'" (*Jub.* 17:14). Genesis does not refer to this episode, although it mentions Nebaioth as the first of Ishmael's twelve sons (Gen 25:13). Nebaioth means "prophets." It is Hagar and not Ishmael's wife who says God "was near to me when I called to him," referring to the angelic encounter in the wilderness when she was sent away from Abraham's encampment and ran out of water. As Kugel mentions in his comment on this verse, there is no clear connection between the name Nebaioth and Hagar's statement about God being near.[30]

29. Rothstein, "Text and Context," 245.
30. Kugel, "Jubilees," 355.

The final verses in this *Jubilees* chapter make specific mention of Hagar and Ishmael, noting that sending them away was a trial for Abraham, through which he proved his faithfulness to God. The rabbis likewise refer to these tests. In the various midrashic sources, there is general agreement that the tenth and most difficult of Abraham's trials was the Binding of Isaac. In *Jubilees*, it is Sarah's death that is listed as Abraham's tenth trial (*Jub.* 19:7–8). Nonetheless, there are variations about the specificity of the trials. In some sources, like *Jubilees*, the expulsion of Hagar-Ishmael is listed (*Jub.* 17:17). When that expulsion is mentioned, *Jubilees* suggests that Abraham felt grievous loss over "his maidservant and because of his son that he should drive them away from him" as a result of Sarah's emotional tirade (*Jub.* 17:5).

Jubilees 19

Jubilees 19 is a condensed version, with both omissions and additions to Gen 23–27, the narratives that cover Sarah's death through Jacob's attainment of the family blessing. The final reference to Hagar in *Jubilees* reads: "And Abraham took a third wife and her name was Keturah, from the daughters of his household servants because Hagar died before Sarah" (*Jub.* 19:11). While this is not an endogamous marriage, neither is it with a foreigner. The author's distaste for this marriage is presumably the reason he leaves out their grandchildren and great-grandchildren, noted in Gen 25:3–4.

This verse seems to raise a question: Had Hagar not died, would Abraham have married Keturah or remarried Hagar?[31] Abraham's marriage to Keturah appears in Gen 25:1. While Sarah's death and burial receives considerable attention in Gen 23, just as it does in *Jub.* 19, no mention is made of Hagar's death in the biblical text. As will be noted later in the rabbinic section, according to several, but not all, rabbinic traditions, Keturah and Hagar are the same person.

Philo

Philo of Alexandria (ca. 20 BCE–50 CE) suggests that "Abraham's mating with Hagar prior to Sarah's conception of Isaac . . . allegorically represents Abraham's pursuit of encyclical studies (or preliminary curriculum, symbolized by Hagar) before he can mate productively with Sarah—that is,

---

31. Rothstein, "Text and Context," 256 n. 37. An Ethiopic manuscript states that Abraham married Keturah "because" Hagar had died.

acquire virtue."[32] Furthermore, "Philo juxtaposes the simple-mindedness of Hagar, the maidservant, with the wisdom of Sarah, the mistress: it was natural for the former who is compared with 'savages,' to take the angel for God [in Gen 16]; Sarah the Wisdom would never be so naive."[33]

Josephus

Josephus tells of God commanding Sarah to give Abraham "one of her handmaidens, an Egyptian," thus taking away Sarah's responsibility for the ensuing conflict. This woman then "had the insolence to abuse " Sarah and was "assuming queenly airs." Josephus downplays Sarah's harshness to Hagar. When Hagar flees, Josephus has the angel telling her to apologize to Sarah, which she presumably does. When she "returned to her master and mistress [she] . . . was forgiven" (*Ant.* 1.10.4). As mentioned in our chapter on Sarah, Josephus notes that Sarah cared for Ishmael for many years: "Sarah at first . . . cherished [Ishmael] . . . with an affection not less than if he had been her own son . . . when she herself gave birth to Isaac, she held it wrong that her boy should be brought up with Ishmael who was the elder child and might do him an injury after their father was dead" (*Ant.* 1.12.3). According to Josephus, Abraham was very reluctant to accede to Sarah's wish to cast out Hagar and Ishmael, "thinking nothing could be more brutal than to send off an infant child with a woman destitute of the necessaries of life." In the end, he conceded his position because Sarah's behests "were sanctioned also by God" (*Ant.* 1.12.3). Sarah's demand to expel Hagar is morally problematic for Josephus, as is Abraham's concession to her wish. By having God approve of Sarah's point relieves Abraham of some of his culpability. As mentioned earlier in this book, Josephus is writing his history of the Jews in order to mediate between his contemporary Jewish and Greco-Roman Greek-speaking audiences, so he wants to cast the Jews in the best possible light.

---

32. Birnbaum, "On the Life of Abraham," 918. "Philo's interest in the story of Sarah and Hagar is fueled . . . by that of a platonist and philospher . . . he cautions his readers against being mislead by the literal storyline of Genesis" (Thompson, *Writing the Wrongs*, 25).

33. Topchyan and Muradyan, "Questions and Answers," 836. See also Thompson, *Writing the Wrongs*, 24–27 on Philo and ibid., 27–28 on Josephus.

The Genesis Apocryphon

In the *Genesis Apocryphon*, column 20, the Pharaoh gives Sarai (later Sarah) many gifts, including silver and gold, fine clothing, and Hagar as well. Although the text does not specifically designate Hagar as Pharaoh's daughter, she is part of a list of valuable items. While this statement is predicated on the power of, and presumably the virtues of, the house of Sarah-Abraham, it also locates Hagar as a high-status Egyptian woman. She is not just *an* Egyptian; she is of royal stock, and therefore will be a fitting companion in Sarah's household. Furthermore, she will be an appropriate birth mother for Abraham's future heir.[34]

The Rabbis' Hagar

Demonizing "Others" in General and Ishmaelites in Particular

In the ancient world of the Near East and in the centuries that followed, family, clan, and tribal connections were all-important. Later, people thought in terms of community units. The ancient Israelites, no less than their neighbors, thought in terms of "them" versus "us." There are numerous examples of this mindset. Egyptians are conscious of their being different from their neighbors (Gen 46:34). Amorites and Moabites distrust Israelites (Num 21:23; 22:1–4). Moses instructed the Israelites to clear away the native population of Canaan (Deut 7:1–2). Philistines do not trust Hebrews (1 Sam 29:1–5).[35] Divisions between "them" and "us" were commonplace in many cultures. As was mentioned in our chapter on Sarah, "All foreign peoples were portrayed in a negative light, for example, in the Greco-Roman world the Roman satirists depicted Egyptians, Syrians, Jews and other non-Romans" in an unflattering light. This demonizing of "Others" was standard fare; it was not a uniquely Jewish trait. It was, in fact, "totally consistent with pre-modern thinking in the West and Middle East."[36]

In the minds of the sages of the rabbinic period, Hagar was doubly an "Other." As an Egyptian, she was not an Israelite. Furthermore, she was an "Other" simply because she was the mother of Ishmael. Beginning in the biblical era and continuing into Greco-Roman times, Ishmael's nominal

34. The *Genesis Apocryphon* (1Q20) is part of the Dead Sea Scrolls. See Machiela, "Genesis Apocryphon."

35. These facts do not preclude biblical leaders from making military or political alliances with former enemies when it is in their perceived self-interest to do so.

36. Reuven Firestone, personal communication to David Zucker, September 1, 2000.

descendants, the Ishmaelites, became a generalized figure for Israel's Semitic neighbors, whether they were Ammonites, Edomites, Midianites, or Moabites. For example, the caravan that takes Joseph to Egypt is led by Midianites. The text also describes them as Ishmaelites (Gen 37:25, 27–28).[37] Consequently, both in the Bible and Rabbinic literature, distrust and hostility toward Israel's neighbors, "Ishmaelites," was an expression of the tensions between Israel and those tribes, and later for the Jewish community and its neighbors, those Semitic and/or Arab and later Islamic groups with which it was in competition.[38] Reuven Firestone explains that the "ancient Israelites were keenly aware of their geographic, linguistic and cultural kinship with Arab peoples." Although they were conscious of a close affinity between Israelites and Arabs or other Semites, the biblical writers tried to maintain a discrete distance. While peoples with Arabic names carried on interacting with Israelites, Firestone adds that those relations were "inevitably portrayed with little love lost." In the postbiblical world during the Hellenistic and the Roman periods, such relations between Jews and Arabs persisted: "Arabs continue to be mentioned in the Talmud . . . where they are sometimes referred to as Ishmaelites."[39] The term "Arab" is not used in Genesis because that designation "does not appear in written sources before the ninth century B.C.E."[40] It is first used in the Bible in Isa 13:20 (*'aravi*). With this as part of the cultural background in biblical times, it is no accident that when Hagar is first introduced, she is depicted as an outsider: "Now Sarai . . . had an Egyptian slave-girl whose name was Hagar" (Gen 16:1). Techni-

37. Note that there are those who contend that the Midianites and Ishmaelites were two separate groups and that the reference to them in the Joseph narrative is neither a scribal error nor an indication that the two tribes really were the same (Plaut, *Torah: A Modern Commentary, Revised Edition*, 257).

38. Following the birth of Islam, the historical progenitor of which is Ishmael, calumnies increase. Indeed, after ca. 650 CE, "Ishmael" becomes a code word for "Islam." The midrash collection *Pirke de Rabbi Eliezer*, composed ca. 725 CE in the land of Israel during the closing days of the Umayyad dynasty, even contains Arab legends. In *Pirke de Rabbi Eliezer* ch. 30, Abraham's son Ishmael is featured as having two wives named Ayesha and Fatima. Those women are respectively a wife and daughter of Mohammed, who will live two millennia in the future. These are not coincidental references. Later territorial disputes between various Jewish communities and Arab—or, in the case of Islam, territorial and religious disputes—are retrojected to the time of the Patriarchs and Matriarchs in Genesis so that it appears that Isaac and Ishmael had a long-standing history of conflict. For a discussion about the artificiality of this "conflict" between Isaac and Ishmael, see Zucker, "Conflicting Conclusions," and Reiss, "Ishmael, Son of Abraham." See also Thompson, *Writing the Wrongs*, 54–57.

39. Firestone, *Journeys in Holy Lands*, 3–4. For an example of Arabs-as-Ishmaelites portrayed in a negative light, see *Lamentations Rabbah* 2.2.4. Egyptians and Ishmaelites are both denigrated in *Esther Rabbah* 1.17.

40. Sarna, *Genesis*, 171.

cally, as an Egyptian, Hagar is not an Arabian, but she is a Semite and so she is included in this general term.

The Rabbis' Views of Hagar

On the whole, because of her "Other-ness," Hagar receives short shrift from the rabbis. Yet there were those who spoke well of her.

Chapter 16

HAGAR CAME FROM ROYAL LINEAGE

> Rabbi Simeon bar Yoḥai said: Hagar was Pharaoh's daughter. When Pharaoh saw what had been done on Sarah's behalf in his own house [Gen 12:17, the plagues visited upon Pharaoh], he took his daughter and gave her to Sarah, saying "Better let my daughter be a handmaid in this house than a mistress in another house." (*Genesis Rabbah* 45.1; *Pirke de Rabbi Eliezer* ch. 26)

SARAH URGES HAGAR TO MARRY ABRAHAM

Sarah, according to the rabbis, goes out of her way to convince her handmaiden that Hagar will benefit from her marriage with Abraham: "[Sarah] persuaded her [Hagar] with words, 'Happy are you to be united with such a holy man'" (*Genesis Rabbah* 45.3.)

HAGAR IS ABRAHAM'S WIFE, NOT HIS CONCUBINE

Hagar's relationship to Abraham, whether as wife or concubine, is not a new controversy, for the rabbis also weighed in with their views. A midrash proclaims Hagar is Abraham's wife, not his concubine: "To be a wife, but not a concubine" (*Genesis Rabbah* 45.3.) Yet she remains in a lesser role than Sarah. According to *Pirke de Rabbi Eliezer*, Sarah was Abraham's partner or companion, not like Hagar, who was his "servant" (*Pirke de Rabbi Eliezer* ch. 30).

HAGAR CONCEIVES IMMEDIATELY

The biblical text explains that Abraham "went in to Hagar, and she conceived" (Gen 16:4). She conceived on their initial attempt at intimacy, explains Rabbi Levi bar Ḥayta (*Genesis Rabbah* 45.4). Given the difficulties surrounding pregnancy that so many of the Matriarchs and Patriarchs experience, this immediate success is noteworthy. Although not explicitly stated, this suggests that the Hagar-Abraham union had divine approval. That argument is nonetheless countered by another midrashic view that claims, "A woman never conceives by the first intimacy." Then an objection is raised on the basis of the episode of Lot and his daughters. In that instance, each daughter lay with her father but one night and immediately conceived (Gen 19:36; *Genesis Rabbah* 45.4). There may well be a subtext to this rabbinic observation. Lot's daughters seduced their father and committed incest with him. The resulting children were the eponymous ancestors of the Moabites and Ammonites, two of Israel's traditional tribal enemies. Just as that earlier cohabitation was an immoral relationship, likewise there is a hint that Hagar is of questionable moral character.

HAGAR MOCKS AND SPEAKS ILL OF SARAH

"When she saw that she had conceived, [Hagar] looked with contempt on her mistress" (Gen 16:4). A midrash explains that Hagar compares her limited sexual experience with Abraham to the many years Abraham and Sarah were married. Reflecting the concept that fertility and the resulting children means divine favor, and infertility or childlessness means divine disfavor, Hagar's unspoken message is clear. She is a person of high moral character because she conceived so rapidly. The midrash explains that female visitors would come to talk to Sarah. Sarah in turn referred them to Hagar. Then "Hagar would tell them: 'My mistress Sarai is not inwardly what she is outwardly: she appears to be a righteous woman, see how many years have passed without her conceiving, whereas I conceived in one night!'" (*Genesis Rabbah* 45.4; *Midrash ha Gadol*, Gen1.244). This midrash accomplishes two goals: it praises Sarah for referring her guests to Hagar, but it also speaks ill of Hagar.

SARAH AND ABRAHAM'S REACTIONS

Despite the fact that she had arranged the Hagar-Abraham connection, Sarah holds Abraham responsible for this state of affairs. She confronts her husband, and in her anger, she demands that he reverse Hagar's special role in their household. Let her become a slave again, she suggests. Abraham counters that this is not possible. He points out to Sarah that if a woman has been sold as a slave, and then given higher status—such as becoming a wife to the master—she cannot be re-enslaved, even if she has displeased the master. To buttress his case, Abraham cites these words taken from the book of Exodus: "He shall have no right to sell her to a foreign people" (Exod 21:8; *Genesis Rabbah* 45.6).[41] Logically, there seems to be a disconnection here. All of these characters lived prior to the time of the Exodus revelations. The rabbis, however, would explain that despite the fact that Abraham lived centuries earlier, he was still aware of what would be normative Jewish law. As we noted earlier, for the rabbis in terms of midrashic explication, there is no such thing as linear or chronological time in the biblical era.

Genesis presents Abraham as capitulating to Sarah. He says, "Your slave-girl is in your power; do to her as you please" (Gen 16:6). Sarah mistreats Hagar. Since Genesis does not provide details about this abusive behavior, the rabbis fill in with examples. Sarah prevented Hagar and Abraham from engaging in sexual relations. Additionally, Sarah slapped Hagar and made her perform menial tasks such as carrying water and bringing towels to the bathhouse (*Genesis Rabbah* 45.6). The medieval commentator Nahmanides criticizes Sarah for her behavior toward Hagar.[42]

HAGAR IN THE WILDERNESS: THE ANGEL(S) OF THE LORD

As the Genesis text explains, although she is pregnant, Hagar runs away from her tormentor; she heads off to the desert wilderness. When she is quite alone, Hagar has an encounter with what are either many angels or perhaps a single angel:

> Rabbi Hama bar Rabbi Hanina [in some editions, Rabbi Yosi bar Rabbi Hanina] said: There were five [angels], for each time "speech" is mentioned it refers to an angel. The Rabbis said: Four, this being the number of times the word "angel" occurs. (*Genesis Rabbah* 45.7; 75.4; *Exodus Rabbah* 3.16)

Hagar took this angelic encounter in stride, because in "Abraham's household there were prophets [literally "watchers," understood as angels], so she

---

41. See the collection *Midrash on Proverbs*, Prov 26. The midrash puts these words into Abraham's mouth to prove a moral point. This is not necessarily an accurate (or inaccurate) evaluation of Near-Eastern laws and traditions at the time of Abraham.

42. See "Sarah's Harsh Treatment of Hagar Has Later Repercussions" in "The Rabbis' Sarah" section above.

[Hagar] was accustomed to them" (*Genesis Rabbah* 45.7). Hagar expresses delight that she could see the angel(s) in her own right. Previously she had been in the company of her mistress when she saw such figures. For a non-Israelite to see an angel, much less converse with one, is a rare event (*Genesis Rabbah* 45.10).[43]

In a midrash, Hagar says, "I am running away from my *mistress* Sarai" (*Genesis Rabbah* 45.7). In this instance, the rabbis have a reason to praise Hagar, for even though she had risen in status, Hagar still recognized Sarah as having a more prominent role in the household.

HAGAR PRAYED, PART 1

Sforno comments on the fact that the angel "found" Hagar (v. 7). This means that the angel found her in a frame of mind ready to receive divine wisdom. She had prepared herself through prayer.

HAGAR PRAYED, PART 2

Sforno comments on Hagar saying that God is the God of vision (*'el-roi*) (Gen 16:13). He explains that Hagar acknowledges that God "sees everywhere, not only in the house of Abram." Sforno then refers to the Talmudic statement that God always hears the cries of [the tears of] wrongdoing (Babylonian Talmud *Baba Metzia* 59a).

Chapter 21

HAGAR, SARAH, ABRAHAM (AND ISHMAEL)
FOLLOWING ISAAC'S WEANING

Genesis 21:9ff. details Sarah's response when she sees Ishmael "playing" (or "laughing," or "mocking"). This is either during the festivities surrounding Isaac's weaning or some time after that occasion. Sarah says, "Cast out this slave woman with her son." According to a midrash, Sarah demands that Abraham immediately divorce Hagar. He complies and gives her a bill of divorcement (*Pirke de Rabbi Eliezer* ch. 30). Although he honors Sarah's demand that he send Hagar and Ishmael away, Abraham is upset about this turn of events. The biblical text explains, the "matter was very distressing to

---

43. Later on, this midrash states that when Sarah and Hagar were together, only Hagar sees the angels.

Abraham on account of his son" (Gen 21:11). The text is ambiguous about the subject of Abraham's concern. Is he distressed about the effect on Ishmael, or on Isaac? Whatever the answer, it is noteworthy that nothing is mentioned about his concern for Hagar, who is his second wife and the mother of his firstborn son.

ABRAHAM'S CONCERNS ABOUT HAGAR

As noted earlier in this volume, there is a rabbinic tradition that Abraham faced ten trails and overcame all of them. While there is a broad consensus that overlaps many of these trials, there are differences in the specifics. According to one tradition, the expulsion of Hagar was one of Abraham's ten trials (*Midrash Psalms*, Ps 18.25). Some medieval commentators, such as Naḥmanides and Rabbi Jonah Gerondi (Spain, thirteenth century), agreed that this expulsion was one of Abrahams trails.[44] Another midrashic collection addresses how Abraham coped. Before Hagar left, he ties some kind of sash around her. The cloth will leave a mark in the sand as she travels. Then, at some future time, he can go to visit her (*Pirke de Rabbi Eliezer* ch. 30).

HAGAR AND ISHMAEL LOST IN THE DESERT

Hagar finds herself lost in the desert wilderness. She runs out of water. One might assume that Abraham was culpable for this dilemma, as he had not provisioned her sufficiently. The fault was not Abraham's, explains a midrash, for it was entirely because of Hagar's actions: "By the merit of our father Abraham the water did not fail in the bottle. When, however, she reached the entrance of the wilderness, she began to go astray after the idolatry of her father's house. Immediately the water in the bottle was spent" (*Pirke de Rabbi Eliezer* ch. 30).

A different midrash blames Sarah for Hagar and Ishmael's plight in the desert. Sarah put a spell on Ishmael. He became feverish and quickly exhausted the water they brought with them (*Genesis Rabbah* 53.13). There is no criticism of Sarah in this midrash, yet later commentators voice their disapproval of the way Sarah treated Hagar and Ishmael.[45] Understandably aggrieved, Hagar raises her voice in pain. Hagar "said, 'Do not let me look on the death of the child' . . . she lifted up her voice and wept" (Gen 21:16).

---

44. Rothstein, "Text and Context," 246 n. 12.

45. See the section below, "Some Concluding Thoughts About the Rabbinic Views of Hagar."

According to the midrashic tradition, Hagar confronts God and challenges God's seeming inconsistency. She says, "Yesterday you promised me, 'I will greatly increase your seed' [Gen 16:10] and now my son is dying of thirst!" (*Genesis Rabbah* 53.13).[46] God replies to her, sending a message via an angel. God expresses concern for both Hagar and Ishmael. The biblical text explains that "God heard the voice of the boy; and the angel of God called to Hagar from heaven, and said to her, 'What troubles you, Hagar? Do not be afraid; for God has heard the voice of the boy where he is.'" God then reiterates that Hagar, through Ishmael, will be the Matriarch of many peoples: "I will make a great nation of him" (Gen 21:17–18). Hagar subsequently sees a well and fills her container with water. Even that simple act is taken as a mark of her faithlessness. She did not have sufficient belief that the well would remain full (*Genesis Rabbah* 53.14).

Hagar Returns to Paganism

In the mind of the rabbis, because Hagar finds an Egyptian wife for Ishmael, this is proof that she returns to her pagan origins (*Genesis Rabbah* 53.15).

Hagar as a Righteous Convert

Not all the midrashim, however, view Hagar's Egyptian origins as an impediment to monotheism. *Yalkut Shemoni* . . . lists Hagar first among nine righteous converts, including such important figures as Zipporah, Moses' wife, and Shifra and Puah, the Egyptian midwives who saved the Jewish boys from being drowned in the Nile.[47]

---

46. Hagar's plaint to God that aforetime God had promised Ishmael would prosper, and now Ishmael is on the edge of death, is in contrast to a midrash in which we might have expected Abraham to say the same thing in terms of Isaac on Mount Moriah. According to rabbinic tradition, Abraham instead demonstrates his faithfulness and subservience to God's request. Abraham says to God, "Even though you asked me to sacrifice Isaac I was willing to do this. I, Abraham, did not say to you, earlier on you had promised that through Isaac you would have descendants" (*Pesikta Rabbati, Piska* 40.6; *Pesikta de Rab Kahana: Piska* 23.9; *Leviticus Rabbah* 29.9).

47. Reinhartz and Walfish, "Conflict and Coexistence in Jewish Interpretation," 106. The authors cite *Yalkut Shemoni, Remez,* 9.

Beer-lahai-roi Again

As noted earlier, taken as a whole, the rabbinic view about Hagar is at best ambivalent. The Bible clearly says that Hagar "lifted up her voice and wept," presumably calling upon the God of Abraham. Yet the angel says, "God has heard the voice of the boy where he is." According to the *Pirke de Rabbi Eliezer*, it was Ishmael, not Hagar, who called to God, entreating, "Oh God of my father, Abraham" (*Pirke de Rabbi Eliezer* ch. 30). Although the Bible does not list the locale of this well of water, according to the midrashic tradition, this was none other than the spot where she had first had an angelic encounter: Beer-lahai-roi. Hagar places Ishmael under some bushes. Punning on the word "bushes," *sihim*, "Rabbi Yosé the son of Halafta maintained: It was the place at which an angel had spoken [*suah*] to her previously" (*Midrash Tanhuma Yelammedenu, Genesis*, And He Went Out, 7.5, p. 190; *Genesis Rabbah* 53.13). Indeed, this very well was one of the special items that God created on the eve of the first Sabbath in the week of creation (*Pirke de Rabbi Eliezer* ch. 30).[48]

Chapter 25

HAGAR IS THE SAME PERSON AS KETURAH

Following Sarah's death, Abraham married again: "Abraham took another wife, whose name was Keturah. She bore him" six sons (Gen 25:1–2). Who was Keturah? She was Hagar. With the exception of a reference to Hagar in the Ishmael genealogical chart (Gen 25:12), Hagar does not appear past Gen 21. Following the death of Sarah, the rabbis argue, Abraham was able to reconcile with Hagar and to remarry her. How was this so? A number of midrashim suggest that Hagar and Keturah are the same person (*Genesis Rabbah* 61.4; *Midrash Tanhuma, Genesis. Hayye Sarah* 5.9 Gen 25:1ff., Part 3; *Pirke de Rabbi Eliezer* ch. 30), although this view is also challenged (*Midrash Tanhuma Yelammedenu, Genesis*, 5.8, And the Life of Sarah). Not only does Abraham remarry Hagar, he does so with the cooperation and approval of his son Isaac! In an extraordinary teaching, a midrash explains that it was Isaac himself who brought Hagar/Keturah to Abraham so that they could marry: "Then Abraham took a wife again. It is simply that when Isaac took Rebekah, Isaac said: Let us go and bring a wife to my father. Hagar and Keturah are the same person" (*Midrash Tanhuma, Genesis. Hayye Sarah* 5.9

---

48. See also *Mishnah Avot* 5.6, where the well alternatively refers to the spring that fed the Israelites in the desert (Num 21:16–18).

Gen 25:1ff., Part 3; *Genesis Rabbah* 60.14; *Midrash Tanhuma Yelammedenu, Genesis* 5.8, And the Life of Sarah). Were that not enough, there also is a rabbinic tradition suggesting that God commanded Abraham to (re-)marry Hagar. Furthermore, she was named Keturah because she united (*kitrah*) piety and nobility (in herself) (*Genesis Rabbah* 61.4).

Hagar Is Not (Necessarily) Keturah

Although many midrashim equate Hagar with Keturah, that view is disputed by many of the medieval exegetes, such as Rashbam (Rabbi Shmuel ben Meir, France, twelfth century), Abraham Ibn Ezra (Spain, twelfth century) and Ḥizkuni (Ḥezekiah ben Manoaḥ, France, thirteenth century).

Some Concluding Thoughts about the Rabbinic Views of Hagar

As explained in the introductory chapter, one cannot accurately speak of *the* rabbinic view on any matter; there are no singular rabbinic views in Jewish teaching. There are often multiple opinions, some of which appear to contradict other rabbinic views. The rabbis often differed amongst themselves about the possible meanings of certain words or passages. The rabbis sought to promulgate Jewish values for the Jewish community. They wanted to bring people closer to both their religious traditions and to the presence of God. Midrash was one way to inculcate such values. As mentioned earlier, the rabbinic "sages utilized every sort of literary and rhetorical technique to make this material attractive and compelling to their audience."[49]

Some rabbis were sympathetic to Hagar and saw her as a positive figure. Others regarded Hagar as insincere and only too ready to return to her pagan roots. On one level, Hagar is credited with royal lineage, as being Pharaoh's own daughter. She prays to God, and angels speak to her, as does God, even if it is through the mediation of these angels. Rabbi Obadiah Sforno (Italy, sixteenth century) asserts that when Hagar "called" on the name of God in Gen 16:13, she was actually displaying her piety by praising and praying to God. The angel, moreover, having found her "ready for the divine vision," yet proceeds to warn her that her flight will take her from "a house of the righteous . . . to an unclean place of wicked people."[50]

---

49. Heinemann, "Nature of the Aggadah," 47.

50. Sforno, *Commentary on the Torah*, 78 comment on Gen 16:7–8. See also Thompson, *Writing the Wrongs*, 57–60.

Nonetheless, Hagar is an "Other," someone who comes from outside of the community. Hagar's most serious fault is that she is Ishmael's mother, for Ishmael's descendants, the Ishmaelites, become a generalized figure for Israel's neighbors (the Ammonites, Edomites, Midianites, etc.), with whom territorial and religious disputes often arose. Later, following the birth of Islam—the historical progenitor of which is Ishmael—calumnies increase. Indeed, after ca. 650 CE, "Ishmael" becomes a code word for Islam. Hagar's role is further complicated because the rabbis have a strong predilection to favor "Sarah Our Mother" (*Sarah imeinu*) as Matriarch and "Abraham Our Father" (*Avraham avinu*) as Patriarch and to feature them positively.

There are occasional exceptions to this view. Nahmanides (Ramban) says Sarah's harsh treatment of Hagar and Ishmael is why the Egyptians enslaved the Israelites in Egypt: "Sarah sinned in afflicting [Hagar] and also Abraham for permitting it. God hearkened to Hagar's cry, and as a result her descendants persecute and afflict the seed of Abraham and Sarah" (comment on Gen 16:6).[51] The medieval commenter Abraham Ibn Ezra (1092–1167 CE) wrote in terms of the expulsion of Hagar and Ishmael in Gen 21: "Many are amazed at Abraham's behavior." He further explains that Abraham, in fact, may have given Hagar some gold or silver after all, despite the silence of Scripture here (comment on Gen 21:14). Abraham provided "enough bread and water to last her till she reached Beersheba." He also suggests that she got lost in the desert (a view shared by Rashbam, Rabbi Samuel ben Meir, Troyes, ca. 1085–1158). Sforno, in his comment on Gen 21:14, suggests that Abraham sent Hagar away with asses, camels, and laborers. He also refers to a similar interpretation in *Genesis Rabbah* 53:15 that mentions those items.

The rabbinic view of Hagar develops out of the biblical corpus. The rabbis, for the most part, are wary of her. Hagar is insolent to Sarah. Later, when Sarah demands Hagar's expulsion, God voices approval of this decision to Abraham. Hagar is the mother of Ishmael and therefore irretrievably connected with Ishmaelites (i.e., Arabs or other Semitic groups). Ishmael is understood as the historical progenitor of Islam, and religious tensions exist with Islam. Yet, as we have seen, there are a variety of rabbinic views towards Hagar. With their expanded portraits, the rabbis offer a broader and deeper picture that provides additional ways for people to understand Hagar.

---

51. Later, when Hagar and Ishmael are expelled, Nahmanides blames Sarah for Abraham not giving them appropriate provisions: "All this occurred to Abraham because he had been commanded to do whatever Sarah said, and she commanded that he send him [Ishmael] away immediately, and it was at her command that he did not give them silver and gold, servants, and camels to bear them" (Nahmanides, *Genesis*, comment on Gen 21:15).

Targum Pseudo-Jonathan

Targum Pseudo-Jonathan has different traditions about Hagar. She is the daughter of Pharaoh and granddaughter of King Nimrod (Gen 10:8–10). This lineage thus associates Hagar and Ishmael with both royalty and idolatry. Sarah hated Hagar because of Hagar's relation to Nimrod, the king who, according to rabbinic tradition, had threatened Abraham's life. According to the Targum, God accuses Ishmael of being an idolater, and consequently his numerous descendants will be criminals.[52] By the third verse of the sixteenth chapter of *Targum Pseudo-Jonathan*, Hagar is a free woman. As one scholar comments, "The reason . . . is certainly to prevent Abraham from becoming the father of a slave's child, something that could bring dishonor upon the patriarch." Hagar is also understood as Abraham's wife, because "when he sends her away he gives her a proper bill of divorce, a *get*, something a slave would not have received."[53]

Contemporary Scholarship

A Complex Character

As one scholar writes, "Hagar is a complex character: not simply victim and not simply heroine. The same diversity of interpretation, of course, holds for Sarah."[54]

Adoption as Anti-infertility Device

The adoption process by Sarah (and later by Rachel) was intended as a stimulant to fertility.[55] In real life, there are examples of childless couples who, following the adoption of a child, "suddenly" become biological parents in their own right.

---

52. Martinez, "Hagar in *Targum Pseudo-Jonathan*."
53. Ibid., 267–68.
54. Levine, "Beer-lahai-roi," 19.
55. Kardimon, "Adoption as a Remedy," 123–26.

Hagar Is Sarah's Property

Hagar was presumably given some undefined rights of a wife, albeit a secondary wife. She is young, fertile, and "the object of Abram's embrace."[56] Yet, in chapter 16, "when Hagar becomes [Abraham's] wife (v. 3), she does not cease to be [Sarah's] slave; when Abraham surrenders Hagar to [Sarah's] authority (v. 6), he acknowledges that his wife has prior claims that supersede his."[57]

Hagar: A Rival Drunk with Success

Hagar's continuing change of status is dizzying. She moves from *shifḥah*, a maidservant or female slave, to the master's wife (*'isha*), and then while pregnant she returns to her status as a *shifḥah*. For Hagar, this was emotionally overwhelming. She succeeded where her mistress had failed. That she might smirk with her swollen belly is understandable, albeit unwise. Sarah's angry reaction, whether borne out of rivalry-filled jealousy or the realization that her own childlessness is now public, is also understandable. Hagar has defenders, but she also has critics. Nehama Leibowitz characterized Hagar's attitude toward Sarah in chapter 16 as "suffering caused by the arrogant bearing of the rival drunk with success."[58]

"Looked with Contempt"

The word "looked with contempt" in Hebrew is *vateykal*. It has different possible shades of meaning. Speiser offers "with contempt," while NJPS gives "her mistress was lowered in her esteem," NEB has it "she despised her mistress," and NIV offers "despise." The New Jerusalem Bible (Roman Catholic) gives "her mistress counted for nothing in her eyes," and the New American Bible (Roman Catholic) has "she looked on her mistress with disdain," while Robert Alter's *Genesis* translates it as "her mistress seemed slight in her eyes." Phyllis Trible, like Alter, suggests "her mistress became slight in her eyes." The NJPS seems to come close to the original meaning of the word in this context ("her mistress was lowered in her esteem"), for in Hagar's mind her own status has risen in relationship to Sarah, and she treats her mistress accordingly. Sarah, reacting to Hagar's unexpected

---

56. Fewell and Gunn, *Gender, Power, and Promise*, 46.

57. Niditch, "Central Commentary, *Lech L'cha*," 71.

58. Leibowitz, *Studies in Bereshit*, 155.

change of demeanor, goes to Abraham wanting to return to their previous relationship. Abraham, instead of responding by talking to Hagar and dealing with her as his wife, gives Hagar back as a slave to Sarah.

Punning on Pregnancy

The statement that Hagar "looked with contempt"—or more literally that Sarah became "became light in her eyes"—offers an excellent pun: light as now "lightweight" as well as light compared to Hagar's weight-gain.[59]

God Speaks to a Woman

In Gen 3:16, God speaks to the woman in the garden of Eden. When God speaks to Hagar, this is only the second instance in Genesis of God speaking to a woman, and she is a non-Israelite.

Hagar Names God

Hagar is the only person in the Bible who names God. She addresses the emissary—or perhaps God—who visits her by the spring and says, "You are El-*roi*'; for she said, 'Have I really seen God and remained alive after seeing him?" Therefore, one scholar adds,

> In the Bible, an essential ingredient in asserting a character's [and a place's] individuality is the assigning of a name. In fact, the Bible begins with God defining [God's] inanimate creations by naming them. The heavens, the earth, the seas, the day, and the night are all given distinction through their names. Later, emulating God, Adam affirms the particular nature of individual species of animals and fowl by naming them . . . The Bible uses names to preserve the memory and accomplishments of outstanding, and often godly, individuals.[60]

59. Thanks to Amy-Jill Levine for pointing out this pun (Amy-Jill Levine, personal communication to David Zucker, December 2013). See also Levine, "Beer-lahai-roi," 22–23.

60. Klitsner, *Subversive Sequels*, 46–47.

The Different Faces of Hagar

Although chapters 16 and 21 are clearly connected, there are differences between them as well. Noting two different sources for these narratives, primarily a J source in 16, and an E source in 21, Speiser writes of the different reasons given for Hagar's departure.[61] In chapter 16, she leaves in response to Sarah's mistreatment. In chapter 21, she is sent away, not because of something that she does or fails to do, but as a result of Sarah's anger or fear about something in Ishmael's behavior at Isaac's weaning ceremony. Hagar's voice is both defiant and proud in chapter 16. In chapter 21, she grieves over the fact that death seems imminent. Earlier, Hagar was "spirited but tactless," while in the latter account, she is "the downtrodden slave throughout."[62]

Child or Lad? Or Both at the Same Time? Part 1

As noted earlier in this book's chapter on Sarah, Ishmael is about sixteen or seventeen at the time of the expulsion. Commonly, the term for such a lad would be *na'ar* (Gen 22:3, 5), and that exact term is used by God, the angel, and the narrator to describe Ishmael (Gen 21:12, 17–20). However, when referring to Ishmael Hagar uses the word *yeled*, "child." To Hagar, nevermind that he may now be a teenager, he is still her precious child. It is that same word, *yeled*, or "child," that the narrator uses when Abraham hands over Ishmael to Hagar prior to their departure (v. 14). Abraham complies with Sarah's ultimatum, but he is fully aware that he is sending away his own child.[63]

61. Speiser, *Genesis*, 156–57.

62. Ibid., 120, 157.

63. Pinker, "Expulsion of Hagar and Ishmael," 14 n. 51 refers to P. T. Reis, who seems to argue a similar thought. Reis writes: "My reading is that 'lad' and 'child' are aptly employed to illustrate different points of view. God calls Ishmael a lad because that is what he is. When the perspective is Abraham's or Hagar's, Ishmael is a child, the more tender term, for, to them, he is their child whatever his age. Syntactically, v. 14 can be read so that Abraham places bread and water on Hagar's shoulder and also gives their child into her charge. He may well, however, have set Ishmael's hand on his mother's shoulder. The boy may have felt somewhat frail and in need of support. If he had to close his eyes or squint against the morning light, he may have needed guidance. For Ishmael, after all, it is the morning after the night before" (Reis, "Hagar Requited," 100).

Child or Lad? Or Both at the Same Time? Part 2

When they are in the desert wilderness and have run out of water, different
Bible translations use significantly different verbs to describe what happens
next: Hagar "left," "places," "thrust," or "cast" the lad (*yeled*) under some
bushes. This seems a strange action if Ishmael is a teenager of sixteen or
seventeen. One reasonable explanation is that he is unwell; he is as weak
as a child.

Parallels between Hagar and Sarah, Part 1

Sarah's call for the expulsion of Hagar and Ishmael is located in her desire to
protect her own child, Isaac. Hagar now has a similar role; she is trying to
protect her child. In chapter 21, the angel specifically tells Hagar that she is
not to give in to her fears about his impending death, but rather to "lift up
the boy and hold him fast with your hand" (v. 18). She not only gets water
for him, she also continues as his protector. Just as Abraham will arrange for
a wife for Isaac in chapter 24 (Sarah having died in the previous chapter), so
here Hagar "got a wife for [Ishmael] from the land of Egypt."

Parallels between Hagar and Sarah, Part 2

Sarah and Hagar are powerful and resourceful characters. Each becomes the
Matriarch of a nation. Hagar's Ishmael will father "twelve princes according
to their tribes" (Gen 25:16). Sarah's heritage will come through her grandson Jacob, who fathers at least thirteen children and whose twelve sons
will be the titular heads of Israel's tribes. Sarah and Hagar have a complex
relationship. At times interdependent upon each other, they also know moments of conflict. In Abraham they share a husband prone to strange visions
and behaviors, especially when he hears what he believes to be the divine
voice. Their common husband appears indifferent and certainly insensitive
to the personal welfare of his wives. He is ready to sacrifice the welfare of
their children. These two women are cast as rivals for the attention of their
husband and for the privilege of bearing him an heir. Although much sepa-
rates them, they share many common experiences. A close reading of the
relevant biblical texts (Gen 12, 16, 18, 21) in which Sarah and Hagar (and
Abraham) appear—or where their presence is felt—features many parallels
in the language of the narratives dealing with these characters.[64]

64. See Zucker, "Seeing and Hearing." Also see in the Sarah chapter the "Parallels
between Sarah and Hagar" section under "Contemporary Scholarship."

Sympathy for Hagar

The biblical text treats Hagar with great sympathy in both chapters. As Sarna commented in terms of chapter 16, "As between Sarai and Hagar, there is no doubt as to where the sympathies of the Narrator lie. God, the guardian of the weak and the suffering, reveals Himself to the lowly Egyptian maidservant, bringing her a message of hope and comfort."[65] While in chapter 21 God does take Sarah's side, the heavenly response to Hagar's plight again shows God as the guardian of the weak and of those who suffer.

Abraham Was Becoming Comfortable with Hagar

There is no doubt that God sides with Sarah on the issue of expelling Hagar and Ishmael: "Whatever Sarah says to you, do." Aron Pinker makes a persuasive case when he suggests that Abraham had bonded to Hagar and had appropriately warm feelings toward his firstborn son:

> God's communication to Abraham reveals also something that Abraham gallantly tried to conceal and Sarah with her womanly intuition sensed. Abraham was becoming comfortable with Hagar. She is young, dynamic, proud, a free spirit. She is also the mother of his oldest son . . . In Sarah's eyes the slave and her boy became family breakers. In Hagar's eyes she had found a comfortable niche with solid prospects for her son.[66]

Hagar's Destination: Gerar

Pinker notes that it is possible that Hagar was not an Egyptian, but rather from Muzrim. He quotes Gunkel, noting, "an opinion by Winckler that Mizraim (Egypt) and the North Arabian tribe of the Muzrim, to whom Gerar belonged, have been confused. In this process, Hagar, who was a Muzrim woman, became a woman of Mizraim." [67] If Muzrim was confused with Mizraim, then Hagar could have kinship with the people of Gerar, and Gerar would be a natural destination for her. Abraham and his household lived in Gerar, so Gerar was familiar to her. It is possible that Abraham lived nearby, and Hagar had a relatively short distance (maybe five miles) to walk to Gerar. Abraham could have found or even arranged accommodations for

65. Sarna, *Genesis*, 120.

66. Pinker, "Expulsion of Hagar and Ishmael," 9.

67. Ibid., 15. Pinker refers to Gunkel, *The Legends of Genesis*, 102.

Hagar and Ishmael and maintained a relationship with them. Perhaps it was Abraham's plan to settle Hagar and Ishmael in Gerar.

Hagar's Destination: Beer-lahai-roi

The text suggests that Sarah is both protecting her own son's interests and ridding herself of a long-hated rival. There may be a very different explanation. It is entirely possible that Sarah's sending Hagar away was part of a mutually conceived plan between the two women. This plan would permit Sarah and Isaac to subsequently join Hagar and Ishmael at a certain place.[68] Abraham sends away his wife and son without a pack animal carrying sufficient food, in contrast to when Abraham and Isaac take along an ass for a three-day journey in chapter 22. This detail is important. It suggests Hagar had a clear destination, one not far away. Although this is not explicitly stated, it is likely that Hagar and Ishmael intended to travel to and then dwell at the oasis at Beer-lahai-roi, which lies between Kadesh and Bered, where years ago Hagar had found refuge.

Angry Hagar

A very different interpretation of Hagar's actions in the desert when she is sent away from the Abrahamic encampment suggests that she deliberately sabotaged her journey in the desert around Beersheba. She feels angry and scorned by Abraham. Hagar's "disappointment, frustration, fear of the future, injured self-dignity, combine into a feeling of deep injustice and contempt toward her self . . . Hate and a need to take revenge now drive her."[69] Understanding that Ishmael was still precious to Abraham, she takes out her anger at Abraham by "throwing" or "flinging" her son, who was possibly in a weakened state, under some bushes.[70]

---

68. For a discussion of this plan and that Beer-lahai-roi is Hagar's destination, see the "Addition/Excursus" in our chapter on Sarah.

69. Pinker, "Expulsion of Hagar and Ishmael," 19. "She cast the child" (NRSV).

70. Phyllis Trible challenges the interpretation that Hagar abandons her child: "Contrary to some translations, Hagar does not cast away, throw out, or abandon her son; instead, she prepares a deathbed for 'the child' (yeled)" (Trible, "Ominous Beginnings," 48).

Hagar Is Not (Necessarily) Keturah

Sarna suggests that the report in Gen 25 relates not "to a time subsequent to Sarah's death and Isaac's marriage, but to many years before."[71]

Feminist Thought

Hagar: A Throwaway Character?

Cynthia Gordon points out that the story of Hagar in chapter 16 begins, "Now Sarai Abram's wife, bore him no children. She had an Egyptian slave-girl whose name was Hagar" (Gen 16:1). The relationship between the two women is immediately established. Sarah then speaks to Abraham, "You see that the LORD has prevented me from bearing children; go into my slave-girl, it may be that I shall obtain children by her" (v. 2). Sarah does not need to mention that Abraham was childless, for the narrator has emphasized Abraham's problem. Hagar's name is not even mentioned, she is simply Sarah's maid. Abraham obeys, taking "Hagar the Egyptian maid . . . as a wife" (Gen 16:3). Hagar is seen as a "throwaway" character.[72]

Neither Victim Nor Heroine

Cynthia Gordon's comments about Hagar being a throwaway character notwithstanding, the matter is more complex: "A careful reading of the Hagar and Ishmael stories shows that commentators who take Hagar to be either persecuted victim or exemplary heroine oversimplify. None of the human characters is a paragon of virtue; all are flawed."[73]

---

71. Sarna, *Genesis*, 172.

72. Gordon, "Hagar: A Throw-Away Character." Aron Pinker, cited earlier in this chapter, lists several sources in the second footnote to his article where the Hagar-Ishmael "human-interest" episode has been "subjected to considerable analysis, in particular from the feminist and womanist perspective." In addition to authors that are part of this book's bibliography, he suggests: "J. Van Seters, *Abraham in History and Tradition* (New Haven: Yale University Press, 1975), 193–94; K. P. Darr, *Far More Precious than Jewels: Perspectives on Biblical Women* (Louisville: Westminster John Knox, 1991), 132–63; J.C. Exum, *Fragmented Women: Feminist (Sub)version of Biblical Narratives* (Valley Forge, PA: Trinity, 1993), 130–47; N. Steinberg, *Kinship and Marriage in Genesis: A Household Economics Perspective* (Minneapolis: Fortress, 1993), 35–86."

73. Robinson, "Characterization," 198.

Surrogate Motherhood: Religious Ritual?

Savina J. Teubal takes a controversial position by suggesting that Sarah is a priestess. Teubal argues that there may also be a religious or ritual aspect to the matter of surrogate motherhood. Therefore, this act, through which Hagar is to become pregnant, is part of a formalized ritual.[74] She goes on to suggest that there is "a prior understanding—an oral or written agreement—between the participants in the ritual, which both Sarah and Hagar were duty-bound to honor and which was witnessed by the divinity."[75]

Hagar's Pregnancy

According to Teubal, the "immediacy of conception as described in the text supports the notion that this was, indeed, a ritual union rather than the beginning of a lengthy period of concubinage."[76] Although Teubal does not elaborate on this point, the inference is that once Hagar became pregnant, she had fulfilled her purpose.

Hagar Runs Away

Tammi J. Schneider raises the question what dangers Hagar faced by running away. In ancient law codes such as that of Lipit-Ishtar, Eshnunna, or the Code of Hammurabi, there are severe penalties for not turning over a runaway slave or for harboring a runaway slave (although we are not told the penalty for the runaway slave). If this was prevailing law, Hagar must have felt very angry and oppressed to take such action.[77]

Naming God, Part 1

That Hagar names someone—in this case, God—reflects the idea that someone has finally paid attention to Hagar as a person in her own right, as Sarah and presumably Abraham had not done. Furthermore, she was given good news, despite having to go back to her oppressor.[78]

---

74. Teubal, *Hagar*, 77. See also Teubal's earlier work, ibid., *Sarah*.

75. Ibid., *Hagar*, 78.

76. Ibid., 77.

77. Schneider, *Mothers of Promise*, 109.

78. Ibid., 110.

Naming God, Part 2

Hagar came into "contact with angels [but that] in itself is not prophecy," and therefore "Hagar is not listed among the female prophets. She did, however, give [God] the Name 'God of Vision' (Gen 16:13)."[79]

A Troubling Narrative

Oppression in any form is a difficult matter, but some view the Sarah-Hagar relationship as a particularly disturbing subject: "From a feminist perspective, the call for the expulsion of Hagar raises troubling questions. The story portrays the oppression of one woman by another."[80]

Neither Befriended Nor Protected

Phyllis Trible describes Hagar as befriended and protected neither by Abraham, nor by God. She writes, "God supports, even orders [Hagar's] departure to the wilderness, not to free her from bondage but to protect the inheritance of her oppressors."[81] Trible's comment is well taken, but it is needlessly critical. A close reading of the Hagar passages shows that God makes it clear to both Hagar and Abraham that Ishmael will prosper; he will become a mighty nation.[82] Twice God takes note of Hagar—once in chapter 16 and once in chapter 21.

Power and Powerlessness

Phyllis Trible's writing style is marked by powerfully stated contrasting language. She explains that Hagar is undoubtedly in an inferior position to Sarah:

79. Antonelli, *Image of God*, 36.

80. Eskenazi and Weiss, *Torah: A Women's Commentary*, 98. "The violence that is practiced by Abraham against Sarah," forcing her to accept the role of sister rather than wife in Gen 12 and 20 and therefore, as Plaskow writes, setting up "her potential rape" by Pharaoh or Abimelech, "she now recapitulates in relation to the most vulnerable person in her own household. Thus, the cycle of abuse goes on" (Plaskow, "Contemporary Reflection, *Vayeira*," 107). See also the observation noted earlier, "This passage is a difficult one in biblical ethics" (Niditch, "Genesis," 35).

81. Trible, *Texts of Terror*, 25.

82. See the comments to Hagar (Gen 16:10; 21:18) and comments to Abraham (Gen 17:20; 21:13).

Sarai the Hebrew is married, rich, and free but also old and barren. Hagar the Egyptian is single, poor, and slave but also young
and fertile. Power belongs to Sarai; powerlessness marks Hagar
... To enhance her own status, Sarai would make Hagar a surrogate mother. The fertility that God has denied Sarai, she can
achieve through the maid whose name she never utters and to
whom she never speaks.[83]

Reordering the Relationship

The rabbis largely favor Sarah over Hagar. Trible often goes in the other
direction and places the best possible interpretation on Hagar's behavior:
"Structurally and substantively, new understanding encircles Hagar's view
of herself and her mistress. Hierarchical blinders drop. The exalted mistress
decreases; the lowly slave increases. Not hatred or contempt but a reorder-
ing of the relationship emerges."[84] The problem that Trible ignores is the
obvious fact that no matter what her inner feelings, Hagar is not in a position to slight—never mind to show contempt toward—her legal and social
superior, a woman who is still her mistress. Hagar has no power to "reorder
the relationship," for when she does show contempt toward Sarah, it is to
Hagar's own detriment.

A Powerless Slave: A Larger Divine Plan

Ellen Frankel, in her commentary, describes Hagar as "a powerless Egyptian
slave, a shadow to Wife Number One, a surrogate womb." Sarah, in Frankel's
fictional/midrashic work, in turn explains that her actions were motivated
by a larger divine plan, as a foreshadowing of the experience of slavery. Yet
she acknowledges, "But it cost me everything—for from that moment on,
I disappear from my own story. I am not heard from again in the Bible."[85]

The Fateful Swing of History's Pendulum

Frankel also comments that with the expulsion of Hagar and Ishmael, there
"begins the fateful swing of history's pendulum: Abraham banishes Ishmael;
two generations later, the Ishmaelites sell Abraham's great grandson Joseph

83. Trible, "Ominous Beginnings," 38.
84. Ibid., 39.
85. Frankel, *Five Books of Miriam*, 18.

into Egyptian slavery. Sarah banishes Hagar the Egyptian; later, Egypt enslaves Sarah's descendants for four hundred years."[86]

Hagar and Abraham

There are curious similarities between the actions of Hagar and Abraham. In the desert wilderness, Hagar's

> treatment of her son parallels Abraham's treatment of Hagar. Even the verbs sound alike [*shala̲h̲, shalakh*] Abraham sent [*shala̲h̲*] Hagar away, and Hagar placed [*shalakh*] Ishmael under a bush on the ground . . . The mother is powerless to stop the march of death against her son . . . She is incapable of arresting death as Abraham was in attempting to thwart Sarah.[87]

Co-opting Hagar

In recent years, some African-American and Hispanic women have written about the figure of Hagar, seeing her as reminiscent of power relations between masters and slaves, between white mistresses and black slave women, and the use of poor women as sexual instruments and domestic servants in modern societies. Such writers argue that the "African American community in North America has already appropriated the story with Hagar as the central human figure rather than Sarah or Abraham."[88]

Hagar Triumphs

In his analysis, Kari Latvus suggests that the "culmination is in the expulsion story, because it contains the possibility of total destruction but leads to an experience of empowerment. At the end, Hagar is able to also make her own decisions: to find her own place and to take a wife for her son."[89]

* * * *

86. Ibid., 19.
87. Hamilton, *Genesis*, 83.
88. Williams, *Sisters in the Wilderness*, 8.
89. Latvus, "Reading Hagar in Contexts," 273.

Summary and Conclusion

Hagar, an Egyptian, is one of Sarah's servants (Gen 16). When Sarah cannot conceive, she gives Hagar to Abraham "as a wife" with the purpose of producing an heir. Hagar is not consulted about this role. When Abraham impregnates Hagar, the relationship between the two women changes. Hagar holds herself as superior to her mistress. Not long thereafter, Sarah mistreats Hagar, and in response, Hagar leaves and seeks refuge at some kind of oasis or spring, where she has a divine encounter. An angel tells Hagar that she will bear a son; she is to name him Ishmael. The angel comforts Hagar: "So she named the LORD who spoke to her, 'You are El-*roi*'; for she said, 'Have I really seen God and remained alive after seeing him?'" Hagar returns and gives birth to Ishmael. At this point, Ishmael is the heir apparent. In Gen 21, at Isaac's weaning ceremony, or some time thereafter, Sarah sees Ishmael "playing," perhaps with Isaac. Something upsets Sarah; she demands that Abraham send away both Hagar and Ishmael: "Cast out this slave woman with her son; for the son of this slave woman shall not inherit along with my son Isaac." Sarah effectively dismisses the relationship between Abraham and Hagar by not mentioning Hagar by name. Although upset, Abraham defers to his wife's ultimatum. In the vastness of the desert wilderness Hagar loses her way; soon she runs out of water. She finds shelter for Ishmael and places him under a bush. An angel calls out to her, promising that Ishmael will become a great nation, and then God opens her eyes, and Hagar sees a well of water. Towards the end, this narrative explains that Ishmael dwelled in the wilderness of Paran and that "his mother got a wife for him from the land of Egypt."

In the early extra-biblical literature dealing with Hagar, in *Jubilees* the family disharmony featured in Genesis is ignored. Likewise, Hagar's visitation by the angel(s) or God is completely omitted. Like *Jubilees*, Josephus downplays Sarah's harshness to Hagar. When Hagar does flee away, Josephus describes the angel telling her to apologize to Sarah, which she presumably does.

The rabbis generally are critical of Hagar. Hagar was doubly an "Other." She was Egyptian and Ishmael's mother, and was thereby connected to Ishmael's nominal descendants, the Ishmaelites, who became a generalized figure for Israel's Semitic or Arab neighbors. Yet some rabbis speak well of Hagar. She is Pharaoh's daughter and therefore of royal lineage—a fitting companion in Sarah's household and an appropriate birth mother for Abraham's future heir. Hagar is Abraham's wife, not his concubine, explains a midrash. Furthermore, Hagar recognized Sarah's more prominent role in the household. When lost in the desert, Hagar began to go astray after the idolatry of her father's house. Immediately, the water in the bottle she carried evaporated. In the mind of the rabbis, because Hagar found an Egyptian wife for Ishmael, this was proof that she returned to her pagan origins. Yet a medieval midrash collection includes Hagar as the first among nine righteous converts. According to rabbinic tradition, Abraham's wife Keturah is the same person as Hagar, although this view also is challenged.

One contemporary scholar points out Hagar's complexity as a character—Hagar is neither simply a victim nor a heroine. This is true of Sarah as well. Although married to Abraham, Hagar still remains Sarah's property. Hagar is also the only character in the Bible to name God. In terms of the Sarah-Hagar conflict, another contemporary scholar explains that God is sympathetic to Hagar's plight, and that while in chapter 21 God takes Sarah's side, God is also the guardian of the weak and of those who suffer. Feminists have been sympathetic to Hagar. Sarah's call for Hagar's expulsion raises troubling questions, for this portrays the oppression of one woman by another. Yet another scholar notes that Hagar finally makes her own decisions; she finds her own place and arranges a wife for her son.

In conclusion, Hagar is a Matriarch of Genesis, although not a Matriarch of Judaism. She is not mentioned in the Qur'an. In Islamic tradition, as the wife of Abraham and the mother of Ishmael, Hagar holds a place of honor. In Islam, Hagar is mentioned in many of the stories about the prophets, which are broadly parallel to midrash. Biblical Hagar has a troubled and troubling relationship with Sarah, one that reflects understandable (if not always commendable) tensions between the two women. Like Sarah, Hagar has strong opinions, especially about matters concerning her child, and what she does directly influences the lives of her husband and her son. *Jubilees* downplays the Sarah-Hagar conflict and is unique in mentioning Hagar's death. The rabbis' Hagar is most often cast in a negative light, although there are midrashim that suggest Abraham remarried Hagar. This idea contrasts the explicit statement in *Jubilees* that Abraham married Keturah after Hagar died. Contemporary scholars and feminist scholars take note of Hagar's strengths and her anger. Some regard Hagar as a victim or a throwaway character. Others see Hagar as a more complex figure, for neither she nor those with whom she interacts are paragons of virtue—indeed, all are flawed.

We turn now to the second generation of Matriarchs to explore the life of Rebekah in Genesis, in early extra-biblical writings, rabbinic literature, contemporary scholarship, and feminist thought.

4

Rebekah

Biblical Rebekah

Introducing Rebekah

IN JEWISH (AND CHRISTIAN) tradition, Rebekah is the Bible's second Matriarch. She marries Isaac, the second Patriarch. She lives initially in Aram-Naharaim, the city of Nahor (Gen 24:10).[1] She is the daughter of Bethuel and the sister of Laban. While we do not know the name of her mother, her paternal grandparents are Nahor (a younger brother of Abraham) and Milcah. When she is a young woman, Rebekah agrees to marry her cousin Isaac, who is living in Canaan. Like her mother-in-law Sarah, Rebekah has trouble conceiving children. After twenty years of marriage, she bears twin sons, Esau and Jacob. While Isaac seems to have a special affinity with their son Esau, Rebekah favors Jacob. Although most of her married life is spent in Canaan, for a brief period of time Rebekah and Isaac live in the neighboring Philistine town of Gerar. If measured by words quoted in Genesis, Rebekah is the most verbal of the Matriarchs. Rebekah is also unique amongst the Matriarchs, for God reveals to her something about the nature of the coming generation, although that information is quite ambiguous. God only speaks to Sarah in an aside to gently chide her that she lied (Gen 18:15). God neither speaks to Leah nor Rachel, despite their being Matriarchs.

Genesis 22: The Announcement of Rebekah's Birth

Readers of the book of Genesis rightly associate Gen 22 with the major subject of that chapter, the dramatic narrative of the Binding of Isaac (*Aqedah, Aqedat Yitzhaq*). Genesis 23 then commences with the death of Sarah and

---

1. Also termed *Paddan-aram* (Gen 25:20) or *Haran* (Gen 27:43).

the preparations for her burial. Yet the last section of Gen 22 (vv. 20–24) provides important information: the birth of Rebekah to Abraham's nephew Bethuel. As Tammi J. Schneider comments, "Rebekah, the matriarch for the next generation, appears immediately before the previous one, Sarah, dies. This passage emphasizes the women in the lineage and highlights the importance of women in the 'patriarchal' line of the people of Israel."[2] Rebekah's grandmother Milcah is also mentioned as part of this special line of people. She seems to have had an important place in the life of Rebekah, or perhaps of the family or clan. Details about Milcah appear towards the close of Gen 11, in the same pericope that mentions that Sarah was married to Abraham but that she "was barren, she had no child" (Gen 11:30). Years later, when Rebekah meets Abraham's servant, she self-identifies as "the daughter of Bethuel son of Milcah, whom she bore to Nahor" (Gen 24:24).

Genesis 24: Rebekah Agrees to Marry Isaac

Chapter 24 of Genesis is the longest in that book; it is a series of scenes in which the personalities of the characters are developed through details concerning their actions rather than by narrative description. Rebekah appears in chapter 24, when she becomes betrothed to Isaac. Isaac is Abraham's heir-apparent, but he is forty years old and unmarried. Abraham sends his unnamed senior servant [*'eved*],[3] on a mission to the home country to fetch a wife for Isaac.

The first part of the chapter focuses on the conditions of the servant's assignment. Speiser writes, "(1) Isaac must not take a wife from among the Canaanites, for that would affect the purity of the line through which God's covenant is to be implemented; and (2) he is not to be repatriated to Mesopotamia, for the covenant is bound up with the Promised Land."[4]

2. Schneider, "Central Commentary, *Vayeira*," 103.

3. The term "servant" or "slave" (*'eved*) is related to the Hebrew word for "work," *'avodah*. The servant or slave is an unpaid worker who lacks freedom and is regarded as the master's property. This differs from a hired person who receives wages. The slave, male or female, is a member of the master's household (Gen 24:2; Lev 22:11). The word for "servant" or "slave" also refers to a person involved in production or in the household. Likewise, it is used for someone who is in a subordinate position, such as in regard to the ruler, where "slave" could mean "courtier" as a means to refer to oneself when addressing someone of higher rank. In the Bible, a female servant, maidservant, or slave might be called a *shifhah* or an *'amah*; the terms seem to be interchangeable.

4. Speiser, *Genesis*, 183. On the importance of in-family marriage, see Engelmayer, "Ivri: Naming Ourselves," 13–26. This stress on endogamy would be followed in the next generation when Jacob is sent back to Mesopotamia to find a wife. Jacob marries within the family, which is in contrast to Esau's exogamous marriage to local

Yet it is more than an issue of repatriation—Isaac is not even to visit Mesopotamia, something that Jacob does in the next generation. Abraham lacks
confidence in Isaac. He is fearful that if Isaac were to leave the new land,
he might not return. Abraham explains to his servant that God will send a
divine emissary or angel to go before him to aid him in his search.

When the servant and his retinue arrive at his destination, he offers a
prayer to the God of his master that he will be successful in his assignment.
The text explains that it was toward evening, the time when women go to
draw water from the wells.[5] Even before his prayer is completed, Rebekah
appears with a pitcher on her shoulder. She is described as "very fair to look
upon, a virgin, whom no man had known" (Gen 24:16). Attracted to her,
the servant approaches Rebekah and asks if he may have some water from
her pitcher. She immediately invites him to drink. Unbidden, she volun-
teers to draw water for all of his ten camels, no small feat in its own right,
considering how much camels drink. He silently watches her at work. He
then presents her with generous gifts even before he asks who she is. He
seeks her identity and inquires about accommodation at her father's house.
She identifies herself and mentions that there is plenty of food and room
to meet his needs. When he learns that she is the daughter of Bethuel and
the granddaughter of Milcah/Nahor, he bows and gives thanks to God for
having connected him with Abraham's kin. Hearing his reply, Rebekah runs
back to her mother's home and relates what has happened.[6]

Laban, Rebekah's brother, goes to the spring to greet Abraham's servant and his entourage. He invites them to lodge at the family house. He
provides room, food, and water for the men and their animals. Food is set
before them, but first the servant wishes to explain his purpose in coming
to Aram-Naharaim. He addresses Bethuel and Laban. He describes at some
length his commission and how he met Rebekah at the water-fount. He
credits God with their fortuitous meeting. He concludes with his request,
"Now then, if you will deal loyally and truly with my master tell me; and if
not, tell me, so that I may turn either to the right hand or to the left" (Gen
24:49). Bethuel and Laban immediately agree that this is God's doing. They

---

women (cf. Gen 27:46; 28:8–9).

5. The verb for "draw water" is in the feminine plural, sho'avot; i.e., it is women
drawing water (Gen 24:11).

6. As noted in the introduction, the "Bible calls the household 'mother's household' rather than the usual 'father's household' in several passages concerned with marriageable daughters (Gen 24:28; Ruth 1:8; Song 3:4; 8:2) . . . Such a role took women
out of their own domestic contexts and gave them input into matters affecting land and
property. It gave them direct influence over aspects of life that transcended their own
immediate milieu" (Meyers, "Every Day Life," 249).

tell the servant that he is to take Rebekah to be Isaac's wife. The servant is delighted. He brings out precious gifts for the family: silver and gold objects and various articles of clothing. The next day, the servant is eager to return. The family wishes to delay his departure for a few days. He is insistent that he should return. It is at this point that Rebekah's voice is once more heard. The family says, "'We will call the girl and ask her.' And they called Rebekah and said to her, 'Will you go with this man?' She said, 'I will'" (Gen 24:57–58). The family then sends Rebekah off, accompanied by her wet nurse and her attendants (na-ʿaroteiha). They bless her with words that are fittingly reminiscent of the blessing given to Abraham and his offspring in Gen 22—that she should be vastly numerous, and that she should be triumphant in her endeavors (Gen 24:60, cf. 22:17).

Rebekah is pictured leaving her homeland in the morning, mounted on a camel. The next sentence changes locales. Obviously it is several weeks later. Isaac, who has settled in the area of Beer-lahai-roi in the Negev, is strolling at twilight; he notices the arrival of the camels. The scene shifts to Rebekah. Seeing Isaac striding in the fields to greet them, she dismounts and asks the servant, "Who is that man?" Informed that it is Isaac, Rebekah covers herself with a veil. The final verse in the chapter explains that Isaac took Rebekah into his mother's tent; they married, he loved her, and Isaac was comforted following the death of his mother.

Genesis 25: Rebekah Becomes a Mother; Esau and Jacob

Twenty more years pass by. Isaac is now close to sixty.[7] The text explains that Rebekah is childless, as was initially true of her late mother-in-law, Sarah. The same Hebrew term for childlessness or infertility, ʿaqarah, is used in both passages. Isaac pleads on her behalf. Through God's intervention, Rebekah becomes pregnant. It is a difficult pregnancy, for she is carrying twins and the children clash within her. She questions her existence and goes to seek an answer from God. God then answers her, explaining that Rebekah is not only carrying twins, but that there will be a rivalry between her sons. Furthermore, they are each to become nations. God appears to explain that one will be stronger than the other, and the older shall serve the younger (v. 23).[8] Does Rebekah relate this revelation to Isaac? The biblical

---

7. As explained in the chapter on Sarah, in many cases when one halves the ages of people in the post-diluvian generations in Genesis, the narrative makes greater sense. See Zucker, "Ages of the Matriarchs and the Patriarchs."

8. See "Who Serves Whom?" under the "Contemporary Scholarship" section later in this chapter for Friedman's suggestion that the matter is ambiguous.

text is silent on this point. One of the co-authors of this book, Reiss, believes that Rebekah did not tell Isaac.[9] The other co-author of this book believes that she did share her revelation with Isaac.[10] Isaac's being (or not being) privy to this information sheds light on his role in Gen 27, when Jacob surreptitiously "steals" the primogeniture blessing.

Rebekah gives birth to Esau and Jacob. While he is the second child, Jacob is holding on to the heel ('*akev*) of his brother, as if he is "attempting to forestall the prior birth of his twin." Sarna explains that Jacob's name, in terms of "folk etymology . . . is here derived from Hebrew '*akev*, 'heel.'"[11] In time, Esau becomes a skillful hunter, but Jacob grows to be a quiet man, keeping to the tents. Because of his own fondness for game, Isaac loves Esau, while Rebekah loves Jacob. That Isaac loves Esau's hunting ability does not mean that Isaac does not also love Jacob. Likewise, that Rebekah loves Jacob does not imply that she has any less feeling for Esau. Later in Gen 27, it is clear that Esau keeps his best clothes with his mother. It appears that Rebekah has a good relationship with *both* of her sons. The rest of the chapter deals with some tensions between the brothers and the alleged sale of the right of primogeniture.

Genesis 26: Rebekah and Isaac Visit Gerar

Chapter 26 is the third of what are often termed as the wife-sister motifs in Genesis. The first two occasions are when Abraham, initially with Pharaoh in Egypt (Gen 12) and then with King Abimelech of Gerar (Gen 20), falsifies his real relationship with his wife, claiming that Sarah is his sister, not his wife. As discussed in the chapter on Sarah, there are a number of ways to interpret these situations. They range from Abraham asking or pleading with Sarah to do this to his coercing her, which means that Abraham was pimping Sarah, to the possibility that this is a mutually agreed-upon plan, which suggests Abraham and Sarah are tricksters by which the relatively powerless can outwit the powerful. In Egypt, it went well for Abraham because of his claims (Gen 12:11–16). Likewise, Abraham prospered in Gerar (see Gen 20:1–16). In the meantime, Sarah seems to have no recourse to her husband's demands that she be presented as a sister, not as his wife. In each case God brought difficulties to the respective monarchs, and they discerned that Abraham and Sarah were spouses, not siblings, as had been claimed. Isaac and Rebekah now repeat that pattern of behavior in the next

---

9. Reiss, "God of Abraham."

10. Zucker, "Deceiver Deceived," 49.

11. Sarna, *Genesis*, 180.

generation. In this case, however, no one approaches Rebekah sexually, although that possibility is very real, as the ruler of Gerar will attest to Isaac (vv. 10–11). Rebekah is mentioned by name in this chapter, but she has no speaking voice.[12]

"So Isaac settled in Gerar. When the men of the place asked him about his wife, he said 'She is my sister'; for he was afraid to say, 'My wife,' thinking, 'or else the men of the place might kill me for the sake of Rebekah, because she is attractive in appearance'" (Gen 26:6–7). One day the ruler of Gerar, Abimelech, looks through a window and sees Rebekah and Isaac acting like a married couple.[13] He confronts Isaac, who admits that he was deceitful. The ruler indignantly complains that such action could have brought disgrace to his kingdom. In the eleventh verse, he instructs people that anyone who touches that man or his wife will be put to death. After a time, Isaac and Rebekah and their family leave Gerar and return to the area of Beersheba. The chapter then concludes (vv. 34–35) with the announcement that Esau, at age forty, took a couple of Hittite women as wives, a matter that was distressing, for "they made life bitter for Isaac and Rebekah."

Genesis 27: Rebekah, Isaac, Jacob, and the "Theft" of the Blessing

Rebekah overhears Isaac instruct Esau to go to hunt some game and then prepare a dish so that he, Isaac, will give Esau the special primogeniture blessing. When Esau leaves, Rebekah tells Jacob to take two goat kids and pretend to be Esau. Jacob, at least initially, appears reluctant, even afraid, to take on this role. He voices his fears that he will end up cursed instead of blessed by Father Isaac: "Rebekah appears to be in charge of the events in this episode, actively putting her plan into action . . . Not being the head of the household, she lacks the authority to give Jacob the blessing directly."[14] In any case, Rebekah persuades Jacob to play-act the role of his older brother. She prepares the food, and then she takes Esau's choicest garments, which she had stored at her tent, and dresses Jacob in them. Rebekah also wraps Jacob's neck and hands in goatskins. Finally she takes the prepared meal, along with some bread, gives them to Jacob. and sends him on his way to receive the primogeniture blessing. Rebekah then drops out of sight until the end of the chapter.

12. Niditch, *Prelude to Biblical Folklore*, 23–69; Exum, "Who's Afraid?" 141–56.

13. See the discussion in "Fondling, Caressing, Laughing? *Metzaheq*" under the "Contemporary Scholarship" section below.

14. Eskenazi and Person, "Central Commentary, *Tol'dot*," 142.

Some time after Jacob has been successfully blessed, Rebekah learns that Esau is threatening revenge; he is so angry, hurt, and disappointed that he wants to kill Jacob. This information comes to her anonymously: "the words of her elder son Esau were told to Rebekah" (v. 42). Rebekah then initially goes to Jacob and urges him to leave immediately for the home of her brother in Haran, some five hundred and more miles to the north. She explains that in time, Esau's anger will dissipate. Then she will be able to send for Jacob. She says, "Why should I lose both of you in one day?" (v. 45). Next, Rebekah goes to Isaac and complains to him that she is weary of Esau's Hittite wives. She worries that Jacob will also marry local women. If he does, she says, "What good will my life be to me?" (v. 46). Rebekah frames this as her personal concern, but in reality it is a problem for both Isaac and Rebekah. As noted earlier, this is a reference to Esau's recent marriage to two Hittite women, for "they made life bitter for Isaac and Rebekah" (Gen 26:35). In Rebekah's and clearly in Isaac's view, Jacob should marry, and he needs to marry someone from the direct family circle. In fact, "Rebecca's concern that Jacob marry according to the matrifocal traditions of her homeland reflects her attempt to maintain her own customs against the profound changes symbolized by Esau's Hittite wives."[15] That Isaac concurs with Rebekah's assessment becomes immediately apparent in the next chapter. Rebekah may be the force behind this idea, but Isaac has bought into it. How do we know? Life is bitter for him as well.

* * * *

The theft of the blessing is already controversial in the biblical era (Jer 9:4 [3H]; Hos 12:3 [4H]).[16] On the whole, and certainly in contemporary times, Rebekah is castigated for her behavior, suggesting that she instigated a situation by which Jacob took shameless advantage of his father's infirmities. There is no doubt that she is at the forefront of the deception. The twenty-seventh chapter of Genesis, however, is a wonderful example of a deeper plot moving beneath the plain text. Undoubtedly there is intrigue, but who is really in the dark? Is it Isaac, or are there other possible—even more likely—explanations?[17]

15. Plaskow, *Standing Again at Sinai*, 42. See Teubal, *Sarah*, 42, 45.

16. The connection to Jacob is not readily clear in English, but it is in Hebrew. The Hebrew in Jer 9:4 [3H] puns on the word *'aqev*, or "supplanter," which contains the same letters as the word for "Jacob," *Ya'aqov*. See Gen 27:36. The reference in Hosea is readily clear.

17. See the discussion in "The Theft of the Blessing: A Matter of Some Controversy" in the "Contemporary Scholarship" section below, as well as "Searching beneath the Surface: Who Is in the Dark? An Alternative View" at the close of this chapter.

Genesis 28: Jacob Sent to Uncle Laban, Rebekah's Brother

Rebekah voices her concerns to Isaac. He immediately calls for Jacob and blesses him, telling him he is not to marry any of these local women but must leave immediately to find a wife from among the daughters of Laban, his maternal uncle (Gen 28:1–2). As the fifth verse explains, "Thus Isaac sent Jacob away; and he went to Paddan-aram, to Laban son of Bethuel the Aramean, the brother of Rebekah, Jacob's and Esau's mother." Although she thought it would be a relatively short time before she could send for Jacob to return, this was not to be. Rebekah will be cited by name later in chapter 29, when Jacob identifies himself to Rachel. She will also be mentioned in passing at Gen 35:8 and 49:31, but the dramatic events of chapter 27 are the last time she is seen alive.

Early Extra-Biblical Literature's Rebekah

Jubilees

As explained in the introductory chapter, *Jubilees* promotes certain values. Two of these are endogamous marriages and contented families. The *Jubilees* author offers alternative narratives to the Genesis text in order to create ideal family situations with Isaac and Rebekah. They celebrate feasts with Abraham and at times provide gifts of food. When Abraham dies, the wider family both finds his body and then mourns him. Jacob is present at all of these events, and Rebekah is there for many of them. *Jubilees* downplays the deception in the Genesis narrative when Jacob acquires the primogeniture blessing from Isaac, as well as Rebekah's role in this venture. It features Jacob as the special son, a thought clearly enunciated by Abraham, and having the mark of God's approval (*Jub.* 19:15–31; 22:19–20):

> Although the author of *Jubilees* can be very harsh in his treatment of women, especially foreign women (*Jub.* 25:1–2), he does devote an unusual amount of attention to Rebekah, developing for her a role that goes far beyond the biblical text (she counsels Jacob about his marriage 25:1–3, gives a lengthy maternal blessing 25:11–23, and speaks a final testament 35:1–27); although the revised picture of Rebekah is shaped by certain theological and exegetical concerns, the result is that "a woman has taken

her place in the company of men; a matriarch has joined the patriarchs."[18]

Rebekah's advice to Jacob as to whom to marry and her blessings reflect the importance the book of *Jubilees* places on endogamy and the prohibition against exogamy: "*Jubilees'* author created an exchange between mother and son on the subject of intermarriage, one of his favorite themes."[19]

The presentation of Rebekah in *Jubilees* is considerably different than that seen in Genesis. To highlight but three matters: The courtship of Rebekah, which is described in considerable detail in Gen 24, is eliminated. This kind of romantic detail is not important to the *Jubilees* author. Second, her seeming childlessness is ignored. Finally, in *Jubilees* there is a special relationship between Abraham, Rebekah, and Jacob that is missing in the biblical narratives. While she is a major figure in *Jub.* 25, Rebekah's role is larger than just that one chapter. Kugel terms her "*the* powerful woman of *Jubilees*."[20]

Jubilees 19

The first nine verses of chapter 19 center on Sarah's death and burial. Rebekah makes her first appearance in the tenth verse, which details her lineage. This is different from the Genesis text, where Rebekah is featured briefly within a pericope at the close of chapter 22, which suggests that someone came to Abraham with news of his family in Aram-naharaim, information that mentions Rebekah's birth. In Genesis, the death of Sarah and Abraham's subsequent need to negotiate for a burial site takes up all of chapter 23. Chapter 24 then begins with Abraham instructing his servant to search for a wife for Isaac in the old country. Rebekah does not make her appearance as a full-blown character until Gen 24:15, where the text sets out her lineage even as she comes to the spring with a water jug on her shoulder. In *Jubilees*, unlike Genesis, Laban is introduced as Rebekah's brother at this early point in the chapter (v. 10). In Genesis, Laban is first mentioned further along in the text. In Genesis, there is a wealth of information addressing Abraham's instructions to his servant regarding his search for a wife for Isaac. There also are many details surrounding the encounter between Abraham's servant and the girl at the well at Aram-naharaim. In *Jubilees*, we simply learn that Abraham "took a wife for his son, Isaac, and her name was Rebekah,"

---

18. Endres, *Biblical Interpretation in the Book of Jubilees*, 25–26, quoted in Schuller, "Women of the Exodus," 183.

19. Kugel, "Jubilees," 382.

20. Ibid., 415, emphasis in original.

although it also gives Rebekah's family's lineage. The poignant details found in Genesis—that Isaac took Rebekah into his mother Sarah's tent, that he loved her, and that he was comforted after his mother's death (Gen 24:67)— all are absent in the *Jubilees* account.

The *Jubilees* text then turns to Abraham for two verses and follows with the report that Rebekah bore two sons to Isaac, "Jacob and Esau." It ignores the specific biblical statements that Rebekah was unable to conceive for twenty years and that Isaac prayed on her behalf. There is no mention of the struggle of the children in her womb or of her seeking guidance from God. Although at a later point in *Jub.* 24 and 37 it will be clear that Esau was the firstborn child, in *Jub.* 19 his name follows that of Jacob. The *Jubilees* text goes on to say that Abraham favors his grandson Jacob over Esau, in part because Jacob is literate while Esau is a man of war (vv. 14-16). Abraham also knows that Rebekah loves "Jacob more than Esau," even as Isaac "loves Esau more than Jacob." Although the distinction is subtle, *Jubilees* conveys the message that both parents do love their other sons, but that they prefer one over the other. Abraham tells Rebekah to watch over Jacob, for the covenantal blessing will be through Jacob, not Esau. God will choose Jacob to be a blessing among people throughout the earth (vv. 17–20). Furthermore, Abraham tells Rebekah that he loves Jacob more than all of his own sons. Technically, this could refer to children by Keturah as well, but the inference is that Abraham prefers his grandson Jacob to his own sons, Isaac and Ishmael.

Abraham says that Rebekah's hands should be strong and her heart should rejoice in Jacob (v. 21). Then Abraham uses language similar to the blessings he himself heard regarding his own descendants, that they shall be innumerable (Gen 15:5; 22:17). Abraham's ignoring Isaac, his biological son, to discuss the future of his grandson Jacob with Rebekah is extraordinary on several levels. She is his daughter-in-law and she is a woman. Abraham seems to have been so put off by Isaac's love for Esau and so convinced that Rebekah loves Jacob that the Patriarch assumes Isaac would, of necessity, give the covenantal blessing to Esau. Abraham seems to think, "Better I make an alliance with Rebekah than leave Isaac to make this decision." As explained in the "Biblical Rebekah" section above, Abraham does not place a lot of confidence in Isaac's decision-making. This may well have resulted from the events of the *Aqedah* (Binding of Isaac) described in Gen 22. It was, to use a modern term, traumatic for both father and son. In *Jubilees*, Abraham calls Jacob, and standing before Rebekah, Abraham kisses Jacob and blesses him. Abraham addresses Jacob as the "firstborn son" as the chapter closes (v. 29). This particular phrase was probably meant as an allusion to the time that God tells Moses to inform Pharaoh "Israel [i.e., Jacob] is my firstborn son" (Exod 4:22).

Jubilees 22

In this chapter, Isaac and Ishmael visit Abraham for the late spring holiday, the Feast of Weeks. Rebekah makes some grain cakes, and Isaac sends a "good thank offering," both of which they give to Jacob to bring to Abraham to eat and then to use as a blessing to God. Abraham takes these offerings and blesses God. Abraham then speaks to Jacob and blesses Jacob in language not dissimilar to the blessing that Isaac "unwittingly" gave to Jacob as faux Esau, "May the nations serve you, and all the nations bow down before your seed" (v. 11; Gen 27:29). Abraham also uses language reminiscent of the priestly blessing in Num 6: "May God bless you and keep you." He specifically instructs Jacob not to marry among the local inhabitants (v. 20).

Jubilees 23

Jacob and Abraham sleep in one bed. During the night, Abraham dies. Jacob awakes to find his grandfather dead. He then wakes Rebekah, who in turn goes to get Isaac in the middle of the night. Ishmael is also present and mourns his father. This is followed by the burial of Abraham by both of his sons, Isaac and Ishmael, in the cave where Sarah had been buried.

Jubilees 25

In this chapter, Rebekah goes to Jacob and informs him that he is to marry within the clan and, more specifically, a woman from her own father's house, for then his children will be a righteous generation and a holy seed (v. 3). Rebekah addresses Jacob twice; first briefly (*Jub.* 25:1–3), and then she blesses him extensively (*Jub.* 25:15–23). In the meantime, she lifts her face to heaven and extends the fingers of her hands (v. 11), almost priestlike. She kisses her son (v. 23) and will do so again (*Jub.* 31:6), as Abraham had done beforehand (*Jub.* 22:11). Later, with Isaac nearby, she will bless and embrace two of her grandchildren when they return from their time in Paddan-aram (*Jub.* 31:7). These blessings, especially those in proximity to the presence of Isaac, are unexpected for a woman. These incidents are not found in Genesis. In her comments to Jacob in chapter 25, Rebekah stresses endogamy. She contrasts this with Esau, who has married local women who are evil and indulge in fornication and lust (v. 1). Rebekah professes her great love for Jacob. Jacob replies that he is pure of heart and soul and would never take a wife from the women of Canaan. He remembers the words of his grandfather Abraham, who instructed him in a similar manner. He also tells Rebekah that he has heard that "daughters had been born to your brother Laban. And I have set my heart upon them that I might take a wife from among them" (v. 6).[21]

Rebekah replies with a long and involved blessing to God that fills the rest of the chapter. This blessing describes Jacob as a "blessed and holy seed," asks for progeny for Jacob, that they may arise according to the months of the year (i.e., twelve), and that their children should be many and great as beyond the stars of heaven and sands of the sea. She asks that she may see her own grandchildren (v. 18). Rebekah uses very evocative language when she speaks to her son: "And just as you have given rest to your mother's soul in her lifetime . . . My affection and my breasts are blessing you; and my mouth and tongue are praising you greatly." She continues, "Increase and overflow in the land, and may your seed be perfected in every age in the joy of heaven and earth" (*Jub.* 25:19–20). She includes language reminiscent of God's early blessing to Abraham as well as Isaac's blessing to Jacob, "The one who blesses you will be blessed, and all flesh which curses you falsely will be cursed" (v. 22, cf. Gen 12:3; 27:29). Ironically, in *Jub.* 26 Isaac will, perhaps unwittingly, mimic those very words when he blesses Jacob as faux Esau.

This chapter "establishes Jacob's obedient character and his mother's appropriate usurpation of the paternal role in blessing her son—something she could do because she, like Abraham and unlike Isaac, recognized his true character and superiority over his older brother . . . . Something simply had

---

21. To offer some historical context for this stress on endogamy, *Jubilees* is written about the second century BCE, or even earlier. At this point, Hellenistic assimilation is a serious threat to Judaism. This time frame also follows the injunction by Ezra and Nehemiah not to marry foreign wives. While the tradition of matrilineal descent will develop at a point in the late Second Temple period and thereafter, it is likely that there were concerns about proper in-family marriages. The historian Salo W. Baron posited that conversion to Judaism was fairly common in this era. He estimated the Jewish population at the time of the destruction of the First Temple (586 BCE) at 150,000, and by the time of the Second Temple's destruction (70 CE), eight million. This would require extensive conversions between these periods, a time of little world population growth (Baron, "Population," 869–71). For a different view on population growth, see McGing, "Population and Proselytism," 106. Even if one discounts Baron's figures to a quarter of that number, it would still have been a formidable increase in the number of Jews over a six-hundred-year period.

Judith Baskin has written that historically, "conversion became common in the centuries after the Babylonian Conquest" (Baskin, *Pharaoh's Counsellors*, 45). There is a statement in Esth 8:17 that many people of the land professed to be Jews. Adele Berlin comments that she understands this not as conversion, but that "they sided with the Jews." She does note, however, that there "is a body of interpretation advocating the meaning that some non-Jews converted to Judaism." Berlin also explains that religious conversion in the technical sense probably is later than the period of the book of Esther, for religious "conversion begins in Hellenistic times" (Berlin, *Esther*, 80).

to be done to avert his [Isaac's] ill-conceived plan, one that ran contrary to the insights of Abraham and Rebecca into the souls of the two young men."[22]

Jubilees 26

This chapter is very similar to Gen 27, the so-called "theft of the blessing." Here too, Isaac sends Esau out to hunt game, Rebekah convinces Jacob to play the role of Esau, and Jacob has a momentary scruple about this. This *Jubilees* chapter even includes the famous line, "The voice is the voice of Jacob, but the hands are the hands of Esau." According to the *Jubilees* text, Isaac did not know who was truly before him "because the change was from heaven in order to distract his mind, and Isaac was unaware" (v. 18). Indeed, "Whereas in Genesis Rebecca's conniving and Jacob's compliance seem underhanded, in *Jubilees* they appear as commendable efforts by concerned people to thwart a disaster."[23]

Jubilees 27

This chapter begins with Rebekah learning about Esau's threat against Jacob. The Genesis text explains that Esau planned his revenge in his heart, but then someone tells her (Gen 27:41–42). The *Jubilees* author chooses the medium of a dream as the way for Rebekah to become aware of this knowledge. The net result is the same. She goes first to Jacob and urges him to leave so that Esau will not kill him. Jacob, full of bravado, says he will kill Esau before Esau can kill him. Rebekah replies that she would not be bereft of her sons in one day. Then Rebekah approaches Isaac and complains about Esau marrying local women. She urges him to send Jacob back to the old country to find a proper wife. He does this, complete with—as in Genesis—an additional blessing that mentions Abraham. Next, we learn that Rebekah's spirit grieved over her absent son. Isaac offers her great comfort, telling her that Jacob will do well, that he would go in peace and return in peace, and that they would see him again.

Jubilees 29, 31–33

There is a passing reference to Rebekah in chapter 29. Upon Jacob's return to the land of his birth, in addition to gifts he sent regularly to his father,

22. VanderKam, *Book of Jubilees*, 62.
23. Ibid., 62.

Isaac, Jacob sent quarterly presents to his mother. In chapter 31, Jacob returns to his parents' home. He brings his sons Levi and Judah. There they are greeted and welcomed. Rebekah is thrilled to see her son and two of her grandchildren. Jacob is on his way to Bethel, where he had promised to offer up a sacrifice upon his return. He wants his parents to accompany him. Isaac demurs, claiming he is too old and unwell, but he sends Rebekah to accompany Jacob and his sons. Although there are other details in these chapters, in terms of Rebekah, in chapter 32 we only learn that following the sacrifice at Bethel, she returned to Isaac at their encampment, accompanied by Jacob's gifts. In chapter 33, Rebekah is mentioned briefly: Jacob went to live near his parents. When they meet up again, Jacob's family shows obeisance to Isaac and Rebekah, and they bless Jacob and his family.

Jubilees 35, 37, 38

Chapter 35 contains material that is not found in in the Genesis account. There are some attractive touches regarding Rebekah's physical health. Rebekah "was not suffering loss of strength, because she was coming and going and seeing (clearly), and her teeth were sound, and no disease had touched her all the days of her life" (v. 7). Rebekah goes to Isaac and requests that he tell Esau not to harm Jacob. The tensions between the brothers stem from the "theft of the blessing." Isaac agrees to this. Isaac admits that now he loves Jacob more than Esau (v. 13). He also tells her that the "protector of Jacob is greater and mightier and more honored and praised than the protector of Esau" (v. 17). Nonetheless, Rebekah seems to know that she will soon die and she has some unfinished business to conduct with her sons. Rebekah first calls Esau and asks for his personal pledge that she is to be buried in the ancestral burial ground next to Sarah. She further requests that he and Jacob act peacefully and respectfully towards each other. Esau affirms both requests. Rebekah then calls Jacob and asks him to promise to make the same two commitments, which he willingly does (vv. 18–26). The chapter closes with her death and burial at the family sepulcher. The siblings' promises of mutual non-aggression will come to naught. In *Jub.* 37 and the beginning of 38, open warfare breaks out between the brothers and Jacob kills Esau—matters again at variance with the biblical text. In Genesis when the brothers meet, Esau welcomes Jacob and kisses him. They converse a bit, and then Esau returns to his home at Seir. Later, the two brothers come together to bury Isaac (Gen 33:4–16; 35:29). *Jubilees* is clear that Esau's sons, not Esau, begin the conflict.

In the book of *Jubilees*, Jacob is the model Patriarch[24] and Rebekah is the model Matriarch: "For the mid-generation . . . Rebekah . . . emerges as the central character."[25] John Endres argues that in "*Jubilees* Rebekah's status was highly elevated, far beyond any reasonable expectations." One of the reasons he suggests is "the possibility of re-defining spousal relationships and responsibilities."[26] Rebekah openly offers blessings to Jacob, something that only Isaac does in Genesis. She acts almost priest-like. She openly discourses with Abraham.

Josephus

In Josephus' account, the details about Rebekah are considerably condensed. The servant does not search for an unnamed wife for Isaac. Instead, when Isaac was forty, Abraham specifically "decided to give him to wife [Rebekah] the granddaughter of his brother Nahor" (*Ant.* 1.16.1). The servant is sent to Mesopotamia to bring expensive gifts and to return with Rebekah. Josephus notes Rebekah's nobility and goodness of heart, not her beauty and virginity, as noted in Genesis. After marrying Isaac, Rebekah almost immediately conceives. Isaac asks God about his wife's pregnancy and is told of the twins and of the younger's primacy. Despite this revelation, Isaac favors Esau, while Rebekah favors Jacob. Although Esau married local girls and Isaac was unhappy, he held his peace, not wanting to create ill will with his son (*Ant.* 1.18.4). Josephus tells of Isaac dwelling in Gerar but makes no mention of the wife-sister motif. Later, Rebekah manipulates Jacob so that he receives the blessing from Isaac. Then she sees to it that Jacob will visit his uncle Laban in order to marry and to save him from Esau's anger. Isaac simply acquiesces. Jacob tells Laban that his mother got him the blessing and suggested going to Laban to marry. While not calling her a prophet, Josephus describes Rebekah's powers of wisdom (*Ant.* 1.18.8; 1.19.1). This is also noted in the *Targum Jonathan* Gen 27:5, 42. In Josephus, as with *Jubilees* beforehand, Rebekah is the dominant personality of the couple.

Joseph and Aseneth

As mentioned in our chapter on Sarah, in the opening verses of the pseudepigraphical work *Joseph and Aseneth*, Aseneth is compared to the Matriarchs

24. Endres, *Biblical Interpretation*, 155.

25. Ibid., 50. See also ibid., 51–84.

26. Ibid., 49.

of old. In contrast to other Egyptian women, Aseneth "was in every respect similar to the daughters of the Hebrews and she was tall like Sara, *attractive like Rebekka*, and beautiful like Rachel" (*Jos. Asen.* 1:5).

The Rabbis' Rebekah

Advance Announcement

Genesis 22 closes with the announcement that Abraham's brother Nahor had a number of children, including Bethuel, who in turn fathered Rebekah. According to rabbinic tradition, Abraham received news of the name of his son's future wife while still at Mount Moriah (*Genesis Rabbah* 57.1). According to another tradition, she was destined to be Isaac's wife even while in her mother's womb (*Pirke de Rabbi Eliezer* ch. 16).

A Virgin, No Man Had Known Her, Part 1

According to Gen 24:16, Rebekah was a virgin whom no man had known. That is, no man had approached her with a wicked thought (*Midrash Psalms*, Ps 125.2).

A Virgin, No Man Had Known Her, Part 2

Heathen women protected their hymens but engaged in other sexual practices, explain the rabbis. Not only was Rebekah a physical virgin, but she had also refrained from any sexual activity (*Genesis Rabbah* 60.5).

The Sun Rises and the Sun Sets

Based on the verse that "the sun rises and the sun sets" (Eccl 1:5), the rabbis note that before the sun of Sarah set, so did the sun of Rebekah arise (*Ecclesiastes Rabbah* 1.5.1), based on Gen 22:23, the announcement of Rebekah's birth, which comes just before the announcement of the death of Sarah in Gen 23:1.

As a Lily among Thorns

Rebekah came from a family of deceivers, explains a midrash, punning on the word "Aram," the name of the land where the family lived, suggesting that it is connected to the word *ram'ai*, "deceiver." She was different, a "lily among the thorns" (*Genesis Rabbah* 63.4; *Song of Songs Rabbah* 2.2.1).

A Woman Needs to Give Her Consent for Marriage

When Rebekah's family ask her whether she will accompany the servant to go to marry Isaac, she gives her consent. According to the rabbis, this is the basis for a woman being required to give her consent to a forthcoming marriage (*Genesis Rabbah* 60.12).

Conflicting Views about Rebekah as an "Independent" Woman

The rabbis have conflicting views about Rebekah. On one hand, she appears to have independent views and is willing to share them. She is not demure or self-effacing towards men, something they do not count in her favor. Yet, on the other hand, she is willing to stand up to her *pagan* kinfolk and say that she is going with the servant to go marry Isaac. Rebekah is self-determining. She tells her brothers she will go to marry Isaac whether or not they wish it (*Genesis Rabbah* 60.12).

Wishing Rebekah Many Heirs

Rebekah's brothers wish many heirs for her, saying, "May you, our sister, become thousands of myriads" (Gen 24:60). The literal Hebrew means thousands, even ten thousands. As the rabbis explain, thousands through Esau, ten thousands through Jacob (*Genesis Rabbah* 60.13).

When Rebekah Met Isaac

The Hebrew verb describing Rebekah's action when she saw Isaac is *tipol*, which means, in its most literal sense, that she fell (from off the camel). The clear sense is that she *descended* from her camel. The rabbis go out of their way to explain that she did not fall but instead came down from her mount

(*Genesis Rabbah* 60.15; Naḥmanides comment on Gen 24:64). Sforno has a different view: she bowed her head to Isaac as a sign of respect.[27]

Rebekah Compared Favorably to Sarah

When Isaac finally marries Rebekah, he "brought her into his mother Sarah's tent . . . and she became his wife; and he loved her. So Isaac was comforted after his mother's death" (Gen 24:67). As the first Matriarch, Sarah holds a special place in the minds of the rabbis. Taking Rebekah into Sarah's tent gives the rabbis a chance to compliment (and complement) Sarah and Rebekah each in her own right: "As long as Sarah lived, a cloud [signifying the divine presence] hung over her tent; when she died the cloud disappeared; but when Rebekah came, it returned. As long as Sarah lived, her doors were wide open; at her death that liberality disappeared; but when Rebekah came, that openhandedness returned" (*Genesis Rabbah* 60.16). These items represent a sense of grace, warmth, security, comfort, and sanctity in the home.

Rebekah Is a Pious Woman

Rebekah is depicted as a pious woman; she performs several traditional ritual acts associated with women, such as separating dough from the *hallah* and lighting candles (*Genesis Rabbah* 60.16). These are home-based rituals associated with preparations for Shabbat (the Sabbath). These rituals are instituted hundreds of years after the time of Rebekah in the post-biblical Rabbinic period. This does not bother the rabbis. Rebekah is simply portrayed as doing what a pious Jewish woman does.

Rebekah Is One of Seven Childless Women

Rebekah is one of seven biblical women who had difficulty conceiving children: Sarah, Rebekah, Rachel, Leah, Manoah's wife, Hannah, and Zion. In each case, as noted in the chapter on Sarah, God intervenes to see that the woman will give birth. This is based on Ps 113:9: an infertile "woman . . . making her the joyous mother of children." Just as the first six overcame

---

27. A variant of this matter suggests that Rebekah did fall from the camel, and in the process lost her virginity. She is able, however, to prove that this was an accident. *Yalkut Shimoni* on Genesis para. 109, quoted in Shinan and Zakovitch, *From Gods to God*, 231–32. See also *Pirke de Rabbi Eliezer*, ch. 16.

their difficulties, so too will Zion know redemption (*Pesikta de Rab Kahana, Piska* 20.1).

Isaac and Rebekah Pray Together

Isaac prostrated himself in one spot, and Rebekah prostrated herself opposite him (*Genesis Rabbah* 63.5).

Isaac and Rebekah at Mount Moriah

Isaac took Rebekah to Mount Moriah to pray that she would become pregnant. Later, she goes there on her own to inquire of God (*Pirke de Rabbi Eliezer* ch. 32).

Isaac and Rebekah's Prayers

Isaac and Rebekah work in tandem. He prayed to God, "May all the children which you will grant me be from this righteous woman," and she prayed likewise (*Genesis Rabbah* 63.5).

Rebekah Was Lacking an Ovary

Rebekah could not conceive because she lacked an ovary, but then God formed one for her. There is a similar midrash concerning Sarah (*Genesis Rabbah* 63.5; see *Genesis Rabbah* 53.5). Rebekah is not termed as androgynous—that is not the point. Rather, the implication is that because of her righteousness and that of Isaac, God mercifully creates an ovary for her.

God Answered Isaac's, Not Rebekah's, Prayers

A midrash suggests that God answered Isaac's entreaty for a child because he was a righteous person, the child of a righteous person. God would not have responded merely to Rebekah's request, for she was the child of wicked people (Babylonian Talmud *Yevamot* 64a).

Both Isaac and Rebekah Were Childless

While most midrashic sources regard Rebekah as the spouse that was infertile, according to a Talmudic passage, both Rebekah and Isaac were unable to conceive children until God intervened on their behalf (Babylonian Talmud *Yevamot* 64a).

Rebekah Seeks Womanly Advice

Rebekah went to "women's houses and asked them: Did you suffer so much in your time?" (*Genesis Rabbah* 63.6).

Pain, Regrets, or a Relationship with God?

Rebekah asks God, "If it is to be this way, why do I live? (Gen 25:22). Does Rebekah regret the pain of her pregnancy, as Rashi (France, eleventh century) suggests? Does she regret this even unto death, as Ḥizkuni (Hezekiah ben Manoaḥ, France, thirteenth century) posits? Is she simply anxious, or seeking a relationship with God, as Naḥmanides (Spain, thirteenth century) wonders.[28]

What God Revealed to Rebekah

In their explanation about what God revealed to Rebekah, the rabbis draw on metaphorical images: the garden of Eden is paradise, Gihinnom is something like the Jewish view of Hell. "The Holy One made known to her everything <about them> [the twins within her] . . . You are like a field that is sown and thrives . . . Let there be prosperity within this belly . . . fill up the Garden of Eden with righteous <offspring> [i.e., the children of Jacob] and Gihinnom with wicked <offspring> [i.e., the children of Esau]" (*Midrash Tanhuma, Genesis. Bereshit* 1.31 Genesis 5:1ff., Part 6).

---

28. See Rashi, Ḥezekiah ben Manoaḥ, and Naḥmanides' comments on Gen 25:22–23.

Rebekah Was Able to See the Twelve Tribes Even While Pregnant

Rebekah, like all the Matriarchs, is regarded as possessing the gift of prophecy: "Even Rebekah saw {them} [the twelve tribes]." Then comes a kind of counting: two nations, two peoples—one stronger and one weaker, one elder and one younger—twins, children (*Midrash Tanhuma, Genesis. Wayehi* 12.16 Genesis 49:27ff., Part 4). The midrash counts the plural nouns as two each.

Why Rebekah Only Had One Pregnancy

Esau brought great grief to his mother. When leaving the womb, he ripped it so Rebekah could not have more children. He also prevented her from (directly) giving birth to the twelve tribes, even though she deserved to do so, being pious (*Pesikta de Rab Kahana, Piska* 3.1).

Rebekah Praised for Her Role in the "Theft" of the Blessing, Part 1

When Rebekah urges Jacob to fetch two goat kids from the flocks, she explains that, if necessary, he should take them from her dowry gift. She likewise told Jacob that two goats would in future bring blessings to his descendants, referring to the rites for the Day of Atonement found in Lev 16:5, 15–22, 30 (*Genesis Rabbah* 65.14).

Rebekah Praised for Her Role in the "Theft" of the Blessing, Part 2

Rebekah, according to the rabbis, also tells Jacob that she is willing to go to Isaac to tell her husband that Jacob is righteous and Esau is wicked (*Genesis Rabbah* 65.15).

Rebekah Was Buried at Night

Esau's wickedness was the reason that—contrary to normal custom—Rebekah was buried at night. The midrash says that this is shown obliquely. When she died, people reasoned, who will go before her? Abraham is dead, Isaac is at home and cannot see, Jacob is away in Paddan-aram, and the wicked Esau should not go before her. Hence they buried her at night. Jacob only learns about this when he buries Deborah, Rebekah's nurse at Allon-bacuth. "Bacuth" translates as "weeping," while 'allon in Greek means "other" or "another," thus another weeping—a second weeping—one for Deborah and one for Rebekah (*Midrash Tanhuma, Numbers-Deuteronomy. Ki-Tetse* 6.4 Deut 25:17ff., Part 1).[29]

Rebekah Was a Prophet

Rebekah knew ahead of time that Esau intended to kill Jacob; she was a prophet (*Midrash Psalms*, Ps 105.4; *Genesis Rabbah* 67.9). In Gen 27:45, Rebekah asked Jacob rhetorically, "Why should I lose both of you in one day?" In a fanciful story, the rabbis suggest that Esau and Jacob were buried on the same day, and in that sense, Rebekah's prophecy was fulfilled (Babylonian Talmud *Sotah* 13a).

Rebekah's Interpretation of Esau's Intent

According to Rashi, Rebekah explains to Jacob that Esau seeks to comfort himself *for the loss of the blessing* by killing Jacob (comment on Gen 27:42).

Targum Onqelos

Genesis 24:64 features Rebekah dismounting from the camel she is riding. As noted above, the verb *tipol* could be construed as "she fell." *Targum Onqelos* uses the verb *it'r'khenat*, which means "to descend." Genesis 24:67 explains that Isaac brought Rebekah into Sarah's tent and she became his wife, so he was comforted after his mother's death. *Targum Onqelos* says that he brought her into the tent (not Sarah's tent). Isaac then saw that her deeds were constructive like his mother's had been, and therefore he took Rebekah, and she became his wife.

29. See also *Pesikta de Rab Kahana* 3.1; *Genesis Rabbah* 81.5; and *Pesikta Rabbati* 12.4, where Rebekah herself requests this.

Contemporary Scholarship

The Vitality of the Line

Rebekah is credited with being even more important than Isaac in ensuring that the Abrahamic line would continue successfully: "Isaac . . . is important chiefly as a link in the patriarchal chain. Continuity is essential, but the vitality of the line will now depend on the woman who is to become Jacob's mother."[30]

The Meaning of the Word "Rebekah"

Rebekah, or in Hebrew, *Rivqah*, can be translated as "tying" or "connecting." She is the connection that will continue the line of Abraham and Sarah. It is suggested that there may be some wordplay on the Hebrew term *baqar*, meaning "cow" or "cattle." The root letters of *Rivqah* are *r b q*, and the letters for "cow" or "cattle," in a different order, are *b q r*. This allows for an analogy "to other names in the patriarchal narratives, such as Rachel ('ewe'), or Leah ('cow'), and Zilpah (short-nosed animal)."[31]

A Virgin of Marriageable Age

Where the NRSV translates the word "virgin" from the Hebrew *b'tulah* (Gen 24:16), a newer translation uses the phrase "of marriageable age."[32] As one scholar explains, "The word *b'tulah* is often translated as 'virgin' but has a broader meaning than a biological one. In the ancient world, women often married shortly after puberty; therefore one can assume that Rebekah is very young. Isaac, her future husband, is forty years old (25:20)."[33]

Marriage, Negotiation, Financial Arrangements

> In the societies of the ancient Near East, a woman's sexuality was generally under the control of a man in her family. A father controlled his daughter's sexuality, and a husband his wife's. The

30. Speiser, *Genesis*, 182.

31. Beck, "Rebekah (Person)," 5:630.

32. Plaut, *Torah: A Modern Commentary, Revised Edition*, 118.

33. Amit, "Central Commentary, *Chayei Sarah*," 118. Genesis does not specify Rebekah's age.

marriage of a young woman was a matter of negotiation and
financial arrangements between the groom . . . and the father or
leading male of the bride's family.[34]

Rebekah's Assertive Behavior

In Gen 24, on five occasions when referring to Rebekah as a young woman,
grammatically the Hebrew actually features the word for a young man:
na'ar, not *na'arah*. Once may have been a scribal error, even twice. To have
this appear five times (Gen 24:14, 16, 28, 55, 57) suggests that something
is being consciously conveyed. The five occasions are when Rebekah is initially with Abraham's servant, when she goes back to her home to inform
the family that she has met her great-uncle Abraham's servant, when the
offer of betrothal is being considered (by her or by the family—the text is
somewhat ambiguous), and when she is asked whether she will accept this
offer. Rebekah, in succeeding chapters, is portrayed as somewhat independent in her thinking and strong-willed. Perhaps by using the word *na'ar*
instead of *na'arah*, the text is suggesting that she has some strong masculine
traits in that she is assertive in her character.[35]

A Woman of Faith

Rebekah is the most verbal of all the Matriarchs. Yet we do not hear of Rebekah's anguish over her childlessness, but simply a single verse that she
has no progeny. No attention is drawn to the fact that Rebekah had been
married and without issue for two decades, a considerable period of time.
Unlike Sarah and Leah or Rachel, Rebekah does not opt for the maidservant-as-surrogate womb connection. Nor apparently, unlike Rachel with
Jacob, did she speak to Isaac about the problem. She has faith and chooses
to wait for God to intervene.

34. Hackett, "1 and 2 Samuel," 156.

35. This would be consistent with Endres and Halpern-Amaru's comments; see
Reiss, "God of Abraham."

A Mutual Goal

The Genesis text states more than just that Rebekah conceived, but says *his wife Rebekah* conceived, which suggests how much this was a mutual goal on their part.

Existential Language

During her pregnancy, the Genesis text explains, "the children struggled within her and [Rebekah] said 'If it is to be this way, why do I live?' So she went to enquire of the LORD" (Gen 25:22). Rebekah's query is rhetorical; her statement has the sense of an existential question. What is the *meaning* of my life? Her statement is, "If so, why do I exist [*lamah zeh 'anokhi*]?" (Gen 25:22). *'Anokhi* has a somewhat different meaning than "am I"; it is "am I really."[36] It is similar to the question that the angel put to Hagar when she ran away to the wilderness. In that instance, the angel asks momentous questions: "Where have you come from and where are you going?" (Gen 16:8). At the same time, there are several levels to those queries. On an existential level, the angel is asking Hagar to consider where she is on her spiritual life's journey. Rebekah also wants to know where she is on her spiritual life's journey. Hagar's answer is "I am running away [*'anokhi bora<u>h</u>at*]." This may not be such a different answer from Rebekah's "why do I live." Each woman uses the more formal archaic term, *'anokhi*, versus the other word for I, *'ani*. Rebekah, like Hagar, finds her current life intolerable.

"Why Do I Live?"

It is strange that this formerly childless woman does not simply bless God for granting her—or granting them—the most desired wish, which she and her husband had prayed and even pleaded for. She asks, "Why do I live?" Literally, her words are "Why am I?" As Eskenazi and Person explain:

> Interpreters often say that Rebekah is bemoaning her physical pain. However, the text mentions only that the pregnancy is unsettling, not that it is painful. Instead, what prompts her question may be the prospect of multiple children, which in the Bible typically signals a special destiny. Far from complaining about her condition, Rebekah is wondering about her role in

---

36. See Zornberg's discussion on this point in Zornberg, *Genesis*, 159. Rebekah "frames her distress in existential terms, revealing her character as the most introspective and philsophical of the matriarchs" (Rosenblatt, *After the Apple*, 65).

such destiny. God's answer (v. 23) confirms such a reading, since it refers to the children's future.[37]

Seeking God

Rebekah is the first person to seek out God.[38]

God Speaks to Rebekah

God responds to Rebekah's plaint concerning her pregnancy. This is a rare occurrence among biblical women, never mind the Matriarchs. God either gently chides—or, as some would say, criticizes—Sarah to tell her that she did laugh (Gen 18:15), but God never speaks to Leah or Rachel, much less Bilhah and Zilpah, despite their being Matriarchs. Hagar is an interesting contrast, for despite not being considered a Matriarch (to Jews), God speaks to her twice, both times to bless her (Gen 16:10–12; 21:17–20). Rebekah hears the voice of God before Isaac does, who will only be addressed in Gen 26:2. When it comes to God's revelation, the message is more important than man or woman.[39]

Punning on Rebekah's Name

When Rebekah is pregnant, the children struggle within her. The Hebrew for the words "within her" are b'qirbah [bet quf resh bet hey], and these self-same letters, when scrambled, could say, "within Rebekah," or b'Rivqah" [bet resh bet (vet) quf hey].

Ambiguous Language

God addresses pregnant Rebekah and tells her she is bearing twins, although there will be a rivalry between her sons, both of whom are to become founders of nations. In addition, one will be stronger than the other, and the older shall serve the younger (Gen 25:23). God does not stipulate when or how long the older shall become subservient to the younger, or which nation will be the stronger one. Although not stated specifically, there is a theological

---

37. Eskenazi and Person, "Central Commentary, Tol'dot," 136.

38. Zornberg, "Her Own Foreigner," 215.

39. Friedman, Commentary on the Torah, 87 comment on Gen 25:23.

aspect to this pronouncement. It is the nation that is the more God-fearing and righteous that will prosper.

A Rivalry That Begins in Utero

Speiser translates Gen 25:23 as "Two nations are in your womb, two peoples at odds while still in your bosom." The "nations" or "peoples" have been "drawing apart ever since . . . they were implanted within your womb."[40]

Rebekah's Special Mission

In Gen 25:23, God explains to Rebekah that the older child shall serve the younger. This could be a simple statement of fact, but likewise it could be a command to Rebekah: you are called to see that the older shall serve the younger. In this latter case, Rebekah would be unique among the Matriarchs—and among biblical women in general—to be asked by God to undertake a special mission. This task was to ensure that God's blessing would rest with the correct figure in the third generation. Nonetheless, the younger will only continue to know this blessing if the younger is deserving.

Who Serves Whom?

Friedman challenges the idea that the oracle from God is clear-cut. Pointing out that at this point, Genesis features "subtle, exquisitely ambiguous biblical wording. The text does not in fact say that the elder son will serve the younger son . . . It can mean: 'the elder will serve the younger' But it equally can mean: 'the elder, the younger will serve.'"[41]

Fondling, Caressing, Laughing? Metzaḥeq

At Gen 26:8 Rebekah and Isaac interact in way that the ruler of Gerar understands them to be a married couple. NRSV translates the verb as "fondling," as does Speiser, NAB [the New American Bible, a Roman Catholic translation], the JPS' *The Contemporary Torah*, and NJPS-TANAKH. NIV has "caressing," and NEB "laughing." Capturing the flexibility of the word

---

40. Speiser, *Genesis*, 194.
41. Friedman, *Commentary on the Torah*, 88 comment on Gen 25:23.

metzaheq, and recognizing its particular context here, Everett Fox, in *The Five Books of Moses*, offers the phrase "laughing-and-loving."

The Hebrew verb is *metzaheq*. It has as its root letters *tzadeh het quf* – (*tz h q*). These are the same root letters that make up the name "Isaac," or *Yitzhaq*. The punning on his name is deliberate. As noted earlier in this volume, this verb can have a multiplicity of meanings. It is the same verb—and indeed the same exact verbal form—used to described Ishmael's behavior at, or some time after, the celebrations surrounding Isaac's weaning. There the proper translation is something like "laughing" or "playing"—see the discussion about this verb in the "Contemporary Scholarship" section in our chapter on Sarah. As noted before, Isaac's name literally means, "one will laugh," or "he will laugh."

Rebekah Loved Jacob . . . and Esau as Well?

Much is made of the fact that the Genesis text states that Rebekah loved Jacob and Isaac loved Esau (Gen 25:28). Yet it is clear that Rebekah is close to both of her sons. Esau may be forty and a married man with two wives, but he leaves his best clothes with his mother. When it is time to dress up Jacob in Esau's clothes, they are located in the house with her (*'ita babayit*) (Gen 27:15). Following Jacob's receiving the blessing, Esau is upset and in his anger threatens to kill Jacob. Rebekah then suggests to Jacob that he leave for a while. She says, "Why should I lose both of you in one day" (Gen 27:45). As Nehama Leibowitz points out, the text "wished to teach us that Rebecca rescued Jacob from death, not just in her role as the mother of Jacob. She was acting as the mother of Esau, too, in preventing him murdering his brother."[42]

"Listen to My [Her] Voice"

When Rebekah suggests to Jacob that he should impersonate his brother Esau, she says, "obey my word" or "listen to my voice" [*sh'ma b'qoli*]. This phrase echoes God's statement to Abraham that when it comes to Sarah, he should "listen to her voice" (*sh'ma b'qolah*); and in both cases the matter centers on assuring that the major inheritance will go to the "correct" child (Gen 27:8; 21:12).

---

42. Leibowitz, *Studies in Bereshit*, 289.

Dividing the Blessing?

Two nineteenth-century rabbinic commentators have suggested that Isaac and Rebekah discussed the blessing but disagreed on the strategy. Isaac wanted to separate the blessing. He felt that Jacob had the ability to lead spiritually, while Esau had the ability to lead in terms of the material world as a warrior. They then would form a partnership. Rebekah disagreed. She was convinced that the blessing had to be bestowed fully on one son and that Jacob was the sole choice.[43]

Lady Macbeth, or a Woman of Steadfast Kindness?

One contemporary commentator calls Rebekah the "Lady Macbeth" of the Bible.[44] This is too harsh a description. When Rebekah first appears on the scene, it is her selfless acts that cause the servant to praise God for having shown "steadfast kindness," or _hesed ve-emet_ (Gen 24:27). It is Rebekah's own "steadfast kindness" in drawing water for the man and his camels that elicited this praise of God.

The Theft of the Blessing: A Matter of Some Controversy

The narrative of Gen 27 features Isaac giving the primogeniture blessing to Jacob instead of his actual firstborn son, Esau. This appears to be the handiwork of Rebekah, who, along with the connivance of her son Jacob, takes advantage of Isaac's limited sight. In the Anchor Bible commentary on Genesis, E. A. Speiser titled this section, "Isaac Deceived."[45] Nahum N. Sarna writes of "Jacob's moral lapse in his treatment of his brother and father."[46] Elsewhere, he describes this episode as one where Jacob "purloins the patriarchal blessing by means of crafty deception."[47] W. Gunther Plaut writes that Jacob "practices outrageous deceit on a helpless father and a

---

43. Hirsch, _Genesis_, 393–94. See also Malbim, _Commentary on the Torah_. Rabbi Meir Leibush (Malbim, Russia, 1809–1879) and Rabbi Samson Raphael Hirsch, (Germany, 1808–1888).

44. Vawter, _On Genesis_, 299.

45. Speiser, _Genesis_, 205.

46. Sarna, _Understanding Genesis_, 184.

47. Sarna, _Genesis_, 397; see Excursus 21, "Jacob: The Moral Issue."

guileless brother."[48] Gerhard von Rad sees this as a plot engineered solely by Rebekah. He calls chapter 27 "The Cunning Acquisition of the Blessing,"[49]

Consequences and Unintended Consequences

Rebekah understands the consequences of her actions (Gen 27:42–46). She says to Jacob, "flee at once to Haran, to my brother Laban, and stay with him for a while, until your brother's fury turns away . . . Why should I lose both of you in one day?" As a mother, she understands that despite the blessing Isaac gave to Jacob granting him power over his older brother, this is an unlikely event in the immediate future. She is concerned that she may indeed lose both sons. Her actions have already cost Rebekah her relationship with Esau, at least in the short term. He will realize that his mother orchestrated the stolen blessing event, not his passive brother. Rebekah calculates that her manipulative brother Laban—whom she understands well—might find a way to keep Jacob for years by playing up Jacob's fear of Esau. She may never see Jacob again, despite her words to him that when his brother Esau's anger abates, she will send for Jacob and bring him back (v. 45). Nonetheless, she is more fearful of the possible consequences of Esau's anger. The word she uses for "I lose" in Hebrew, 'eshkol, is made up of the root letters *shin kaf lamed*. They are a pun away from the word for "insight" or "understanding," *sekhel* (*sin kaf lamed*). In her mind, Rebekah suddenly understands the full consequences of her action. She may not see either of her children ever again—Esau because he is so angry and disappointed with her, Jacob because he is living so far away.

A Couple That Works in Tandem

Isaac loves Rebekah and finds comfort in her presence. When they are unable to conceive, instead of taking the route of surrogate pregnancy through a maidservant or second wife, Isaac prays on her behalf, and she becomes pregnant. In the midst of her difficult pregnancy, she inquires of God, who reveals matters about the children she is carrying. Since Isaac had prayed

---

48. Plaut, *Torah: A Modern Commentary, Revised Edition*, 185.

49. von Rad, *Genesis*, 273. Fox writes of "Deceit and Blessing," in Fox, *Five Books of Moses*, 122. "Jacob's theft of Isaac's blessing" is the remark in Laymon, *Interpreter's One-Volume Commentary*, 21. "Jacob cheats Esau out of the blessing," explains a *NOAB* commentary. "Jacob and Rebekah defraud Esau of his Father's Blessing" (Bennett, *Genesis*, 271). A different way to understand the narrative of Gen 27 is found in the section below, "Searching beneath the Surface: Who Is in the Dark? An Alternative View."

to God on their behalf, one reasonable assertion is that she would tell her husband about God's revelation. At Gerar, they collude to disguise their true relationship as husband and wife. This is a couple that thinks in tandem and works in tandem.

Feminist Thought

Shrewd and Potent, Rebekah Makes Crucial Decisions

Rebekah is "the shrewdest and the most potent of the matriarchs . . . in her actions and speech we see her energy, her considerable courtesy, her sense of quiet self-possession."[50] Jeansonne observes that Rebekah "made the continuation of Abraham and Sarah's line possible, and has ensured that God's blessing will be continued through the son that God chose." Rebekah is a crucial character in Israel's history. For her part, she is more important than Isaac because she determines that the promise of Abraham is fulfilled. Jeansonne continues, the presentation of her person "shows that women in Israel were viewed as persons who could make crucial decisions about their futures, whose prayers were acknowledged, who might have known better than men what God designed, and who could appropriately take the steps necessary to support God's plans for the community."[51] Rebekah is arguably the boldest Matriarch in Israel's history and one of the first women with whom God has direct communication. She is a determined and independent woman, and most importantly, she assists in the fulfilment of the covenantal promise of land, descendants, and blessing of the future. To recall a statement found in the introductory chapter, the "matriarchs of Genesis are all strong women. As independent personalities, fiercely concerned for their children, they often seem to have an intuitive knowledge of God's plans for their sons. Indeed, it appears from the stories of Sarah and Rebekah that they understand God better than their husbands."[52]

Rebekah as Skeletal Archetype

Betsy Halpern-Amaru believes that "the biblical portrait of Rebekah provides a skeletal archetype for the facilitator role of all the matriarchs in

---

50. Alter, *Art of Biblical Narrative*, 54.

51. Jeansonne, *Women of Genesis*, 68–69.

52. Plaskow, *Standing Again at Sinai*, 3–4.

Jubilees. The Rebekah of Genesis is aware of the future; the knowledge is revealed to her directly; and her actions correct the inclinations of her husband."[53]

Viewing Rebekah

Alice Ogden Bellis explains that although

> Rebekah is often viewed as a positive character from a feminist point of view, she is not well liked by male interpreters. The reason perhaps lies in the psychological realm. Biblical and modern women are often stereotyped as constantly fighting among themselves. The jealousy and fighting between Sarah and Hagar, for example, are seen as typically feminine. If a man is involved in the rivalry, and especially if the woman wins the fight, the situation is evaluated differently. Sarah's behavior toward Hagar was cruel and far worse than Rebekah's deception of Isaac. Nevertheless, in the eyes of many, Sarah is the more ethical character. Abusing a woman servant is acceptable; deceiving a man, even to achieve God's mission is not.[54]

The division that Bellis makes between feminists and male interpreters is overstated. Many feminists are males. Were she to have claimed that many male interpreters view Rebekah's role in Gen 27 negatively, we would have agreed.

A Powerful, Influential Matriarch, Rebekah Is Gutsy

Rebekah is described as "a powerful, influential matriarch." The narrator "does not judge her behavior; he simply tells her story. Her influence over Jacob and Isaac is evident: both seem to do her bidding, with little or no protest. Rebekah appears to be a master of intrigue . . . She is strong and daring and bold."[55] Rebekah seems to be fearless. She "addresses God directly, and . . . God responds to her with equal directness (v. 23). The earlier picture of Rebekah as gutsy, independent, and resourceful (Genesis 24) thus continues."[56]

---

53. Halpern-Amaru, *Empowerment*, 80.

54. Bellis. *Helpmates, Harlots, and Heroes*, 83.

55. Nunnally-Cox, *Foremothers*, 15.

56. Eskenazi and Person, "Central Commentary, *Tol'dot*," 136.

Isaac and Rebekah Pray Together

The Hebrew for the words "for his wife," as in "Isaac prayed to the LORD for his wife," is literally "in front of his wife." This implies that "Rebekah is present" when Isaac entreats God on her behalf.[57]

Respect for Rebekah's Feelings

While Isaac, like his father Abraham before him, and Jacob his son, "could have taken other wives to try to solve the problem of continuity . . . he apparently does not. Isaac's sensitivity to Rebekah stands out in contrast to Jacob, who chastises his barren wife Rachel when she asks for children ([Gen] 30:2)."[58] It also speaks of their mutual affection.

God Addresses Rebekah

While Rebekah may (or may not) have informed Isaac about God's revelation to her, it is noteworthy and a credit to her stature that "God replies to Rebekah directly, informing her—not Isaac—about their sons' future."[59]

Attractive in Appearance

When first introduced to the reader in Gen 24:16, Rebekah is termed "very fair to look upon." Now, many years later, she still is regarded as "attractive in appearance," at least in the sight of her husband, for he fears that the inhabitants of Gerar may kill him on account of Rebekah (Gen 26:6–7). A modern commentary observes, that the "difference . . . is that Isaac thinks his wife is irresistibly attractive, but apparently no one else does."[60] A different reading of the text, however, suggests that Rebekah still is desirable, for as noted above, the ruler of Gerar is concerned lest someone lay with her and bring suffering and guilt upon Gerar's population (vv. 10–11).

57. Ibid., 135.
58. Ibid.
59. Ibid., 136.
60. Ibid., 139.

Repeating History?

According to one scholar, Gen 26 is more like Gen 12 than Gen 20:

> From a feminist perspective, this story [of Rebekah, Isaac, and
> Abimelech] more closely resembles Gen 12 [about Sarah, Abra-
> ham, and Pharaoh] than Gen 20 [about Sarah, Abraham, and
> Abimelech]. Isaac lied, risking his wife to secure his own wellbe-
> ing. He was more important than her, and if one should suffer,
> quite logically it should be the woman. Isaac is not punished for
> his lie . . . [Like Sarah in Gen 12] Rebecca never speaks, never
> has a choice, never makes a decision. She is a passive character,
> passed between men, a tragic example of patriarchal culture.[61]

This is one perspective. Conversely, it could be that Rebekah and Isaac
planned this together, an example of the couple as tricksters.

Genesis 26: Rebekah and Isaac Act Together

An alternative view is that Isaac and Rebekah consciously follow in the
pattern set by Abraham and Sarah in earlier chapters. In this interpretation, husband and wife again "cooperated in outwitting a powerful man,
Abimelech king of Gerar (Gen 26). As Abraham and Sarah had done before
them, the couple presented [Rebekah] as [Isaac's] sister in order to keep the
husband alive among covetous strangers."[62]

The Woman's Body as a National Boundary

Many years after the episodes depicted in Genesis, the Israelites viewed the
events in Egypt and then in Gerar in national terms. The woman's body was
not just her body, it was representative of the nation itself: "The severe penalties suffered by the Egyptian and Canaanite kings for their involvements
with Sarah and Rebekah are meted out not only in response to the violation
of conjugal boundaries but also for the violation of national boundaries, as
the Israelite woman's body is not to be claimed by a non-Israelite."[63] The severe penalty meted out to the Hivites (Gen 34) reflects a similar viewpoint.

---

61. Laffey, *Introduction to the Old Testament*, 32.

62. Bledstein, "Binder, Trickster, Heel," 287.

63. Fuchs, "Intermarriage, Gender, and Nation," 80. Fuchs' use of the word "Israelite" is anachronistic in terms of Sarah and Rebekah.

Rebekah's Spiritual Insight

The Genesis text hints at Rebekah's spiritual insight. God's revelation to her suggests one son will be stronger than his brother. She understands this strength is spiritual, not material, for it refers to the covenant with God. Rebekah intuits that this refers to Jacob. Isaac, at least publically, seems unaware of Jacob's future. Rebekah is so convinced that she is willing to appear to deceive her husband as to who will receive the blessing. Nothing in Genesis explicitly explains her knowledge, motivation, or actions as they enhance covenantal history.

Rebekah's Carefully Phrased Words

In Gen 27:6, Rebekah is very specific in how she words her statement to Jacob. She wants to highlight for him how he is personally connected to each family member. She "is careful to identify Isaac and Esau in relation to Jacob and not to herself. Thus Isaac is *your father* (not 'my husband') and Esau is *your brother* (not 'my son')."[64]

The Theft of the Blessing: A Feminist Explanation

As noted in the "Contemporary Scholarship" section, the so-termed "theft of the blessing" in chapter 27 is a matter of some controversy. Was this entirely Rebekah's doing, or is there a more beneficent explanation, one that involves Isaac as a co-conspirator? Most commentators, including Reiss, the co-author of this book, think that Rebekah deceived Isaac to ensure that Jacob would receive the family blessing. They agree with Tamara Cohn Eskenazi and Hara E. Person in their analysis of this situation, which suggests that Rebekah "works through Isaac, albeit without his explicit knowledge or consent."[65] Eskenazi and Person suggest that Rebekah needs to act in that way because in this patriarchal society, only male heads of households make those decisions.

The other co-author of this book, Zucker, believes that Isaac was a co-conspirator, arguing instead that this is a jointly preplanned Rebekah-Isaac project.[66] In this latter case, Rebekah is not the scheming, manipulative, deceitful wife taking advantage of her husband's frailty. Rather, she is a loving

---

64. Hamilton, *Genesis*, 215.
65. Eskenazi and Person, "Central Commentary, *Toldot*," 142.
66. See "Addition/Excursus" below.

partner who joins her husband in a mutually conceived plan in which she plays her part, as does he. Rebekah remains someone who schemes and manipulates, but the object of her (or their) actions is Jacob, who needs to be motivated to leave and then marry within the clan. In this interpretation, rather than Rebekah taking advantage of her husband's infirmity, they work together to achieve mutual goals.

Rebekah Loves Both Her Sons

David W. Cotter points out that Rebekah does love both of her sons. Following Esau's outburst claiming that he would kill Jacob, "Rebekah identifies herself for the first time as the mother of both of her sons, and she acts in a such a way as to preserve both of their lives."[67]

A Quick Thinker, but . . .

"Rebekah continues to emerge as a quick thinker, the mistress of all emergencies." Yet her advice to Jacob that he "needs stay away" only a short time "is actually unrealistic." She will never see him again.[68]

Addition/Excursus

Searching beneath the Surface: Who Is in the Dark?
An Alternative View

As noted earlier in this chapter, in the Bible, Gen 27 describes how Jacob receives the primogeniture blessing from his shortsighted father. A plain reading of the text suggests that Rebekah comes up with this idea and that she orchestrates the whole deception. Rebekah has been both praised and condemned for this. She has been lauded for being more insightful than her husband as to the true nature of their mutual children. She is praised in *Jubilees*, as VanderKam explains, for her "appropriate usurpation of the paternal role in blessing her son—something she could do because she [Rebekah], like Abraham and unlike Isaac, recognized his [Jacob's] true character and superiority over his older brother . . . Something simply had to be done."[69] The rabbis also have good things to say about Rebekah's role in assuring

---

67. Cotter, *Genesis*, 205.

68. Hamilton, *Genesis*, 230.

69. VanderKam, *Book of Jubilees*, 62.

that Jacob would be blessed (*Genesis Rabbah* 65.14–15). Feminists praise Rebekah for her strength and independence. Most importantly, Rebekah assists in the fulfillment of the covenantal promise of land, descendants, and blessing of the future.[70]

At the same time, some modern commentators have condemned the "theft" as a moral lapse and as a cunning acquisition of the blessing earned through the deceit of a disloyal wife. One commentator describes Rebekah as "the Machiavellian matriarch manipulating Jacob to defeat the purpose of her blind and dying husband."[71] That there was deception is not in question. That Jacob consciously, purposefully, and with guile sought to mislead his father also is not in debate. The issue is not *if* someone was in the dark about this whole matter, but *who* is it that was deceived? A careful and close reading of the text suggests that it is not Isaac who is "in the dark," it is Jacob. Rebekah and Isaac together manipulate Jacob to act, so that he believes he is "stealing" the blessing. Throughout the chapter, there are clues and coded messages that suggest Jacob's parents have planned this "deception." Jacob is forty years old; he remains unmarried and is still living at home. His parents plan this ruse that will force him to leave home, and at their direction, seek a wife from the old country, from the family of his uncle Laban.

Susan Niditch argues persuasively for the narrative pattern of the trickster: "One of the biblical authors' favorite narrative patterns is that of the trickster. Israelites tend to portray their ancestors, and thereby to imagine themselves, as underdogs, as people . . . who achieve success in roundabout, irregular ways."[72] Women can be tricksters, as well as men (e.g., Jacob and David). Sometimes men and women collude together to serve as tricksters. The example of the wife-sister motif described earlier may be one set of cases in point, and here, the Isaac-Rebekah collusion provides another instance of this honored tradition.

Nothing in the earlier Isaac-Rebekah narrative suggests anything but a close relationship between these two figures. Isaac loved Rebekah and finds comfort in her (Gen 24:67). They seem to pray together for a child (Gen 25:21). When the children are born, in the very act of their naming, the text itself underscores "Rebekah's greater involvement in the future of her children." Esther Fuchs points out that whereas "in the case of Isaac, YHWH endows Abraham with the exclusive right to name his son, here the children are named by *both parents*: 'The first came forth . . . *they* called his name

---

70. Jeansonne, *Women of Genesis*, 68–69.

71. Wenham, *Genesis 16–50*, 208.

72. Niditch, "Genesis," 36.

Esau'" (Gen 25:25).[73] Sometime following the "theft" of the blessing when Esau threatens Jacob, all that Rebekah needs to do is to complain to Isaac and he immediately sends Jacob away to Paddan-aram (Gen 27:46–28:5). Not only does Isaac send Jacob on his way, he adds additional blessings! This would not happen if Isaac had felt deceived or betrayed by his wife and son. Isaac displays no anger toward Rebekah for her part in the blessing going to Jacob. Likewise, he displays no animosity towards Jacob. This hardly reflects the action of a man who had felt manipulated or misused. At the beginning of chapter 27, Isaac explains to Esau that he is old and that he does not know the time of his death, but he will live another eighty years (Gen 35:28 [cf. Gen 25:26; 26:34]). Goatskins on Jacob's hands and neck do not feel like human hair. Furthermore, Isaac knows full well who is in front of him. This is evident when he speaks his most famous lines, "The voice is Jacob's voice, but the hands are the hands of Esau" (Gen 27:22). The text depicts Isaac as having limited sight, not limited insight.[74]

* * * *

Summary and Conclusion

While Abraham's servant negotiates with Rebekah's family, the final decision to move to Canaan rests with Rebekah herself (Gen 24). Isaac takes Rebekah into his mother's tent; he loves her and finds comfort following his mother's death. Rebekah is childless; Isaac pleads on her behalf, and through God's intervention, she becomes pregnant. It is a difficult pregnancy, for she is carrying twins, so she questions her existence. Rebekah seeks an answer from God and learns that there will be a rivalry between her sons. Isaac loves Esau, while Rebekah loves Jacob (Gen 25). Chapter 26 repeats the wife-sister motif, seen earlier with Abraham and Sarah. Here, Isaac and Rebekah interact with King Abimelech of Gerar. Later, Rebekah overhears Isaac instruct Esau about the primogeniture blessing and instructs Jacob to pretend to be Esau (Gen 27). She makes the proper preparations. Subsequently, Rebekah learns that Esau is threatening revenge against Jacob. She persuades Isaac to send Jacob to his uncle Laban in Paddan-aram (Gen 28).

73. Fuchs, "Literary Characterization," 130.

74. That this is a cleverly construed conspiracy engineered in tandem by Isaac and Rebekah, see Zucker, "Still Stranger Stratagem"; ibid., "Rescuing Rebecca's Reputation"; ibid., "Choosing Jacob." An alternative view could be that Isaac is fully aware of what is going on and that he approves of the scheme of Rebekah and Jacob (Wray, *Good Girls, Bad Girls*, 37).

Jubilees offers additional narratives in order to create ideal family situations. Mention of Rebekah's childlessness is omitted. Isaac and Rebekah celebrate feasts with Abraham. *Jubilees* downplays the deceptive quality of Jacob acquiring the primogeniture blessing from Isaac—as well as Rebekah's role in this venture—for Jacob is the special son, approved by Abraham and God. Rebekah gives several long speeches. She informs Jacob he is to marry within the clan, and more specifically, a woman from her own father's house, for then his children will be a righteousness generation and a holy seed (*Jub.* 25:3). These blessings, in proximity to the presence of Isaac, are unexpected for a woman and are not found in Genesis. In *Jubilees*, Jacob is the model Patriarch, and Rebekah is the model Matriarch.

In the writings of Josephus, the details about Rebekah are considerably condensed. The servant does not go to find a wife for Isaac; Abraham specifically "had decided to give him to wife [Rebekah] the granddaughter of his brother Nahor." Josephus notes Rebekah's generosity and good behavior, not her beauty and virginity. Rebekah conceives almost immediately. God tells Isaac about his wife's pregnancy and the younger twin's primacy. Isaac favors Esau, while Rebekah prefers Jacob. There is no mention of the wife-sister motif. Later, Rebekah manipulates Jacob so that he receives the blessing from Isaac. In Josephus' account, as with *Jubilees* beforehand, Rebekah is the dominant personality of this couple. In the opening chapter of the pseudepigraphical work, *Joseph and Aseneth*, Aseneth is described as being as attractive as Rebekah.

The rabbis stress Rebekah's purity of body and mind, yet they are ambivalent about her. She is neither demure, nor self-effacing towards men. Yet she stands up against her pagan kinfolk. Like Sarah, Rebekah is pious; she performs several traditional ritual acts associated with women, such as separating dough from the *hallah* and lighting candles. Rebekah is one of seven biblical women who had difficulty conceiving children: Sarah, Rebekah, Rachel, Leah, Manoah's wife, Hannah, and Zion. Rebekah is praised for her role in the "theft" of the blessing. When she urges Jacob to fetch two goat kids from the flocks, she explains that two goats would, in a future time, bring blessings to his descendants, referring to the rites for the Day of Atonement found in Lev 16:5, 15–22, 30.

A contemporary scholar notes that Rebekah is the most verbal of all the Matriarchs. She does not anguish over her childlessness, nor does she opt for the maidservant-as-surrogate womb connection. Having faith, she waits for God's intervention. Many modern scholars criticize Rebekah's behavior in the "acquisition of the blessing," using such words as "cunning," "moral lapse," and "outrageous deceit," but there are alternative explanations that redeem her reputation. Many feminist scholars see Rebekah as a determined and independent woman—someone who is powerful and influential, daring and bold. Rebekah intuits Jacob's special future, and she is willing to appear to deceive her husband to achieve this end.

In conclusion, Rebekah is the strongest and most vocal of the Matriarchs. Genesis portrays her as a woman who is independent of mind and action. God reveals to Rebekah something about the destiny of her children. She has a distinctive sense of what this means. When the occasion allows, she sees to it that, contrary to the accepted practice of primogeniture inheritance that would mean her son Esau receives the blessing, this benediction goes to Jacob. This act may or may not have been done with the sure knowledge of Isaac. The Rebekah of *Jubilees* is an even stronger and more prominent figure; she is a woman who makes multiple speeches and is shown as a confidante of Abraham. *Jubilees* commends Rebekah's actions to secure the blessing for Jacob, and indeed, her intervention is seen as averting disaster. Josephus suggests that Rebekah manipulates Jacob to get the patriarchal blessing, and while stopping short of calling her a prophet, he commends her wisdom. The rabbis do call her a prophet, and many approve her role in the theft of the blessing. Rebekah is also compared favorably to Sarah. Contemporary scholars and feminist scholars praise Rebekah for assuring that the vitality of the line will continue to the next generation. She is lauded as a woman of both faith and action. Many criticize her involvement in the acquisition of the blessing, but others praise her for her spiritual insight.

We turn now to the third generation of Matriarchs, exploring first the life of Leah, then Rachel, and subsequently Bilhah and Zilpah in Genesis, early extra-biblical writings, rabbinic literature, contemporary scholarship, and feminist thought.

5

Leah

Biblical Leah

Introducing Leah

LEAH IS MARRIED TO Jacob.[1] In terms of Jewish (and Christian) tradition, Leah, along with her younger sister, Rachel, constitutes the third generation of Matriarchs, following Sarah and then Rebekah. In a technical sense, it is Leah and Rachel, as well as Bilhah and Zilpah, who form the third generation of Matriarchs.[2]

Leah is Jacob's first wife, but she is not the woman he thought he married. Leah is Rachel's older sister. On the night that Jacob believed he was wedding Rachel, the girls' father, Laban, placed Leah in the bridal tent. Jacob only realized this fact the next morning. Jacob will eventually be married to four women concurrently: Leah, Rachel, Bilhah, and Zilpah. These four women will collectively give birth to at least thirteen children—twelve sons and a daughter. The twelve sons become the eponymous ancestors of the twelve tribes of Israel. The Leah-Jacob-Rachel triangle is fraught with understandable tensions, as shall be explained in this chapter. In time, the two sisters appear to make peace with each other. They work in concert with Jacob when it is time to leave their homeland at Haran near the upper Euphrates River for the land of Canaan, about five hundred miles to the south.

Leah is the mother of six sons and one daughter. In order, they are: Reuben, Simeon, Levi, Judah, Issachar, Zebulon, and Dinah. Leah also gives Jacob her handmaid Zilpah, who in turn bears him two additional sons, Gad and Asher. Although both Rachel and Leah predecease Jacob, it is Leah

---

1. As this volume was in its concluding stages, we learned that the Jewish Publication Society had just published Jerry Rabow's work, *The Lost Matriarch: Finding Leah in the Bible and Midrash* (2014). Rabow covers some similar ground that we do in this chapter, although he approaches his material differently.

2. For further discussion about this, see our chapter on Bilhah and Zilpah.

who is buried with Jacob at the family sepulcher at Machpelah in Hebron/
Kiriyat Arba.

Genesis 29: Leah Is Jacob's First Wife;
Rachel Is His Second Wife

Although Leah is first mentioned by name in chapter 29, there is a general
reference to her in the previous chapter when Isaac tells Jacob to flee to
Paddan-aram, the home of Rebekah's father Bethuel as well as her brother
Laban: "Go at once . . . and take as wife from there one of the daughters
of Laban, your mother's brother" (Gen 28:2). As will be explained in our
chapter on Rachel, she is the woman Jacob meets first when he arrives at
Haran, as well as the woman he deeply loves. Jacob arrives at Haran more
or less with the clothes on his back. He brings no dowry price. Instead, he
offers to work for seven years for his uncle to earn the right to marry Rachel.
Just before this offer is made, the text notes that Laban has two daughters,
an older one, Leah, and a younger, Rachel: "Leah's eyes were lovely, and
Rachel was graceful and beautiful" (Gen 29:17).[3] Laban promises Rachel
to Jacob, but at the crucial moment, in the darkness of the marriage tent, he
substitutes Leah for Rachel. Following the wedding feast, "in the evening . . .
[Laban] brought [Leah] to Jacob; and he went in to her . . . When morning
came, it was Leah!" (Gen 29:23, 25).

Jacob, filled with righteous indignation, confronts Laban with his
treachery: "What is this you have done to me? Did I not serve you for Rachel? Why then have you deceived me?" (v. 25). Laban offers what is clearly
a frail excuse, one that may or may not be true. He says it is local custom to
marry the older daughter before the younger. Laban continues, saying that
if Jacob honors the bridal celebration week[4] with Leah, he may have Rachel
as well. The necessary condition is that Jacob will have to earn her with
another seven years of labor. The text also explains parenthetically that at

---

3. The Hebrew word translated here as "lovely," *rakkot*, defies clear definition in
this context. See references to "Leah's eyes" in the "Rabbis' Leah" and "Contemporary
Scholarship" sections below. Given the context, the statement about Leah's eyes probably is meant pejoratively, and a better translation might be "weak" or "lacked luster."

4. Does the text really refer to a "bridal week," or is Laban suggesting that Jacob
needs to work another seven years before earning Rachel as his wife? See the explanation under "Did Leah Have a Week's 'Bridal Celebration' with Jacob, or Were They Married Seven Years before Rachel Became Jacob's Second Wife?" in the "Contemporary
Scholarship" section below, as well as the explanation under "Seven or Fourteen years?
How Long Did Jacob Work *before* Marrying Rachel?" in the "Contemporary Scholarship" section in our chapter on Rachel.

this time, "Laban gave his maid Zilpah to his daughter Leah to be her maid" (Gen 29:24). The narrative is clear that Jacob has a favored wife; he "loved Rachel more than Leah" (v. 30). The biblical text then continues to say that when it was clear Leah was "unloved" by Jacob, God "opened her womb; but Rachel was barren" (v. 31).[5] Leah is a fruitful vine. She conceives and bears a son, Reuben. The root meaning of the word "Reuben" is "See, a son," from the Hebrew *r'eu, ben (r'eu ven)*. Having borne a son to Jacob, Leah believes— or at least she hopes—that this will change Jacob's attitude toward her. Her actual words are, "Because the LORD has looked on my affliction; surely now my husband will love me" (Gen 29:32). The next verses report that she bears three more sons: Simeon, Levi, and Judah. In each case, Leah offers an explanation for why she gave her son that name. Her explanation puns on the child's name and gives readers insight into Leah's difficult relationship with Jacob. Leah connects her first three sons' names with her hopes that Jacob will now love her. With Judah she instead praises God, perhaps feeling that her destiny is motherhood, if not the affection of her husband.

- For Simeon, the text says, "'Because the LORD has *heard* that I am hated, [God] has given me this son also'; and she named him Simeon" (v. 33). The root letters of the word "Simeon" contain the same Hebrew root letters as the word "heard," *shin mem 'ayin*.

- For Levi, the text says, "Again she conceived and bore a son, and said, 'Now this time my husband will be *joined* to me, because I have borne him three sons'; therefore he was named Levi" (v. 34). The root letters of the word "Levi" contain the same Hebrew root letters as the word "joined," *lamed vav hey*.

- For Judah, Leah says, "'This time I will *praise* the LORD; therefore she named him Judah" (v. 35). The root letters of the word "Judah" contain the same Hebrew root letters as the word "praise" or "thanks," *yud dalet hey*.

Genesis 30: More Children for Jacob

The narrative of Genesis then focuses on Rachel and her inability to get pregnant. In her frustration, Rachel offers her maid Bilhah to Jacob to produce offspring. Bilhah bears two sons, first Dan and then Naphtali. Leah, assuming that she is no longer fertile, takes her maid Zilpah and gives her to Jacob "as a wife." Zilpah in quick succession bears two sons, Gad and Asher.

5. See "Jacob's Feelings for Leah" in the "Contemporary Scholarship" section below.

Although it is Zilpah who gives birth to the children, Leah takes personal credit for these additions to the family. Similar to the births of her own sons, Leah names these boys, and their names involve wordplay once again.

- For Gad, she says, "'Good *fortune!*'" so she named him Gad" (Gen 30:11). The root letters of the word "Gad" contain the same Hebrew root letters as the word "fortune," *gimmel dalet.*

- For Asher, Leah says, "'*Happy* am I! For the women will call me *happy*'; so she named him Asher" (v. 13). The root letters of the word "Asher" contain the same Hebrew root letters as the word "happy," *aleph shin resh.*

One late summer's day, Reuben finds some mandrakes and brings them to his mother, Leah. Rachel addresses Leah and asks for some of the plants. In all probability, the mandrakes were thought to be some kind of aphrodisiac or to have some magical powers. There is palpable tension between the two sisters. Leah says to Rachel, "Is it a small matter that you have taken away my husband? Would you take away my son's mandrakes also?" (v. 15). Rachel concedes the point and agrees that in exchange for the plants, Jacob will come to Leah's tent that evening. When Jacob returns from the field, Leah goes out to greet him and she says, "'You must come in to me; for I have hired you with my son's mandrakes.' So he lay with her that night" (v. 16). Not only does Leah conceive once again, she conceives yet another time, producing more sons for Jacob: Issachar and then Zebulon. Next she bears a daughter, Dinah. As with her own previous biological sons and her surrogate sons, Leah names them and connects those names with her desire to be loved by Jacob. Notably, there is no "explanation" regarding the birth of Dinah. A translation of the name "Dinah" may mean something to do with the Hebrew word for "judgment," or "vindication." The absence of a biblical pun for Dinah's name is another example of male-centered narratives in the biblical text. Were there additional children? Genesis 37:35 refers to Jacob being comforted by all his sons and all his daughters, but this may refer to daughters-in-law.

- For Issachar, Leah says, "'God has given me my *hire* because I gave my maid to my husband'; so she named him Issachar" (v. 18). The root letters of the word "Issachar" contain the same Hebrew root letters as the word "hire," *sin khaf resh.*

- For Zebulon, she says, "'God has endowed me with a good dowry [or gift]; now my husband will *honor* me, because I have borne him six sons'; so she named him Zebulon" (v. 20). The root letters of the word

"Zebulon" contain the same Hebrew root letters as the word "honor,"
zayin bet lamed.[6]

- Finally, Rachel becomes pregnant, and she gives birth to Joseph. Rachel says, "May the LORD *add* to me another son" (v. 24). The root letters of the word "Joseph" contain the same Hebrew root letters as the word "add," *yud samekh fey.*

The rest of chapter 30 details how, despite the lack of cooperation on the part of his father-in-law and uncle, Laban, Jacob managed to prosper and became a wealthy man who owned abundant flocks, female as well as male slaves, camels, and donkeys (Gen 30:43).

Genesis 31: Tensions Mount; Jacob's Family Leaves for Canaan

Close to twenty years have passed since Jacob left his homeland to go to live with his uncle Laban. He has married and has four concurrent wives: Leah, Rachel, Bilhah, and Zilpah. He has at least twelve children—eleven sons and a daughter. Materially, he is successful, but there are tensions not only with Laban, but also with Jacob's brothers-in-law, who feel that he has done well at their expense. Now, after many years, once again God speaks to Jacob. God tells him that it is time to return to Canaan, to the land of his kin (v. 3). Jacob then consults with his primary wives, Rachel and Leah. He makes a case for why this is the time to leave their homeland and to move to the place of his birth. Both women concur. Together they voice their support for his decision. The women resent the shabby way their father has treated them. They call Laban avaricious and selfish. They are fearful that if they stay, he will find a way to disinherit them, putting their own and their children's futures in jeopardy. They side with the decision of Jacob and Jacob's God:

> Then Rachel and Leah answered him, "Is there any portion or inheritance left to us in our father's house?[7] Are we not regarded by him as foreigners? For he has sold us, and he has been using up the money given for us. All the property that God has taken away from our father belongs to us and to our children; now then, do whatever God has said to you." (Gen 31:14–16)

---

6. Brown, Driver, and Briggs, *Hebrew and English Lexicon*, s.v. *zayin bet lamed.* See also Sarna, *Genesis*, comment on Gen 30:20.

7. This phrase is echoed in 1 Kgs 12:16 and 2 Chron 10:16.

Although there will be references to Leah in terms of Laban's visit to Leah's tent later in this chapter (v. 33), she does not have a speaking voice again in Genesis. She is referred to when Jacob meets Esau (33:1–2).

Genesis 34: Shechem Violates Leah's Daughter, Dinah; Dinah's Brothers' Reaction

Chapter 34 details the rape of Dinah, Leah and Jacob's only daughter, and its aftermath. In terms of the history of the Matriarchs, in the opening line Dinah is mentioned as the daughter of Leah. Later in the chapter, all of Jacob's sons are outraged at Shechem's act (v. 7). As a group they give their answer to Hamor, Shechem's father (v. 13). It is two of Dinah's older brothers by Leah, Simeon and Levi, however, who then follow through on the attack on the Hivites and "rescue" their sister Dinah (vv. 25–26). All of the brothers partake in the plunder of the city "because their sister had been defiled" (Gen 34:27). When Jacob confronts Simeon and Levi, it is they who reply to him that the very honor of the family was at issue.

Leah is mentioned again in Genesis in terms of her children (35:23; 46:15) and her surrogate sons (46:18). In his final words to his sons, Jacob mentions that he buried Leah in the family sepulcher in Machpelah (49:31). The last biblical reference to Leah is in the book of Ruth, where she is held up as an example of someone who, along with Rachel, built up the house of Israel (Ruth 4:11).

Early Extra-Biblical Literature's Leah

Jubilees

The themes of endogamous marriages and contented families are seen in the treatment of Leah in *Jubilees*. Conflict may be present, but it is played down or sanitized.

Jubilees 28

Jubilees acknowledges Leah's eyes, calling them weak, but then goes on to say that like her sister Rachel, Leah's "appearance was very beautiful" (v. 5). As in Genesis, the morning following the bed-switch, Jacob confronts Laban. He tells his father-in-law that he can take Leah back, for Jacob is threatening to leave: "Take your daughter, and I will go because you have done evil

against me." Laban's defense of his actions is remarkable. Following the expected statement taken from the Genesis account that local custom dictates
that the elder is married before the younger, Laban then goes on to say that
this is a custom "ordained and written in the heavenly tablets." Furthermore,
Laban explains that God would have this as a command for "the children
of Israel so that they will not do this thing: 'Let not the younger woman be
taken or given without the elder one being first (given) because that is very
evil'" (*Jub.* 28:7). That there were no "children of Israel" at this point, nor is
there a biblical verse in the rest of the Torah to support this contention, does
not seem to bother the author(s) of *Jubilees*. Furthermore, Laban refers to
the "heavenly tablets"—a reference to the Torah, which at this point in the
understanding found in *Jubilees*, is written but presumably still in heaven,
having not yet been given to Moses.

The *Jubilees* translation suggests that Leah was "hated" (v. 12) as opposed to a softer word.[8] Unlike the Genesis account, *Jubilees* does not explain why she names her sons as she does, but in its place *Jubilees* offers the
exact dates on which the sons were born. *Jubilees* leaves out the mandrakes
episode. It suggests that Zebulon and Dinah, Leah's sixth and seventh children, are twins born on the same day.

Jubilees 29

As in Genesis, Jacob consults his wives before leaving for his homeland. In
the Genesis account, Jacob sends for Rachel and Leah (Gen 31:4), but in
Jubilees the names are reversed and appear in birth order, for he calls for
Leah and Rachel (v. 2). The women then speak in one voice, words reminiscent of Ruth's statement to Naomi: "We will go with you anywhere you go,"
which probably is a deliberate choice of words by *Jubilees*' author(s) because
Rachel and Leah are referenced at the close of the book of Ruth as women
who built up the house of Israel (see Ruth 1:16; 4:11).

Jubilees 33

Leah appears here when Jacob takes her to visit Father Isaac. In the *Jubilees*
version, this provides the occasion for Reuben to sneak into Billah's bed to
violate her. While Genesis does mention a specific visit by Jacob to Isaac,
there is no mention of Leah (Gen 35:27).

---

8. See "Jacob's Feelings for Leah" in the "Contemporary Scholarship" section
below.

Jubilees 36

Leah's death and burial at the special double cave is mentioned in this chapter. It explains that Jacob's sons came to support him in his time of grief. *Jubilees* also brings in new material suggesting that Jacob held Leah in high regard, a matter that is not at all clear in the Genesis account, but this is consistent with the recurring themes in *Jubilees* of contented families and little familial strife:

> And Leah, his wife, died [twenty-four years after the death of Rachel]. And he buried her in the cave of Machpelah near Rebekah, his mother, and north of the tomb of Sarah, his father's mother. And all of her children and his children went out to weep with him for Leah, his wife, and to comfort him concerning her because he was lamenting her. For he loved her very much after Rachel, her sister, died since she was perfect and upright in all of her ways, and honored Jacob. And in all the days that she lived with him he never heard a harsh word from her mouth because she possessed gentleness, peace, uprightness, and honor. And he remembered all of her deeds that she had done in her life, and he lamented greatly for her because he loved her with all his heart and all his soul. (*Jub.* 36:21–24)

Jubilees intends the reader to understand that during these two-and-a-half decades, Leah was instrumental in helping Jacob mourn the death of his own parents, Isaac and Rebekah, and sustaining him during the period of his supposed loss of Joseph. This is quite a remarkable addition in *Jubilees*, making Leah in many ways an equal wife to Rachel.[9] There are a few other references to Leah in *Jubilees*, and these are basically in terms of listing her as the mother of her seven children.

Other References in the Pseudepigrapha

Leah does appear by name in several other pseudepigraphical works, such as *Demetrius the Chronographer*, *Joseph and Aseneth*, *Pseudo-Philo*, and the

---

9. Some Jewish mystics relate to the period of Jacob's life prior to Rachel's death as exemplifying his earthly role (e.g., overtaking Esau and Laban, amassing wealth, and building his family). At the second stage of his life with Leah alone, Jacob reflects his more spiritual side, through which he ultimately develops as Israel, his God-given name (Dresner, *Rachel*, 60). Gershom Scholem describes the *Shekhinah* as having two faces: one is Rachel as the exiled one from God and lamenting, and the other is Leah as reunited with God (Scholem, *On the Kabbalah*, 149). In this way, Leah helps Jacob develop himself into Israel, the Patriarch of Israel.

Testaments of the Twelve Patriarchs. In these works, however, it is only to point out a genealogical reference, i.e., Leah was the mother of Reuben, Simeon, etc. A fragment in the work of Theodotus refers to the fact that Laban substituted Leah for Rachel.

Josephus

While the Genesis text addresses Leah's eyes (which were possibly weak, tender, lovely, or delicate), Josephus simply points out that Leah was both older and "devoid of beauty" (*Ant.* 1.19.6). He likewise makes no reference to Leah being unloved, much less hated, but rather says that Leah was "grievously mortified by her husband's passion for her sister" and therefore Leah "made continuous supplication to God" that she might bear children. When she did, Josephus explains, "her husband's affection consequently being drawn towards her" (*Ant.* 1.19.7). None of these explanations are biblically based.

The Rabbis' Leah

Leah and Rachel Were Twins

While the fact that Esau and Jacob were twins is clear, some midrashim suggest that Leah and Rachel likewise were twins: "In the hour that Rebekah gave birth to Jacob and Esau, two daughters were born to Laban" (*Midrash Tanhuma, Genesis. Wayyetse* Gen 7.20; Gen 30:22ff., Part 5).[10]

The Power of Prayer

Leah had been betrothed to Esau, but she prayed that this would not happen, and it did not. Great is the power of prayer (*Genesis Rabbah* 70.16). In this example the rabbis are not only praising prayer itself, but also more specifically the prayer of a woman. A variation of this explanation proposes that after Jacob married Leah, Rachel was supposed to be married to Esau.

---

10. A medieval midrashic text known as *Sefer ha-Yashar* also suggests that Leah and Rachel were twins (*Yashar,* Toledot 43a–43b, quoted in Ginzberg *Legends of the Jews,* 5:281 n. 71). See the *Jewish Encyclopedia* "Yashar, Sefer ha-," 12:588–89. Under the entry devoted to Rachel, the encyclopedia notes that *Seder Olam Rabbah* 2 suggests that the girls were twins. Furthermore, they were fourteen when Jacob arrived (*The Jewish Encyclopedia,* s.v. "Rachel" 10:305–7).

Jacob and Leah then prayed that this would not happen, and so that marriage was averted (*Midrash Psalms*, Ps 55.4).

Leah and Rachel Were Equally Beautiful

The rabbis often pun on words. The Hebrew words for "two" (*sh-t-y*) and for "equal" (*sh-ww-t*, from the root letters *sh-w-h*) are similar enough to allow for a midrash to explain that "Leah . . . was as beautiful as Rachel, as stated (in Gen 29:16). Laban had two (*ShTY*) daughters. They were equal (*ShWWT*) in beauty, in loveliness, and in stature" (*Midrash Tanhuma, Genesis. Wayyetse* Gen 7.12; Gen 29:31ff., Part 3).

Leah's Eyes

Genesis 29:17 comments on Leah's eyes. The biblical text says that they were *rakkot*, a word often translated as "weak," but that has many possible translations. An unnamed contemporary of Rabbi Yohanan suggests that they were weak, presumably myopic. Another view is that they had become weak because she wept so much. She wept because she thought that she was destined to marry the wicked Esau. She was the elder daughter and it would have been presumed that she would have to marry the elder son, Esau, instead of Jacob (*Genesis Rabbah* 70.16).

Pre-arranged Marriage

Another midrash suggests that the Esau-Leah marriage had been pre-arranged by their parents: "When Rebekah bore Esau [and Jacob] there were born to Laban two daughters, Leah and Rachel. They sent letters to each other and agreed among themselves that Esau would take Leah and Jacob, Rachel (*Midrash Tanhuma, Genesis. Wayyetse* Gen 7.12; Gen 29:31ff., Part 3).

Why Jacob Did Not Want to Marry Leah

In a very well-thought-out explanation, the rabbis make a case for why Jacob did *not* want to marry Leah. Following the idea that as Laban's older daughter Leah had been betrothed to Esau (Isaac and Rebekah's older son), Jacob reasoned this way:

If I marry Leah, who knows what Esau will do? He could say, "Was it not enough for you to take my birthright and my blessing, that you should take my betrothed as well!" He therefore said to Laban (in Gen 29:18) I shall serve you for seven years for <your younger daughter> Rachel. Apart from such a situation, would a man taking a wife leave the older and take the younger? because in the absence of sons, the elder daughter would receive the double portion of the firstborn (cf. Num 27:8) (*Midrash Tanhuma, Genesis. Wayyetse* Gen 7.12; Gen 29:31ff., Part 3).

Why Wedding Feasts Are a Week Long

The tradition for a week-long wedding celebration follows the custom established by the bridal week of Jacob and Leah explains a midrashic collection (*Pirke de Rabbi Eliezer* ch. 16).

Punning on Leah's Name

A midrash suggests that on their wedding night, during the darkness, local townspeople were praising Laban, calling out in exclamation, *hi leah, hi leah* (something like "hooray"). This phrase is a close homonym to the words in Hebrew "This is Leah, this is Leah" (*Genesis Rabbah* 70.19).

Like for Like . . .

In the morning, Jacob realizes that he has been duped; he married Leah, not Rachel. He turns to Leah and calls her a cheat: "The whole night he called to her, 'Rachel' and she answered him. In the morning, however, behold it was Leah. He said to her, 'You are a deceiver, the daughter of a deceiver!' She retorted, 'Is there a teacher without students, your father called you "Esau" and you answered him! [Gen 27:24] So did you call to me and I answered you!'" (*Genesis Rabbah* 70.19).

Leah Was Hated Because She Scolded Jacob

A midrash says Leah was hated because she scolded Jacob, claiming he was hypocritical. This midrash adds additional reasons to those cited in *Genesis Rabbah* 70.19. God then takes note and says the only way to solve this problem is for Leah to have sons, for then Jacob will desire her (*Midrash Tanhuma, Genesis. Wayyetse* Gen 7.11; Gen 29:31ff., Part 2).

Leah Was Hated by Many

Many held Leah in contempt: sea travelers, land travelers, and local women. They said that Leah leads a double life. She pretends to be righteous, but this is not so. If she were righteous, she would not have deceived her sister (*Genesis Rabbah* 71.2).[11]

Leah Was Hated Because Some of Her Descendants Would Be Hated Kings

The Davidic monarchy (David is a descendant of Judah, Leah's fourth son) contained some hated (i.e., evil) kings such as Jehoram, Jehoash, Ahaz, Manasseh, and others. The midrash lists these wicked kings, offering biblical quotations citing their offenses, and suggests that is why Leah was hated (*Midrash Tanhuma, Genesis. Wayyetse* Gen 7.14; Gen 29:31ff., Part 5).

The Angels Hated Leah

In the midrash collection *Midrash Tanhuma Yelammedenu*, the guardian angels ask God why Leah was to be given sons, since the descendant of one of them would be Zimri (of the tribe of Simeon). Through Zimri's perfidy, twenty-four thousand people were killed by a plague (Num 25:6–9; 14–15). God answered, "I will not deprive her of her sons (because of future generations) . . . *[God] saw that Leah was hated*" (Gen 29:31), *Midrash Tanhuma Yelammedenu, Genesis,* And He Went Out, 7.5, p. 190. Similar reasoning— that God judges people where they are, not on some future events—is found in midrashic explanations about Ishmael following the expulsion from the Abrahamic encampment (*Genesis Rabbah* 53.14).

Leah's Reward for Being Disfavored

God saw that Leah was disfavored, so as a reward her seven pregnancies were only seven months each (*Pirke de Rabbi Eliezer* ch. 36).

---

11. See "Hagar Mocks and Speaks Ill of Sarah" under "The Rabbis' Hagar" section in this volume, where a similar accusation is leveled against Hagar.

Jacob Wanted to Divorce Leah

Jacob was so upset at being deceived that he wanted to divorce Leah. Then, when she began to have children, he changed his mind. He said, "Shall I divorce the mother of these children?" (*Genesis Rabbah* 71.2). This may be an ironic contrast to Abraham "divorcing" Hagar, or an insight by the rabbis that children themselves might form a bond between parents.

Leah Originally Lacked a Uterus

Although originally infertile, God fashioned a womb for Leah so that she bore seven children: six sons and a daughter (*Genesis Rabbah* 72.1). As mentioned in our chapter on Sarah, the word for "ovary," *'ikar*, is connected to one of the words for "womb," *'ikurah mibayit*.

Endogamy: Leah's Male Children Married Their Sisters

The "daughters of Jacob were the wives of his sons. All of the seed of Jacob married their sisters and their blood-relations, so that they should not intermarry with the people of the lands, therefore they were called a true seed, as it is said, 'Yet I have planted you a noble vine, a wholly true seed' (Jer 2:21)" (*Pirke de Rabbi Eliezer* ch. 39). A variation of this is found in a different midrash collection. Each of Leah's sons was born with a female twin, whom they then married (*Genesis Rabbah* 82.8, 84.21).[12]

Exogamy

A quite different explanation about the marriage partners of Jacob's sons is found in *Midrash Rabbah*. According to Rabbi Nehemiah, the tribal ancestors married Canaanite women (*Genesis Rabbah* 84.21).

Leah's Descendants Were Heroes of Israel

A midrash highlights a number of Leah's famous descendants. Among them are Moses, a Levite, and King Hezekiah of Judah (*Genesis Rabbah* 70.15).

---

12. That such marriages are at variance with later Levitical legislation is explained below. See "Marrying Sisters" in the "Contemporary Scholarship" below.

Leah's Descendants Created Dynasties of Princes and Priests

Among Leah's descendants are the dynasty of David, through Judah, and the dynasty of Aaron, through Levi (*Genesis Rabbah* 70.15).

Leah and Rachel's Descendants Were Kings, Prophets, and Judges

What Leah produced, Rachel produced. Leah produced kings (the line of David, a descendant of Judah), and so did Rachel (Saul is a Benjaminite, and his son, Ish-boshet, ruled briefly). Leah produced prophets (Isaiah and Ezekiel), and so did Rachel (Samuel and Jeremiah). Leah produced judges (Elon and Samson), and so did Rachel (Ehud and Deborah) (*Midrash Tanhuma, Genesis. Wayyetse* Gen 7.13; Gen 29:31ff., Part 4). Elon was from the tribe of Zebulon (Judg 12:11), while Samson was from the tribe of Dan (Judg 13:2, 24).

Punning on the Sons' Names

Just as Leah and Rachel punned on their children's names when they gave birth, the rabbis also added some puns regarding Simeon, Levi, and Judah (*Genesis Rabbah* 71.4).

Leah Praises God

Leah was the first person to praise God (Babylonian Talmud *Berakhot* 7b). The rabbis base this on the line, "'This time I will praise the LORD,' therefore she named him Judah" (Gen 29:35).

Leah Is Now Satisfied, She Has Borne Four Sons

Ibn Ezra, the twelfth-century Spanish commentator, suggests that Leah's thanks is her declaration that she is satisfied with her four sons and wants no more.[13]

---

13. Quoted in Rabow, *Lost Matriarch*, 79.

Leah's Brazen Acquisition of Jacob Rationalized

Genesis 30:14–16 relates how Leah "traded" her son Reuben's mandrakes for the chance to bring Jacob to her bed. She was so anxious to do this that she did not even let him wash his feet. This kind of forward behavior on a woman's part troubled the rabbis. They explained it away by suggesting that her intent was honorable: "The Holy One, Blessed be God saw her motive was none other than to produce tribes" (*Genesis Rabbah* 72.5).

Leah's Brazen Acquisition of Jacob Condemned

As some rabbis praised Leah's demeanor when she greeted Jacob in the matter of the mandrakes, some criticized her.[14] This following example reflects the misogynist view of at least this rabbinic source, for not only is Dinah held responsible for her being raped (blaming the victim) but Leah, her mother, is also censured. Commenting on the verse "Dinah the daughter of Leah . . . went out" (Gen 34:1), this midrash observes, "Like the daughter is the mother . . . when Leah went out to meet Jacob, she dressed like a harlot" (*Genesis Rabbah* 80.1).

Leah Prays That Rachel Will Have a Son, Part 1

At one point, Leah prays that Rachel will not only conceive, but that she should bear a son (*Midrash Tanhuma, Genesis. Wayyetse* Genesis 7.19; Gen 30:22ff., Part 4).

Leah Prays That Rachel Will Have a Son, Part 2

Leah's saintliness[15] is depicted in a midrash that explains that when Rachel finally conceived, her fetus was female. In the previous verse, we are told, "Afterwards she [Leah] bore a daughter, and named her Dinah" (Gen 30:21). The word "afterwards" in this midrash is interpreted to mean that Leah prayed that her sister's fetus would be transformed into the son she was

14. In the introductory chapter, we explained that the rabbis often disagree among themselves. To say that something is *a* rabbinic view, or even *the* rabbinic view, does not mean that all rabbis support that position or that interpretation.

15. The text tells us that Jacob "loved Rachel *more* than Leah," *gam et Rachel mi-Leah* (Gen 29:30). The Hasidic Rabbi Levi Yitzhak of Berdychev (1740–1809) translates the *gam*, or "more" to mean that Jacob loved Rachel more because she brought with her Leah, the saintly one (*Kedushat Levi*, 53, quoted in Dresner, *Rachel*, 71–72).

carrying and that she, Leah, would give birth to the daughter, Dinah. Rachel then gave birth to a son, Joseph (Babylonian Talmud *Berakhot* 60a). *Genesis Rabbah* 72.6 explains that Dinah was born as a female because Rachel prayed for this outcome.

The Matriarchs Join Together to Pray for Leah

Generally, the superiority of sons over daughters is made rampantly clear throughout the book of Genesis. Exceptions exist. According to Rabbi Hanina, "All the matriarchs assembled and prayed, 'We have sufficient [*dayyenu*] males, let her [Rachel] be remembered'" in her own time, but now let Leah give birth to a daughter, Dinah (*Genesis Rabbah* 72.6). There is a pun here on the Hebrew words *dayyenu* and "Dinah."

Leah's Granddaughter Will Be Joseph's Wife

According to a midrashic source, Leah's daughter, Dinah, will give birth to Aseneth, who will become Joseph's wife (*Pirke de Rabbi Eliezer* ch. 36).

Leah Is Buried with Jacob

Mamre is Kiriyat Arba, the City of the Four. The four couples who are buried there are Adam and Eve, Abraham and Sarah, Isaac and Rebekah, and Jacob and Leah (Babylonian Talmud *Eruvin* 53a).

Targum Onqelos

While the Genesis text says that Leah's eyes were weak (*rakkot*), according to *Targum Onqelos*, they were lovely (*ya-ain*).

Contemporary Scholarship

Marrying Sisters

That Jacob marries two sisters while both are living violates later Levitical law (Lev 18:18). Sarna points out that it is clear that no "attempt was made to rewrite [this ancient narrative] . . . in conformity with the morality and law of a later age."[16] Likewise, the tradition mentioned earlier in the midrash collection *Pirke de Rabbi Eliezer*—that Jacob's sons married their sisters—would be explained in a way that the later legislation had not yet been enacted. Another issue of conflict with later Levitical legislation is similarly resolved in the book of *Jubilees*, as we will explain in our chapter on Bilhah and Zilpah. In any case, on many levels marrying two sisters simultaneously is a sure recipe for disaster. The tensions in Jacob's house must have been enormous.

Did Leah Have a Week's "Bridal Celebration" with Jacob, or Were They Married Seven Years before Rachel Became Jacob's Second Wife?

As will be explained in our chapter on Rachel, there is some debate on how long Jacob waited until he married Rachel. There is no doubt that he committed to a fourteen-year "service debt" to Laban in order to marry Rachel. But did he serve his initial seven years and then an additional week more with Leah as part of her "bridal celebration," or did he need to work another seven years before attaining Rachel as his wife? The morning after Jacob's wedding to Leah, Jacob confronts Laban. Laban then says to Jacob, "Complete the *sh'vu'a* [translated as "week" or "seven-year period"] . . . and we will give you [Rachel]." The Hebrew is ambiguous. Most modern translations follow the bridal "week" interpretation, including the NRSV, NJPS-TANAKH, the Contemporary Torah, NIV, NEB, JB, NJB, the Schocken Bible's *The Five Books of Moses*, and NAB, as well as von Rad, Speiser, and Alter. An exception is the revised edition of *The Torah: A Modern Commentary*, which, following Nahmanides, favors a period of seven years.

Seven

The number seven [*shev'a*] often is a sacred number in biblical texts and in later Judaism: seven days of the week, the Sabbath being the seventh day of the week; seven branches on the menorah; the seventh or sabbatical year; and the like. "Seven" in Hebrew contains the same letters as the word for "oath" or "swear," and so Beersheba can mean "the well of seven" or "the well of the oath." Yet sometimes it would seem to be a more generalized word, less literally "seven" than something akin to more than a handful, perhaps

16. Sarna, *Genesis*, 205 n. 28.

"several." In this context, Laban may have meant, "Work for me for a few years more."

Jacob's Feelings for Leah

Leah's relationship with Jacob is prejudiced by the way she became his wife; in effect, she was forced upon him. Consequently, she becomes the focal point for his misplaced anger, which should more appropriately be directed at Laban. The biblical text says that Leah is *s'nu'ah* (Gen 29:31). This word is translated differently. The KJV has "hated," and this word is also used in the Soncino *Midrash Rabbah* series, which used the English from the Jewish Publication Society's 1917 translation of the Bible. Alter's *Genesis* has the word "despised," while the NRSV features the word "unloved," as does Speiser, NAB, NJB, NJPS-TANAKH, and *The Contemporary Torah*. The NEB and NIV give "not loved," while the revised edition of *The Torah: A Modern Commentary* has "disfavored" and JB has "neglected," all of which are softer translations than KJV or Soncino give and, we suggest, are more accurate ways of describing Jacob's feelings for Leah.

Who Really Hates or Disfavors Leah?

The biblical text (Gen 29:31) states that Leah is hated, unloved, disfavored, or neglected. The text does not specify who feels this way toward her. It could refer to the feelings of Laban, who puts Leah in an impossible position; it could be the feelings of Jacob, who takes out his anger on Leah (who is but a pawn in this power play) because he was duped by Laban; it could be the feelings of Rachel, who would be rightfully jealous of having to share Jacob's affections and attention; or it could be any combination of these possibilities.

"Hated" or "Disfavored" May Have Sexual Connotations

Sharon Pace Jeansonne points out that the word "'hated' . . . may have connotations of sexual revulsion."[17]

---

17. Jeansonne, *Women of Genesis*, 74. See instances of where the same word is used: Amnon's feelings toward Tamar after he raped her in 2 Sam 13:15, and also legislation in Deut 22:13, 16; 24:3.

Leah's Self-Evaluation of Jacob's Feelings for Her

As noted above, in Gen 29:31, Leah is termed as *s'nu'ah* –a word that has been translated various ways. Two verses later, Leah says of herself that because God "has heard that I am . . . *s'nu'ah* [hated, despised, or neglected], [God] has given me this son also" (Gen 29:33). In this context, Jacob is the reference for this emotion. The earlier statement in Gen 29:31 is the voice of the narrator describing Leah's situation. In the thirty-third verse, she is describing what she feels personally within herself. Here again, different versions of the Bible take the exact same word, *s'nu'ah*, and in this context, offer either the same or a more nuanced translation. The KJV and Soncino's *Midrash Rabbah*: give it as "hated"; NRSV has "unloved" or "hated"; Speiser, NJPS-TANAKH, *The Contemporary Torah*, NAB, and NJB give it as "unloved"; NEB and NIV have it as "not loved"; Alter translates it as "despised"; JB gives it as "neglected", and the revised edition of *The Torah: A Modern Commentary* translate it as "disfavored" or "despised."

Leah Gives Zilpah to Jacob "as a Wife"

When Leah presents Zilpah to Jacob, the Hebrew says, "as a wife" (*l'isha*). This is the exact phrase that Sarah uses with Hagar when she presents her to Abraham as a wife, not as a concubine. This does not change the fact that Zilpah and Bilhah remain servants[18] of Leah and Rachel, respectively. Bilhah and Zilpah are secondary wives.

Leah's Eyes Were . . .

Different translations address the matter of Leah's eyes (Gen 29:17): the NRSV gives "lovely"; NIV has "weak" with an alternative reading of "delicate"; NJB gives "lovely"; NAB translates it as "lovely" with an alternative reading of "weak"; KJV gives "tender"; NEB has "dull-eyed"; JB translates it as "no sparkle"; NJPS-TANAKH and *The Contemporary Torah* give it as "weak"; the Schocken Bible's *The Five Books of Moses* has "delicate"; Speiser offers "tender" with alternative readings of "dainty" or "delicate"; Alter gives it as "tender," although he notes that this too is uncertain. Alter suggests that this wording may be meant to contrast Leah's specific positive quality as opposed to Rachel's general beauty.

18. See Sarna, *Exodus*, 120.

Were the Girls (Also) Twins?

While the text does not state so specifically, we might reasonably wonder whether Leah and Rachel were also twins, as were Esau and Jacob. In the midrash collection *Midrash Tanhuma*, it suggests the sisters were equal. All that Genesis states is that Leah was the older sister. Similar language is often used for Esau in terms of Jacob. If they were indeed twins, there would be a biblical kind of balance between the two sets of children: first, the younger twin subverts the older (as Jacob subverts Esau's primogeniture blessing); (Rachel becomes betrothed before Leah), then the older sibling subverts the younger. Leah, at least passively, subverts Rachel's plan to marry Jacob, and in this subversion Leah asserts her primogeniture right to be the first married. Esau, through his descendant Edom, attacks Judah (the country, but in a sense, the descendants of Jacob) following the Babylonian destruction of Jerusalem (Lam 4:18–21; Obad vv. 11–18).

Mandrakes

Mandrakes are part of the nightshade family, *Mandragora officinarum*. It reputedly has medicinal, magical, or even aphrodisiacal powers: "The aphrodisiac association is reinforced in the Hebrew by a similarity of sound (exploited in the Song of Songs) between *duda'im*, 'mandrakes,' and *dodim*, 'lovemaking.'"[19]

Sibling Rivalry, Sibling Cooperation

At times, Leah and Rachel are rivals; at times, they work in tandem. According to rabbinic tradition, Rachel gave Leah certain "signs" known only to Rachel and Jacob, whereby Leah could disguise that it was she, not Rachel, in the marriage bed that first night. Later, Leah "changed" the gender of her child in utero from male to female so that Rachel would birth a male child.[20] When they agree to leave Haran, they work in tandem, agreeing to separate from their father and brothers. Clearly, like all humans, the sisters are inconsistent. Sometimes they fought together, and sometimes they worked together in common cause.

---

19. Alter, *Genesis*, 160.

20. See the discussion in "Rachel Complicit in the Marriage-bed Switch" under "The Rabbis' Rachel" below and "Leah Prays That Rachel Will Have a Son" under "The Rabbis' Leah" above.

Balancing the Past

Rabow takes note of the midrash that suggests that Leah, while pregnant herself, prayed that Rachel, who had finally conceived, would bear a son, even if this meant changing the gender of their respective fetuses in utero: "According to this telling, the story of Jacob's married life in Haran, which began with the switch of Leah and Rachel in the wedding tent, now closes with the switch of the sisters' children, Dinah and Joseph, in their wombs."[21]

Feminist Thought

A Wife's Worth

"In the ancient Near East, one vital measure of a wife's worth was her ability to bear sons—to tend the fields, herd the flocks, defend land and honor, and carry on the family name. For the woman herself, unable to inherit on her own, sons represented security in her old age."[22]

These Female Heroes Name Their Heirs

"Where the male heroes seek to conquer, claim, and sanctify land, the female heroes strive to inscribe their memory on the body of their heirs; the acts of birthing and naming function as the counterpart to those of inaugurating and settling territory."[23] It is momentous that unlike Hagar, Sarah, and Rebekah, both Leah and Rachel name their own children. Abraham names Ishmael and Isaac, while an anonymous "they"—probably Isaac and Rebekah together—name Esau, and the literal Hebrew verb says, "he was named Jacob" (Gen 25:26). Only after Rachel dies does Jacob change his son's name from Ben-Oni (son of my sorrow) to Benjamin (son of [my] right hand).

Leah's Isolation and Her Longing

Leah not only names her children, but those words are "soliloquies [which] . . . underline her isolation and her longing for Jacob's affection."[24]

21. Rabow, *Lost Matriarch*, 116.
22. Frankel, Five Books of Miriam, 54.
23. Havrelock, "Central Commentary, *Vayeitzei*," 164.
24. Wenham, *Genesis 16–50*, 243.

Leah's Nightmare

The Matriarchs all face difficult situations in their lives: "In each generation of this family . . . there is a nightmare for a woman. In the first generation, Abraham gave away his wife not once, but twice [Gen 12, 20] . . . Isaac gave his wife away once [Gen 26] . . . Leah's years of being hated must have been a nightmare for her."[25] Hagar is treated badly, and later she is exiled. Rachel's inability to get pregnant was her nightmare. Neither Zilpah nor Billah's voice is ever heard, and then Bilhah is sexually violated by her stepson Reuben.

From Lament to Praise

When naming her first three sons—Reuben, Simeon, and Levi—Leah verbalizes the (unrealized) hope that Jacob will now love her. With Judah's birth (Judah means "God will be praised), Leah "makes no mention of her hope for improved relations with her husband . . . She may not enjoy her husband's affection, but God has given her four sons, and she must be grateful for that . . . here . . . [her] lament turns to praise."[26]

From Rivalry to Cooperation, Part 1

Leah and Rachel are pitted against each other; the two sisters become pawns in Laban's plan to indenture Jacob for a further seven years. Then they become rivals for Jacob's affection. In a world that valued and defined a woman's worth by her ability to bear children, Leah earns public admiration but her sister's antagonism: "The turning point in the sisters' relationship comes with their readiness to enter into an exchange—to give each what the other lacks. Symbolically, Leah is willing to give fertility (via the mandrakes [see Gen 30:14–17]) to her barren sister and, in turn, Rachel gives Jacob to Leah, who longs for his love."[27]

From Rivalry to Cooperation, Part 2

When Jacob decides to return to his homeland, he consults both of his primary wives, and they speak with one voice in their agreement (Gen 31:14–16). Indeed, "Previously the sisters have employed language as a mode of

25. Cotter, *Genesis*, 252.
26. Wenham, *Genesis 16–50*, 244.
27. Havrelock, "Central Commentary, *Vayeitzei*," 167.

competition; but here they speak with one voice, indicating their common desire and alliance with Jacob—and, implicitly, with each other."[28] One contemporary scholar underscores just how rare an occasion this is: "Jacob's wives reply [Gen 31:14–16] is extraordinary . . . they express their feelings in a way that is . . . unique in Scripture: they speak in unison."[29]

Recognizing the Rights and Power of Rachel and Leah

When, in chapter 31, Jacob decides to leave for his homeland, he has his primary wives brought to the fields, where he consults with them: "Recognizing that a break with Laban and Laban's sons at this point would put an irrevocable breach between his own immediate family and that of his wives, Jacob solicits their agreement." Jacob relates the way their father has mistreated all of them, and "Rachel and Leah, for the first time speak in a united voice . . . It is appropriate that they disown their father in the formulaic words that are reminiscent of other important family ruptures in the Hebrew Bible, 'Do we yet have a portion or inheritance in our father's house?'"[30] Since this was a patriarchal society, Jacob could have simply told his wives they were leaving. His solicitation of their cooperation marks his respect for their power and position within his immediate family structure.

Conception Requires Intimacy with Both Humans and God

> Genesis acknowledges that conception issues from sexual relations. But the subtext . . . indicates that its success requires intimacy not only between a man and a woman but also between a woman and God. Following the birth of a child, the mother encodes the memory of her specific path from barrenness to fertility in the name that she bestows as a legacy to her child.[31]

For example, when she names her firstborn son, Reuben, Leah says, "Because the LORD has looked on my affliction; surely now my husband will love me" (Gen 29:32). When she gives birth to her second son, Simeon, she

---

28. Ibid., 171.

29. Cotter, *Genesis*, 234.

30. Jeansonne, *Women of Genesis*, 80. See 1 Kgs 12:16 and 2 Chron 10:16. Niditch points out that the sisters "describe themselves in their relationship to their father as exploited and dispossessed slaves, treated as foreign women unrelated to him" (Niditch, "Genesis," 39).

31. Havrelock, "Central Commentary, *Vayeitzei*," 157.

says, "Because the LORD has heard that I am hated, [God] has given me this son also" (Gen 29:33). Later, when she names her son Joseph, Rachel will say, "God has taken away my reproach . . . may the LORD add to me another son!" (Gen 30:23–24).

The Problematic Ethics of Surrogacy

Just as Sarah did, first Rachel and then Leah "offer" their maidservants to their respective husbands to serve as surrogate wombs. It "is deeply problematic that the matriarchs potentially force their servants into undesired sexual relations."[32]

Birthing Is a Collective Effort between Women

> In biblical narrative, birth is a moment of female collaboration when the boundaries between distinct bodies collapse, an occasion in which multiple female bodies operate in tandem. All females on the narrative stage at the moment of birth function as a collective body absorbed in the process and implication of birthing.[33]

* * * *

Summary and Conclusion

Leah and her younger sister, Rachel, are part of the third generation of Matriarchs. Leah is Jacob's first wife but not the woman he intended to marry. Jacob will have four concurrent wives: Leah, Rachel, Bilhah, and Zilpah. They give birth to at least thirteen children—twelve sons and a daughter. The twelve sons become the eponymous ancestors of the twelve tribes of Israel. Leah is the mother of six sons and one daughter: Reuben, Simeon,

---

32. Ibid., 166. A counter-argument is that a concubine/wife gained enormous status when she "married" the master. Tsevat explains, "the honor of bearing a child to the master would probably have satisfied most slave women and compensated them [through their higher status] for any contingent deprivations" (Tsevat, "Hagar and the Birth," 55). See the cultural context of such legalized surrogate motherhood in Speiser, *Genesis*, 119–21; Sarna, *Understanding Genesis*, 127–29; Sarna, *Genesis*, 119 comment on v. 2; Sarna, *Exodus*, 120; Matthews and Benjamin, *Old Testament Parallels*, 48f., 110.

33. Havrelock, "Central Commentary, *Vayeitzei*," 166. See Gen 35:17–18; 38:29; 1 Sam 4:19–22; Ruth 4:17.

Levi, Judah, Issachar, Zebulon, and Dinah. She offers an explanation for her sons' names. Leah gives Jacob her handmaid, Zilpah, who bears him Gad and Asher. The Leah-Jacob-Rachel triangle is fraught with (understandable) tensions. In time, the two sisters appear to make peace with each other; they work in concert with Jacob when it is time to leave their homeland at Haran. Both Rachel and Leah predecease Jacob. Only Leah is buried with Jacob at the family sepulcher at Machpelah in Hebron/Kiriyat Arba.

In the early extra-biblical literature, the themes of endogamous marriages and contented families are seen in the sections in *Jubilees* that mention Leah. Conflict may be present, but it is played down or sanitized. Nonetheless, the *Jubilees* translation suggests that Leah was "hated" as opposed to a softer word. *Jubilees* says Leah's eyes are weak but then continues that like her sister, Leah's "appearance was very beautiful." *Jubilees* does not explain the sons' names, but it offers the exact dates on which the sons were born. Zebulon and Dinah, Leah's sixth and seventh children, are twins born on the same day. Leah dies nearly twenty-five years after Rachel. She helps Jacob mourn the death of his own parents, Isaac and Rebekah, and sustains him during the period of his supposed loss of Joseph. Leah, in many ways, is an equal wife to Rachel.

According to some rabbinic sources, Leah and Rachel were twins. After Jacob married Leah, Rachel was supposed to be married to Esau. Jacob and Leah prayed that this would not happen. Leah and Jacob were evenly matched. On the morning following their wedding night, Jacob realizes that he has been duped; he turns to Leah and calls her a cheat. He says to her, "You are a deceiver, the daughter of a deceiver!" She retorts, "Is there a teacher without students, your father called you 'Esau' and you answered him! So did you call to me and I answered you!"

Jacob wanted to divorce Leah. Then, when she began to have children, he changes his mind. He said, "Shall I divorce the mother of these children?" Leah has famous descendants, including Moses, a Levite, and King Hezekiah of Judah. Leah was the first person to praise God.

Contemporary scholars point out that Leah's relationship with Jacob is prejudiced by the way she became his wife, for she was effectively forced upon him. Consequently, she becomes the focal point for his misplaced anger, which more appropriately should be directed at Laban. The biblical text (Gen 29:31) states that Leah is "hated," "not loved," "unloved," "disfavored" or "neglected." It does not specify who feels this way toward her. It could be Laban, who puts her in an impossible position; it could be Jacob, who takes out his anger on Leah (who is but a pawn in this power play); it could be Rachel, who would be rightfully jealous of having to share Jacob's affections and attention; or it could be any combination of these possibilities. Unlike

Hagar, Sarah, and Rebekah, the two sisters name their own children. When Jacob decides to leave for his homeland, he has his wives brought to the fields, where he consults with them. Since this was a patriarchal society, Jacob could have simply told his wives they were leaving. His solicitation of their cooperation marks his respect for their power and position within his immediate family structure.

In conclusion, Leah is the first wife in the third generation of Matriarchs. Although she will give birth to (at least) seven of Jacob's children—six sons and a daughter—Genesis, at least initially, describes her as "unloved," "hated," or "despised." Jacob, understandably angry about the bridal switch, appears to vent his resentment on Leah. After many years of sisterly rivalry, Leah and Rachel end up working in tandem to help Jacob extricate his family from Laban's influence as they head for Jacob's homeland. *Jubilees* does not obscure the difficult role that Leah plays in the family dynamic, at least over the initial years of their marriage. Later, she and Jacob have a good relationship. The rabbis' opinions of Leah are quite mixed. Some suggest that she was hated or despised by many groups, and she is likewise criticized for her brazen behavior in the matter of the mandrakes. Other rabbis commend Leah and take note of her famous descendants. In gynecologic terms, according to some midrashim, Leah, like the other primary Matriarchs, lacks ovaries or a womb, which is then created by God. Contemporary scholars puzzle over the true meaning of what it means for Leah to be "unloved," "hated," "despised," or "neglected," and they propose a variety of answers beyond just her husband's feelings. Likewise, the nature of Leah's eyes elicits various answers. Feminist scholars take note that Leah as well as Rachel name their own children.

We turn now to the life of Rachel in Genesis, in early extra-biblical writings, rabbinic literature, contemporary scholarship, and feminist thought.

6

Rachel

Biblical Rachel

Introducing Rachel

RACHEL IS MARRIED TO Jacob. Along with her older sister, Leah (and the maidservants Bilhah and Zilpah, who are also Jacob's wives), she is the third generation of the Matriarchs in terms of Jewish (and Christian) tradition. Rachel is born, grows up, and lives most of her married life in Haran. Located in the wider area of Aram-Naharaim in what today would be southeast Turkey or northwest Syria near the upper Euphrates River, Haran at various points is also called Paddan-aram. Rachel is Jacob's favorite wife. She is the woman he intended to marry and for whom he pledged seven years of labor to his future father-in-law, his uncle Laban. As explained in our chapter on Leah, Laban replaced Rachel with Leah in the bridal tent, a fact that Jacob only realized the morning after his wedding night. Rachel will give birth to two of Jacob's children, Joseph and Benjamin. She dies following Benjamin's birth and is buried on the road to Ephrath (alternately, Ephrata or Ephratha), which is Bethlehem. The relationship between Rachel, her husband Jacob, and her sister, Leah, is complicated. Initially, and for many years, there is a great deal of expected tension, especially between the sisters. Nonetheless, over the next dozen-plus years they spend in the women's homeland, the family members appear to eventually reconcile their individual issues to work in tandem with Jacob for the good of their ever-growing family.

Genesis 29: Rachel Meets Jacob
and Becomes His (Second) Wife

Rachel first appears as a major figure in chapter 29. In the preceding chapter, which takes place in Beersheba, there is an oblique note that back in the ancestral homeland of Paddan-aram, Rebekah's brother Laban has fathered daughters. Isaac's instructions to Jacob are to go there, some five hundred or so miles to the north, and marry one of his cousins: "Go at once . . . and take as wife from there one of the daughters of Laban, your mother's brother" (Gen 28:2). Even prior to this, at the close of Gen 27 Rebekah had instructed Jacob, in order to avoid Esau's anger, to "flee at once to my brother Laban in Haran, and stay with him a while until your brother's fury turns away . . . and he forgets what you have done to him" (Gen 27:43–45).

When Jacob arrives at the vicinity of Haran, he sees a well in the field with a large stone covering it. He also sees a number of flocks surrounding it. The text explains that when the flocks were gathered, several people working together would roll the stone off of the mouth of the well. He makes inquiries with some of the local shepherds, seeking to learn from where they hail. They explain that they are from Haran. Jacob then inquires if they know Laban (grand)son of Nahor, and whether all is well with him. The shepherds reply affirmatively and note that Laban's daughter Rachel is coming with some sheep (Gen 29:4–6). Jacob clearly wants to make contact with Rachel, but he wants to do so more privately. He urges the shepherds to water their flocks and then pasture them somewhere else. They reply that their general practice is for all the flocks to be gathered and then, following the work of moving the large stone, the flocks are watered. When Jacob sees his cousin Rachel, he not only moves the stone from the well's mouth by himself (presumably a feat of great strength) but he then waters his uncle's flocks himself (vv. 7–10). Although it is not specifically stated, the inference is that the other shepherds have also watered their flocks and moved on to pasture them. At this point, Jacob goes up to Rachel and kisses her, after which he announces their kinship.[1] He weeps aloud, presumably with a combination of relief at having arrived safely at his stated destination, but also with happiness in having linked up with his relatives. Jacob explains that he is family, the son of Rebekah, Rachel's father's sister. Rachel then runs home to tell her father this news (vv. 11–12). Laban comes to greet Jacob and invites him to dwell with them. After about a month, he asks Jacob what he would like by way of wages. The text mentions that while Laban had two daughters, it was "Rachel [who] was graceful and beautiful" (Gen 29:17). The narrator then explains that Jacob loved Rachel. Jacob says to Laban that he would serve his uncle for seven years in order to marry Rachel. Jacob has come to Haran without bringing gifts for a dowry price; he therefore needs to earn his keep: "So Jacob served seven years for Rachel, and they seemed to him

---

1. A man kissing a woman in the Bible in public is unique, with the exception of perhaps "Let him kiss me with kisses of his mouth" (Song 1:2). "If Jacob kissed her, can we not assume that Rachel allowed herself to be kissed?" (Dresner, *Rachel*, 34).

but a few days because of the love he had for her" (v. 20). Then Jacob goes to his uncle Laban to arrange the wedding. Laban gathers the people for a feast. In the dark of the night, however, Laban substitutes Leah for Rachel, and Jacob makes love to Leah, thinking she is Rachel. In the morning when he finds he has been duped, Jacob furiously confronts Laban, accusing him of deceit. Laban explains that local custom dictates that the older daughter is always married before the younger. He also tells Jacob that if he commits to working for an additional seven years, he can marry Rachel as well. Laban then says, "When you complete the seven [days? years?] you can marry Rachel." Most translators and commentators understand this to mean that after Jacob completes the seven-day bridal festivities with Leah, then he can marry Rachel. Another possibility is that Jacob, while still married to Leah, will need to complete his additional seven years of servitude *before* he can marry Rachel.[2]

Whether he married Rachel a week or seven years after wedding Leah, eventually the couple is united. That Jacob served a total of fourteen years is not in dispute. The text mentions in passing that at this time, Laban gave his maid Bilhah to Rachel to serve as her maid (Gen 29:29). The narrator likewise explains that Jacob "loved Rachel more than Leah" (Gen 29:30). The next verse notes that because Leah was unloved, God "opened her womb"—a biblical phrase meaning she was able to get pregnant—but that Rachel remained childless. In short order, Leah bears four sons, each time giving them names that express her hopes for a better relationship with Jacob, or her acceptance of her role as mother.

Genesis 30: Rachel's Plight; Surrogate Motherhood; The Mandrake Bargain; Rachel's Pregnancy; Jacob Prospers

This chapter commences immediately after Leah's first four children are born and named, as Rachel enviously views the fertility of her older, less-loved sister. With pathos, Rachel turns to Jacob and says, "Give me children, or I shall die!" (Gen 30:1). Surprisingly, Jacob responds in anger instead of with sensitivity. He replies that he is not God; he is not the one who has withheld fruit from her womb. In desperation and sorrow, Rachel takes her maid, Bilhah, and offers her to Jacob as a substitute for herself—a surrogate womb: "'Here is my maid Bilhah; go in to her, that she may bear upon my knees and that I too may have children through her.' So she gave him her maid Bilhah *as a wife* [*l'ishah*]" (Gen 30:3–4). Bilhah conceives,

---

2. See the discussion in "Seven or Fourteen Years? How Long Did Jacob Work before Marrying Rachel?" in the "Contemporary Scholarship" section below.

twice. Similar to the pattern with Leah, Rachel gives each surrogate child (Dan, then Naphtali) a name that connects to her situation. Their naming underscores her need for motherhood.[3]

- For Dan, Rachel says, "'God has *judged* me, and has also heard my voice and given me a son'; therefore she named him Dan" (v. 6). The root letters of the word "Dan" contain the same Hebrew root letters as the word for "judged," *dalet nun*.

- For Naphtali, Rachel says, "'With mighty *wrestlings* I have *wrestled* with my sister, and have prevailed,' so she named him Naphtali" (v. 8). The root letters of the word "Naphtali" contain the same Hebrew root letters as the word for "wrestled," *peh tav lamed*.

Some years later at the time of the wheat season, Reuben, Leah's oldest son, finds some mandrakes in the fields and brings them to his mother. It is evident that the sisters, although rivals for Jacob's affections and presence, are living in close proximity. Rachel sees the mandrakes and says to Leah, "Please give me some of your son's mandrakes." As explained in our chapter on Leah, mandrakes were thought to have aphrodisiacal, medical, and even magical powers. Apparently Rachel believes that if she had access to some of these flowers, she might become pregnant in her own right. Leah responds, reflecting her bitterness with their situation and her disquiet with both Jacob and Rachel: "Is it a small matter that you have taken away my husband? Would you take away my son's mandrakes also?" Rachel is desperate and concedes Jacob's presence, offering what she can in this bad bargain: "Then he may lie with you tonight for your son's mandrakes" (Gen 30:14–15). As explained in our chapter on Leah, Leah claims her prize and becomes pregnant with her fifth son, Issachar. Before long she will become pregnant again with Zebulon, and then their daughter, Dinah. Following the mandrake bargain, some years seem to pass. Finally, Rachel becomes pregnant: "God remembered Rachel, and God heeded her and opened her womb. She conceived and bore a son" (vv. 22–23).

As in the parallel situations with Leah and her biological and surrogate sons, and Billah's sons (Rachel's surrogate children), Rachel names her son and contextualizes his name with her existential situation.

- Rachel says, "'God has taken away my reproach'; and she named him Joseph, saying 'May the LORD *add* to me another son!'" (vv. 23–24). The root letters of the word "Joseph" contain the same Hebrew root letters as the word for "add," *yud samekh feh*.

3. Dresner, "Rachel and Leah," 152–53.

Jacob then goes to Laban and says that he wants to return to his home-land. The rest of the chapter deals with Laban's attempt to defraud his son-in-law/nephew and details the ways in which Jacob outwits Laban and is able to prosper despite Laban's efforts: "Thus the man [Jacob] grew exceed-ingly rich, and had large flocks, and male and female slaves, and camels and donkeys" (v. 43).

Genesis 31: Plans to Head out for Jacob's Homeland; Rachel's Theft of Her Father's Teraphim, or "Household Gods"

Tensions are arising in the relationship between Jacob and Laban, as well as between Jacob and Laban's sons. Fortunately, this is matched by the ap-parent fact that tensions between the sisters are subsiding. Jacob sends for his primary wives, bringing them out to the fields. There he laments the situation in which they find themselves. Jacob points out that Laban has cheated him (which really means that Laban has shortchanged all three [or five] of them and their children) and accuses Laban of changing his wages ten times. Nonetheless, Jacob continues, "God did not permit him to harm me [us]" (v. 7). Jacob goes on to explain that he had a visitation from an angel of God telling him to return to the land of his birth. Implicit in his words is that Jacob desires his wives' cooperation in leaving their home-land and heading out to his family in Canaan. The women, speaking with one voice for the first time, quickly agree. As explained in our chapter on Leah, both of Jacob's wives are resentful of the callous, uncaring way they and their families have been treated. They consider Laban to be rapacious and greedy. The sisters see greater gains in leaving than in staying. Rachel and Leah reply, "Is there any portion or inheritance left to us in our father's house? Are we not regarded by him as foreigners? For he has sold us, and he has been using up the money given for us. All the property that God has taken away from our father belongs to us and to our children; now then, do whatever God has said to you" (Gen 31:14–16). In short order, the family is on its way from Paddan-aram to Canaan. Jacob and his entourage cross the Euphrates, heading south toward the hill country of Gilead. Laban learns of their flight and gives chase, accompanied by his own family kin. A week later, they catch up with the travelers. The night before the confrontation, God appears to Laban with a warning, "Take heed that you say not a word to Jacob, neither good or bad" (v. 24). Since Laban reports these very words to Jacob when they finally meet, it is clear that the older man does not take God's words literally, although he may have taken them seriously.

What is particularly irksome to Laban is that someone has stolen his household gods—the *teraphim*.[4] Laban goes on at length about how he would have feted his children and grandchildren with song and music before they left. He then concludes his tirade with what is really on his mind: the purloining of his household gods. Laban suspects Jacob, but Jacob is innocent of this theft. Since Jacob feels that he is in the right and that Laban is being duplicitous *yet again*, he claims his innocence. Thinking that this will be an empty promise he can make without fear of repercussion, he says that the life of the person with whom those gods are found is forfeit. Jacob has no idea that, in fact, it is Rachel who has stolen her father's property. Filled with self-righteousness, Jacob invites Laban to look throughout his camp. In an attempt to retrieve the stolen goods, Laban conducts a thorough search. Finally he comes to Rachel's tent. The next two lines in the text describe what happens:

> Now Rachel had taken the household gods and put them in the camel's saddle, and sat on them. Laban felt all about in the tent, but did not find them. And she said to her father, "Let not my lord be angry that I cannot rise before you, for the way of women is upon me." So he searched, but did not find the household gods. (Gen 31:34–35)

As to the question of whether Rachel was speaking truthfully or if there were other implications to her words, see the appropriate comments in the "Contemporary Scholarship" and the "Feminist Thought" sections below. When Laban comes up empty-handed, Jacob feels completely vindicated, so he berates his father-in-law/uncle for Laban's mean-spirited and churlish behavior. The two men ultimately conclude a treaty of non-aggression, and each party leaves on its way.

Genesis 32: Before Meeting Esau

In this chapter, Jacob learns that his older brother, Esau, is aware of his return. Esau is coming to greet them, accompanied by four hundred men. Jacob takes defensive action. In his fear and distress, Jacob divides his family into several sections. He places the maids and their children at the front, then Leah and her children, and finally Rachel with their son, Joseph. He places himself last of all. He thinks to himself, "If Esau comes to the one company and destroys it, then the company that is left will escape" (Gen

---

4. See the discussion under 'Teraphim or 'Household Gods'" in the "Contemporary Scholarship" section below.

32:8). That Jacob places Rachel and Joseph in the most protected position addresses his family priorities, indicating that he continues to favor their lives above the rest his family. This is followed by the nighttime encounter with the stranger, through which Jacob earns his new name, Israel.

Genesis 33: Actually Meeting Esau

At the final moment, Jacob goes alone ahead of all of his wives and children, making obeisance to Esau. To Jacob's surprise, Esau welcomes him and his retinue. Jacob's family—first the maids and their children, then Leah and her children, and then Rachel and Joseph—each come and bow before Esau in their turn.

Genesis 35: Rachel's Pregnancy, Death, and Burial

Rachel does not appear in chapter 34. At the beginning of chapter 35, God tells Jacob to go to Bethel and settle there. In that area around Bethel, Deborah, Rebekah's nurse, died and was buried at Allon-bacuth. Shortly afterwards, God appears again to Jacob and bestows an additional name upon him: Israel. God also promises Jacob a brilliant future. (This is a different source for Jacob's additional name. The first source comes in Gen 32, the episode of the famous night-wrestling.) The family then leaves Bethel for Ephrath, which according to the nineteenth verse is Bethlehem. While they were still some way from their destination, Rachel, who is pregnant, goes into labor. With her last breath, Rachel names her son, calling him Ben-oni, meaning "Son of my sorrow." Jacob, however, renames his son Benjamin, "Son of the right hand" (vv. 16–18). Jacob buries Rachel there, sets up a pillar over her tomb, and then journeys on to the area of Eder. The biblical text does not address the question of why Jacob does not take Rachel's body the short distance south from the place of her death to the cave at Machpelah, a proper burial site for members of Abraham's family. A number of midrashim offer suggestions for why Rachel is buried where she is, as will be discussed in "The Rabbis' Rachel." The chapter concludes with several important details: Reuben sexually violated his stepmother Bilhah; a listing of Jacob's sons in terms of their respective mothers; Jacob reunited with Isaac at Mamre; and that following their father's death, Esau and Jacob buried Isaac at the family sepulcher. Rachel will be mentioned again in chapter 46 in terms of her sons and her maidservant, Bilhah, as well as in chapter 48, when Jacob refers to her death. The other references to Rachel are a geographic mention of her tomb (1 Sam 10:2); Jeremiah's allusion to Rachel as Mother Israel weeping for her children as they are exiled to Babylon (Jer 31:15); and finally in the book of Ruth, where alongside her older and more prolific sister, Leah, Rachel is offered as the example of someone who built up the house of Israel (Ruth 4:11).

Early Extra-Biblical Literature's Rachel

Jubilees

The broad outlook and various emphases of *Jubilees* have been mentioned in previous chapters.

Jubilees 28

Rachel is first mentioned in *Jub.* 28. *Jubilees* ignores completely the scene by the well where Jacob initially encounters Rachel. Instead, Jacob meets Rachel, and then he is with his uncle Laban. After a period of seven years he demands Rachel as a wife. The *Jubilees* version of Laban's switching Leah for Rachel and his explanation to Jacob is dealt with in our chapter on Leah, as is *Jubilees'* comments about the physical qualities of the two sisters.

Jubilees 29

Leah and Rachel appear together in this part of *Jubilees*, as was covered in our chapter on Leah. *Jubilees* mentions that Jacob left Mesopotamia without telling Laban and that Laban then gave chase. Nothing is mentioned here about Rachel's theft of the household *teraphim* or "household gods," much less how Rachel duped her father. Likewise, the confrontation with Esau is completely ignored, as is Jacob dividing his camp into sections and sending Leah and her children to greet Esau before Rachel and her son. *Jubilees* states simply that the brothers met and were reconciled (*Jub.* 29:13). This is very consistent with *Jubilees'* typical downplaying of family conflict.

Jubilees 31

In the opening verses of Gen 35, God tells Jacob to move to Bethel, settle there, and to set up an altar. By way of preparation, Jacob instructs his family to get rid of the foreign gods they had with them. They respond to his request: "So they gave to Jacob all the foreign gods that they had, and the rings that were in their ears; and Jacob hid them under the oak that was near Shechem" (Gen 35:4). In *Jubilees*, the family heads out to Bethel at Jacob's orders. They also rid themselves of the foreign objects. It is at this point that *Jubilees* mentions the stolen idols, but there is no reference to Laban's unsuccessful search or to Rachel's deceptive behavior. More specifically here, Rachel brings these images to Jacob, and he destroys them: "And they handed over the strange gods and what was on their ears and what was on their necks and the idols which Rachel stole from Laban, her father, and she gave everything to Jacob, and he burned it and crushed it and destroyed it and hid it under an oak which was in the Land of Shechem" (*Jub.* 31:2).

Jubilees 32

Towards the close of this chapter, the family is at a place called the land of Kabratan. They dwell there, and Rachel, who is pregnant, gives birth at night. In the final verses of this chapter, *Jubilees* repeats much of the Genesis record, but then, as with his older brothers, it adds the specific day that Benjamin was born. "And Rachel bore a son in the night and called him 'son of my sorrow,' because she suffered when she bore him, but his father called him Benjamin, on the eleventh of the eighth month in the first year of the sixth week of that jubilee. And Rachel died there and she was buried in the land of Ephrata, i.e., Bethlehem. And Jacob built a pillar on the tomb of Rachel, on the road above her tomb" (*Jub.* 32:33–34).

Jubilees 33

As noted in our chapter on Leah, this is where it is reported that Reuben sexually violated his stepmother, Bilhah, Rachel's attendant. It also refers to Rachel as the mother of her two sons.

Jubilees 34

This chapter reflects the narrative of Gen 37. Instead of repeating Joseph's arrogance and the conflicts between the brothers, it instead offers a pastiche of verses similar to the battle of the five monarchs versus the four monarchs in Gen 14. *Jubilees* does report that Joseph's brothers sell him to Ishmaelite merchants going to Egypt and that the brothers falsely tell Jacob about finding Joseph's bloodied garments. The news of Joseph's reputed death so devastates the family that both Bilhah and Dinah die. They are then buried near to Rachel:

> And on that day Bilhah heard that Joseph had perished and she died while mourning for him. And she was dwelling in Qafratef. And Dinah, his daughter, also died after Joseph perished. And these three lamentations came upon Israel in a single month. And they buried Bilhah opposite the tomb of Rachel, and they also buried Dinah, his daughter, there. (*Jub.* 34:15–16)

There are a few other references to Rachel in *Jub.* 44, but these are in terms of listing her as the mother of her children.

The Testaments of the Twelve Patriarchs

The *Testaments of the Twelve Patriarchs* (the twelve sons of Jacob) with its subsection, the *Testament of Issachar*, is part of the Pseudepigrapha.[5]

The Testament of Issachar

The first two chapters of the *Testament of Issachar* refer to the mandrakes episode in Gen 30, but then it embroiders on the biblical text. According to this testament, Reuben had brought in two pieces of this fruit from the field, but Rachel took them from him. In a new translation of the text, the mandrakes are defined as "fragrant apples" (*T. Iss.* 1:5).[6] Leah objected, and the sisters argued. Then Leah was mollified when Rachel gave one back to her, keeping one for herself. The bargain was that Leah would have Jacob as a bed partner that evening—an act that resulted in the birth of Issachar. The second chapter explains that Rachel then bargained with Leah for the second mandrake in exchange for Leah spending a second night with Jacob. God saw that Rachel's desire for the mandrakes was rooted in her wish to have children by Jacob; it was not lustfulness on her part (*T. Iss.* 2:1–3). Consequently, God saw to it that Rachel would have two sons. The text then explains that although Rachel desired the mandrakes, she did not actually eat them. Instead, she offered them "to the priest of the Most High, who was there at that time" (*T. Iss.* 2:5).

---

5. *Testaments of the Twelve Patriarchs: The Testament of Issachar*, the fifth son of Jacob and Leah.

6. Kugel, "Testaments of the Twelve Patriarchs," 1772.

The Testament of Joseph

The *Testament of Joseph* is a subsection of the *Testaments of the Twelve Patriarchs.*[7] Joseph, upon his deathbed, instructs his sons to take "your mother Aseneth to the road of Ephrat, and bury her next to Rachel your mother," understanding Rachel as their maternal ancestor (*T. Jos.* 20:3).

Josephus

Josephus retells the story of Rachel and Jacob by expanding on the Genesis text using flowery language. Unlike *Jubilees,* which ignored the romantic descriptions concerning the search for a wife for Isaac, Josephus adds indulgent details about how Jacob and Rachel met. He explains that upon seeing Rachel, Jacob was immediately smitten: "Jacob was not so much moved by their relationship or the affection consequent thereon, as overcome with love for the maid; he was amazed at the sight of beauty such as few women of those days could show" (*Ant.* 1.19.4). Jacob then gives a long-winded recitation of the family connections between them, mentioning Abraham and Sarah as well as Isaac and Rebekah and Rachel's kin as well. Rachel, upon hearing these family connections, is the one who weeps and embraces Jacob. In Genesis, it is Jacob who weeps and kisses Rachel. Jacob's initial meeting with Laban is likewise greatly expanded upon in the Josephus text. Jacob tells Laban that he wants to marry Rachel. Laban wants Jacob to remain in Haran because Laban "would not send his daughter among the Canaanites; indeed he regretted that his sister's [Rebekah's] marriage had been contracted over there" (*Ant.* 1.19.6). As explained in our chapter on Leah, Josephus does report that Laban placed Leah and not Rachel in the wedding tent. As in Genesis, Jacob agrees to another seven years of labor in order to acquire Rachel. In Josephus' account, Jacob first works the additional period and then marries Rachel. "*After the lapse of seven years more* he won Rachel" (*Ant.* 1.19.6, emphasis added).

The various pregnancies are noted, as well as the puns on the sons' names. The mandrake episode is also featured in Josephus similarly to its description in Genesis. In the Josephus account, Jacob does consult with his wives, although here they are not mentioned by name. Josephus, however, includes at this point Rachel's theft of the *teraphim*: "Rachel, taking with her even the images of the gods which the religion of her fathers made customary to venerate, escaped along with her sister and the children of both wives,

7. *Testaments of the Twelve Patriarchs: The Testament of Joseph, the eleventh son of Jacob and Rachel.*

the handmaids with their sons, and their possessions" (*Ant.* 1.19.8). Josephus adds explanations for Rachel's actions—words that are not supported in the biblical text. In the biblical text, one assumes Rachel either wants to use the images as a bargaining chip with her father, or perhaps to pray to them to protect herself and her family. Josephus explains, "Rachel, who carried the images of the gods, had indeed been taught by Jacob to despise such worship, but her motive was that, in case they were pursued and overtaken by her father, she might have recourse to them to obtain pardon" (*Ant.* 1.19.8). The eventual confrontation between Jacob and Laban is much expanded, but Laban's visit to Rachel's tent in search of the household images is fairly similar to the Genesis account. When Laban came to her, she had "deposited the images in the pack-saddle . . . and sat upon it, professing to be incommoded by the functions natural to women" (*Ant.* 1.19.10). Later, we learn that Jacob "lit upon the gods of Laban, being unaware that Rachel had stolen them; these he hid in the ground beneath an oak at Sikim [Shechem]" (*Ant.* 1.21.2). That chapter also mentions Rachel's death in childbirth and her burial at Ephrata. Josephus conflates the Genesis account in terms of Jacob naming his son. The reason for the name comes from Rachel's words, but it is Jacob who names his son: "He called the child whom she bore Benjamin because of the suffering which he had caused his mother" (*Ant.* 1.21.3). Josephus, at this juncture, specifically mentions Rachel in terms of her being Joseph's mother, a point not found in Gen 37 (*Ant.* 2.1.1).

Joseph and Aseneth

As noted earlier in the sections on Sarah and Rebekah, Aseneth is compared favorably to those Matriarchs, and in addition, she is said to be beautiful like Rachel.

The Rabbis' Rachel

Rachel's Arrival at the Well Foreshadows Future Events

Rachel's connection with her cousin Jacob at the well at Haran foreshadows Jeremiah's reference to Rachel weeping as her children are exiled to Babylon (Jer 31:15). Just as the family was reunited earlier, so too will the family of Rachel (the exiles) be reunited in the land of Israel at a future time (*Genesis Rabbah* 70.10).

Rachel Was Safe to Mingle with the Other Shepherds

A midrash explains that in the olden days, people used to lead chaste lives; therefore, Rachel did not need to worry for her virtue but could intermingle with the male shepherds (*Numbers Rabbah* 20.9).[8]

Rachel Lived in a Godly Environment; Consequently, She Was a Virtuous Woman

Another midrash offers a variation on the ideas previously suggested. Here a differentiation is made between the locale in which Rachel grew up and that of Zipporah. Rachel and Zipporah, as well as Zipporah's sisters, were all shepherds. In the latter case, even though there were several women, the local shepherds harassed them. No one bothered Rachel because, unlike Zipporah in Midian, she lived in a righteous environment, which translated itself to Rachel herself and protected her (*Genesis Rabbah* 70.11).

Public Displays of Affection

The rabbis discourage public displays of affection, especially such displays between the sexes. They make an exception with Jacob kissing Rachel in public because this is kin kissing kin (*Genesis Rabbah* 70.12; *Exodus Rabbah* 5.1).

Both Leah and Rachel Are on Jacob's Mind

When Laban offers to pay Jacob wages (at half their worth), Jacob replies that he has come to Haran "only for the sake of your two daughters" (*Genesis Rabbah* 70.14).

Leah and Rachel Were Twins, Part 1

The Jewish Encyclopedia, in its entry on Rachel, quotes *Seder Olam Rabbah* 2, which suggests Leah and Rachel were twin sisters and furthermore that they were fourteen when Jacob arrived.[9] Sforno explains that the seven

---

8. A variation of this appears in *Midrash Tanhuma, Numbers. Balaq* Numbers 7.8 Numbers 22:2ff., Part 8. Both examples refer to Rachel and to Moses' wife, Zipporah, who also shepherded sheep.

9. *The Jewish Encyclopedia*, s.v. "Rachel" 10:305–7.

years Jacob agreed to work for Rachel both allowed her to attain marriage-able age, but also time for Laban to find a spouse for Leah (comment on Gen 29:18).

Leah and Rachel Were Twins, Part 2

As noted in our chapter on Leah, according to rabbinic tradition, Leah and Rachel were twins and were born at the same time as Esau and Jacob (*Midrash Tanhuma, Genesis. Wayyetse* Gen 7.20; Gen 30:22ff., Part 5).

Rachel Complicit in the Marriage-bed Switch

The rabbis praise Rachel. When she warned Jacob that her father might try to cheat him by replacing her with Leah, Jacob gave Rachel some secret signs to indicate, while in the darkness of the marriage tent, that it was really her. When Rachel saw that her fears were realized, she decided that she did not want her sister to be humiliated; hence Rachel gave Leah the appropriate signals, thereby becoming complicit in the deception but showing filial kindness (Babylonian Talmud *Baba Batra* 123a). Another version of Rachel's complicity is found in *Midrash Rabbah*. Here Rachel not only gives Leah the signals, she literally lies under their bed and speaks the words while Leah remains silent (*Lamentations Rabbah* Proem 24).

When Did Jacob Marry Rachel?

Although most medieval commentators, including Rashi and Abraham ibn Ezra, suggest that Jacob married Rachel following the week of bridal festivities for Leah, Naḥmanides suggests Jacob worked the additional seven years and *then* married Rachel. Laban says in Gen 29:27 that Jacob is to wait out the *sh'vu'a* before he marries Rachel. This could be seven days, or it could be seven years.[10]

Rachel Almost Married Esau

As noted in our chapter on Leah, Rachel was scheduled to marry Esau (*Midrash Psalms*, Ps 55.4).

---

10. See "Seven or Fourteen Years? How Long Did Jacob Work *before* Marrying Rachel?" in the "Contemporary Scholarship" section.

Rachel's (Eventual) Descendants Were Heroes of Israel

The midrash holds up several of Rachel's descendants. Among them are the judge Gideon, who was from the tribe of Manasseh, Joseph's son; and Mordecai, who was of the tribe of Benjamin (*Genesis Rabbah* 70.15).

Rachel's Descendants Had Temporal Power for a Limited Time

Joseph and Saul (a Benjaminite) all held temporal office but did not leave a dynasty (as did Aaron and David, who are both descendants of Leah) (*Genesis Rabbah* 70.15).

Rachel Was Not Childless, She Was Special

The Hebrew of Gen 29:31 says that Rachel was childless, or *'aqarah*. Do not read this as *'aqarah*, but as *'iqar*—(the midrash puns), special or the chief person of the house (*Genesis Rabbah* 71.2).

Rachel Envied Leah

Genesis locates Rachel's envy of Leah in her sister's pregnancies. A midrash says she envied Leah's good deeds, reasoning that were Leah not righteous, why would she bear children? (*Genesis Rabbah* 71.6).

"Give Me Children, or I Shall Die."

Rachel laments to Jacob, "Give me children, or I shall die" (Gen 30:1). The rabbis confirm that one who is childless is as if dead (Babylonian Talmud *Nedarim* 64b).

Jacob Reprimanded

When Rachel laments to Jacob, he is very terse with her, saying "Am I in the place of God?" (Gen 30:2). This draws God's ire, and God criticizes Jacob, saying, "Is that a way to answer a woman in distress?" God then goes on to tell Jacob that at a future time, Jacob's very own children will stand before a descendant of Rachel, who will say to them, "Am I in the place of God?"

(Gen 50:19). This refers to Joseph's statement to his brothers in Egypt (*Genesis Rabbah* 71.7).

Why Rachel Gave Bilhah to Jacob

Building upon the Genesis text, the midrash reports additional dialogue between Rachel and Jacob when he dismisses her plaint. He suggests to Rachel that she should act as his grandmother Sarah had, namely by giving him her maid to wed in order to produce surrogate sons. She agrees to this plan and gives Bilhah to Jacob. In the words of the midrash, Rachel says to Jacob, "What did [Sarah] do?" He explains, "She brought her rival into her home." Rachel then says, "If that is the obstacle, behold my maid Bilhah, go into her . . . And I may be built up through her" (Gen 30:3; *Genesis Rabbah* 71.7).

Rachel's Thinking

The sixteenth-century Italian biblical commentator and physician Obadia Sforno interprets Rachel's hope in terms of a biological process. In his view, Rachel's statement, "I shall obtain children by her," or *'ibbaneh . . . mimenah*—literally, "I will be built up by her," which is the same expression used by Sarah in terms of Hagar (Gen 16:2)—expresses Rachel's wish that the jealousy she expects to feel for Billah will stimulate her own reproductive system so that it will function normally.[11] As an editorial note in the volume on Sforno listed in the bibliography explains, the word "through her" or "from her," *mimenah*, is taken by Sforno to mean that Rachel understands this quite literally: "From Bilhah's ability to conceive and give birth to a child whom I will raise, the functioning of my reproductive system hopefully will be aroused."[12]

Rachel Feels Both Condemned and Vindicated

When Bilhah gives birth to Rachel's surrogate son, Rachel names him Dan, a pun on the word "judge." The midrash offers the thought that Rachel feels that God has judged her and condemned her (Rachel's childlessness), but also that she has been divinely judged and vindicated (which results in her claiming a child, her stepson, Dan) (*Genesis Rabbah* 71.7).

11. Sforno, *Commentary on the Torah*, 158 comment on Gen 30:3.
12. See ibid.

Rachel Criticized for Slighting Jacob

As explained in our chapter on Leah, Leah is both praised and condemned for her brazen behavior greeting Jacob in the mandrakes episode. Rachel is criticized for her behavior, which slights Jacob. This is given as the reason she was not buried with her husband. Rachel is buried near Ephrath (Ephrata), while Jacob is buried at the ancestral burial ground at Machpelah (Gen 35:19–20; 50:13; *Genesis Rabbah* 72.3).

God Remembered Rachel

God remembered Rachel, and she became pregnant (Gen 30:22). God did this in response to Rachel's own prayers, as well as those uttered by Leah and Jacob on her behalf. God also allowed Rachel to get pregnant for the sake of the Matriarchs (*Genesis Rabbah* 73.3). Additional reasons why God remembered Rachel were that she remained silent even though she knew that Leah would be substituted for her, and furthermore that she gave Bilhah to Jacob, thereby consciously setting up another rival for Jacob's affection (*Genesis Rabbah* 73.4).

Jacob Inadvertently Caused Rachel's Death

When Laban came to seek his stolen household gods, in all innocence Jacob said, "Anyone with whom you find your gods shall not live" (Gen 31:32). This judgment then was applied to Rachel (*Genesis Rabbah* 74.4; *Ecclesiastes Rabbah* 10.5.1).

Rachel Apologizes to Her Father; She Cannot Rise Before Him

Nahmanides questions Rachel's statement that she cannot arise before her father. Surely, he writes, women who are menstruating can rise and stand. His explanation is that in ancient days, women who were menstruating were kept very isolated, and that Laban respected this custom.

Rachel's Real Reason For Stealing
The Household Gods, Part 1

A midrash suggests that the real reason Rachel stole the household gods was to deprive her father of the opportunity for idol worship (*Genesis Rabbah* 74.5).

Rachel's Real Reason For Stealing
The Household Gods, Part 2

Another midrash takes a different view: "*Now Rachel had taken the teraphim . . . Why did she steal them?* To prevent them from informing Laban that Jacob had fled with his wives, his sons, and his flock. Do *teraphim* actually speak? They do indeed, as it is written: *The teraphim have spoken vanity* (Zech 10:2)" (*Midrash Tanhuma Yelammedenu, Genesis*, 7.12, And He Went Out, p. 198). This midrash also explains that alternatively, she wanted to eradicate idolatry from her father's house.

Rachel Was One of Three Women to Die in Labor

In addition to Rachel, the wife of Phinehas (Samuel's son) as well as David's wife Michal, die in labor (1 Sam 4:19 ff.; 2 Sam 6:23). The midrash understands Michal to have died in labor; she had no child until the day of her death (*Genesis Rabbah* 82.7).

Rachel Gave Birth to Twins

Benjamin, Rachel's son, had a twin sister (*Midrash Tanhuma, Hayye Sarah. Gen 5* 5.10 Gen 25:1ff., Part 4; *Genesis Rabbah* 82.8ff.). The one exception to a tribal leader being born with a twin was "Joseph, whose partner was not born with him, for Aseneth, the daughter of Dinah, was destined to be his wife." The reason for mentioning these twin sisters is to allow the sons of Jacob to marry their half-sisters rather than intermarry with the people of the land (Gen 24:3; *Pirke de Rabbi Eliezer* ch. 36).

Why Rachel Was Buried at the Road to Ephrata

Jacob foresaw that many years in the future, his descendants would be exiled from their homeland. They would pass by the spot of Rachel's death. He buried her there so that she would ask for mercy on their behalf (*Genesis Rabbah* 82.10ff.). A variation on this idea suggests that Jacob wanted to bury Rachel at the family tomb at Machpelah in Hebron. God, however, specifically directed Jacob to bury her at the road to Ephrata, at Ramah, because the future exiles from Jerusalem would "embrace the tomb of Rachel" and ask mercy from God (*Pesikta Rabbati, Piska* 3.4).

Rachel Pleads Successfully with God for Her Children

In a proem, or introductory section, to the book of *Lamentations Rabbah*, Jeremiah calls upon Abraham and Moses to plead for mercy for the exiles from Jerusalem. They do so, but God refutes their claims. Finally, Rachel arises and makes her case. Then God relents and says, "For your sake Rachel, I will restore Israel to their place" (*Lamentations Rabbah* Proem 24). A variation of this midrash suggests the same teaching and then offers an additional thought through a play on words. Do not read Rachel [*resh ḥet lamed*], but rather *Ruaḥ 'El* [*resh vav ḥet 'alef lamed*], the "Spirit of God," that is, Rachel caused the Spirit of God to weep for the exiles (*Tanna Debe Eliyyahu, Eliyyahu Rabbah* ch. [30] 28, ER p. 148 [pp. 325–26]).

Rachel Associated with the Shekhinah, God's Feminine Presence

According to the *Zohar*, when in a future time, the *Shekhinah* will return with Israel's exiles, they shall come to Rachel's tomb. Then, "Rachel, who lies on the way, will rejoice with Israel and with the *Shekhinah*" (*Zohar, Vayishlah,* 2.175a–b).

Jacob Grieves for Rachel

Jacob said, "Rachel's death was a greater grief than all the misfortunes which befell me" (*Genesis Rabbah* 97—MSV. See also *Pesikta Rabbati, Piska* 3.4).

The Four Primary Matriarchs Compared to the Lulav

At the autumn harvest festival of *Sukkot* (Booths), the Bible dictates that people are to rejoice with four species: the fruit of the Hadar tree, palm branches, leafy trees, and willows of the brook (Lev 23:40). In Jewish tradition, the Hadar tree is equated with a citron, the *etrog*. These four species, known collectively as the *lulav*, are each connected to one of the primary

Matriarchs. The Hadar tree connects to Sarah because God honored (*hidderah*) her with old age. The palm branches symbolize Rebekah. Palm trees have edible fruit as well as prickles. Rebekah had two sons—one righteous, one wicked. The boughs of leafy trees connect to Leah, who was fecund with children. Finally, the willow wilts before the other species, just as Rachel died earlier than all the other Matriarchs (*Leviticus Rabbah* 30.10).

The Importance of Rachel

"Rabbi Simeon ben Yoḥai stated as follows: Because so many matters of moment in Israel's past go back to Rachel, therefore the children of Israel are called by her name: *Rachel weeping for her children* (Jer 31:15). They are not only called by her name, but by her son's name" and her grandson's name (with references to Amos 5:15, where they are called Joseph, and to a line in Jer 31:20, where they are called Ephraim) (*Pesikta de Rab Kahanah, Piska* 20.2.)

Targum Onqelos

In chapter 30 of the Genesis text (Gen 30:17 with Leah, and Gen 30:22 with Rachel), God listens (*sh'ma*) to the woman and she becomes pregnant. In both of these verses, *Onqelos* uses different terminology, namely the phrase that God *accepted* their prayers (*qabil tzlota*).

Contemporary Scholarship

Watering Flocks

When Jacob first meets Rachel, he draws water for the flocks she is bringing to the well. This action is reminiscent of Rebekah, Jacob's mother, who draws water for the stranger who has come to Paddan-aram with a large entourage. In both cases, the act of drawing water for the animals is unsolicited (Gen 24:19–20; 29:9–10).

Negotiating for Rachel

As explained in our chapter on Rebekah, daughters were considered part of their father's responsibility, certainly in terms of approving and arranging details concerning the daughter's marriage. As noted in that chapter, "In the societies of the ancient Near East, a woman's sexuality was generally under the control of a man in her family. A father controlled his daughter's sexuality, and a husband his wife's. The marriage of a young woman was a matter of negotiation and financial arrangements between the groom and . . . the father or leading male of the bride's family."[13]

The Bed-trick: A Literary Trope or Plot Device

The bed-trick is a literary trope or plot device that involves a sex act with someone who the person in question thinks is someone else. The most common form is a man having an assignation with a woman but then finding out that someone else has been substituted in her place. This is a universal phenomenon found throughout the literature of many cultures.[14]

Seven or Fourteen Years? How Long Did Jacob Work before Marrying Rachel?

Most biblical translations suggest that Jacob worked seven years before he married Rachel. Or did he work fourteen years? What did Laban say to Jacob the morning after the subterfuge? The dower or bride-price for Rachel was another seven years of unpaid labor, to which Jacob agreed. The question is whether Laban told Jacob to honor the "week" of his wedding celebration with Leah, and then he would give him Rachel as a wife, or whether Laban told Jacob to first work another seven years, and then he would give Jacob Rachel as a wife. The Hebrew is ambiguous. The term used is *sh'vu'a*, which means "week" but could in this context mean "a week of years."

The revised edition of *The Torah: A Modern Commentary* explains why it favors the idea of seven years. It understands

> *sh'vua* (usually denoting seven days) to mean seven years (as in Daniel 9:24–27). According to this translation (following Nachmanides), Jacob must first serve seven more years before he can marry Rachel. However, other medieval and modern

13. Hackett, "1 and 2 Samuel," 156.
14. Doniger, *Bedtrick*, 164–65.

interpreters following Rashi and ibn Ezra, understand Laban to stipulate that Jacob will wait out "this [bridal] week" and then may marry Rachel, thus obtaining his beloved "on credit" and paying off it in seven yearly installments.[15]

In reading *sh'vu'a* as an additional seven years *before* marrying Rachel, this translation also reflects Josephus' understanding of this situation.

Be Careful for What You Ask

There is an adage, "Be careful for what you ask, for you may get it. You may not get it when you want it, and you may not want it when you get it." In Gen 30:1, Rachel says to Jacob, "Give me children, or I shall die." Years later, she gives birth to Joseph, but when she gives birth to Benjamin, she dies because of complications (Gen 35:16–19).

Rachel Passed on Her Good Looks to Joseph

Both Rachel and Joseph are described as having wonderful physical qualities. Rachel is termed *y'fat to-'ar v'yafat mar-'eh* (Gen 29:17), translated in NRSV as "graceful" and "beautiful." Joseph is termed *y'fey to-'ar vifey mar-'eh* (the masculine equivalents, Gen 39:6), translated in NRSV as "handsome" and "good-looking."

Who Names the Children?

In the first generation, Abraham and Sarah, it was the Patriarch who named his children (Gen 16:15; 21:3). Technically, God told Hagar what her son's name would be, but it was Abraham who named him Ishmael. In the second generation, Isaac and Rebekah, both parents name their children (Gen 25:25–26). In the third generation, Leah and Rachel the primary mothers name their biological and adoptive children (Gen 29:32–35; 30:6, 8, etc.), although Jacob then changes the name of his twelfth son to Benjamin.

---

15. Plaut, *Torah: A Modern Commentary, Revised Edition*, 198. This newly revised translation differs from the 1981 edition of this work, which favored the bridal week explanation.

Rachel and Jacob as Doubles

The narrative of Rachel and Jacob "is the Torah's greatest love story. In it the lovers—Rachel and Jacob—figure as doubles. Their lives are in many ways parallel. Each of them works as a shepherd, flees from home, steals a father's legacy, contends with siblings and God alike, tricks others and is in turn tricked, and bargains for the blessing of having children."[16]

Selling His Daughters

When Rachel and Leah agree to leave Haran, they characterize their father as having sold them:

> The language of [Gen] 31:15 is very strong. Though men are said to acquire wives with the verb that often means "to buy," nowhere else in the Hebrew Scriptures is a proper marriage described as a father's selling (*makar*) his daughters . . . Thus, bitterly, and poignantly, the daughters of Laban describe themselves in their relationship to their father as exploited and dispossessed slaves, treated as foreign women unrelated to him . . . The sisters' complaint is a remarkably critical statement by women about their treatment and status.[17]

Teraphim, or "Household Gods," Part 1

These household gods, at least in the case of Laban,

> were small enough to be hidden under a saddle. Their use reflects the custom in Aram, and perhaps they were similar to the numerous figurines, many of them of deities, found throughout the Near East. Other passages indicate that *teraphim* were used in divination (Ezek 21:21; [21:26 H]; Zech 10:2). Their use is condemned in 1 Sam 15:23 and 2 Kgs 23:24.[18]

16. Havrelock, "Central Commentary, *Vayeitzei*," 157.
17. Niditch, "Genesis," 39.
18. Curtis, "Idol, Idolatry," 3:379.

Teraphim, or "Household Gods," Part 2

A body of thought links *teraphim* "with clan leadership or inheritance rights,"[19] perhaps something like household deeds. This offers another reason why Rachel stole these items—to protect the interests of her own family:

> Rachel was in a position to know, or at least to suspect, that in conformance with local law her husband was entitled to a specified share in Laban's estate. But she also had ample reason to doubt that her father would voluntarily transfer the images as formal proof of property release . . . tradition remembered Rachel as a resolute woman who did not shrink from taking the law—or what she believed to be the law—into her own hands.[20]

Willful Defilement, Part 1

Rachel's secreting the appropriated teraphim reflects a powerful message.

> In light of Israelite notions of purity and impurity, as set forth in Leviticus 15:19–24, the description of Rachel's act constitutes . . . an attitude of willful defilement and contemptuous rejection of the idea that Laban's cult objects had any religious worth.[21]

Willful Defilement, Part 2

Given the fact that the "ancients widely regarded menstrual flow as a potentially contaminating substance,"[22] Rachel is more than merely punishing her father for his past perfidy by appropriating these items; she is actively defiling them because she and he believe that they do have religious worth.

Rachel's Anger

There is another, psychological level to Rachel's sitting on the camel saddle with the *teraphim* secreted underneath her, claiming that she had her menstrual period. Rachel is understandably furious with her father for his lack of filial support for her and her family. There are the slights over the years.

19. Havrelock, "Central Commentary, *Vayeitzei*," 172.
20. Speiser, *Genesis*, 250.
21. Sarna, *Genesis*, 219.
22. Ibid.

Yet Rachel's anger goes back further. It has been well over a dozen years since the bait-and-switch of Leah's wedding night. Just as Laban had deprived her of something she deeply valued—her fiancé, Jacob—so now it is payback time: she is depriving Laban of something he deeply values, his household gods, signs of leadership, or property deeds.

Is Rachel Pregnant?

Sometime after this encounter, Rachel gives birth to Benjamin (Gen 35:16–18). If Rachel were pregnant with Benjamin at the occasion of Laban's visit, which seems possible, it is unlikely that she would be menstruating.

Feminist Thought

Rachel Was a Shepherd

The Bible draws attention to Rachel's occupation.

> The first description of Rachel does not emphasize her beauty—as is sometimes the case when a female character is introduced (Rebekah, Gen 24:16; Abigail, 1 Sam 25:3; Bathsheba, 2 Sam 11:2). Rather, it declares her occupation. Rachel's very name means "ewe."[23]

Beauty Is Dangerous for Women

Rachel is described as beautiful. In terms of beauty, in "the Hebrew Bible it is dangerous for women. Abram charges that Sarai's beauty threatens his life ([Gen] 12:11–12), and Amnon rapes Tamar supposedly because of her beauty (2 Sam 13) . . . Samson marries a Philistine woman because of her appearance (Judg 14:1–3), and the results are disastrous."[24]

Struggles between Sisters Contextualized

In the biblical period, bearing sons was highly valued.

---

23. Havrelock, "Central Commentary, *Vayeitzei*," 162.
24. Schneider, "Another View, *Vayeitzei*," 176.

The struggle between Rachel and Leah clearly arises from a context of patriarchal structures and expectations. The narrator presents a society that determines the value of women by the number of sons that they bear . . . these women are desperate to become pregnant and bear sons in order to have the esteem of both men and women.[25]

"Un-wholeness"

Neither Rachel nor Leah understands herself to be a complete person.

The problem for Rachel and Leah is indeed one of un-whole-ness. Neither are allowed to be whole persons. From the beginning they were introduced to us only as parts, as though neither were complete in herself (29:16–17) . . . each woman possesses something the other does not . . . Rachel is the wife, the lover, the one desired by her husband. Leah is the mother, the "other," and fertile to a fault, it seems. They each want to be the other. Rachel may have her husband's love but what she really wants is children . . . Leah, on the other hand, has plenty of children, sons . . . [but what] Leah wants, however, is her husband's love . . . She, like Rachel, is caught in a vain attempt to change her life.[26]

Imitative Magic

When Rachel offers Bilhah to Jacob as a surrogate womb for herself, she has multiple reasons for doing this. First, she will then "adopt" the child as her own. Second, she hopes that this will somehow help Rachel herself to become pregnant: "Rachel performs a kind of imitative magic in which she plays the Deity—causing a woman to conceive in the hopes that the Creator will likewise fertilize her."[27]

25. Jeansonne, *Women of Genesis*, 79.
26. Fewell and Gunn, *Gender, Power, and Promise*, 78.
27. Havrelock, "Central Commentary, *Vayeitzei*," 166.

Women Making Choices for Men as a Kind of Subversive Activity

"The mandrakes incident [Gen 30:14–16] includes the information that the women could decide which of them would have sex with their husband."[28] In this instance, the two sisters make decisions about their rights concerning reproduction. They claim their own power in the realm of their sexuality: "Leah gives her sister the fruit that fertilizes (cf. the fruit of the tree that gave sexual knowledge in Gen 2) while Rachel sends her the husband. This encouraging story rests on the efforts the two women accomplish to break out of the narrow limits set by their father and husband. The exchange is thus thoroughly subversive."[29]

Rachel Delighted

When Bilhah gives birth to her son Dan, Rachel feels that she is justified in her decision to offer her maidservant as a substitute womb: "Unlike Sarah (cf. 16:5–6, 21:9–13), Rachel is delighted by the new baby [Bilhah's son Dan, who Rachel "adopts"]. This is divine vindication; 'God has vindicated me' (*dananni*) is a play on the boy's name, Dan."[30]

Did God Forget Rachel?

What does it mean that God "remembered" Rachel?

> Why is it written: "Now God remembered Rachel" (30:22)? Why had God forgotten her? . . . God never forgot her! When Rebecca, Rachel, and [Sarah] had difficulty conceiving, it was Ha-Rahaman, the Womb-of-the-World, who intervened . . . In each case, the Torah uses a different verb to describe God's intercession: God *visited* (*pakad*) Sarah (21:1); *responded* to Isaac's plea (*ye-ater*) to help his wife conceive (25:21); and here "God remembered [*va'yizkor*] Rachel; God heeded [*va-yishma*] her and opened her womb" (30:22).[31]

28. Huwiler, *Biblical Women*, 13.

29. Bal, *Lethal Love*, 85.

30. Wenham, *Genesis 16–50*, 245.

31. Frankel, *Five Books of Miriam*, 59. The word *Ha-Rahaman*, generally translates as "the Merciful One"; it shares a similar root meaning with the word *rehem*, or "womb."

Stealing the Teraphim: Power Issues

As a woman in that society, Rachel did not have the same overt rights or power as the men in her family, including her husband, father, or brothers. Consequently, she acts in such a way as to circumvent the law: "Rachel steals the *t'rafim* because her status as a woman in a patriarchal household prevents her from confronting her father with her own grievances about her rightful inheritance. Therefore she goes about getting justice from her father through devious and extra-legal means."[32] As another commentator explains, "Laban's paternal and therefore male authority—an authority related to his ownership of his household gods—is undermined by his female offspring's clever exploitation of that which makes her most markedly female. Covert woman's power in this one brief scene dominates man's overt authority."[33]

"Strategies of the Disempowered"

A different view makes a similar point in even more direct language. It also draws our attention to a detail about the story, one that plays on the common phrase of being in charge when one is "in the saddle":

> Rachel hides [the *teraphim*] . . . in a camel cushion and sits on them . . . Unlike the men in her family—father, brothers, husband, son—who can negotiate power directly, through physical struggle, bargaining, or covenant, Rachel as a woman can only resort to indirect means. In this case, she relies upon the camouflage of menstrual taboo. In so doing, she escapes the harness of social control and places herself in the saddle.[34]

Mixed Motives

David W. Cotter points out that it "is not entirely clear why Rachel takes [her father's *teraphim*]. It may be as simple as an act of spite against her father; it may be an act where she derogates Laban's gods as powerless to help him; she may also be laying claim to her share in Laban's wealth."[35]

---

32. Lapsley, "Voice of Rachel, 238, quoted in Zierler, "Contemporary Reflection, *Vayeitzei*," 179.

33. Niditch, "Genesis," 40.

34. Frankel, *Five Books of Miriam*, 63.

35. Cotter, *Genesis*, 234.

Rachel's Angry and Ironic Words

When Laban enters Rachel's tent, she does not rise before him, pleading that he will understand since she is in the way of women: "Rachel's plea that Laban not be angry is profoundly ironic considering how angry *she* is with *him*."[36]

A Discourse of Resistance

Rachel's words

> reveal something true both about the inequity of her own situation in the context of the story and that of women in ancient Israelite culture more generally. Beyond possessing mere descriptive power, however, Rachel's words also constitute a discourse of resistance, a subtle protest against the patriarchal discourse and social structures that attempt to silence her.[37]

Rachel's speech has three levels of meaning. She deceives her father by claiming she is menstruating; she is asserting that in the world in which she lives, women do "not have access to the same legal process" that men do; and therefore, she "has chosen extra-legal means to get justice,"[38] all of which she asserts in her statement that this is "the way of women" in which she finds herself.

Rachel, Jacob, and Naming Benjamin

Rachel dies in childbirth, but she names her son. Jacob changes his name:

> Appropriately, Rachel names her son Ben-oni, meaning "son of my anguish" (35:18). After her death, Jacob renames the child Benjamin, meaning . . . "son of my right hand" (35:18) . . . This renaming should not be seen as an example of Jacob's encroachment on Rachel's right to name her son but should be interpreted as a sign of hope. Indeed, Jacob expresses his love for Rachel even in death. He sets up a monument to her.[39]

---

36. Lapsley, "Voice of Rachel," 238, emphasis in original.
37. Ibid., 234.
38. Ibid., 243.
39. Jeansonne, *Women of Genesis*, 85.

A Life of Disappointment

Judith Z. Abrams suggests that Rachel's life was one of disappointment. She asks, "Was [Rachel] . . . a passive and frustrated person, seen as an object by those who supposedly loved her? . . . Rachel's story is one of disappointment, desperation and indifference of others to her needs." Does Rachel ever desire anything other than Jacob's child? Yet, after giving birth to Joseph, she immediately finds him insufficient. She then dies giving birth to her second son, Benjamin. The text says that either Rachel, or the midwife on her behalf—for the words are ambiguous—names the boy Ben-oni, "son of my sorrow" (Gen 35:18).[40]

Rachel's Voice at Ramah

Rachel is buried at Ramah, on the road to Ephrata. She then pleads for the exiles from Jerusalem in the sixth century BCE: "The Jewish people will be restored from exile because of a woman who, in the midst of incredible rivalry, put sisterhood above all else" by stepping aside and allowing Leah to marry Jacob first.[41]

Rachel: An Image of Motherhood

There is yet another twist that surfaces from the Rachel story. Rachel, who spent most of her life childless and died young in childbirth, is ultimately transformed into an image of motherhood. Her tomb remains a pilgrimage, a landmark (1 Sam 10:2), and a testimony to her. Indeed, Rachel's tomb continues to be a site associated with women facing fertility issues.[42]

* * * *

Summary and Conclusion

Rachel is married to Jacob and is his favorite wife. Along with her older sister, Leah, who is Jacob's first wife (and the maidservants Bilhah and Zilpah, who are also Jacob's wives, albeit secondary wives) she constitutes part of the third generation of the Matriarchs. She is born, grows up, and lives most

40. Abrams, "Rachel," 213.
41. Antonelli, *Image of God*, 79.
42. Sered, "Rachel's Tomb," 9.

of her married life in Haran. Jacob pledges seven years of labor to his future father-in-law, his uncle Laban, as a bride-price for Rachel. For a long time Rachel remains childless, but then she bears two of Jacob's children, Joseph and Benjamin. When the family leaves Haran, unknown to Jacob, Rachel takes her father's *teraphim*, or household gods. When Laban searches for his property, he cannot find them, for Rachel is sitting on them. Some time later, shortly after giving birth to Benjamin, Rachel dies and is buried near Ephrath, which is Bethlehem.

In the early extra-biblical literature, *Jubilees* ignores the scene by the well when Jacob first encounters Rachel. The *Jubilees* version of Laban's switching Leah for Rachel and his explanation to Jacob is dealt with in our chapter on Leah, as is *Jubilees'* comments about the physical qualities of the two sisters. *Jubilees* effectively deletes Rachel's theft of the *teraphim*, or household gods, as depicted in Genesis. In the *Antiquities of the Jews*, Josephus retells the story of Rachel and Jacob. He adds romantic details of how they met. Josephus expands the initial meeting between Jacob and Laban. Josephus reports on the bridal switch and Jacob's pledge to provide another seven years of labor in order to acquire Rachel: "*After the lapse of seven years more* he won Rachel." Josephus mentions Rachel's theft of the *teraphim* and adds words not supported in Genesis. In the section related to Joseph, Josephus specifically mentions Rachel in terms of her being Joseph's mother, a point not found in Gen 37. In *Joseph and Aseneth*, Aseneth's beauty is compared to that of Rachel.

The rabbis connect Rachel and Jacob's first meeting with Jeremiah's reference to Rachel weeping as her children are exiled to Babylon (Jer 31:15). Just as the family was reunited earlier, so too will the family of Rachel, the exiles, be reunited in the land of Israel at a future time. Leah and Rachel were twins born at the same time as Esau and Jacob. Rachel warned Jacob that her father might try to cheat him. Jacob gave Rachel secret signs to indicate that it was really she. Rachel did not want Leah humiliated, so she gave Leah the appropriate signals, thereby becoming complicit in the deception but showing filial kindness. Rachel has distinguished descendants, including Gideon and Mordecai. Finally, God is pictured as indifferent to the sufferings of the exiles from Jerusalem until Rachel arises and makes her case.

Contemporary scholars note the parallels between Rebekah and Rachel and their presence in the drawing of water for strangers. The bed-trick is a literary trope that involves a sex act and a mistaken identity; it is found throughout the literature of many cultures. Later, concerning the *teraphim*, Rachel is more than merely punishing her father for his past perfidy by appropriating these items; she is depriving Laban of something he deeply values. Feminists point out that in the mandrakes incident, the two sisters make decisions about their rights concerning reproduction. They claim their own power in the realm of their sexuality. Likewise, Rachel's appropriating and holding on to the *teraphim* shows that women's covert power is more than a match for men's overt power. Regretfully, much of Rachel's life is facing one sorrow after another.

In conclusion, Rachel is Jacob's favored wife, the woman for whom he pledged his time and efforts. He had met her at the community well in Haran and had fallen in love with her instantly. Nonetheless, Genesis is clear that their marriage also has times of turbulence, especially when Rachel finds it impossible to become pregnant. Rachel is the more daring of the sisters: she bargains with the rights to Jacob's company, and she is willing to steal her father's *teraphim* when she thinks this is in her family's best interests. While *Jubilees* offers a less romantic but also a less conflict-driven view of Rachel, Josephus embroiders on the Genesis text. Here Rachel kisses Jacob, while in Genesis the opposite it true. The rabbis' Rachel is praised in many ways, not the least being that she steals the *teraphim* as a way to wean Laban from his idolatrous practices. Contemporary scholars note that Jacob and Rachel are similar in many ways. They also speculate on the story behind the story of why she steals and then defiles the *teraphim*. Feminist scholars have written about Rachel's anger and the irony of her words, noting that, regretfully, much of Rachel's life was a series of disappointments.

We turn now to the lives of Bilhah and Zilpah in Genesis, in early extra-biblical writings, rabbinic literature, contemporary scholarship, and feminist thought.

7

Bilhah and Zilpah

Biblical Bilhah and Zilpah

Introducing Bilhah and Zilpah, the Secondary Matriarchs

SARAH, REBEKAH, LEAH, AND Rachel are the primary Matriarchs of the people of Israel. They are joined by Bilhah, Rachel's attendant and then, presumably concurrently, both Jacob's secondary wife and Rachel's attendant. They are also joined by Zilpah, Leah's attendant and then, presumably concurrently, both Jacob's secondary wife and Leah's attendant.[1] Bilhah is the birth mother of Dan and Naphtali, just as Zilpah is the birth mother of Gad and Asher. Both Bilhah and Zilpah are part of the extended household, and they will eventually accompany the family to Canaan. As the biological mothers of Dan, Naphtali, Gad, and Asher, these women are also Matriarchs of the tribes of Israel, although secondary Matriarchs. This family dynamic, whereby a secondary wife is also a primary wife's attendant or servant as well as the birth mother of surrogate children, is fraught with emotional and psychological complications and charged with potential conflicts.

Genesis 29: Bilhah and Zilpah Are Introduced and Become Leah and Rachel's Maidservants

Mention of Zilpah precedes that of Bilhah. When Leah marries Jacob, Laban gives her a maidservant, Zilpah, as an attendant in her own right (v. 24). When Jacob eventually marries Rachel (whether it is a week after he marries Leah, or seven years later) Laban gives his maidservant Bilhah to Rachel as an attendant in her own right (v. 29).

1. "Zilpah and Bilhah, however, are legitimately Jacob's wives (albeit subordinate to Leah and Rachel); they become concubines, who in the ancient word typically had certain legal rights when they bore sons for a household" (Ahearne-Kroll, "Joseph and Aseneth," 2570). See also Sarna, *Exodus*, 120.

Genesis 30: Rachel Gives Bilhah to Jacob "As a Wife"; Leah Gives Zilpah to Jacob "As a Wife"

When Rachel sees that she is unable to bear children, she gives her maid-servant, Bilhah, to Jacob "as a wife" (v. 4). Rachel appoints Bilhah as her (i.e., Rachel's) surrogate womb. She says to Jacob, "'Here is my maid Bilhah; go in to her, that she may bear upon my knees and that I too may have children through her.' So she gave him her maid Bilhah as a wife; and Jacob went in to her" (vv. 3–4). In short order, Bilhah gives birth to Dan and then to Naphtali. As explained in our chapter devoted to Rachel, Rachel names and claims these surrogate sons as her own. Some time later, Leah believes that she has stopped being able to bear children. She then turns to Jacob and offers Zilpah "as a wife": "When Leah saw that she had ceased bearing children, she took her maid Zilpah and gave her to Jacob as a wife" (v. 9). Not long thereafter, Zilpah births first Gad and then Asher. As explained in our chapter on Leah, Leah claims these surrogate sons as her own and names them herself (vv. 10–13).

Genesis 35: Bilhah's Stepson Reuben Sexually Abuses Her

Bilhah is next mentioned in chapter 35, when the narrator notes that Reuben, Jacob's first son, defiles his stepmother's bed. The possible reasons for his action will be discussed in the "Contemporary Scholarship" section below. The relevant Genesis text relates: "While Israel lived in that land, Reuben went and lay with Bilhah, his father's concubine; and Israel heard of it" (v. 22). The Hebrew term used here is not *'isha*, "wife," but rather *pilegesh*, "concubine." As Sarna notes, "Only here is Bilhah so called. The term has sociolegal implications within the context of the situation described."[2] Bilhah's name comes up again at the end of this chapter in a genealogical reference with her sons.

Genesis 37, 46, and 1 Chronicles 7: Further References to Bilhah

Here again, as in the latter part of chapter 35, the references to Bilhah are in terms of her being the mother of her sons.

---

2. Ibid., *Genesis*, 245. These implications will be discussed in the "Contemporary Scholarship" and "Feminist Thought" sections. We use there the word "violated," although others would use the word "rape." In the biblical context, this appears as forcible, non-consensual sexual intercourse. See Gravett, "Reading 'Rape.'"

Genesis 37 and 46: Further References to Zilpah

Here, as in the latter part of chapter 35, the references to Zilpah are in terms of her being the mother of her sons.

Early Extra-Biblical Literature's Bilhah and Zilpah

Jubilees

Jubilees' emphases and outlook are discussed in previous chapters.

Jubilees 28

In this chapter, *Jubilees* not only notes that Bilhah was given to Rachel as a maidservant or attendant, but also that Bilhah is Zilpah's sister. Laban "gave to Rachel, Bilhah, the sister of Zilpah, as an attendant" (v. 9). Earlier, the text had explained that Laban gave Zilpah to Leah. Laban "gave to her Zilpah, his handmaid, as an attendant" (v. 3). As in Genesis, in *Jubilees* both Bilhah and Zilpah produce surrogate sons for Rachel and Leah, respectively—sons Rachel and Leah then name and claim as their own.

Jubilees 33

Bilhah next appears several years later. The biblical context is Gen 35:22: "While Israel lived in that land, Reuben went and lay with Bilhah, his father's concubine, and Israel heard of it." In *Jubilees*, that one sentence is expanded to an entire chapter. By this point, Jacob and his large family have returned to the land of Canaan. One day, Jacob and Leah go to visit Isaac. Reuben then sees Bilhah bathing, and he lusts for her. That night, he surreptitiously enters her bed and defiles her. She awakes and tries to fend him off. He runs away. This part of the narrative has echoes of Judah and Tamar and Joseph with Potiphar's wife, but the details are scrambled. In the Judah-Tamar story, Judah lies with Tamar but does not know it is her, and in the Joseph-Potiphar's wife episode, she pursues him, but he resists her importuning (Gen 39):[3]

---

3. Menn discusses the parallels with the Judah-Tamar and the Joseph-Potiphar's wife episodes as well as connections with *The Testaments of the Twelve Patriarchs*. See Menn, *Judah and Tamar*, 172.

> And Jacob went and dwelt toward the south of Magdaladra'ef. And he and Leah, his wife, went to his father, Isaac, on the first day of the tenth month.[4] And Reuben saw Bilhah, the attendant of Rachel (and) his father's concubine, washing in the water privately, and he desired her. And hiding at night, he entered Bilhah's house at night and found her sleeping in her bed, alone in her house. And he lay with her. And she woke up and looked, and behold, Reuben was lying with her on the bed. And she uncovered the hem of her (skirt)[5] and seized him and screamed and recognized that it was Reuben. And she was ashamed because of him and released her hand from upon him. And he fled. (*Jub.* 33:1–5).

Bilhah is mortified and ashamed. Indeed, "*Jubilees* was at pains to assert that Bilhah was completely innocent and, as soon as she woke up, did all she could to restrain Reuben."[6] At first, she says nothing, but then she confesses to Jacob, telling him what his firstborn son had done:

> And she lamented greatly concerning this matter. And she did not tell anyone at all. And when Jacob came and sought her, she said to him, "I am not clean for you since I have become polluted for you because Reuben has defiled me and lay with me at night, but I was sleeping and I was unaware until he had uncovered my skirt and lain with me." (*Jub.* 33:6–7)

Jacob is appropriately angry with Reuben, but he does not reprimand him at this time. The *Jubilees* text then explains that Jacob refuses to approach Bilhah again. She attains what is termed "living widowhood."[7] The text then makes reference to the heavenly tablets (the Torah) and paraphrases Lev 18:8 and Lev 20:11 (see Deut 22:30 [23:1 H]):

> And Jacob was very angry with Reuben because he had lain with Bilhah, for he had uncovered his father's robe. And therefore

---

4. The date that *Jubilees* suggests is significant. It is the new moon, a time of maximum darkness, without any moonlight. Bilhah was consciously modest in her behavior.

5. Kugel explains that the hem of her skirt, or the hem of her clothing, is a reference to the Hebrew word *kenaf* (kaf nun feh). "Reuben exposed her [*kenaf*] which was the exclusive right of her husband and, in that sense 'his'" (Kugel, *Walk through Jubilees*, 162). See Deut 22:30 [23:1 H]; 27:20: "No man shall marry his father's former wife, so as to remove his father's garment [*kenaf*]" (NJPS). See Tigay, *Deuteronomy*, 209 comment on Deut 23:1.

6. Kugel, "Jubilees," 409. See also ibid., "Reuben's Sin with Bilhah," 533; ibid., *How to Read the Bible*, 188.

7. See the comment "Three Reasons Why Reuben Violated Bilhah" in the "Contemporary Scholarship" section below.

Jacob did not draw near her since Reuben had defiled her. And the deed of any man who uncovers his father's robe is very evil because he is despicable before [God]. Therefore it is written and ordered in the heavenly tablets that a man should not lie with his father's wife, and he should not uncover his father's robe because that is defilement. They shall certainly die together, the man who lies with his father's wife and also the wife because they have made defilement upon the earth. And there shall be no defilement before our God among the people whom [God] has chosen . . . as a possession. And again it is written a second time: "Let anyone who lies with his father's wife be cursed because he has uncovered his father's shame" (*Jub.* 33:8–12).

As one commenter explains, "This biblical sentence ['The man who lies with his father's wife has uncovered his father's nakedness; both of them shall be put to death; their blood is upon them' (Lev 20:11)] raised an unsettling problem because Genesis says nothing about the execution of Reuben and Bilhah here, and in fact Reuben figures prominently later in the Joseph stories."[8] The author(s) of *Jubilees* resolved this problem by positing "that there was a progressive revelation of law and that individuals were responsible for obeying only the laws in force at their time."[9] Reuben and Bilhah lived several generations earlier, so they were exempt from this legislation.

In short, the laws regarding this kind of incest were not yet revealed at the time of Reuben and Bilhah. In addressing the issue, the angel tells Moses[10] that from this point on, since Moses is writing down these commands, people will be held responsible if they violate the law:

For the ordinance and judgment and law had not been revealed till then (as) completed for everyone, but in your days (it is) like the law of (appointed) times and days and an eternal law for everlasting generations. And this law has no consummation of days. And also there is no forgiveness for it but only that both of them should be uprooted from the midst of the people. On the day when they have done this they shall be killed.

And you, Moses, write for Israel, and let them keep this. And let them do according to these words. And let them not commit a sin worthy of death because . . . our God is a judge who does not accept persons or gifts. And say to them these words of the ordinance that they might hear and guard them and watch

8. VanderKam, *Book of Jubilees*, 73.

9. Ibid.

10. As mentioned in the introductory chapter, *Jubilees* takes the form of an angel dictating to Moses the prior history of Israel while Moses is on Mount Sinai.

themselves concerning them and they will not be destroyed or
uprooted from the earth. For defiled, and an abomination, and
blemished, and polluted are all who do them upon the earth
before our God. And there is no sin greater than the fornication which they commit upon the earth because Israel is a holy
nation to . . . God, and a nation of inheritance, and a nation of
priests, and a royal nation, and a (special) possession. And there
is nothing which appears which is as defiled as this among the
holy people (*Jub.* 33:16–20).

Jubilees 33 then closes with a mention of Bilhah and Zilpah in terms of
a genealogical reference to their sons.

Jubilees 34

Bilhah's death is recorded in *Jub.* 34; she dies mourning the supposed death
of her stepson Joseph. She is buried near the tomb of Rachel near Ephrat.

Jubilees 44

Jubilees 44 mentions Bilhah and Zilpah one final time in terms of a genealogical reference to their sons.

The Testaments of the Twelve Patriarchs

The *Testaments of the Twelve Patriarchs*, including its subsections the *Testament of Reuben* and the *Testament of Judah*, are part of the Pseudepigrapha.[11]

The Testament of Reuben, Testament of Judah

The *Testaments of the Twelve Patriarchs* are considered highly misogynistic
in their approach, particularly the *Testament of Reuben*.[12]

---

11. *Testaments of the Twelve Patriarchs: The Testament of Reuben, the first son of Jacob and Leah; The Testament of Judah, the fourth son of Jacob and Leah.*

12. "The *Testaments of the Twelve Patriarchs* espouse some of the most sweepingly misogynous rhetoric in ancient Jewish literature. The testaments of Reuben, Judah, and Joseph especially contain vitriolic warnings against the evil sexual threat that women represent and provide advice as to how to avoid succumbing to their dangerous power" (Rosen-Zvi, "Bilhah the Temptress," 65).

REUBEN SEXUALLY VIOLATING BILHAH

According to the *Testament of Reuben*, Reuben saw Bilhah bathing naked in a hidden place. Seeing her naked did not let him sleep (*T. Reu.* 3:11–12). This obvious comparison to David seeing Bathsheba bathing is an attempt to lessen Reuben's guilt; it offers a kind of mitigating circumstances for his sexual violation of Bilhah:

> For while Jacob our father had gone off to [visit] his father Isaac
> ... Bilhah got drunk and lay down and fell asleep uncovered in
> the bedroom. And I entered and I saw her nakedness and I did
> that impiety, and leaving her asleep, I went out. Thereafter, an
> angel of God revealed to my father Jacob concerning my impi-
> ety, and he came and grieved over me, and he touched her no
> more. (*T. Reu.* 3:13–15)

Bilhah's bathing where she could be observed, her sleeping naked, and her drunkenness are, of course, intended to imply the dangers of women as temptresses.

The *Testament of Reuben* features important differences from the *Jubilees* account that describe the Reuben-Bilhah incident. In *Jubilees*, Bilhah tells Jacob about the incident and claims that she is no longer pure for him; they never sleep together again. She is not drunk when she goes to sleep, nor is she sleeping naked. In *Jubilees*, there is a long discussion of the evils of incest (*Jub.* 33:10–17), which is followed by a statement that "there is no greater sin than the fornication which they commit on earth because Israel is a holy nation to ... God" (*Jub.* 33:20). Bilhah being described as drunk in the *Testament of Reuben* is noteworthy, given the general view of drunkenness in the *Testaments of the Twelve Patriarchs*:

> Do not get drunk with wine, since wine turns one's mind away
> from the truth and instills the passion of lust and leads the eyes
> astray. For the Spirit of licentiousness uses wine as [its] errand
> boy when it comes to [exciting] pleasure in the mind ... it rattles
> the mind with filthy thoughts ... and heats up the body [with
> the desire] for sexual intercourse, so that if the opportunity to
> [fulfill his] lust should present itself, the person will unasham-
> edly perform the sin. (*T. Jud.* 14:1–3)

In both *Jubilees* and the *Testament of Reuben*, it is Bilhah's nakedness while bathing that provokes Reuben's illicit act. In the *Testament of Reuben*, she never awakened during the entire event, which could only occur if Bilhah were seriously drunk. The innocence of Bilhah is made much clearer in *Jubilees* than in the *Testament of Reuben*. *Jubilees* also states that Reuben desired Bilhah when he saw her in the *private* place where she bathed (*Jub.* 33:2). In *Jubilees*, Bilhah did awake—she grabbed Reuben and screamed out before he escaped. The differences are startling. The *Testament of Reuben* places blame on Bilhah; she is dangerous. She bathes in a place where it is possible for Reuben to see her. She is so inebriated that she is unaware of his entrance into her living quarters and continues unaware as he has sexual relations with her. This is a form of misogynistic "blaming the victim." *Jubilees* ends this story with a warning against incest. In contrast, the author of the *Testament of Reuben* states, "For women are evil . . . they resort to guile to draw [men] to themselves by [their physical] charms" (*T. Reu.* 5:1).[13] Esther Marie Menn explains that the *Testament of Reuben* uses the Reuben-Bilhah narrative to serve as a warning "concerning the dangers of feminine beauty and adornment, the weakness of women to the deceptions of Beliar [Beliar, or Belial, is a demon], and the advisability of maintaining a safe distance from them."[14] This finds parallels in the *Testament of Judah*, which mentions the dangers of women and wine (*T. Jud.* 13:5–8; 14:1).

The Testament of Naphtali[15]

ZILPAH AND BILHAH ARE SISTERS

In the *Testament of Naphtali*, there is a figure named Rotheus (or, in other translations, Rotheos) who is the brother of Deborah, Rebekah's nurse:

> Rotheus was from Abraham's family—a God-fearing Chaldean, a free man of noble birth . . . taken captive, he was bought by Laban . . . and [Laban] gave him his servant-girl Aina [in other translations, Hannah], as a wife, and she gave birth to a daughter and he called her Zilpah [in other translations, Zelpah] . . . Then she gave birth to Bilhah. (*T. Naph.* 1:10–12)

As one scholar explains, "Through this genealogy, *T. Naph.* tells us that Bilhah's father is a descendant of Abraham; as a result she [Bilhah] is a

---

13. These verses have "surprising parallels in rabbinic literature" (cf. *Mishna Kiddushin* 4.12) and there seem to be some parallels (see *T. Reu.* 3:10) with some of the late canonized texts, such as Prov 6:24 and 6:29 (Rosen-Zvi, "Bilhah the Temptress," 72–73). See also Najman, "Rewriting as Whitewashing."

14. Menn, *Judah and Tamar*, 171. See also ibid., 166–74. For a parallel views in rabbinic writings, see Babylonian Talmud *Berakhot* 61a; *Avodah Zarah* 20a–b.

15. *Testaments of the Twelve Patriarchs: The Testament of Naphtali, the eighth son of Jacob and Bilhah*. A text (4Q215 T.Naph) called *Testament of Naphtali* was found in the Dead Sea Scrolls with almost the exact same information.

descendant of Abraham."[16] That their lineage traces back to what Ezra terms the "holy seed" (Ezra 9:2) is vitally important in the late Second Temple period and beyond.[17] The *Testament of Naphtali* also mentions that Bilhah and Rachel were born on the same day (*T. Naph.* 1:9).

The Testament of Benjamin[18]

Benjamin mentions that "since my mother Rachel died giving birth to me, I had no milk. So I was nursed by Bilhah, her servant-girl" (*T. Benj.* 1:3).

Joseph and Aseneth

Joseph and Aseneth is part of the Pseudepigrapha.

A Sad Legacy

The favoritism that Jacob showed to Rachel's sons, Joseph and Benjamin, had a kind of ripple effect, as interpreted by the author of the Pseudepigraphic book *Joseph and Aseneth*. If Rachel's sons were primary in Jacob's mind and Leah's children secondary, then the children of the maidservants Zilpah and Bilhah were tertiary. They envied their older stepbrothers: "Simeon and Levi, the brothers of Joseph and the sons of Leah, alone joined in escorting them [Joseph and Aseneth], but the sons of Zilpah and Bilhah, the servants of Leah and Rachel (respectively) did not join in escorting them because they envied them and they were at enmity with them" (*Jos. Asen.* 22:11). Not only are these brothers jealous of Simeon and Levi, they are also envious of Joseph and Aseneth. They then join the Pharaoh's son in a plot against this couple (*Jos. Asen.* 24:2). It is probable that the author of *Joseph and Aseneth* hints here at Joseph's "bad report" about those brothers, which is written about in Gen 37:2

---

16. Hillel, "Why *Not* Naphtali?," 286. As Halpern-Amaru notes, "Birth within Laban's household . . . indicates that Zilpah and Bilhah . . . are not Canaanite in origin" (Halpern-Amaru, *Empowerment*, 106).

17. Reiss and Zucker, "Co-opting the Secondary Matriarchs."

18. *Testaments of the Twelve Patriarchs: The Testament of Benjamin, the twelfth son of Jacob and Rachel.*

Josephus

Josephus adds some details in his presentation of Bilhah and Zilpah. As in Genesis, Laban presents them to the sisters. They were "in no way slaves, but subordinates" (*Ant.* 1.19.7). It is likely that Josephus was trying to represent the status of Bilhah and Zilpah in a positive light to his intended audience. Whatever that distinction might mean, Rachel has the power to put Bilhah into Jacob's bed. In the same manner, Leah puts Zilpah into Jacob's bed. Both Bilhah and Zilpah are credited with birthing their respective biological sons, even as the sisters claim them as their own. There is no mention of Reuben's violating the bed of Bilhah in Josephus' account.

The Rabbis' Bilhah and Zilpah

Bilhah and Zilpah Were Laban's Daughters

A midrash suggests that both Bilhah and Zilpah were the biological daughters of Laban. A comment on this midrash explains they were his daughters through a concubine (*Genesis Rabbah* 74.13; 74.14; *Pirke de Rabbi Eliezer* ch. 36). The point of their being Laban's daughters is that they are part of the Abrahamic family, or to use an anachronistic term, proto-Jews. This is of vital importance in the late Second Temple period and beyond. It bears directly on the issue of endogamy versus exogamy.[19]

Zilpah's Pregnancy

When Bilhah gives birth, notice is given beforehand that she conceived. When Zilpah gives birth, the text says simply that she that she bore Jacob a son. The rabbis explain that Zilpah was very young and her pregnancy was not noticeable (*Genesis Rabbah* 71.9).

Bilhah and Zilpah Were Set Free

According to Sforno, in adopting their stepchildren, Rachel and Leah "agreed to set . . . Bilhah and Zilpah . . . free. Since these children were accepted as sons, they would not have the status of slaves, since their mothers were no longer maidservants . . . For this reason they no longer subjugated (their maidservants) as Sarah did with Hagar" (Sforno, comment on Gen 30:6).

---

19. See footnote 17 above.

Reuben and Bilhah, Part 1

The overwhelming preponderance of talmudic and midrashic comments takes the Genesis text at face value and condemns Reuben for going to Bilhah's bed (Babylonian Talmud *Megillah* 25a–b; *Baba Kama* 92a; *Genesis Rabbah* 82.11; 87.5; 92.9; *Numbers Rabbah* 6.2; 9.17; 13.18; *Sifre Deuteronomy, Piska* 347[20]; *Midrash on Proverbs* 1 [n. 68]; *Midrash Tanhuma Yelammedenu, Genesis,* 9.1, And Jacob Sat, p. 223). Nonetheless, a number of midrashim rationalize Reuben's presence in Bilhah's tent. They suggest he was merely removing Jacob's couch and placing it in his mother's tent (Babylonian Talmud *Shabbat* 55b; *Genesis Rabbah* 79.1; *Zohar, Vayishlah,* 2.175a–b). The focus of these rabbinic texts is to regard Reuben as a good son who is reminding his father, Jacob, of the loyalty of the Patriarch's first wife, Leah.[21]

Reuben and Bilhah, Part 2

Babylonian Talmud *Shabbat* 55b offers an additional, slightly different explanation. Reuben removed two couches, one belonging to the *Shekhinah*, God's feminine presence, and one belonging to his father, Jacob. Rashi, in his comments to this passage in the Talmud, explains that Jacob set a couch for the *Shekhinah* in the tent of each of his wives. Where the *Shekhinah* came to rest was where Jacob spent the night. Nahmanides offers a different explanation: Reuben wanted to insure that Jacob would not have any more children. By defiling Bilhah, she would be disqualified. His own mother, Leah, was elderly, and Nahmanides suggests that Zilpah had perhaps died.

Bilhah Reared Joseph Following Rachel's Death

Since Bilhah was Rachel's maid, it made sense that she would be the one to rear Joseph following Rachel's death (*Genesis Rabbah* 84.11).

Bilhah and Zilpah Were Not Full Matriarchs

A midrash discounts Bilhah and Zilpah, relegating them to a secondary status because they were called maids, or 'amahot (*Numbers Rabbah* 14.11).

---

20. Hammer, *Sifre: A Tannaitic Commentary.*
21. Antonelli, *Image of God,* 100–101.

Bilhah and Zilpah Were Full Matriarchs; All the Tribes and All the Matriarchs Were Equal

Other midrashim suggest Bilhah and Zilpah were full Matriarchs: "Six corresponds to the six matriarchs [*shisha imahot*]—Sarah, Rebekah, Rachel, Leah, Bilhah, and Zilpah" (*Esther Rabbah* 1.12; *Song of Songs Rabbah* 6.4.2). Furthermore, there was parity among the tribes: "You should not think that the children of the wives [i.e., Leah and Rachel] come first, and that of the handmaidens [Bilhah and Zilpah] last, but . . . these were not greater than the others" (*Exodus Rabbah* 1.6).

The Matriarchs Leah, Rachel, Bilhah, and Zilpah Were All Prophets

Each of the Matriarchs thought she would raise up three tribes, explains *Genesis Rabbah* 71.4. The supercommentary to *Genesis Rabbah*, the *Matnot Kehuna* of Rabbi Issachar Katz-Berman (Germany, sixteenth century), explains that all of the Matriarchs knew this through prophecy, or *nevu'ah* (comment on *Genesis Rabbah* 71.4 [in some editions, 71.6]).

Bilhah and Zilpah Are Jacob's Wives

Nahmanides suggests that during Leah and Rachel's lifetimes, Bilhah and Zilpah were called "handmaids," but after those women died, Jacob took Bilhah and Zilpah as wives (comment on Gen 37:2ff.).

When Leah and Rachel Died, God's Presence Moved to Bilhah

During the lives of Leah and Rachel, the *Shekhinah*, God's feminine presence, hovered over them; when they died, it took up abode in the tent of Bilhah (*Zohar, Vayishlah*, 2.175b). This means that God's presence and approval was transferred to the tent of Bilhah.

Bilhah Was a Trusted Go-between

When Jacob died, Joseph's brothers were fearful that Joseph would finally retaliate against them. Therefore, they sent the message of their father's death via Bilhah, presumably relying on Joseph's affection for this particular stepmother (*Midrash Tanhuma, Exodus. Shemot* 1.2 Exodus 1.1ff., Part 2).[22]

Targum Neofiti, Targum Onqelos

The *Targum Neofiti* and the *Targum Onqelos*[23] clearly blame Reuben, stating that as a result of his attack, he lost the birthright, the kingship, and the high priesthood (Gen 49:3–4; cf. 1 Chron 5:1). Similar material is found in the Dead Sea Scrolls Genesis Pesher (4Q252).

Contemporary Scholarship

Endogamy Underscored

The midrashic tradition that both Bilhah and Zilpah are the biological daughters of Laban (*Genesis Rabbah, Pirke de Rabbi Eliezer*) and consequently are half-sisters to their mistresses underscores that all of Jacob's children are from the same Mesopotamian family line. This is a way for the rabbis to emphasize the importance of endogamy. Laban himself is the grandson of Nahor and Milcah, Abraham's brother and sister-in-law. Likewise, in the Pseudepigrapha's *Testament of Naphtali*, Zilpah and Bilhah's father is related to Abraham.

Wives or Concubines?

The Genesis text refers to Bilhah as "a wife," or *'isha* (Gen 30:4) and likewise refers to Zilpah as "a wife," or *'isha* (Gen 30:9). At a later point, however,

> in 35:22 Bilhah is called a "concubine" (Heb. *pilegesh*). Zilpah is designated "wife" in verse 9. In 37:2 both women are termed "wives." The basic difference between a concubine and a wife is that no *mohar*, or bride-price, is paid for the former. The interchange of terminology shows that in the course of time the distinction in social status between the two tended to be effaced.[24]

22. According to Rashi's commentary on Gen 50:16, the message was sent through Bilhah's sons.

23. The *Targum Neofiti* and the *Targum Onqelos* are generally dated about the first century CE, although redacted at a later point, perhaps the fourth century. Martin McNamara dates the *Targum Neofiti* from the fourth century or earlier (McNamara, *Targum Neofiti 1*, 45).

24. Sarna, *Genesis*, 208.

It is possible that chapter 35 represents a different tradition than that of chapters 30 and 37, a tradition whereby Bilhah had a lower status than a full wife.

Wives or Maids?

When the narrator refers to Leah and Rachel before meeting Esau, they are termed "wives," or *nashim*. Bilhah and Zilpah, however, are termed *sh'fahot*, "maids" (Gen 32:23). Later, Zilpah and Bilhah are called *nashim* (Gen 37:2). Did something change? As noted under the "Rabbis' Bilhah and Zilpah" heading, according to Nahmanides, their status changed when their mistresses died. It is also possible that this is a matter of perspective. In the context of Jacob meeting his brother, Esau, Jacob presents Leah and Rachel as Esau's full cousins (sharing the same maternal grandparents), and also as his wives and thus Esau's sisters-in-law. Later, in the context of Jacob's extended family living in Beersheba (Gen 37), Jacob regards Bilhah and Zilpah as full wives, the mothers of four of his thirteen children.

Three Reasons Why Reuben Violated Bilhah

Sarna offers three reasons why Reuben may have entered Bilhah's bed. First, by violating Bilhah, "Reuben makes sure that she cannot supplant or even rival his mother's position as chief wife now that Rachel is dead . . . As a result of Reuben's cohabitation with Bilhah, she would thereby acquire the tragic status of 'living widowhood.'" Second, "As the firstborn son, Reuben, in effect, prematurely lays claim to an inheritance that he would have expected to be his eventually." Third, "It is apparent from several biblical stories and from ancient near Eastern texts that in matters of leadership, possession of the concubine(s) of one's father or of one's vanquished enemy on the part of the aspirant or usurper bestowed legitimacy on the assumption of heirship and validated the succession." Sarna goes on to say that Reuben's act was motivated more by politics than by lust.[25]

---

25. Ibid., 244. See Hamilton, *Genesis*, 387. When Absalom rebelled against his father, King David, he slept with his ten concubines (2 Sam 16:22). Wenham, *Genesis 16–50*, 327. See also Shinan and Zakovitch, *From Gods to God*, 237–41. In a personal communication to author Reiss dated August 2013, James Kugel explained that in his view, Sarna's third point "bestowing legitimacy/validating succession" is the major issue in this episode.

Bilhah Had Replaced Rachel in Jacob's Eyes

That Reuben sleeps with Bilhah as a preemptive tactic (as argued in Sarna's first point above) indicates that certainly in Reuben's mind, and possibly in Leah's, it was likely that Bilhah would, in practical terms, supplant Leah as the "first wife." She might even appear to outrank Leah in the household. According to some midrashim, Reuben did *not* have intercourse with Bilhah—he merely took Jacob's couch from his stepmother's tent and placed it in the tent of Leah, Reuben's biological mother. The implication of these rabbinic insights is that Bilhah did replace Rachel in Jacob's eyes after she died in a kind of double-insult to Leah, a matter that Reuben took deeply to heart. Thus Leah, Reuben's mother, was—or at least felt—further degraded and certainly displaced not only by Rachel but even by Rachel's maid, Bilhah.

Israel Versus Jacob: Spiritual Versus Material

"While Israel lived in that land, Reuben went and lay with Bilhah his father's concubine; and Israel heard of it. Now the sons of Jacob were twelve" (Gen 35:22–23). The text notes that "Israel lived" and "Israel heard," while the next verse refers to "Jacob." The third Patriarch had recently been given the additional name of Israel. According to Jewish mystical tradition, the term "Israel" denoted or reflected his *spiritual* power, while the name "Jacob" was associated with his *material* power. Jacob-as-Israel heard and responded spiritually as a father and at least partially forgave Reuben. Jacob-as-Jacob did not react or answer, just as "Jacob" had kept quiet following Dinah's defilement: "Now Jacob heard that Shechem had defiled his daughter Dinah; but his sons were with his cattle in the field, so Jacob kept his peace until they came" (Gen 34:5).[26]

Feminist Thought

Rachel and Bilhah: A Replay of Sarah and Hagar?

The narratives of the Sarah-Hagar relationship deal with the issues of maternal surrogacy and consequent heirship. In a broad sense, these matters play out again in the third generation: "The reader is reminded of the earlier case of surrogate motherhood, Sarah and Hagar. Might this prompt similar

---

26. Based on a teaching developed by Murray Moshe Kleiman, uncle of author Reiss.

tragedy? Surprisingly, the cases could not be more different. Scant attention is given to Bilhah, who bears two sons."[27]

Attendant or Maid: What Exactly Is Bilhah's Role?

In the passages that mention Bilhah, unlike those that mention Zilpah, various terms are used to explain or define status: "Bilhah's status is more complex than Zilpah's because she is named an *'amah* by Rachel and a *shiphchah, pilegesh,* and *'ishah* by the narrator. We no longer know whether these terms are used interchangeably as a stylistic concern or whether each term carries a different connotation."[28]

Bilhah's and/or Zilpah's Feelings

At no point does the narrator consider either Bilhah's or Zilpah's feelings. Thus, "Viewed from a more individualistic perspective, it is deeply problematic that the matriarchs potentially force their servants into undesired sexual relations."[29]

Giving Birth Is Incidental

As noted earlier, both Rachel and Leah adopt the children that their respective handmaids bear. As one scholar explains, the

> status of the wives of . . . Jacob directly influenced the status of their offspring . . . The sons of Zilpah and Bilhah . . . [need to be] acknowledged by Leah and Rachel as their own offspring . . . The fact that Leah and Rachel's handmaids actually gave birth to some of the children was incidental; the offspring were recognized as having been borne by the matriarchs themselves.[30]

Having children was a mark of status in its own right, one that was credited to the mother whether she was the birth mother or the heir-mother: "It is also clear that in the Leah/Rachel stories that Bilhah and Zilpah are

---

27. Jeansonne, *Women of Genesis*, 76. See also Zucker and Reiss, "Abraham, Sarah, and Hagar." Kramer, however, sees parallels with Hagar (Kramer, "Biblical Women," 223).

28. Schneider, *Mothers of Promise*, 134.

29. Havrelock, "Central Commentary, *Vayeitzei*," 166.

30. Teubal, *Sarah*, 94.

presented to Jacob for the specific purpose of providing the matriarchs with offspring. Jacob has many children when Rachel presents Bilhah to him so that 'through her I too may be built up' (Gen 30:3b)."[31]

The Purpose of the Sh'faḥot, or Maidservants

The maidservants are seen and treated as a means to an end.

> Further the *sh'faḥot* [maidservants or female slaves] have sexual relations with Jacob solely when requested by the matriarchs. The function of the *shifḥah*, then, is to have the honorable purpose of fulfilling the injunction to "be fertile and increase" (Gen 1:28).[32]

In this sense, the *sh'faḥot* provide the means by which Rachel and Leah fulfill the earlier biblical commandment.

Rape, Incest, and Adultery

The phrase that "he went and lay with Bilhah"—*vayeilekh R'euven vayishkav et Bilhah*—is bristling with meaning: "The vast majority of biblical uses of [the verb root *shin kaf bet*] *skb* in a sexual contact refer to illegitimate relations in rape, incest, ritual impurity, adultery and so forth."[33] In the case of Reuben and his family connection to Bilhah, his act is a combination of rape, incest,[34] and adultery.

Bilhah as Pilegesh; Anger at Jacob

Bilhah is a *pilegesh* to Jacob; Bilhah belongs to both Rachel and Jacob. Reuben sexually abuses Bilhah. The object of his perfidy—his crime—is primarily aimed at Jacob. As explained later in Genesis, he "mounted [his] father's

---

31. Ibid., *Hagar*, 56.

32. Ibid.

33. Niditch, "Eroticism and Death," 49. Niditch offers many examples, including "rape and incest [Gen 19:32, 34, 35 (Lot and his daughters); Gen 34:2, 7 (the rape of Dinah); 2 Sam 13:11, 14 (the rape of Tamar)]; of wife-stealing [Gen 35:22 (Reuben's taking Bilhah)]; seduction or adultery [Gen 39:10, 12, 14 (Potiphar's wife)]; and a host of other forbdiden sexual relationships" (ibid.).

34. Davidson, *Flame of Yahweh*, 432.

bed" (Gen 49:4). Reuben may not consider Bilhah a legitimate wife.[35] If he considered her a true wife, the crime would be greater (Lev 18:8).

Sympathy for Bilhah

Like other women in Genesis, such as Hagar and Dinah, Bilhah's plight following Reuben's sexual violation evokes "sympathy at those whose rights are unstable and always at risk."[36]

Disappearing from Our Memories

Bilhah and Zilpah's names are virtually unknown.

> Why have Bilhah and Zilpah vanished from our prayers and memories? In many Jewish prayers and songs . . . we speak of the *four* matriarchs—Sarah, Rebecca, Rachel, and Leah . . . Why then are [Bilhah and Zilpah] absent from our prayers? . . . [Because, like Hagar,] these two women were only concubines, second-class wives . . . Still, Jewish tradition has treated them even worse than [Hagar] and Ishmael . . .[whose] story is read each year on Rosh Hashanah, but poor Bilhah and Zilpah have vanished completely from Jewish worship.[37]

* * * *

Summary and Conclusion

Although Sarah, Rebekah, Leah, and Rachel are the primary Matriarchs of the people of Israel, in the third generation they are joined by two women who are secondary Matriarchs: Bilhah and Zilpah. Bilhah is Rachel's attendant, and then concurrently Jacob's wife. Zilpah is Leah's attendant, and then concurrently Jacob's wife. Bilhah gives birth to Dan and Naphtali. Zilpah gives birth to Gad and Asher. Each of these women is given to Jacob "as a wife" (Gen 30:4, 9). Of the two women, more is written about Bilhah. In Gen 35:22, the text explains that Reuben, Jacob's first son, defiles his stepmother Bilhah's bed: "While Israel lived in that land, Reuben went and lay

---

35. Schneider, *Mothers of Promise*, 137.

36. Niditch, "Genesis," 44.

37. Frankel, *Five Books of Miriam*, 56–57.

with Bilhah his father's concubine; and Israel heard of it." The Hebrew term used here is not *'isha* , or "wife," but rather *pilegesh,* "concubine."

In terms of the early extra-biblical literature, there is more written about Bilhah than Zilpah. *Jubilees* explains that Bilhah is Zilpah's sister. In *Jub.* 33, Reuben sees Bilhah bathing and lusts for her. That night, he surreptitiously enters her bed and sexually violates her. She awakes and tries to fend him off. He runs away. Bilhah is mortified and ashamed. At first she says nothing, but then she confesses to Jacob. *Jubilees* explains that Jacob refuses to approach Bilhah again. She becomes a "living widow." The misogynistic *Testament of Reuben* relates that Reuben saw Bilhah bathing naked in a secluded place. He then entered her bed at night, but being inebriated, she did not realize this. Bilhah's bathing where she could be observed, her sleeping naked, and her drunkenness imply the dangers of women as temptresses. The *Testament of Naphtali* notes that Bilhah and Zilpah were sisters—both daughters of Rotheus, who was of Abraham's tribe, so therefore Zilpah and Bilhah were "family." In *Joseph and Aseneth*, the children of Bilhah and Zilpah are jealous of their other brothers. They join with the Pharaoh's son in a plan to do away with Aseneth and Joseph. Josephus states Bilhah and Zilpah not only were sisters, but they were "in no way slaves, but subordinates." Bilhah and Zilpah give birth to their respective sons, even as Rachel and Leah claim them as their own. There is no mention of Reuben's violating the bed of Bilhah in Josephus.

A midrash suggests that both Bilhah and Zilpah were the biological daughters of Laban by a concubine. This allows them to be proto-Jews, part of the wider Abrahamic family. According to the Italian commentator Sforno, in adopting their stepchildren, Rachel and Leah "agreed to set . . . Bilhah and Zilpah . . . free . . . For this reason they no longer subjugated (their maidservants) as Sarah continued to do with Hagar." The overwhelming preponderance of talmudic and midrashic comments condemn Reuben for going to Bilhah's bed. There are conflicting ideas among the rabbis whether or not Bilhah and Zilpah were full Matriarchs.

Contemporary scholars offer several reasons why Reuben entered Bilhah's bed. He violates her to make sure she will not be a candidate for chief wife. Reuben also prematurely laid claim to his primogeniture blessing. Possession of the concubine(s) of one's father or of one's vanquished enemy bestowed legitimacy and validated succession. Feminist scholars highlight the fact that unlike the Hagar surrogate motherhood narrative, little attention is given to Bilhah and Zilpah in the Genesis text. Yet here too, from an individualistic point of view, the fact that Rachel and Leah "force" their maidservants to marry Jacob without seeking their own views on this matter remains problematic. In terms of Reuben lying with Bilhah, one feminist scholar points out that the particular verb used, *skb*, often refers to some form of illegitimate sexual relations.

In conclusion, Bilhah and Zilpah are Matriarchs of Genesis, but unlike Sarah (and Hagar), Rebekah, Leah, and Rachel, they are secondary, not primary Matriarchs. Aside from their giving birth to Dan and Naphtali along with Gad and Asher, respectively, little is said about them in Genesis, with the exception of Reuben sleeping with Bilhah and some later genealogical references. Their voices are not heard in Genesis. In the pseudepigraphical literature, Zilpah remains mute, but much is written about Bilhah in terms of Reuben's entering her tent. *Jubilees* is sympathetic to Bilhah, seeing her as innocent of wrongdoing. The *Testament of Reuben*, by contrast, seeks to blame Bilhah, making her out as a seductress and a drunk. As noted, most of the rabbinic views of that situation view Reuben as the instigator and culprit. The rabbis also suggest that Bilhah and Zilpah are sisters as well as Jacob's wives. Contemporary writers offer reasons for Reuben's act and also raise the possibility that Bilhah had replaced Rachel in Jacob's eyes. Feminists point out that, surprisingly, the Bilhah and Zilpah episodes are not a replay of those seen between Sarah and Hagar. They also note that this may be another example where women's bodies, possibly against their will, are offered as surrogate wombs.

8

Conclusion

As we noted at the beginning of this book, a people's self-understanding is fashioned on its heroes and heroines. Sarah, Rebekah, Leah, and Rachel—the traditional four Matriarchs—are important and powerful figures in the book of Genesis. Each woman plays her part in her generation. She interacts with and advises her husband, seeking to achieve both present and future successes for their respective families. These women act decisively at crucial points, and through their actions and words, their family dynamics change irrevocably. Unlike their husbands, we know little of their spoken thoughts or actions. The text in Genesis, nonetheless positions these women as perceptive and judicious, often seeing the grand scheme with clarity.

Sarah's silent but important role in Gen 12 impacts her personally as well as her family and even the political and social power structure within Egypt. The biblical text lacks any indication that Sarah gives voice to any objections to Abraham concerning the wife-sister deception, although there is rabbinic material that features Sarah's prayers to God seeking rescue from the Pharaoh's advances. Sarah's apparent acquiescence would be seen again in Gen 20 regarding the ruler and people of Gerar. Sarah's voice is heard for the first time in chapter 16 of Genesis. Her decision to offer Hagar to Abraham as a surrogate birth mother in order to ensure a family inheritance, we suggest, underscores Sarah's strength of character and her commitment to a viable future. Sarah's animus toward Hagar (Gen 16), and later Hagar and Ishmael (Gen 21), shows a conflicted, even darker side of her character.

Hagar has a more limited voice than Sarah and clearly a lot less power. Yet Hagar's role in the chapters in which she appears (Gen 16, 21) shows someone who is highly determined. She acts forcefully. In her state of pregnancy, Hagar is proud and sometimes headstrong. Her role in the Genesis text is secondary to other Matriarchs, but the Bible credits her with the first two angelic encounters mentioned in Genesis. They speak to her, and she speaks to them. Hagar is resilient and resolute. She gives birth to and rears Abraham's first child, Ishmael, a figure who later becomes, as the biblical text explains, "fruitful and exceedingly numerous . . . the father of twelve princes, and [the source of] . . . a great nation" (Gen 17:20).

Rebekah is the most articulate of the Matriarchs. She is a woman who is strong-willed and steadfast. She is portrayed as thoughtful and farsighted. Isaac loves her, and she provides him comfort in his grief for his mother (Gen 24). Rebekah is the only Matriarch who is described as offering "comfort" to her husband. In time, he prays for her to be able to conceive, and when their children are born, Isaac and Rebekah name them together (Gen 25). Rebekah's most discussed and most controversial role is featured in Gen 27. It is then that she appears to collude with Jacob to deceive Isaac and to counter the wishes of her husband. Rebekah works to achieve a divinely inspired and directed goal, which is to see that Jacob will receive the primogeniture blessing, marry within the Abrahamic family line, and produce heirs. Whether Rebekah does this with her husband's knowledge and consent or on her own is a matter of scholarly debate, as we have indicated in the chapter devoted to her. Rebekah's suggestion to Jacob that he should leave the family home and temporarily resettle in Haran with her brother Laban has Isaac's full endorsement (Gen 28). Rachel and Leah initially become rivals for the love and support of their mutual husband, Jacob (Gen 30). Later, they appear of one mind and fully support him and his plan to return to his homeland (Gen 31). Bilhah and Zilpah, Jacob's third and fourth wives, have no voice in Genesis, although the early extra-biblical literature does present Bilhah vocalizing her distress when Reuben sexually violates her. Bilhah and Zilpah each gives birth to two of the eponymous heads of the future tribes of Israel. Bilhah is the birth mother of Dan and Naphtali, just as Zilpah is the birth mother of Gad and Asher. They are deservedly the sixth and seventh of Genesis' Matriarchs.

Too often, biblical women are unable to speak (or are prohibited from speaking) for themselves. Rather, women are portrayed through the male gaze, whereby men and men's experience are central to the narrative, while women and women's voices and experiences are only, if ever, understood through a masculine lens. It is difficult to get to know these women, because the terrain in which they are represented is silent. Women's voices come in three forms in the Bible. The most common is when the omniscient voice of the narrator describes women, or women's actions: "Sarah conceived and bore Abraham a son" (Gen 21:2), or Hagar "sat opposite him, she lifted up her voice" (Gen 21:16). Alternatively, God or a human says something about the woman: "Sarah shall bear [a son] to you" (Gen 17:21), or "We will call the girl, and ask her" (Gen 24:57). Second, when women do speak, it is limited to relating basic factual information as they understand it: "Now Sarah said, 'God has brought laughter for me'" (Gen 21:6), or Leah said, "Now this time my husband will be joined to me because I have borne him three sons" (Gen 29:34). Third, and most rare, is when women describe their feelings: "Then Rebekah said to Isaac, 'I am weary of my life because of the Hittite women'" (Gen 27:46), or Rachel said to Jacob, "Give me children, or I shall die!" (Gen 30:1) Yet even here we remain cautious as to whether these are women's voices speaking or whether it may merely be men representing women's voices and experiences.

This pattern of women being described or spoken about, women actually speaking, and women describing their feelings is true for the Bible and is likewise true for the early extra-biblical writings. Nevertheless, while women's voices do remain fairly limited, pseudepigraphical works such as the book of *Jubilees* offer additional insights into the Matriarchs, as well as opportunities for them to speak and to take action. Likewise, the sermons of the ancient rabbis, through midrashic compilations, offer other opportunities to see and hear the Matriarchs of Genesis through the rabbis' comprehension of—and interaction with—the sacred words of that text.

It is likely that these texts were composed largely, if not exclusively, by men. On many levels, even though there may be women acting and speaking, their actions and words still represent a male understanding, no matter how sympathetic the male compilers may be. *Jubilees*, which is a kind of rewriting or retelling of Scripture, tends to downplay or ignore family conflict. Even as *Jubilees* expunges, it also inserts. For example, the tensions between Sarah and Hagar in Gen 16, as well as Sarah's criticism of Abraham in that chapter, are simply excised in *Jub*. 14. Yet Sarah is depicted as being jealous of Ishmael (*Jub*. 17), an emotion not mentioned in Genesis. She demands that he and Hagar be expelled. *Jubilees*, however, does not give a reason for her jealousy. No mention is made of the surrogate courtship of Rebekah, nor of her problems with fertility. *Jubilees* does feature Rebekah and Isaac celebrating feasts with Abraham, events not found in Genesis. *Jubilees* moderates the deceptiveness behind Jacob's obtaining the primogeniture blessing from Isaac—as well as Rebekah's role in this venture—by featuring Jacob as the special son who has Abraham's specific approval and divine support as well (*Jub*. 19:18). In *Jubilees*, Rebekah counsels Jacob on his marriage and gives him a lengthy maternal blessing (*Jub*. 25:1–3, 11–23). In her dying days, Rebekah tries to make peace between Esau and Jacob (*Jub*. 35:1–27). Undoubtedly, *Jubilees* is unique in privileging women and women's experiences.

Yet the presentations of the pseudepigraphic and rabbinic authors are often not sympathetic at all. Certainly there are exceptions, but in many cases, these ancient authors criticize the Matriarchs. The *Testaments of the Twelve Patriarchs* generally, and especially the *Testament of Reuben*, are noted by scholars for their misogynistic tone. In a similar manner, the rabbis are not at all pleased that Abraham follows Sarah's directions, even when God supports her: "The Rabbis said: She is her husband's ruler. Usually, the husband gives orders, whereas here we read, [God said to Abraham] 'In all that Sarah says to you, hearken unto her voice' (Gen 21:12)" (*Genesis Rabbah* 52.5). Likewise, we read, "Abraham was crowned through Sarah, but not Sarah through Abraham. She was her husband's ruler. Abraham derived honor from Sarah, but not she from him" (*Genesis Rabbah* 47.1). Yet at the same time, others point out that Abraham profits from listening to his wife (*Deuteronomy Rabbah* 4.5). The rabbis were not homogenous in their views; they often expressed a variety of perspectives.

Although the writings of the classical rabbinic period are often sexist and sometimes misogynistic, there are moments when the rabbis praise women. Sarah is credited with being a better prophet than Abraham. She was able to discern that Ishmael was wicked (*Exodus Rabbah* 1.1; *Midrash Tanhuma Yelammedenu, Exodus*, Now These Are the Names, Exodus 1.1). The rabbis provide many examples of Ishmael's distressing acts, which they suggest Abraham was unable to perceive. The rabbis note that angels visit Hagar. The rabbis comment that Hagar seems to take these angelic encounters in stride, because angels had previously visited Abraham's encampment. They explain that Hagar was already accustomed to such encounters (*Genesis Rabbah* 45.7). Furthermore, according to some rabbinic traditions, Hagar is the same person as Keturah, the woman Abraham marries after Sarah's death. There is a tradition that God told Abraham to marry her and that she was named Keturah because she united (*kitrah*) piety and nobility in herself (*Genesis Rabbah* 61.4).

When Rebekah and Isaac marry, Rebekah carries on the traditions of Isaac's mother, which earns her praise in rabbinic tradition: "As long as Sarah lived, a cloud [signifying the divine presence] hung over her tent; when she died the cloud disappeared; but when Rebecca came, it returned. As long as Sarah lived, her doors were wide open; at her death that liberality disappeared; but when Rebecca came, that openhandedness returned" (*Genesis Rabbah* 60.16). These items represent a sense of grace, warmth, security, comfort, and sanctity in the home. Furthermore, Rebekah is a pious woman: she performs several traditional ritual acts associated with women, such as separating dough from the *hallah* and lighting candles (*Genesis Rabbah* 60.16). Leah was the first person to praise God (Babylonian *Talmud Berakhot* 7b). Rather than necessarily being viewed as rivals, the two sisters are seen in many ways as parallel in their accomplishments and certainly in terms of their descendants. This may reflect the observation that like Esau and Jacob, Leah and Rachel were twins (*Midrash Tanhuma, Genesis*.

Wayyetse Gen 7.20; Gen 30.22ff., Part 5). What Leah produced, Rachel produced. Leah produced kings, and so did Rachel. Leah produced prophets, and so did Rachel. Leah produced judges, and so did Rachel (*Midrash Tanhuma, Genesis. Wayyetse* Gen 7.13; Gen 29:31ff., Part 4).

Although one midrashic source discounts Bilhah and Zilpah, relegating them to a secondary status because they were called maids (*Numbers Rabbah* 14.11), other midrashim suggest Bilhah and Zilpah were full Matriarchs. These sources accord Bilhah and Zilpah equal status with Leah and Rachel, for "Six corresponds to the six matriarchs [*shisha imahot*]—Sarah, Rebekah, Rachel, Leah, Bilhah, and Zilpah" (*Esther Rabbah* 1.12), and "You should not think that the children of the wives [i.e., Leah and Rachel] come first, and that of the handmaidens [Bilhah and Zilpah] last, but . . . these were not greater than the others" (*Exodus Rabbah* 1.6). Bilhah also is credited with being the trusted liaison between Joseph and his brothers following the death and burial of Jacob (*Midrash Tanhuma, Exodus. Shemot* 1.2 Exodus 1.1ff., Part 2).

Contemporary scholars from the twentieth and twenty-first centuries have made efforts to revisit (and "rewrite") the lives of the Matriarchs of Genesis. They seek to understand the Matriarchs' experiences through their wider social, political, cultural, ethnic, economic, and religious contexts of their times in the ancient world nearly four thousand years ago. The rabbis credited Sarah with superior powers of prophecy when compared to Abraham; a modern commentator suggests a more psychologically-based reason for her actions, crediting Sarah with a powerful will and a greater sense of reality than Abraham, who was too entangled emotionally with his son Ishmael.

Likewise, contemporary scholars have looked at the crucial word in Gen 21:9, where Ishmael is described as *metzaheq*, which can be understood as "playing," "laughing," or possibly "mocking." The rabbis almost uniformly interpreted this incident in a negative light. Their understanding reflected the social, political, ethnic, national, and economic realities of their time: the ongoing tensions between the Jewish and its neighboring Semitic or Islamic communities. By contrast, contemporary scholars offer more balanced explanations for this matter: that whatever Ishmael did may not have been evil at all. To the contrary, the fact that the brothers were playing with each other as comrades was quite sufficient to evoke a sense of jealousy in Sarah, which brought her to the decision that Ishmael and Hagar had to be expelled. Ishmael's playing may have been no more than his attempt to amuse, rather than abuse, his younger brother. To read sexual play into Ishmael's behavior, some contemporary commentators such as Speiser and Plaut explain, is overreaching.

Scholars in the twentieth and twenty-first centuries analyze and comment on the roles and the actions of the Matriarchs. For example, Rebekah is characterized as an intricate and crucial character in the history of the people of Israel. Rebekah is more important than Isaac for the future of the Abrahamic family because she determines that the covenantal promise of land, descendants, and future blessing given to Abraham is fulfilled. Rebekah is praised because she ensures that Jacob will be the son to continue the special line according to God's will. Rebekah demonstrates that women in Israel could make crucial decisions about their destinies without negative consequences. Their prayers were acknowledged, and they sometimes knew what God designed even better than their husbands; therefore, they took the steps necessary to support God's plans for the community. Rebekah is the strongest Matriarch in Genesis and one of the first women with whom God has direct communication.

Contemporary women scholars writing on biblical women's experiences highlight for readers how the Matriarchs of Genesis served as crucial figures and were central, in their own social and political contexts, in determining the future of their families. In addition to these women scholars' voices writing as women, in the modern world, we have seen important and thought-provoking feminist scholarship. Some women would claim for themselves the term "feminist," while others would not. Feminists, whether male or female, traverse the theological spectrum, including those who self-identify as evangelical. Feminism is both a body of theory and mode of viewing the world that places significance on the experiences of women, as well as a political movement that seeks to end sexism and other systems of oppression. Throughout the writing of this book, we have attempted to be aware of and alert to the worldviews of the biblical authors and their traditional interpreters. We have attempted to highlight their patriarchal biases and sometimes their subtler androcentrism. Although we respect and continue to be influenced by many traditional interpretations, we have sought to challenge and unsettle some of those interpretations. By being deliberately and consciously attentive to feminist thought, we have also sought to share their unsettling challenge to some of the more conventional scholarship by addressing its implicit and sometimes explicit sexism, by calling patriarchy what it is, and by noting how women's experiences are a central organizing principle to understanding the Bible.

The distinctiveness of a feminist approach is that it accounts for women's experiences as women, not women in relation to men as dictated by the male gaze. Similarly, feminists have been effective in unpacking and exposing how patriarchy promotes certain gendered social relations while concealing others. (For example, we are conventionally told to understand the relationship between Sarah and Hagar as asymmetrical and marked by conflict, whereas feminists may argue that women can be friends without necessarily entering into competition or into the service of the immediate male.) In this sense, then, this body of scholarship is able to identify how patriarchal and sexist attitudes exist within a particular context, whereas a non-feminist would likely not consider how or why gender matters. Understanding how patriarchy operates in the ancient world not only helps us understand how men and women's roles operated then, but also how they continue to influence our own world today. Women, but also men, have gained through feminist insights and scholarship.

In the introduction to their groundbreaking work, *Women's Bible Commentary* (2012), Carol A. Newsom, Sharon H. Ringe, and Jacqueline E. Lapsley note that with

> increasing self-confidence and sophistication, feminist study of the Bible has blossomed to become one of the most important new areas in contemporary biblical research. [Women scholars have raised new questions. They] have posed . . . new ways of reading that . . . have challenged the very way biblical studies are done. [Women's and feminist biblical studies take] many different directions . . . Some commentators have attempted to reach "behind the text" to recover knowledge about the actual conditions of women's lives in the biblical period . . . Still others have tried to discover the extent to which even the biblical writings that pertain to women are shaped by the concerns and perspectives of men and yet how it can still be possible at times to discover the presence of women and their own points of view between the lines.[1]

Going beyond the matters of survival and security, a feminist view reaches further; it moves from the public sphere into the private. This deeper level asks several questions: How do people—especially women in relation to men, or women in relation to women—treat each other? What are the implications? How is power organized, and how is it used? Who is (relatively) powerless, and what strategies come into play? All these matters, which often take place at the surface level of description in the text, can tell us a great deal about the lives of the Matriarchs. This line of questioning, inspired by feminist analysis, provides a path to a fuller understanding of the inner family and society-driven dynamics at play, as well as a context to the consequences that take place in the public arena. Feminist analysis

---

1. Newsom, Ringe, Lapsley, introduction to *Women's Bible Commentary*, xxviii. These words are taken from the introduction to the first edition (1992).

covers a broad range of subjects, including religion, class, race, ethnicity, and sexual preference. Furthermore, feminist analysis focuses on the always interrelated and systematic nature of oppressive relations. In our book, we have sought to consider a variety of voices, scholarship, and points of view because of their invaluable contributions to biblical studies. We have also sought to share material that reflects a wide range of scholarly interest and interpretations. As we stated earlier, we do not claim to be exhaustive, but nor do we reproduce the same dominant scholarly outlooks.

In this volume, each chapter considered the individual Matriarch from five perspectives. We began with mining the biblical text. Next, we turned to the early extra-biblical material from the late Second Temple period and beyond. This was followed by insights from the rabbis of antiquity and occasionally of the Middle Ages through the Renaissance period. We concluded with sections devoted to contemporary scholarship and then scholarship from a specifically feminist perspective.

As two men addressing the subject of the Matriarchs of Genesis, from the first days, we were both aware of and sought to be reflexive of our positions as men and our masculine subjectivity. In order to address our own intersubjectivities while examining the textual terrain, we sought advice and insights from a number of women scholars, women pastors, and women rabbis. We also considered the work and insights of our feminist colleagues. We have learned from their comments and their criticism, which helped us to write this book. Nonetheless, we take full responsibility for the words we have written.

Bibliography

Aberbach, Moses, and Bernard Grossfeld, eds. and trans. *Targum Onkelos to Genesis: A Critical Analysis together with an English Translation of the Text based on A. Sperber's Edition*. Denver: Center for Judaic Studies, University of Denver, 1982.

Abrams, Judith Z. "Rachel: A Woman Who Would Be a Mother." *Jewish Bible Quarterly: Dor LeDor* 18 (1990) 213–21. http://jbq.jewishbible.org/assets/Uploads/18/jbq_18.4.pdf.

Adler, Rachel. *Engendering Judaism: An Inclusive Theology and Ethics*. Philadelphia: Jewish Publication Society, 1998.

Ahearne-Kroll, Patricia. "Joseph and Aseneth." In *Outside the Bible: Ancient Writings Related to Scripture*, edited by Louis H. Feldman, James L. Kugel, and Lawrence H. Schiffman, 1:916–50. 3 vols. Philadelphia: Jewish Publication Society, 2013.

Alter, Robert. *The Art of Biblical Narrative*. New York: Basic, 1981.

———. *The Five Books of Moses: A Translation with Commentary*. New York: Norton, 1996.

———. *Genesis*. New York: Norton, 1996.

Amit, Yairah. "Central Commentary, *Chayei Sarah* 23:1–25:18: From Sarah to Rebekah." In *The Torah: A Women's Commentary*, edited by Tamara Cohn Eskenazi and Andrea L. Weiss, 111–26. New York: Women of Reform Judaism, 2008.

Antonelli, Judith S. *In the Image of God: A Feminist Commentary on the Torah*. Northvale, NJ: Aronson, 1995.

Avi-Yona, Michael. "Elusa." In *Encyclopedia Judaica*, 6:690–691. Jerusalem: Keter, 1972.

Avot de Rabbi Natan [Abot de Rabbi Natan]: The Fathers According to Rabbi Nathan. Translated by Judah Goldin. New York: Schocken, 1974.

The Babylonian Talmud. Edited and translated by Isidore Epstein. 18 vols. London: Soncino, 1961.

Bal, Mieke. *Lethal Love: Feminist Literary Readings of Biblical Love Stories*. Bloomington: Indiana University Press, 1987.

Baron, Salo W. "Population." In *Encyclopaedia Judaica*, 13:866–903. Jerusalem: Keter, 1972.

Baskin, Judith R. "Infertile Wife in Rabbinic Judaism." *Jewish Women: A Comprehensive Historical Encyclopedia*. March 1, 2009. http://jwa.org/encyclopedia/article/infertile-wife-in-rabbinic-judaism.

———. *Pharaoh's Counsellors: Job, Jethro, and Balaam in Rabbinic and Patristic Tradition*. Chico, CA: Scholars, 1983.

———. "Women and Post-biblical Commentary." In *The Torah: A Women's Commentary*, edited by Tamara Cohn Eskenazi and Andrea L. Weiss, xlix–lv. New York: Women of Reform Judaism, 2008.

Beck, Astrid Billes. "Rebekah (Person)." In *Anchor Yale Bible Dictionary*, edited by David Noel Freedman, 5:629. London, Yale University Press, 1992.

Bellis, Alice Ogden. *Helpmates, Harlots, and Heroes: Women's Stories in the Hebrew Bible*. 2nd ed. Louisville: Westminster John Knox, 2007.

Bennett, William Howard, ed. *Genesis*. Century Bible 1. Edinburgh: Jack, 1900.

Berlin, Adele. "Central Commentary, Sh'mot." In *The Torah: A Women's Commentary*, edited by Tamara Cohn Eskenazi and Andrea L. Weiss, 305–23. New York: Women of Reform Judaism, 2008.

———. *Esther: The Traditional Hebrew Text with the New JPS Translation*. JPS Bible Commentary. Philadelphia: Jewish Publication Society, 2001.

———. "Writing a Commentary for a Jewish Audience." In *The Book of Esther in Modern Research*, edited by Sidnie White Crawford and Leonard J. Greenspoon, 9–16. London: T. & T. Clark, 2003.

Birnbaum, Ellen. "On the Life of Abraham." In *Outside the Bible: Ancient Writings Related to Scripture*, edited by Louis H. Feldman, James L. Kugel, and Lawrence H. Schiffman, 1:916–50. 3 vols. Philadelphia: Jewish Publication Society, 2013.

Bledstein, Adrien Janis. "Binder, Trickster, Heel and Hairy-man: Re-reading Genesis 27 as a Trickster Tale Told by a Woman." In *A Feminist Companion to Genesis*, edited by Athalya Brenner, 282–95. Sheffield: Sheffield Academic Press, 1993.

Bloom, Harold. *The Book of J*. Translated by David Rosenberg. New York: Grove, 1990.

Bohak, Gideon. "Book of Jubilees." In *The Oxford Dictionary of the Jewish Religion*, edited by R. J. Zwi Werblowsky and Geoffrey Wigoder, 381. New York: Oxford University Press, 1997.

Borgman, Paul. *Genesis: The Story We Haven't Heard*. Downers Grove: InterVarsity, 2001.

Brenner, Athalya, ed. *A Feminist Companion to Genesis*. Feminist Companion to the Bible 2. Sheffield: Sheffield Academic, 1993.

———, ed. *Genesis*. Vol. 1 of *A Feminist Companion to the Bible*. 2nd Series. Sheffield: Sheffield Academic Press, 1998.

Brenner, Athalya, and Carole Fontaine, eds. *A Feminist Companion to Reading the Bible: Approaches, Methods and Strategies*. Sheffield: Sheffield Academic, 1997.

Brenner, Athalya, and Fokkelien Van Dijk-Hemmes. *On Gendering Texts: Female and Male Voices in the Hebrew Bible*. Biblical Interpretation Series 1. Leiden: Brill, 1993.

Bronner, Leila Leah. *From Eve to Esther: Rabbinic Reconstructions of Biblical Women*. Louisville: Westminster John Knox, 1994.

Brown, F., S. R. Driver, and C. A. Briggs. *A Hebrew and English Lexicon of the Old Testament* [BDB]. Oxford: Clarendon, 1907.

Bruns, Gerald. "The Hermeneutics of Midrash." In *The Book and the Text*, edited by Regina Schwartz, 189–213. Oxford: Blackwell, 1990.

Callaway, Mary. *Sing, O Barren One: A Study in Comparative Midrash*. Society of Biblical Literature Dissertation Series 91. Atlanta: Scholars, 1986.

Charlesworth, James H., ed. *The Old Testament Pseudepigrapha*. 2 vols. New York: Doubleday, 1983, 1985.

Chesler, Phyllis, and Rivka Haut. "The Sacrifice of Sarah." *The Jewish Week*, October 26, 2010. *www.thejewishweek.com/editorial-opinion/sabbath-week/sacrifice-sarah*.

Cohen, A. *Everyman's Talmud*. New York: Dutton, 1949.

Cohen, Shaye J. D. *The Beginnings of Jewishness: Boundaries, Varieties, Uncertainties.* Hellenistic Culture and Society 31. Berkeley: University of California Press, 1999.

———. "The Letter of Paul to the Galatians." In *The Jewish Annotated New Testament*, edited by Amy-Jill Levine and Marc Z. Brettler, 332–44. New York: Oxford University Press, 2011.

The Contemporary Torah: A Gender-Sensitive Adaptation of the JPS [Jewish Publication Society] Translation [CJPS]. Edited by David E. S. Stein. Philadelphia: Jewish Publication Society, 2006.

Cotter, David W. *Genesis.* Berit Olam: Studies in Hebrew Narrative and Poetry. Collegeville, MN: Liturgical, 2003.

Curtis, Edward M. "Idol, Idolatry," In *Anchor Yale Bible Dictionary*, edited by David Noel Freedman, 3:379. London, Yale University Press, 1992.

Davidson, Richard M. *Flame of Yahweh: Sexuality in the Old Testament.* Peabody: Hendrickson, 2007.

Davies, Eryl W. *The Dissenting Reader: Feminist Approaches to the Hebrew Bible.* Aldershot, England: Ashgate, 2003.

Delaney, Carol. *Abraham on Trial: The Social Legacy of Biblical Myth.* Princeton, NJ: Princeton University Press, 1998.

Doniger, Wendy. *The Bedtrick: Tales of Sex and Masquerade.* Chicago: University of Chicago Press, 2000.

Dresner, Samuel H. *Rachel.* Minneapolis: Fortress, 1994.

———. "Rachel and Leah." *Judaism* 38 (1989) 151–59.

Endres, John C. *Biblical Interpretation in the Book of Jubilees.* Catholic Biblical Quarterly Monograph Series 18. Washington, DC: Catholic Biblical Association, 1987.

Engelmayer, Shammai. "Ivri: Naming Ourselves." *Judaism* 54 (2005) 13–26.

Eskenazi, Tamara Cohn, and Hara E. Person. "Central Commentary, Tol'dot 25:19–28:9: Shaping Destiny: The Story of Rebekah." In *The Torah: A Women's Commentary*, edited by Tamara Cohn Eskenazi and Andrea L. Weiss, 133–49. New York: Women of Reform Judaism, 2008.

Eskenazi, Tamara Cohn, and Tikva Frymer-Kensky, eds. *Ruth: The Traditional Hebrew Text with the New JPS Translation.* JPS Bible Commentary. Philadelphia: Jewish Publication Society, 2011.

Exum, J. Cheryl. "Who's Afraid of 'The Endangered Ancestress?'" In *Women in the Hebrew Bible: A Reader*, edited by Alice Bach,141–58. New York: Routledge, 1999.

Fewell, Danna Nolan, and David M. Gunn. *Gender, Power, and Promise: The Subject of the Bible's First Story.* Nashville: Abingdon, 1993.

Firestone, Reuven. *Journeys in Holy Lands: The Evolution of the Abraham-Ishmael Legends in Islamic Exegesis.* Albany, NY: State University of New York Press, 1990.

Fox, Everett, trans. *The Five Books of Moses: Genesis, Exodus, Leviticus, Numbers, Deuteronomy.* Vol. 1 of *The Schocken Bible.* New York: Schocken, 1995.

Frankel, Ellen. *The Five Books of Miriam: A Woman's Commentary on the Torah.* San Francisco: HarperSanFrancisco, 1998.

Friedman, Richard Eliott. *Commentary on the Torah: With a New English Translation.* New York: HarperCollins, 2001.

Fuchs, Esther. "Feminist Hebrew Literary Criticism: The Political Unconscious." *Hebrew Studies* 48 (2007) 195–216.

————. "Intermarriage, Gender, and Nation in the Hebrew Bible." In *The Passionate Torah: Sex and Judaism*, edited by Danya Ruttenberg, 73–92. New York: New York University Press, 2009.

————. "The Literary Characterization of Mothers and Sexual Politics in the Hebrew Bible." In *Women in the Hebrew Bible: A Reader*, edited by Alice Bach, 127–39. New York: Routledge, 1999.

————. "Who Is Hiding the Truth? Deceptive Women and Biblical Androcentrism." In *Feminist Perspectives on Biblical Scholarship*, edited by Adela Yarbro Collins, 137–44. Chico, CA: Scholars, 1985.

Gellman, Jerome I. *Abraham! Abraham! Kierkegaard and the Hasidim on the Binding of Isaac*. Burlington, VT: Ashgate, 2003.

Ginzberg, Louis. *The Legends of the Jews*. 7 vols. Philadelphia: Jewish Publication Society, 1967.

Gordon, Cynthia. "Hagar: A Throw-Away Character among the Matriarchs." *Society of Biblical Literature Seminar Papers* 24 (1985) 271–77.

Gottlieb, Lynn. *She Who Dwells Within: A Feminist Vision of a Renewed Judaism*. 1st ed. San Francisco: HarperSanFrancisco, 1995.

Graetz, Naomi. *Silence Is Deadly: Judaism Confronts Wifebeating*. Northvale, NJ: Aronson, 1998.

————. *Unlocking the Garden: A Feminist Jewish Look at the Bible, Midrash, and God*. Piscataway, NJ: Gorgias, 2005.

Gravett, Sandie. "Reading 'Rape' in the Hebrew Bible: A Consideration of Language." *Journal for the Study of the Old Testament* 28 (2004) 279–99.

Greengus, Samuel. "Sisterhood Adoption at Nuzi and the 'Wife-Sister' in Genesis." *Hebrew Union College Annual* 46 (1975) 5–31.

Groothuius, Pierce, and Rebecca Merrill. *Equality: Complementarity without Hierarchy*. Downers Grove: InterVarsity, 2004.

Gruber, Mayer I. "Breast-Feeding Practices in Biblical Israel and in Old Babylonian Mesopotamia." In *The Motherhood of God and Other Studies*, 69–107. South Florida Studies in the History of Judaism 57. Atlanta: Scholars 1992.

Gunkel, Hermann. *The Legends of Genesis: The Biblical Saga and History*. Translated by W. H. Carruth. New York: Schocken, 1964.

Haberman, Bonna Devora. "Divorcing Ba'al: The Sex of Ownership in Jewish Marriage." In *The Passionate Torah: Sex and Judaism*, edited by Danya Ruttenberg, 36–57. New York: New York University Press, 2009.

Hackett, Jo Ann. "1 and 2 Samuel." In *The Women's Bible Commentary*, edited by Carol A. Newsom, Sharon H. Ringe, and Jacqueline E. Lapsley, 85–95. 3rd rev. ed. Louisville: Westminster John Knox, 2012.

————. "Rehabilitating Hagar: Fragments of an Epic Pattern." In *Gender and Difference in Ancient Israel*, edited by Peggy L. Day, 12–27. Minneapolis: Fortress, 1989.

Halevy, Schulamith C. "Sarah, the Enabler: From the Binding of Isaac to the First Israelite Land Purchase in the Promised Land." *Midstream*, 1996. http://www.cs.tau.ac.il/~nachum/sch/PAPERS/Sarah.txt.

Halpern-Amaru, Betsy. *The Empowerment of Women in the Book of Jubilees*. Supplements to the *Journal for the Study of Judaism* 60. Leiden: Brill, 1999.

————. "The First Woman, Wives, and Mothers in 'Jubilees." *Journal of Biblical Literature* 113 (1994) 609–26.

Hamilton, Victor P. *The Book of Genesis: Chapters 18–50*. New International Commentary on the Old Testament. Grand Rapids: Eerdmans, 1995.

Havrelock, Rachel. "Central Commentary, *Vayeitzei* 28:10–32:3: The Journey Within." In *The Torah: A Women's Commentary*, edited by Tamara Cohn Eskenazi and Andrea L. Weiss, 157–75. New York: Women of Reform Judaism, 2008.

Heinemann, Joseph. "The Nature of the Aggadah." In *Midrash and Literature*, edited by Geoffrey H. Hartman and Sanford Burdick, 41–56. New Haven: Yale University Press, 1986.

Hilhorst, Anthony. "Ishmaelites, Hagarenes, Saracens." In *Abraham, the Nations, and the Hagarites: Jewish, Christian, and Islamic Perpectives on Kinship with Abraham*, edited by Martin Goodman, George H. van Kooten, and Jacques van Ruiten, 421–34. Themes in Biblical Narrative 13. Leiden: Brill, 2010.

Hillel, Vered. "Why *Not* Naphtali?" In *Things Revealed: Studies in Early Jewish and Christian Literature in Honor of Michael E. Stone*, edited by Esther G. Chason et al., 279–88. Leiden: Brill, 2004.

Hirsch, Samson Raphael. *Genesis*. Vol. 2 of *The Pentateuch*. New York: Judaica, 1971.

Huwiler, Elizabeth. *Biblical Women: Mirrors, Models, and Metaphors*. Kaleidoscope Series Resource. Cleveland, OH: United Church Press, 1993.

Hyman, Naomi M. *Biblical Women in the Midrash: A Sourcebook*. Northvale, NJ: Aronson, 1998.

Jacobi, Margaret. "Serach bat Asher and Bitiah bat Pharaoh: Names which Became Legends." In *Hear Our Voice: Women Rabbis Tell Their Stories*, edited by Sybil Sheridan, 109–19. London: SCM, 1994.

James, Elaine. "Sarah, Hagar, and Their Interpreters." In *The Women's Bible Commentary*, edited by Carol A. Newsom, Sharon H. Ringe, and Jacqueline E. Lapsley, 67–69. 3rd rev. ed. Louisville: Westminster John Knox, 2012.

Jeansonne, Sharon Pace. *The Women of Genesis*. Minneapolis: Fortress, 1990.

The Jerusalem Bible [JB]. Edited by Alexander Jones. Garden City, NY: Doubleday, 1966.

The Jewish Encyclopedia, s.v. "Rachel" 10:305–7, s.v. "Seder Olam Rabbah," 11:147–49, s.v. "Yashar, Sefer ha-," 12:588–89. New York: Funk & Wagnalls, 1905.

Josephus, Flavius. *Antiquities of the Jews*. Translated by Henry St. James Thackeray. Cambridge: Harvard University Press, 1961.

"Jubilees." Translated by O. S. Wintermute. In vol. 2 of *The Old Testament Pseudepigrapha*, edited by James H. Charlesworth, 34–142. The Anchor Bible Reference Library. New York: Doubleday, 1985.

"Jubilees." Translated by O. S. Wintermute. In *Outside the Bible: Ancient Writings Related to Scripture*, edited by Louis H. Feldman, James L. Kugel, and Lawrence H. Schiffman, 1:272–465. 3 vols. Philadelphia: Jewish Publication Society, 2013.

Kardimon, Samson. "Adoption as a Remedy for Infertility in the Period of the Patriarchs." *Journal of Semitic Studies* 3 (1958) 123–26.

Klitsner, Judy. *Subversive Sequels in the Bible: How Biblical Stories Mine and Undermine Each Other*. Philadelphia: Jewish Publication Society, 2009.

Knobloch, Frederick W. "Adoption." In *Anchor Yale Bible Dictionary*, edited by David Noel Freedman, 1:76ff. London, Yale University Press, 1992.

Kraemer, David Charles. *Responses to Suffering in Classical Rabbinic Literature*. New York: Oxford University Press, 1995.

Kramer, Phyllis Silverman. "Biblical Women That Come in Pairs: The Use of Female Pairs as a Literary Device in the Hebrew Bible." In *Genesis*, edited by Athalya Brenner, 1:218–31. 2nd Series. Sheffield: Sheffield Academic Press, 1998.

Kroeger, Catherine Clark, and Mary J. Evans, eds. *The IVP Women's Bible Commentary.* Downer's Grove: InterVarsity, 2002.

Kugel, James L. "The Apocrypha and the Pseudepigrapha." In *Outside the Bible: Ancient Writings Related to Scripture*, edited by Louis H. Feldman, James L. Kugel, and Lawrence H. Schiffman, 1:7–10. 3 vols. Philadelphia: Jewish Publication Society, 2013.

———. *How to Read the Bible: A Guide to Scripture, Then and Now.* New York: Free Press, 2007.

———. "Reuben's Sin with Bilhah in the Testament of Reuben." In *Pomegranates and Golden Bells: Studies in Biblical, Jewish, and Near Eastern Ritual, Law, and Literature in Honor of Jacob Milgrom*, edited by David P. Wright et al., 525–54. Winowa Lake, IN: Eisenbrauns, 1995.

———. *A Walk through Jubilees: Studies in the Book of Jubilees and the World of Its Creation.* Supplements to the *Journal for the Study of Judaism* 156. Leiden: Brill, 2012.

———, trans. "Testaments of the Twelve Patriarchs." In *Outside the Bible: Ancient Writings Related to Scripture*, edited by Louis H. Feldman, James L. Kugel, and Lawrence H. Schiffman, 2:1697–1855. 3 vols. Philadelphia: Jewish Publication Society, 2013.

Laffey, Alice L. *An Introduction to the Old Testament: A Feminist Perspective.* Philadelphia: Fortress, 1988.

Lapsley, J. E. "The Voice of Rachel: Resistance and Polyphony in Genesis 31:14–35." In *Genesis*, edited by Athalya Brenner, 1:233–48. 2nd Series. Sheffield: Sheffield Academic Press, 1998.

Latvus, Kari. "Reading Hagar in Contexts: From Exegesis to Inter-Contextual Analysis." In *Genesis: Texts @ Contexts*, edited by Athalya Brenner, Archie Chi Chung Lee, and Gale A. Yee, 247–74. Minneapolis: Fortress, 2010.

Laymon, Charles M., ed. *Interpreter's One-Volume Commentary on the Bible.* Nashville: Abingdon, 1971.

Leibowitz, Nehama. *Studies in Bereshit (Genesis): In the Context of Ancient and Modern Jewish Bible Commentary.* 3rd rev. ed. Translated by Aryeh Newman. Jerusalem: World Zionist Organization, 1976.

Levine, Amy-Jill. "Another View, Lech L'cha." In *The Torah: A Women's Commentary*, edited by Tamara Cohn Eskenazi and Andrea L. Weiss, 78. New York: Women of Reform Judaism, 2008.

———. "Settling at Beer-lahai-roi." In *Daughters of Abraham: Feminist Thought in Judaism, Christianity, and Islam*, edited by Yvonne Yazbeck Haddad and John L. Esposito, 12–34. Gainesville, FL: University of Florida Press 2001.

Lieber, David L. et al., eds. *Etz Hayim: Torah and Commentary.* New York: Jewish Publication Society, 2001.

Machiela, Daniel A. "The Genesis Apocryphon (1Q20): A Reevaluation of its Text, Interpretive Character, and Relationship to the Book of Jubilees." PhD diss., University of Notre Dame, 2007. http://etd.nd.edu/ETD-db/theses/available/etd-07022007-205251/unrestricted/MachielaD072007.pdf.

Malbim [Rabbi Meir Leibush ben Yechiel Michel]. *Commentary on the Torah.* Vol. 2. Translated by Zvi Faier. Jerusalem: Hillel, 1979.

Martinez, Florentino Garcia. "Hagar in *Targum Pseudo-Jonathan.*" In *Abraham, the Nations, and the Hagarites: Jewish, Christian, and Islamic Perspectives on Kinship with Abraham,* edited by Martin Goodman, George H. van Kooten, and Jacques van Ruiten, 263–74. Themes in Biblical Narrative 13. Leiden: Brill, 2010. http://kuleuven.academia.edu/FlorentinoGarc%C3%ADaMart%C3%ADnez/Papers/673009/Hagar_in_Targum_Pseudo-Jonathan.

Matthews, Victor Harold, and Don C. Benjamin. *Old Testament Parallels: Laws and Stories from the Ancient Near East.* 3rd rev. ed. Mahwah, NJ: Paulist, 2006.

McGing, Brian. "Population and Proselytism: How Many Jews Were There in the Ancient World?" In *Jews in the Hellenistic and Roman Cities,* edited by John R. Bartlett, 88–106. London: Routledge, 2002.

McKay, Heather A. "On the Future of Feminist Biblical Criticism." In *A Feminist Companion to Reading the Bible: Approaches, Methods and Strategies,* edited by Athalya Brenner and Carole Fontaine, 61–83. Sheffield: Sheffield Academic Press, 1997.

Mekilta de Rabbi Ishmael. Translated by Jacob Z. Lauterbach. Philadelphia: Jewish Publication Society, 1949.

Menn, Esther Marie. *Judah and Tamar (Genesis 38) in Ancient Jewish Exegesis: Studies in Literary Form and Hermeneutics.* Supplements to the *Journal for the Study of Judaism* 51. Leiden: Brill, 1997.

Meyers, Carol L. "Every Day Life: Women in the Period of the Hebrew Bible." In *The Women's Bible Commentary,* edited by Carol A. Newsom and Sharon H. Ringe, 244–51. Louisville: Westminster John Knox, 1992.

———. "Women in Ancient Israel: An Overview." In *The Torah: A Women's Commentary,* edited by Tamara Cohn Eskenazi and Andrea L. Weiss, xli–xlviii. New York: Women of Reform Judaism, 2008.

Midrash Ha-Gadol. Edited by Mordecai Marguiles. Jerusalem: Mossad ha-Rav Kook, 1947.

The Midrash on Proverbs. Translated by Burton L. Visotzky. Yale Judaica Series 27. New Haven: Yale University Press, 1992.

The Midrash on Psalms. Translated by William G. Braude. 2 vols. Yale Judaica Series 13. New Haven: Yale University Press, 1959.

Midrash Rabbah (The Midrash). Edited by H. Freedman, Maurice Simon, and Judah J. Slotki. 10 vols. London: Soncino, 1939.

Midrash Tanhuma, Exodus and Leviticus. Vol. 2 of *Midrash Tanhuma: S. Buber Recension.* Translated by John T. Townsend. Hoboken, NJ: Ktav, 1997.

Midrash Tanhuma, Genesis. Vol. 1 of *Midrash Tanhuma: S. Buber Recension.* Translated by John T. Townsend. Hoboken, NJ: Ktav, 1989.

Midrash Tanhuma, Numbers and Deuteronomy. Vol. 3 of *Midrash Tanhuma: S. Buber Recension.* Translated by John T. Townsend. Hoboken, NJ: Ktav, 2003.

Midrash Tanhuma-Yelammedenu, Genesis and Exodus: An English Translation of Genesis and Exodus from the Printed Version of Tanhuma-Yelammedenu. Edited and translated by Samuel Berman. Hoboken, NJ: Ktav, 1996.

Milne, Pamela J. "Toward Feminist Companionship: The Future of Feminist Biblical Studies and Feminism." In *A Feminist Companion to Reading the Bible: Approaches,*

Methods and Strategies, edited by Athalya Brenner and Carole Fontaine, 39–60. Sheffield: Sheffield Academic Press, 1997.

Morgenstern, Matthew J., and Michael Segal. "The Genesis Apocryphon." In *Outside the Bible: Ancient Writings Related to Scripture*, edited by Louis H. Feldman, and James L. Kugel, and Lawrence H. Schiffman, 1:237–62. 3 vols. Philadelphia: Jewish Publication Society, 2013.

Nahmanides [Nachmanides, Ramban, pseuds.]. *Genesis*. Vol. 1 of *Commentary on the Torah*. Translated by Charles Ber Chavel. New York: Shiloh, 1971.

Najman, Hindy. "Rewriting as Whitewashing: The Case of Rewritten Bible." In *Vixens Disturbing Vineyards: Embarrassment and Embracement of Scriptures; A Festschrift Honoring Harry Fox*, edited by Aubrey L. Glazer et al., 140–53. Boston: Academic Studies, 2010.

The New American Bible [NAB]. Catholic Biblical Association of America. Cleveland, OH: Catholic Press, 1970.

The New English Bible with Apocrypha [NEB]. Joint Committee on the New Translation of the Bible. Oxford: Oxford University Press, 1970.

New International Version [NIV]. *The Holy Bible: New International Version*. International Bible Society. Colorado Springs, CO: International Bible Society, 1984.

The New Jerusalem Bible: The Complete Text of the Ancient Canon of the Scriptures [NJB]. Edited by Henry Wansbrough. New York: Doubleday, 1998.

New Revised Standard Version [NOAB; NRSV]. *The New Oxford Annotated Bible with the Apocrypha: New Revised Standard Version*. Edited by Bernhard W. Anderson, Bruce M. Metzger, Roland E. Murphy, et al. New York: Oxford University Press, 1991.

Niditch, Susan. "Central Commentary, *Lech L'cha* 12:1–17:27: Covenantal Promise and Cultural Self-definition." In *The Torah: A Women's Commentary*, edited by Tamara Cohn Eskenazi and Andrea L. Weiss, 59–77. New York: Women of Reform Judaism, 2008.

———. "Eroticism and Death in the Tale of Jael." In *Gender and Difference in Ancient Israel*, edited by Peggy Lynne Day, 43–57. Minneapolis: Fortress, 1989.

———. "Genesis." In *The Women's Bible Commentary*, edited by Carol A. Newsom, Sharon H. Ringe, and Jacqueline E. Lapsley, 27–45. 3rd rev. ed. Louisville: Westminster John Knox, 2012.

———. *A Prelude to Biblical Folklore: Underdogs and Tricksters*. Urbana, IL: University of Illinois Press, 2000.

Niehoff, Maren R. "Mother and Maiden, Sister and Spouse: Sarah in Philonic Midrash." *Harvard Theological Review* 97 (2004) 413–44.

Nikaido, S. "Hagar and Ishmael as Literary Figures: An Intertextual Study." *Vetus Testamentum* 61 (2001) 219–42.

Noth, Martin. *Numbers: A Commentary*. Translated by James D. Martin. Philadelphia: Westminster, 1968.

Nunnally-Cox, Janice. *Foremothers: Women of the Bible*. San Francisco: Harper & Row, 1981.

Otwell, John H. *And Sarah Laughed: The Status of Women in the Old Testament*. Philadelphia: Westminster, 1977.

Paul, Robert A. *Moses and Civilization: The Meaning behind Freud's Myth*. New Haven: Yale University Press, 1996.

Pesikta de Rab Kahana: Rabbi Kahana's Compilation of Discourses for Sabbaths and Festal Days. Translated by William G. Braude, and Israel J. Kapstein. JPS Classics. Philadelphia: Jewish Publication Society, 1975.

Pesikta Rabbati: Discourses for Feasts, Fasts, and Special Sabbaths. Translated by William G. Braude, 2 vols. Yale Judaica Series 18. New Haven: Yale University Press, 1968.

Pinker, Aron. "The Expulsion of Hagar and Ishmael (Gen 21:9–21)." *Women in Judaism: A Multidisciplinary Journal* 6 (2009) 1–24.

Pirke de Rabbi Eliezer (The Chapters of Rabbi Eliezer the Great): According to the Text of the Manuscript Belonging to Abraham Epstein of Vienna. Translated by Gerald Friedlander. Judaic Studies Library 6 New York: Sepher-Hermon, 1981.

Plaskow, Judith. "Contemporary Reflection, *Vayeira.*" In *The Torah: A Women's Commentary*, edited by Tamara Cohn Eskenazi and Andrea L. Weiss, 107–8. New York: Women of Reform Judaism, 2008.

———. *Standing Again at Sinai: Judaism from a Feminist Perspective.* San Francisco: HarperSanFrancisco, 1991.

Plaut, W. Gunther. *The Torah: A Modern Commentary.* New York: Union of American Hebrew Congregations, 1981.

———. *The Torah: A Modern Commentary, Revised Edition.* Edited by David E. S. Stein. New York: Union of Reform Judaism, 2005, 2006.

Porton, Gary G. "Midrash." In *Anchor Yale Bible Dictionary*, edited by David Noel Freedman, 4:819. London, Yale University Press, 1992.

Rabow, Jerry. *The Lost Matriarch: Finding Leah in the Bible and Midrash.* Philadelphia: Jewish Publication Society, 2014.

Rashkow, Ilona N. *The Phallacy of Genesis: A Feminist-Psychoanalytic Approach.* Literary Currents in Biblical Interpretation. Louisville: Westminster John Knox, 1993.

Rashi. *The Pentateuch and Rashi's Commentary: A Linear Translation into English; Genesis.* Vol. 1. Translated by Rabbi Abraham ben Isaiah and Bernard Sharfman. Brooklyn, NY: S. S. & R., 1976.

Reinhartz, Adele. "Feminist Criticism and Biblical Studies on the Verge of the Twenty-First Century." In *A Feminist Companion to Reading the Bible: Approaches, Methods and Strategies*, edited by Athalya Brenner and Carole Fontaine, 30–38. Sheffield: Sheffield Academic Press, 1997.

Reinhartz, Adele, and Miriam-Simma Walfish. "Conflict and Coexistence in Jewish Interpretation." In *Hagar, Sarah, and Their Children: Jewish, Christian, and Muslim Perspectives*, edited by Phyllis Trible and Letty M. Russell, 101–25. Louisville: Westminster John Knox, 2006.

Reis, Pamela T. "Hagar Requited." *Journal for the Study of the Old Testament* 87 (2000) 75–109.

Reiss, Moshe. "The God of Abraham, Rebekah and Jacob." *Jewish Bible Quarterly* 32 (2004) 91–97.

———. "Ishmael, Son of Abraham." *Jewish Bible Quarterly* 30 (2002) 253–56.

———. "Serah bat Asher." *Jewish Bible Quarterly* 42 (2014) 45–51.

Reiss, Moshe, and David J. Zucker, "Co-opting the Secondary Matriarchs: Bilhah, Zilpah, Tamar, and Aseneth." *Biblical Interpretation* 22 (2014) 307–324.

Robinson, Bernard P. "Characterization in the Hagar and Ishmael Narratives." *Scandinavian Journal of the Old Testament* 27 (2013) 198–215.

Rosenblatt, Naomi Harris. *After the Apple: Women in the Bible; Timeless Stories of Love, Lust, and Longing.* New York: Hyperion, 2005.

Rosenblatt, Naomi Harris, and Joshua Horowitz. *Wrestling with Angels: What Genesis Teaches Us about Our Spiritual Identity, Sexuality, and Personal Relationships.* New York: Dell, 1995.

Rosen-Zvi, Ishay. "Bilhah the Temptress: *The Testament of Reuben* and the 'Birth of Sexuality.'" *Jewish Quarterly Review* 96 (2006) 65–94.

Rothstein, David. "Text and Context: Domestic Harmony and the Depiction of Hagar in *Jubilees.*" *Journal for the Study of the Pseudepigrapha* 17 (2008) 243–64.

Sarna, Nahum M. *Exodus: The Traditional Hebrew Text with the New JPS Translation.* JPS Torah Commentary. Philadelphia: Jewish Publication Society, 1991.

———. *Genesis: The Traditional Hebrew Text with the New JPS Translation.* JPS Bible Commentary. Philadelphia: Jewish Publication Society, 1989.

———. *Understanding Genesis.* New York: Schocken, 1970.

Schneider, Tammi J. "Another View, *Vayeitzei.*" In *The Torah: A Women's Commentary,* edited by Tamara Cohn Eskenazi and Andrea L. Weiss, 176. New York: Women of Reform Judaism, 2008.

———. "Central Commentary, *Vayeira* 18:1–22:24: Between Laughter and Tears." In *The Torah: A Women's Commentary,* edited by Tamara Cohn Eskenazi and Andrea L. Weiss, 85–104. New York: Women of Reform Judaism, 2008.

———. *Mothers of Promise: Women in the Book of Genesis.* Grand Rapids: Baker Academic, 2008.

Scholem, Gershom. *On the Kabbalah and Its Symbolism.* Translated by Ralph Manheim. New York: Schocken, 1965.

Schuller, Ellen. "Women of the Exodus in Biblical Retellings of the Second Temple Period." In *Gender and Difference in Ancient Israel,* edited by Peggy L. Day, 28–42. Minneapolis: Fortress, 1989.

Segal, Michael. *The Book of Jubilees: Rewritten Bible, Redaction, Ideology and Theology.* Leiden: Brill, 2007.

Sered, Susan Starr. "Rachel's Tomb and the Milk Grotto of the Virgin Mary." *Journal of Feminist Studies in Religion* 2 (1986) 7–22.

Sforno, Obadiah ben Jacob. *Sforno: Commentary on the Torah.* Translated by Raphael Pelcovitz. ArtScroll Mesorah Series. Brooklyn, NY: Mesorah, 1997.

Shapiro, Emily. "Approaching the Avot." *Academy for Torah Initiatives and Directions* [ATID] (1999) 1–26. www.atid.org/journal/journal98/default1.asp.

Shargent, Karla G. "Living on the Edge: The Liminality of Daughters in Genesis to 2 Samuel." In *A Feminist Companion to Samuel and Kings,* edited by Athalya Brenner, 26–42. Sheffield: Sheffield University Press, 1994.

Shinan, Avigdor, and Yair Zakovitch. *From Gods to God: How the Bible Debunked, Suppressed, or Changed Ancient Myths and Legends.* Translated by Valerie Zakovitch. Philadelphia: Jewish Publication Society, 2012.

Sifre: A Tannaitic Commentary on the Book of Deuteronomy. Translated by Reuven Hammer. Yale Judaica Series 24. New Haven: Yale University Press, 1986.

Sifsei Chachamim Chumash. Vol. 1 of *Commentary on Genesis.* Translated by Avrohom Y. Davis. Lakewood, NJ: Metsudah, 2009.

Sohn, Ruth H. "Contemporary Reflection, *Lech L'cha.*" In *The Torah: A Women's Commentary,* edited by Tamara Cohn Eskenazi and Andrea L. Weiss, 80–81. New York: Women of Reform Judaism, 2008.

———. "Post-biblical Interpretations, *Vayak'heil*." In *The Torah: A Women's Commentary*, edited by Tamara Cohn Eskenazi and Andrea L. Weiss, 538–39. New York: Women of Reform Judaism, 2008.

Soloveitchik, Joseph Dov. *Man of Faith in the Modern World. Vol. 2 of Reflections of the Rav*. Lectures adapted by Rabbi Abraham Besdin. Hoboken, NJ: Ktav, 1989.

Speiser, E. A., ed. *Genesis*. Vol. 1 of *The Anchor Bible*. Garden City, NY: Doubleday, 1964.

Tanakh: The Holy Scriptures [NJPS]: *The New JPS* [Jewish Publication Society] *Translation According to the Traditional Hebrew Text*. Philadelphia: Jewish Publication Society, 1985.

Tanna debe Eliyyahu: The Lore of the School of Elijah. Translated by William G. Braude and Israel J. Kapstein. Philadelphia: Jewish Publication Society, 1981.

Targum Neofiti 1. In *Genesis*, vol. 1A of *The Aramaic Bible*. Edited by Martin McNamara. Collegeville, MN: Liturgical, 1992.

Testament of Abraham (Recension A and B). In *The Old Testament Pseudepigrapha*, edited by James H. Charlesworth and translated by E. P. Sanders, 1:871–902. Garden City, NY: Doubleday, 1983.

"The Testaments of the Twelve Patriarchs." In *The Old Testament Pseudepigrapha*, edited by James H. Charlesworth and translated by H. C. Kee, 1:775–828. Garden City, NY: Doubleday, 1983.

"Testaments of the Twelve Patriarchs." In *Outside the Bible: Ancient Writings Related to Scripture*, edited by Louis H. Feldman, James L. Kugel, and Lawrence H. Schiffman and translated by James L. Kugel, 2:1697–1855. 3 vols. Philadelphia: Jewish Publication Society, 2013.

Teubal, Savina J. *Hagar the Egyptian: The Lost Tradition of the Matriarchs*. New York: HarperSanFrancisco, 1990.

———. *Sarah the Priestess: The First Matriarch of Genesis*. Athens, OH: Swallow, 1984.

Thompson, John L. *Writing the Wrongs: Women of the Old Testament among Biblical Commentators from Philo through the Reformation*. Oxford Studies in Historical Theology. Oxford: Oxford University Press, 2001.

Tigay, Jeffrey H. *Deuteronomy: The Traditional Hebrew Text with the New JPS Translation*. JPS Torah Commentary. Philadelphia: Jewish Publication Society, 1996.

Tohar, Vered. "Abraham and Sarah in Egypt (Genesis 12:10–20): Sexual Transgressions as Apologetic Interpretations in Post-biblical Jewish Sources." *Women in Judaism: A Multidisciplinary Journal* 10 (2013) 1–14.

Topchyan, Aram, and Gohar Muradyan. "Questions and Answers on Genesis and Exodus." In *Outside the Bible: Ancient Writings Related to Scripture*, edited by Louis H. Feldman, James L. Kugel, and Lawrence H. Schiffman, 1:807–81. 3 vols. Philadelphia: Jewish Publication Society, 2013.

Trible, Phyllis. "Genesis 22: The Sacrifice of Sarah." In *Women in the Hebrew Bible: A Reader*, edited by Alice Bach, 271–90. New York: Routledge, 1999.

———. "Ominous Beginnings for a Promise of Blessing." In *Hagar, Sarah, and Their Children: Jewish, Christian, and Muslim Perspectives*, edited by Phyllis Trible and Letty M. Russell, 33–69. Louisville: Westminster John Knox, 2006.

———. *Texts of Terror: Literary-Feminist Readings of Biblical Narratives*. Lyman Beecher Lectures, 1981–1982, Overtures to Biblical Theology 13. Philadelphia: Fortress, 1984.

Tsevat, Matitiahu. "Hagar and the Birth of Ishmael." In *The Meaning of the Book of Job and Other Biblical Studies*, 53–76. New York: Ktav, 1980.

Tuchman, Shera Aranoff, and Sandra E. Rapoport. *The Passions of the Matriarchs*. Jersey City, NJ: Ktav, 2004.

VanderKam, James C. *The Book of Jubilees*. Guides to Apocrypha and Pseudepigrapha. Sheffield: Sheffield Academic Press, 2001.

———. "Recent Scholarship on the Book of Jubilees." *Currents in Biblical Research* 6 (2008) 405–31.

———. *Textual and Historical Studies in the Book of Jubilees*. Harvard Semitic Monographs 14. Missoula, MT: Scholars, 1977.

Van Ruiten, Jacques T. A. G. M. "Hagar in the Book of *Jubilees*." In *Abraham, the Nations, and the Hagarites: Jewish, Christian, and Islamic Perpectives on Kinship with Abraham*, edited by Martin Goodman, George H. van Kooten, and Jacques van Ruiten, 117–38. Themes in Biblical Narrative 13. Leiden: Brill, 2010.

Vawter, Bruce. *On Genesis: A New Reading*. Garden City, NY: Doubleday, 1977.

von Rad, Gerhard. *Genesis: A Commentary*. Rev. ed. Translated by John H. Marks. Old Testament Library. Philadelphia: Westminster, 1972.

Wenham, Gordon J. *Genesis 16–50*. Vol. 2 of *Word Bible Commentary*. Dallas: Word Books, 1994.

Westermann, Claus. *Genesis 12–36: A Commentary*. Translated by John J. Scullion. Minneapolis: Augsburg, 1985.

Williams, Delores S. *Sisters in the Wilderness: The Challenge of Womanist God-Talk*. Maryknoll, NY: Orbis, 1993.

Witte, Ali. "The Sacrifice of Sarah." *Student Work: Interpretations of the Akeda*, edited by David R. Blumenthal. Spring 2011. http://www.js.emory.edu/BLUMENTHAL/Akeda,%20Ali.htm#_ftn4.

Wray, Tina J. *Good Girls, Bad Girls: The Enduring Lessons of Twelve Women of the Old Testament*. Lanham, MD: Rowman & Littlefield, 2008.

Zierler, Wendy. "Contemporary Reflection, *Vayeitzei*." In *The Torah: A Women's Commentary*, edited by Tamara Cohn Eskenazi and Andrea L. Weiss, 178–79. New York: Women of Reform Judaism, 2008.

———. "In Search of a Feminist Reading of the Akedah." *Nashim* 9 (2005) 10–26.

Zohar. Translated by Harry Sperling, Maurice Simon, and Paul P. Levertoff. 5 vols. New York: Bennet, 1958.

Zornberg, Avivah Gottlieb. *Genesis: The Beginning of Desire*. Philadelphia: Jewish Publication Society, 1995.

———. "'Her Own Foreigner': Rebecca's Pregnancy." In *The Murmuring Deep: Reflections on the Biblical Unconscious*, 208–36. New York: Schocken, 2009.

Zucker, David J. "The Ages of the Matriarchs and the Patriarchs." *Jewish Bible Quarterly* 43 (2015) 49–53.

———. "Betrayal (and Growth) in Genesis 22." *CCAR Journal: A Reform Jewish Quarterly* 46 (1999) 60–72.

———. *The Bible's Prophets: An Introduction for Christians and Jews*. Eugene, OR: Wipf & Stock, 2013.

———. *The Bible's Writings: An Introduction for Christians and Jews*. Eugene, OR: Wipf & Stock, 2013.

———. "Choosing Jacob: The Coded Language of Genesis 27." *Scandinavian Journal of the Old Testament* 2 (2015) forthcoming.

————. "Conflicting Conclusions: The Hatred of Isaac and Ishmael." *Judaism* 39 (1990) 37–46.

————. "The Deceiver Deceived: Rereading Genesis 27." *Jewish Bible Quarterly* 39 (2011) 46–58.

————. "Isaac: A Life of Bitter Laughter." *Jewish Bible Quarterly* 40 (2012) 105–10.

————. "The Mysterious Disappearance of Sarah." *Judaism* 55 (2006) 30–39.

————. "Rescuing Rebecca's Reputation: A Midrash on Genesis 27." *CCAR Journal: A Reform Jewish Quarterly* 48 (2001) 80–87.

————. "Sarah: The View of the Classical Rabbis." In *Perspectives on Our Father Abraham: Essays in Honor of Marvin R. Wilson*, edited by Steven A. Hunt, 221–52. Grand Rapids: Eerdmans, 2010.

————. "Seeing and Hearing: The Interrelated Lives of Sarah and Hagar." *Women in Judaism: A Multidisciplinary Journal* 7 (2010) 1–14.

————. "A Still Stranger Stratagem: Revisiting Genesis 27." *Conservative Judaism* 56 (2004) 21–31.

————. *The Torah: An Introduction for Christians and Jews.* Mahwah, NJ: Paulist, 2005.

————. "What Sarah Saw: Envisioning Genesis 21:9–10." *Jewish Bible Quarterly* 36 (2008) 54–62.

Zucker, David J., and Rebecca Gates Brinton. "'The Other Woman': A Collaborative Jewish-Christian Study of Hagar." In *Perspectives on Our Father Abraham: Essays in Honor of Marvin R. Wilson*, edited by Steven A. Hunt, 339–97. Grand Rapids: Eerdmans, 2010.

Zucker, David J., and Moshe Reiss. "Abraham, Sarah, and Hagar as a Blended Family: Problems, Partings, and Possibilities." *Women in Judaism: A Multidisciplinary Journal* 6 (2009) 1–18.

9 781625 643964